CRITICAL INSIGHTS

Nathaniel Hawthorne

CRITICAL INSIGHTS
Nathaniel Hawthorne

Editor
Jack Lynch
Rutgers University

Salem Press
Pasadena, California   Hackensack, New Jersey

Cover photo: The Granger Collection, New York

Published by Salem Press

© 2010 by EBSCO Publishing
Editor's text © 2010 by Jack Lynch
"The *Paris Review* Perspective" © 2010 by Elaine Blair for *The Paris Review*

∞ The paper used in these volumes conforms to the American National Standard for Permanence of Paper for Printed Library Materials, Z39.48-1992 (R1997).

Library of Congress Cataloging-in-Publication Data
Nathaniel Hawthorne / editor, Jack Lynch.
    p. cm. -- (Critical insights)
    Includes bibliographical references and index.
    ISBN 978-1-58765-604-0 (one volume : alk. paper)
    1. Hawthor̲̅e̲̅, N̲athani̲el, 1804-1864—̲̅Criticism and interpretation. I.
Lynch, Jack (Jo̲̅
    PS1888.N297 20̲̅
    813'.3--dc22

                                                           2009026440

PRINTED IN CANADA

Contents

Resources

About This Volume

Jack Lynch

This contribution to the *Critical Insights* series doesn't presume to reprint everything important in Hawthorne criticism, nor even all the best Hawthorne criticism. The sheer volume of scholarship on Nathaniel Hawthorne would make that impossible. The *MLA International Bibliography* lists 2,884 learned articles on Hawthorne, and the WorldCat library database records 3,993 books devoted to him. Any one-volume collection of criticism necessarily provides nothing more than a sample.

This volume, therefore, brings together some of the representative high points of Hawthorne criticism, ranging chronologically from the 1940s to the present. The essays take a variety of critical and theoretical approaches: some ask biographical questions, while others examine Hawthorne's psychology; still others look at his historical and literary contexts. There are essays on mythology, on politics, and on theology. Together, they trace Hawthorne's reception through changing critical fashions, and illuminate some of the central concerns in Hawthorne criticism: the place of sin and Providence in his fiction, the genres in which he wrote, and the shape of his career as a whole. None of the essays presumes to be the final word on the subject. Instead, each is valuable for offering a starting point for thinking about Hawthorne's work, and for suggesting avenues for further exploration.

The collection opens with two introductory essays and a short biography before moving on to a section on Hawthorne's context and reception, containing a series of wide-ranging overviews of Hawthorne's works and career. A longer section, "Critical Readings," follows, with samples of critical close readings from a number of schools of thought. The volume is rounded out by a chronology of the important events in Hawthorne's life and a bibliography, with suggestions for further reading.

CAREER, LIFE, AND INFLUENCE

On Nathaniel Hawthorne

Jack Lynch

His works have appeared in countless versions, from inexpensive paperbacks to a monumental twenty-three-volume scholarly edition. They can be found in virtually every library in the English-speaking world. No responsible survey course on American literature is complete without *The Scarlet Letter*; no reputable collection of American short stories can omit "The Birth-Mark" or "Rappaccini's Daughter." He stands at the center of nineteenth-century American literature. And yet, for all his familiarity, there remains something strange, something alien, about Nathaniel Hawthorne.

Perhaps we find him difficult because we're too familiar with the realistic novel. The novel has dominated American literature for more than a century, and we spend too much time reading that form to appreciate Hawthorne fully. The novel—a uniquely modern form, whose very name suggests novelty—is characterized by an attention to the minute textures of everyday life. It does away with the fantastic and the supernatural; giants and wizards are banished by middle-class city-dwellers and maidservants. No longer do the plots revolve around dragon-slaying and journeys to the heavenly city; instead, bourgeois heroes and heroines seek inheritances and suitable marriages. In the words of Ian Watt, one of the most influential critics of the realistic novel, the form "arose in the modern period, a period whose general intellectual orientation was most decisively separated from its classical and mediaeval heritage by its rejection—or at least its attempted rejection—of universals" (Watt, 12). The characters are specific people with recognizable idiosyncrasies, not idealized everyman types, and they move in a recognizably real world: "the plot," writes Watt, "had to be acted out by particular people in particular circumstances, rather than, as had been common in the past, by general human types against a background primarily determined by the appropriate literary convention" (Watt, 15). This realistic novel has become the most common form of fiction, the kind on which we're taught to exercise our critical methods.

If we try to read Hawthorne the way we read the realistic novel, though, we're bound to be either disappointed or confused. Hawthorne stands outside this central tradition of realistic fiction. It's true that he was influenced by the realistic novels of Samuel Richardson and Jane Austen, but other writers and other genres contributed more. He borrowed many settings and situations from the Gothic fiction of Ann Radcliffe and Charlotte Brontë—a genre that reintroduced some of the supernatural that had been banished from fiction early in the eighteenth century. Even more important, his sensibility was steeped in the kind of allegorical romance that, while alien to most modern sensibilities, was well known to seventeenth-century Puritans and their nineteenth-century readers. The most famous allegory of that era—John Bunyan's *Pilgrim's Progress*, published in 1678—became one of the most famous English books of all time, and virtually every literate person knew the story of Christian's journey to the Celestial City. Hawthorne, whose fascination with the seventeenth century is evident on nearly every page of his works, had a complicated relationship with the genre that began in earnest in the eighteenth.

Hawthorne's narratives may seem realistic on the surface, but his greatest debt is not to the eighteenth-century novelists but to the seventeenth-century romancers. And he was explicit about his intentions. Hawthorne didn't refer to his works as "short stories" or "novels"; he preferred to call them "tales" and "romances." The choice of vocabulary is significant. "When a writer calls his work a Romance," Hawthorne declares in the preface to *The House of the Seven Gables*, "he wishes to claim a certain latitude, both as to its fashion and material, which he would not have felt himself entitled to assume, had he professed to be writing a Novel." The novel, he goes on to note, "is presumed to aim at a very minute fidelity, not merely to the possible, but to the probable and ordinary course of man's experience." That's a fine description of the work of Jane Austen and George Eliot, but it wasn't what fired Hawthorne's imagination. A romance, on the other hand, claims "a right to present that truth under circumstances, to a great extent, of the writer's own choosing and creation" (Hawthorne, 2:1).

Hawthorne, that is to say, never abandoned his responsibility to tell the truth, but he refused to be limited to "minute fidelity" and the "ordinary course" of life—he insisted on telling the truth under circumstances of his own choosing. His works are set not in the mundane world of his middle-class readers, but in a kind of dreamscape in which the grand dramas of creation were played out. He rarely crosses the line into pure fantasy—Young Goodman Brown, for instance, returns to Salem unsure whether he dreamed the terrible things he saw in the forest; the whole thing may have been imagined—but his stories often border on the supernatural. Hawthorne sought "a neutral territory," as he writes, "somewhere between the real world and fairy-land, where the Actual and Imaginary may meet, and each imbue itself with the nature of the other" (Hawthorne, 1:36).

The eighteenth century, which pioneered the realistic novel, had grown weary of more-than-human heroes engaging in allegorical journeys. Many writers rejected the favorite mode of the seventeenth century; their works were often resolutely literal. Critic Blanford Parker argues that "the idea of the *literal*" was the most important "discovery" of the eighteenth century—and argues that the idea needed discovery, because the earlier "Baroque culture" understood reality in terms of divine analogy (Parker, 20). Hawthorne, who feared that the literal was too limiting for his imagination, worked to bring that older culture back.

Other writers of the Romantic era had begun to roll back the eighteenth-century prejudice in favor of the literal, trying to recover some of the preternatural elements that were fair game before the realistic novel took over, but none did it with more gusto than Hawthorne. He was at heart an allegorist, and when he recorded the details of everyday life, they always pointed to a reality far beyond the everyday.

Not every contemporary reader was pleased. Edgar Allan Poe, for instance, acknowledged that Hawthorne "evinces extraordinary genius, having no rival either in America or elsewhere" (Poe, 577), but he admitted he was put off by the "strain of allegory which completely overwhelms the greater number of his subjects, and which in some measure interferes with the direct conduct of absolutely all. . . . He is infinitely too fond of allegory, and can never hope for popularity so long as he persists in it" (Poe, 582, 587).

Other readers, though, recognized the unique power of Hawthorne's resonant metaphorical imagination and his use of otherworldly phenomena. Herman Melville, another great nineteenth-century allegorist, described the effect Hawthorne's works had on him: "The soft ravishments of the man spun me round about in a web of dreams," he wrote in 1850, "and when the book was closed, when the spell was over, this wizard 'dismissed me with but misty reminiscences, as if I had been dreaming of him'" (Melville, 241). Critics may carp at his fondness for the supernatural, but his immersion in the older forms of fiction make him "immeasurably deeper than the plummet of the mere critic" (Melville, 244).

Focusing too much on Hawthorne's passion for seventeenth-century culture, seventeenth-century genres, and seventeenth-century modes of thought, though, can have the unfortunate side effect of pulling him out of his own age, the nineteenth century. Many have looked on him as a kind of literary hermit, unconnected to the world around him. "Hawthorne's career," wrote the novelist Henry James in 1879, "was passed, for the most part, in a small and homogeneous society, in a provincial, rural community; it had few perceptible points of contact with what is called the world, with public events, with the manners of his time, even with the life of his neighbours" (James, 1). In fact, though, Hawthorne had plenty of "contact with what is called the world"; he lived at the center of an important group of American worthies. At Bowdoin College in Maine, where he studied from 1821 to 1825, one of his classmates was the future president Franklin Pierce. More interesting were his literary acquaintances: Hawthorne knew many of the greatest authors of mid-nineteenth-century America. Another Bowdoin classmate was the poet Henry Wadsworth Longfellow. In August 1850 he met

Herman Melville, fifteen years his junior, who became a fast friend and a promoter of his works: the year after *The Scarlet Letter* was published, Melville's own masterpiece, *Moby-Dick*, appeared with a dedication to Hawthorne, with "admiration for his genius." Though he was never close to Ralph Waldo Emerson, the two were acquaintances, and Hawthorne enjoyed rowing with Henry David Thoreau. He was also close to the early feminist champion Margaret Fuller—critics have suggested that she may have provided the model of Hester Prynne in *The Scarlet Letter.*

It's unsurprising, then, that Hawthorne in many ways embodies what it means to be an American author. He was writing at just the time that American literature was being taken seriously as a rival to the older British tradition. Melville, for instance, was convinced that America's literature would one day surpass England's: "If Shakespeare has not been equalled," he prophesied, "he is sure to be surpassed, and surpassed by an American born now or yet to be born" (Melville, 246). Hawthorne, he hinted, may well be that American Shakespeare. Hawthorne, wrote Henry James a few decades later, "has the importance of being the most beautiful and the most eminent representative of a literature . . .the most valuable example of the American genius" (James, 2).

But Hawthorne would have resented being treated as merely an American author—for all his fascination with the Puritans of Salem, his real concern was humankind as a whole. And in the last 150 years his reputation has spread far beyond New England, beyond America, beyond even the Anglophone world. One important library database records 671 editions of *The Scarlet Letter* in just the twentieth century, but not all are in English: there are now translations into Catalan, Chinese, Czech, Dutch, Finnish, French, German, Gujarati, Hebrew, Hindi, Italian, Japanese, Korean, Persian, Polish, Portuguese, Russian, Slovenian, Spanish, Swedish, Tagalog, and Turkish. The definitive work of nineteenth-century American literature is now a part of world literature.

Works Cited

Hawthorne, Nathaniel. *The Centenary Edition of the Works of Nathaniel Haw-thorne*. Ed. William Charvat et al. 23 vols. Columbus: Ohio State University Press, 1962–97.

James, Henry, Jr. *Hawthorne*. London: Macmillan, 1879.

Melville, Herman. *The Piazza Tales and Other Prose Pieces, 1839–1860*. In *The Writings of Herman Melville: The Northwestern-Newberry Edition*. Eds. Harrison Hayford, Alma A. MacDougall, and G. Thomas Tanselle. Evanston, IL: Northwestern University Press, 1987.

Parker, Blanford. *The Triumph of Augustan Poetics: English Literary Culture from Butler to Johnson*. Cambridge: Cambridge University Press, 1998.

Poe, Edgar Allan. *Essays and Reviews*. New York: Literary Classics of the United States, 1984.

Watt, Ian. *The Rise of the Novel: Studies in Defoe, Richardson, and Fielding*. Berkeley: University of California Press, 1957.

Biography of Nathaniel Hawthorne_____

Frank Day

Early Life

Nathaniel Hawthorne was born July 4, 1804, in Salem, Massachusetts. His great-great-grandfather, John Hathorne, was one of the three judges in the Salem witchcraft trials in 1692; his father, Nathaniel Hathorne, was a sea captain who died in Dutch Guinea when Nathaniel was four years old. Hawthorne added the "w" to his name when he was a young man. Hawthorne's mother, née Elizabeth Manning, came from a Massachusetts family prominent in business. Her brother, Robert Manning, was a well-known pomologist who assumed much of the responsibility for Hawthorne's care after the death of his father.

Hawthorne spent much of his adolescence in Raymond, Maine, where his Manning uncles owned property, and attended Bowdoin College in nearby Brunswick. He was a Bowdoin classmate of Henry Wadsworth Longfellow and Franklin Pierce (who would later become president of the United States). As a student, Hawthorne was adept in Latin and English but was disciplined for gambling and faulty chapel attendance. He was a handsome young man of slender build, with dark hair and eyes. Although quiet, he had a reputation for conviviality and joining friends in clubs and outdoor sports.

Hawthorne took his degree in 1825—he stood eighteenth in a class of thirty-eight—and spent the next twelve years in Salem, where he read extensively and taught himself to write. The product of these twelve years was the indifferent novel *Fanshawe: A Tale* (1828) and more than forty stories and sketches, including such well-known pieces as "The Gentle Boy," "Roger Malvin's Burial," and "My Kinsman, Major Molineux." It was a rewarding apprenticeship in terms of his artistic accomplishment, and although it did not bring him much immediate fame or income, the publication of *Twice-Told Tales* in 1837 successfully launched his career.

In 1838, Hawthorne fell in love with Sophia Peabody of Boston, whom he married in 1842. During their courtship, he spent two years working at the Boston Custom House, and he joined the utopian community at Brook Farm for several months. Both of these experiences later proved fruitful for him as a writer. Hawthorne took his bride to live in the Old Manse in Concord, and there began a life as a happy and devoted husband and father of three children.

A second edition of *Twice-Told Tales* appeared in 1842, and in 1846, the year he left the Old Manse, Hawthorne published *Mosses from an Old Manse*. With these volumes, he began to receive high critical recognition. Edgar Allan Poe praised the second edition of *Twice-Told Tales* in a review that has become famous for its perceptive commentary on Hawthorne's "invention, creation, imagination, originality." When he left the Old Manse, Hawthorne was a mature artist, ready to write the novels for which he became famous.

Life's Work

With the help of influential friends, Hawthorne received in 1846 an appointment as surveyor of the Salem Custom House. He was dismissed from this position in 1849, a victim of the political spoils system, and then wrote his greatest work, *The Scarlet Letter* (1850). In the introduction to *The Scarlet Letter*, Hawthorne settled what he perceived as some old injustices at the customhouse and invented the fiction of having found his story in an old manuscript in the customhouse.

In *The Scarlet Letter*, Hawthorne develops his most powerful theme of the hardening of the heart in what he called the Unpardonable Sin. This theme—essentially an expansion of Saint Paul's admonition in I Corinthians 13 to practice charity—is dramatized in miniature in "Ethan Brand: A Chapter from an Abortive Romance" (1850). Ethan Brand has sought knowledge tirelessly, searching for the Unpardonable Sin, and when he learns that in his quest he has allowed his heart to atrophy, he realizes that he has found the answer in himself: The Unpardonable Sin is the cultivation of the intellect at the expense of one's humanity.

Thus, the Unpardonable Sin in *The Scarlet Letter* is not the very human adultery of Hester Prynne and the Reverend Arthur Dimmesdale, a sin that takes place before the novel opens and which results in Hester's scarlet letter "A" that she has to wear on her bosom, but the relentless, unforgiving persecution of Dimmesdale by Hester's cuckolded husband, Roger Chillingworth. Sadly, Chillingworth is a learned man to whom the implications of his uncharitable obsession with revenge are absolutely clear. The inescapable conflict between nature and civilization stands out tragically in *The Scarlet Letter*: Hester and Chillingworth are united in marriage, a civil institution, but it is a marriage without true feeling for Hester, whereas the passion between Hester and Dimmesdale is deep and natural yet adulterous and unsanctioned. The outcome is tragic for all three of them.

In *The House of the Seven Gables* (1851), Hawthorne returns to the Puritan past and works out another fable of the effects of sin, this time in the form of a hereditary curse. The story of the Pyncheons is a fable of guilt and expiation, of the impossibility of escaping the past. Hawthorne thought it a greater novel than *The Scarlet Letter*.

During his residence at the Old Manse in Concord, Hawthorne had formed friendships with his Transcendentalist neighbors, Ralph Waldo Emerson, Henry David Thoreau, William Ellery Channing, and Bronson Alcott (the Old Manse had been built by Emerson's grandfather). Yet Hawthorne's sensibilities were too burdened by a sense of sin for him to accept the optimism and idealism expressed by these thinkers. Furthermore, his experience at Brook Farm had made him distrust the ideals expressed in the notion of intellectuals living together communally. In *The Blithedale Romance* (1852), he satirized many of the goals and values of Utopian thinkers. The novel is exceptionally acute in its perceptions of human psychology and is a measure of the distance between the student of Puritanism and the sin in the human heart and the Transcendentalists with their lofty vision of human possibilities.

Hawthorne also published in 1852 *The Life of Franklin Pierce*. This campaign biography of his Bowdoin classmate led to Hawthorne's appointment as United States consul in Liverpool, England, a post he held from 1853 to 1857. He left Liverpool to live in Italy for three years, an experience that culminated in *The Marble Faun* (1860). This novel made him one of the first American writers to treat the experiences of his countrymen in Europe, a theme developed by such later writers as Henry James, William Dean Howells, and Ernest Hemingway.

When he came home to the United States, Hawthorne bought a home in Concord, which he named The Wayside. He died four years later while on a tour in Plymouth, New Hampshire. He was buried in Concord. By the time of his death he had earned a considerable reputation for his romances.

From *Dictionary of World Biography: The 19th Century* (Pasadena, CA: Salem Press, 1999): 1064-1067. Copyright © 1999 by Salem Press, Inc.

Bibliography

Bunge, Nancy. *Nathaniel Hawthorne: A Study of the Short Fiction*. New York: Twayne, 1993. Discusses Hawthorne's major short stories in three categories: isolation and community; artists and scientists; and perspective, humility, and joy. Includes excerpts from Hawthorne's journals, letters, and prefaces; also includes excerpts on Hawthorne from Herman Melville, Edgar Allan Poe, Henry James, and several contemporary critics.

Charvat, William, et al., eds. *The Centenary Edition of the Works of Nathaniel Hawthorne*. 23 vols. Columbus: Ohio State University Press, 1962–1997. This continuing multivolume edition of Hawthorne's works will, when complete, contain the entire canon. Somewhat unevenly accomplished by a variety of editors, the volumes contain a considerable amount of textual apparatus as well as biographical and critical information. Volumes 9, 10, and 11 give the texts of all known Hawthorne short stories and sketches.

Doubleday, Neal Frank. *Hawthorne's Early Tales: A Critical Study*. Durham, NC: Duke University Press, 1972. Doubleday focuses on what he calls "the development of Hawthorne's literary habit," including Hawthorne's literary theory and the materials from which he fashioned the stories of his twenties and early thirties. The index, while consisting chiefly of proper names and titles, includes some features of Hawthorne's work ("ambiguity," "irony," and the like).

Fogle, Richard Harter. *Hawthorne's Fiction: The Light and the Dark*. Rev. ed. Norman: University of Oklahoma Press, 1964. One of the first critics to write full analytical essays about the short stories, Fogle examines eight stories in detail as well as the four mature novels. He sees Hawthorne's fiction as both clear ("light") and complex ("dark"). He is particularly adept, although perhaps overly ingenious, in explicating Hawthorne's symbolism.

Keil, James C. "Hawthorne's 'Young Goodman Brown': Early Nineteenth-Century and Puritan Constructions of Gender." *The New England Quarterly* 69 (March, 1996): 33–55. Argues that Hawthorne places his story in the seventeenth century to explore the nexus of past and present in the attitudes of New Englanders toward theology, morality, and sexuality. Points out that clear boundaries between male and female, public and private, and work and home were thresholds across which nineteenth-century Americans often passed.

Kelsey, Angela M. "Mrs. Wakefield's Gaze: Femininity and Dominance in Nathaniel Hawthorne's 'Wakefield.'" *ATQ*, n.s. 8 (March, 1994): 17–31. In this feminist reading of Hawthorne's story, Kelsey argues that Mrs. Wakefield finds ways to escape and exceed the economy of the male gaze, first by appropriating the look for herself, then by refusing to die, and finally by denying her husband her gaze.

McKee, Kathryn B. "'A Small Heap of Glittering Fragments': Hawthorne's Discontent with the Short Story Form." *ATQ*, n.s. 8 (June, 1994): 137–147. Claims that Hawthorne's "Artist of the Beautiful" and "Downe's Wooden Image" are examples of his dissatisfaction with the short story as a form; argues that the fragile articles at the center of the tales mirror the limitations Hawthorne saw in the short-story genre.

Mackenzie, Manfred. "Hawthorne's 'Roger Malvin's Burial': A Postcolonial Reading." *New Literary History* 27 (Summer, 1996): 459–472. Argues that the story is postcolonial fiction in which Hawthorne writes the emerging American nation and recalls European colonial culture; claims that Hawthorne rehearses the colonialist past in order to concentrate and effectively "expel" its inherent violence.

Mellow, James R. *Nathaniel Hawthorne and His Times*. Boston: Houghton Mifflin, 1980. In this substantial, readable, and illustrated biography, Mellow provides a number of insights into Hawthorne's fiction. Refreshingly, the author presents Sophia Hawthorne not only as the prudish, protective wife of the Hawthorne legend, but also as a woman with an artistic sensibility and talent of her own. Mellow's book is a good introduction to a very interesting man. Suitable for the student and the general reader.

Miller, Edward Haviland. *Salem Is My Dwelling Place: A Life of Nathaniel Hawthorne*. Iowa City: University of Iowa Press, 1991. A large biography of more than six hundred pages, illustrated with more than fifty photographs and drawings. Miller has been able to draw on more manuscripts of family members and Hawthorne associates than did his predecessors and also developed his subject's family life in more detail. He offers interpretations of many of the short stories.

Moore, Margaret B. *The Salem World of Nathaniel Hawthorne*. Columbia: University of Missouri Press, 1998. Margaret Moore explores the relationship between Salem, Massachusetts, and its most famous resident, author Nathaniel Hawthorne.

Newberry, Frederick. "'The Artist of the Beautiful': Crossing the Transcendent Divide in Hawthorne's Fiction." *Nineteenth-Century Literature* 50 (June, 1995): 78–96. Argues that the butterfly's appearance is Hawthorne's endorsement of the transcendent power of imagination over nineteenth-century empiricism.

Newman, Lea Bertani Vozar. *A Reader's Guide to the Short Stories of Nathaniel Hawthorne*. Boston: G. K. Hall, 1979. For each of fifty-four stories, this valuable guide furnishes a chapter with four sections: publication history; circumstances of composition, sources, and influences; relationship with other Hawthorne works; and interpretations and criticism. The discussions are arranged alphabetically by title and keyed to a bibliography of more than five hundred secondary sources.

Pennell, Melissa McFarland. *Student Companion to Nathaniel Hawthorne*. Westport, CT: Greenwood Press, 1999. Includes bibliographical references and an index.

Scharnhorst, Gary. *The Critical Response to Hawthorne's "The Scarlet Letter."* New York: Greenwood Press, 1992. Includes chapters on the novel's background and composition history, on the contemporary American reception, on the early British reception, on the growth of Hawthorne's reputation after his death, on modern criticism, and on *The Scarlet Letter* on stage and screen.

Swope, Richard. "Approaching the Threshold(s) in Postmodern Detective Fiction: Hawthorne's 'Wakefield' and Other Missing Persons." *Critique* 39 (Spring, 1998): 207–227. Discusses "Wakefield" as a literary ancestor of "metaphysical" detective fiction, a postmodern genre that combines fiction with literary theory. "Wakefield" raises many of the questions about language, subjectivity, and urban spaces that surround postmodernism.

Thompson, G. R. *The Art of Authorial Presence: Hawthorne's Provincial Tales*. Durham, NC: Duke University Press, 1993. Argues that for Hawthorne the art of telling a story depends on a carefully created fiction of an authorial presence. Examines Hawthorne's narrative strategies for creating this presence by using contemporary narrative theory. Analyzes a small number of early Hawthorne stories and the criticism that has amassed about Hawthorne's fiction.

Von Frank, Albert J., ed. *Critical Essays on Hawthorne's Short Stories*. Boston: G. K. Hall, 1991. Divided into nineteenth- and twentieth-century commentary, with a section of new essays, an introduction, and a chronology of the tales.

Waggoner, Hyatt. *Hawthorne: A Critical Study*. Rev. ed. Cambridge: Harvard University Press, 1963. Waggoner is acute in his tracing of patterns of imagery in Hawthorne's fiction. This book is both a clear exposition and an incentive to plumb Hawthorne more deeply—virtues that have impelled some readers to challenge Waggoner's interpretations. For Waggoner, intuition, rather than biographical data, is the better tool to bring to the study of fiction.

Wineapple, Brenda. *Hawthorne: A Life*. New York: Knopf, 2003. An analysis of Hawthorne's often contradictory life that proposes that many of Hawthorne's stories are autobiographical.

the PARIS
REVIEW

The *Paris Review* Perspective_____

Elaine Blair for *The Paris Review*

Though Nathaniel Hawthorne set only one of his four novels and a handful of stories in the early New England colonies, he has given us our most enduring images of the Puritans—the "stern and black-browed" progenitors who harbor secret guilt over secret sins and fall pointedly short of their own ideals, however zealously they prosecute their neighbors. Hawthorne, however, was no historian. His Puritans were not based on scrupulous research, he did not try to imitate precisely the seventeenth-century language or manners of his subjects in *The Scarlet Letter* or "Young Goodman Brown," and none of his novels has the abundance of elaborate detail that we associate with nineteenth-century realism.

Yet it's not hard to see why Hawthorne was drawn to the subject of the New England colonies. Always interested in the human tendency to hypocrisy and self-deception, he found the perfect setting for these themes in the small communities of religious idealists, isolated between ocean and forest, whose members closely watched one another for any signs of religious apostasy. When Hester Prynne receives her penalty at the scaffold in *The Scarlet Letter*, the better part of the Boston population is there to witness it. Stories like "Young Goodman Brown" and "The Minister's Black Veil" suggest that moral transgressions take place in every society—including those that practice their devotion with the greatest rigor. The conspicuous "A" that Hester is forced to wear on her chest gives her the power to perceive which members of the community have also committed adultery, and the list turns out to be quite long. But Hawthorne's main concern is not so much exposing hypocrisy in general as probing his characters' struggle with conscience, and with private perceptions and intuitions that go against the grain of accepted thought. Hester is not a rebel against the Puritan code; she accepts that she has committed a sin and suffers over it. But her isolation from society nonetheless gives her a subtle measure of independence, a "freedom of speculation, then common enough on the other side of the Atlantic, but which our forefathers, had they known it, would have held to be a deadlier crime than that stigmatized by the scarlet letter."

When he published *The Scarlet Letter* in 1850, Hawthorne made literary history in two senses: the novel was well-loved in the United States and abroad, considered by far the best novel written by an American author. It was also one of the first American works of literature to evoke the American past. Its critical view of the colonies inaugurated a tradition that combined an implicit admiration of foundational American ideals with skepticism about their application. When we think of Hawthorne's contemporaries in Europe (Dickens, Flaubert, Turgenev), it's notable that the American writer—whose native culture was the youngest and most forward-looking—was the one most concerned with the founding myths of national history and the weight of past sins on present generations.

Hawthorne had a suspicion of old families and patrimony rooted in his own family history. His ancestors had lived in Salem, Massachusetts, his birthplace, since 1630. In Europe this would not have been considered an especially long lineage, but by local standards the Hathornes (the author added a "w" to his name) were ancient. A two-hundred-year history in one town was unusual for a nineteenth-century American family: the restless citizenry moved frequently from city to city, East to West, and in any case most Americans were the descendants of more recent immigrants. Hawthorne grew up with a strong sense of his family's history in Salem, of ancestors who had "been born and died, and have mingled their substance with the soil." One suspects that this morbid awareness of his dead forebears sharpened Hawthorne's gothic sensibility, his fascination with ghost stories and supernatural effects. His Salem roots were not a source of pride, at least not in his adult years. He generally felt that too many years in one place, or too long a history of prominent forebears, spawns corruption and mediocrity among the descendants, and most of all allows for the crimes of past generations to accumulate and burden the newer ones. The earliest Hathornes were prominent Puritan leaders who "had all the Puritanic traits, both good and evil," according to Hawthorne. William Hathorne, who came from England to Massachusetts in 1630, was a judge and legislator who, among other more virtuous deeds, had a Quaker woman whipped severely for her heretical faith. His son, Hawthorne writes, "inherited the persecuting spirit, and made himself so conspicuous in the martyrdom of witches that their blood may fairly be said to have left a stain upon him."

His ancestors' ignominious deeds were the basis for Hawthorne's second novel, *The House of the Seven Gables*, about the decline of an old Salem family, the Pyncheons, whose first patriarch built the family fortunes on theft and murder. Colonel Pyncheon, a seventeenth-century Puritan magistrate, acquires the land of a poorer man by having him tried and executed for witchcraft. The poor man curses Pyncheon and his descendants. By the nineteenth-century the Pyncheons are, for the most part, decrepit eccentrics—the curse seems, at least symbolically, to have taken hold. The past, in Hawthorne's stories, is something that inevitably haunts—rather than enriches—the present. Yet it was also a source of inspiration. He was drawn to its thin atmosphere and traveled there regularly in his imagination, and the dispatches that he sent back were his best work. If Hawthorne's fiction still stands at the center of American literature, it's in no small part because of the mixture of skepticism and sympathy with which he approached the American past.

Bibliography

Hawthorne, Nathaniel. *The House of the Seven Gables*. New York: Signet Classic, 1961.

_____. *The Scarlet Letter*. New York: Bantam Classic, 1981.

_____. *Tales and Sketches*. New York: Library of America, 1982.

CONTEXT, RECEPTION, COMPARISON, CRITICAL LENS

Nathaniel Hawthorne and the Canon of American Literature_____

Bridget M. Marshall

Hawthorne worried that his "writings do not, nor ever will, appeal to the broadest class of sympathies," and this, he was convinced, meant they would "not attain a very wide popularity." In this estimate he was too modest, for his work has been at the center of the American canon since the first copies of *The Scarlet Letter* came off the press.

In this overview of Hawthorne's place in American literary history, Bridget Marshall sketches the broad outlines of Hawthorne's career, from his difficult beginnings to his ultimate canonization. She sees an idealistic author buffeted by the unpleasant realities of nineteenth-century politics. Her essay describes some of the ways Hawthorne managed to translate his own biography into fiction, and along the way provides a useful starting point for thinking about Hawthorne as a uniquely American author.   — J.L.

Born in 1804 in Salem, Massachusetts, Nathaniel Hawthorne would eventually become known as a key figure in American letters. Nathaniel Hawthorne's fiction—particularly his short stories "Young Goodman Brown" and "The Minister's Black Veil," and his novel *The Scarlet Letter* (1850)—are some of the most well-known pieces of writing in American literature of this period; however, during his lifetime, Hawthorne struggled to make it as a professional writer and was often uneasy about his place in American literature. According to Stanley Bank, Hawthorne "may stand as a symbol of the nineteenth-century American author and his predicament" (8). Hawthorne struggled throughout his career to make a living as a writer and to create an American literary tradition. Bank explains that he "struggled with the problem of the relevance of the artist to the world and the meaning of art to America" (8). Hawthorne's sometimes ambivalent feelings about the literary life and the literary market are apparent throughout his journals and letters.

Hawthorne was descended from New England Puritans; his was the fifth generation of the family in America. Among his most notable ancestors was John Hathorne, who served as one of the judges in the Salem witch trials of the 1690s. Lore has it that Hawthorne added the "w" to his name to disassociate himself from this ancestor's legacy; however, the reason for the name change is not clear. He did in fact publish two stories under the name "Nathaniel Hathorne" in 1830—"Sights from a Steeple" in *The Token*, and "The Hollow of the Three Hills" in *The Salem Gazette*. He frequently used a variety of pseudonyms for his early writings, but after these two stories in 1830, he never used "Hathorne" again and gave his name as "Hawthorne" from that point on.

Despite what some have called his isolation, Hawthorne led a life filled with connections to the prominent literary and political minds of his day. During his years at Bowdoin College in Maine, where he was a student from 1821 to 1824, he developed friendships with poet Henry Wadsworth Longfellow and future fourteenth United States president, Franklin Pierce. Later in his life, he enjoyed friendships with Ralph Waldo Emerson, Henry David Thoreau, and Herman Melville. His letters and journals tell us much about the pleasure he gained from these relationships, and the reviews that these authors wrote of his work also show that he benefited professionally from his alliances with this circle of writers.

While in college, Hawthorne was concerned about his future ability to support himself (and a family) financially. He was disdainful of a variety of professions. In an 1821 letter to his mother, Elizabeth Hathorne, he dismissed a variety of potential careers—minister, lawyer, physician—for which he felt himself unsuitable, and lamented "Oh that I was rich enough to live without a profession" (295). He further queried his mother, "What do you think of my becoming an Author, and relying for support upon my pen" (295). He suggested (we must assume jokingly) that his qualification to the job was mostly that he thought "the illegibility of my handwriting is very authorlike" (295). However, he (again, perhaps jokingly?) suggests that "Authors are always poor Devils, and therefore Satan may take them" (295–296). Hawthorne would never find the financial remuneration of writing and publishing to be satisfactory, and indeed, he was quite often a "poor Devil" throughout his lifetime.

Hawthorne published ten stories between 1831 and 1833 in yearly gift books called *The Token*, published by Samuel Griswold Goodrich (Wineapple, 76). All were published anonymously and paid Hawthorne very little, probably less than $75.00 for all ten (76). He also had several sketches published in the *Salem Gazette*, but continued to insist upon anonymity (77). Throughout his early career, Hawthorne published many stories and sketches anonymously or pseudonymously in *The New England Magazine*, which later merged with *American Monthly*. For this work he was paid about a dollar a page; however, payment was not always prompt (Wineapple, 81). Through contributions to the *United States Magazine and Democratic Review*, he developed a relationship with its editor, John O'Sullivan. Although O'Sullivan had promised him between $3.00 and $5.00 per page, Hawthorne was rarely paid the full sum, and when he was, it was frequently long after publication (Mellow, 85). Despite the appearance of so many of his tales and sketches in such a wide array of venues, Hawthorne was unable to develop a following, perhaps in part due to the anonymous nature of these publications. These publishing ventures did not offer him improved fame or fortunes, and the tight budget in the Hawthorne household would continue for many years, a fact that chaffed at Hawthorne's sensibilities.

Hawthorne's first publication that earned him any recognition was *Twice-Told Tales*, published in 1837 under his own name rather than anonymously. The book's title came from the fact that all eighteen pieces appearing in it (among which was "The Minister's Black Veil") had previously been published in magazines. Hawthorne sent a copy of his book to former Bowdoin classmate Longfellow. Longfellow reviewed the book positively in the *North American Review*, saying that it came "from the hand of a man of genius" (23), and that "the book, though in prose, is written nevertheless by a poet" (23). Longfellow admired "the beautiful and simple style of the book . . . its vein of pleasant philosophy, and the quiet humor" (24). Hawthorne was grateful for the review and wrote a letter of thanks to Longfellow; this commenced a long-term and mutually enjoyable friendship between the two authors. Despite this and other favorable reviews, the book was not exactly a financial success; the one thousand copies of the first edition, sold at $1.00 a copy, did not sell out before the publisher remaindered them (Mellow, 82). This first venture into the public market was not a favorable one for Hawthorne; it left him deeply disappointed in and skeptical of the American reading public.

Hawthorne frequently confided in Longfellow his doubts about writing and his worries about money. In 1837, in a letter to Longfellow, he lamented that "For the last ten years, I have not lived, but only dreamed about living" (297). It seems that he was dissatisfied by his rather mundane life in Salem, and felt particularly isolated. He indicated that the limitations of his finances (and hence his rather limited travel options) would impede his attempt to become an author; he feared that he faced "another great difficulty, in the lack of materials; for I have seen so little of the world, that I have nothing but thin air to concoct my stories of" (297). Lacking worldly travel or personal adventure, Hawthorne instead used the materials most readily at hand to him—stories and legends of Puritan times and early Massachusetts's colonial intrigues. Although he managed to produce stories that would eventually be much admired, during his life, his early writing brought him no satisfaction; as he wrote in the same 1837 letter to Longfellow, "As to my literary efforts, I do not think much of them—neither is it worth while to be ashamed of them. They would have been better, I trust, if written under more favorable circumstances. I have had no external excitement—no consciousness that the public would like what I wrote, nor much hope nor a very passionate desire that they should do"

(297). Hawthorne's ambivalence here—a sadness that he has not received positive encouragement from the reading public, at the same time that he seems to have a relatively low opinion of that public, would continue throughout his life, even after he achieved some measure of approval from that audience.

Despite his critical success with *Twice-Told Tales* and his continued inclusion in small magazines, Hawthorne's writing was not generating a substantial income, nor did it bring him the kind of literary fame he wished. In 1838 he called himself "the obscurest man of letters in America" (qtd. in Wineapple, 83). As he was unable to make a living through authorship, he sought work in a variety of places in Salem and Boston; he was hired in 1839 to work in the Boston Custom House. The job was tolerable but not entirely satisfactory. He found little time to write while holding down this job; however, he wrote that "The utmost that I can hope to do will be to portray some of the characteristics of the life which I am now living, and of the people with whom I am brought into contact, for future use" (qtd. in Mellow, 162). While he believed that his interactions over the course of his workday might one day provide fodder for his writing, he was also aware that he had little time to write during or after his workday. For a time, the position afforded him a more reasonable salary; however, since the position was a political appointment, he was subject to the whims of political change. In 1840, anticipating a change in political favors, and generally displeased with his position, Hawthorne resigned from the Boston Custom House.

After his stint at the Boston Custom House, he went far afield of such mundane public work. He spent a brief period at Brook Farm, an experiment in communal living. In 1842 he married Sophia Peabody, to whom he had been engaged since 1838. They moved to the Old Manse in Concord, Massachusetts, which they rented from Emerson; it was here that Hawthorne would write *Mosses from an Old Manse* (1846). In Concord, he was more focused on his writing, and was free of other employment, though not of financial worries. He used his immediate surroundings—the house in Concord—as inspiration and setting for many of his stories. This recycling of his real life into his fiction would become a standard characteristic of Hawthorne's writing. He used his experience in various jobs as the basis for creating stories. His time working at the customhouse became "The Custom House," the short story introduction to *The Scarlet Letter*, and his brief experience of living and working on Brook Farm for about eight months in 1841 eventually became the novel *The Blithedale Romance* (1852).

While his early work—particularly the collections of *Twice-Told Tales* and *Mosses from an Old Manse*—was not particularly well-received, it did gain interest from the literary establishment. Although sales were by no means spectacular, as Hawthorne himself bemoaned, his publication of short-story volumes under his own name did at least introduce him to other writers. In his 1851 preface to *Twice-Told Tales*, he explained that "these volumes have opened the way to most agreeable associations, and to the formation of imperishable friendships" (291). These friendships with writers would continue to improve his reputation, and his letters indicate that they helped in large measure to keep his spirits up, and sometimes even helped him financially with donations to supplement his meager salary.

Employing friends and family who wrote letters on his behalf, Hawthorne attempted a return to nonliterary employment in the form of a public position. He desired a position in the post office, but was unsuccessful in gaining one. In 1846, politics favored him once again, and he was appointed surveyor at the Salem Custom House by President James Polk. His job was to determine the quantity and value of goods. Although the job at times gave him pleasure, it is clear that it also kept him from writing as much as he wished. In an 1847 letter to Longfellow, he claimed, "I should be happier if I could write—also, I should like to add something to my income, which, though tolerable, is a tight fit" (219–220). Unfortunately, Hawthorne would never find his financial situation entirely "tolerable," and it seemed that neither the literary nor nonliterary employment he could find would be enough to support his growing family, which now included a daughter, Una (born in

1844), and a son, Julian (born in 1846). Although he wished to write more to supplement his meager salary, he could find no time to write while he continued to work. When the job at the customhouse appeared to be in jeopardy because of politics, he wrote a beseeching letter to G. S. Hillard, another Bowdoin classmate, begging him to intercede on his behalf. The letter indicates Hawthorne's frustration with politics and his job, as well as with his literary stature (or lack thereof). The letter, written March 5, 1849, read in part: "But it seems to me that an inoffensive man of letters—having obtained a pitiful little office on no other plea than his pitiful little literature—ought not to be left to the mercy of these thick-skulled and no-hearted ruffians" (220–221). Hawthorne felt himself ill-used on all fronts, and his disdain for needing to ask for assistance is clear. Despite his own work and the intercession of various friends and writers, Hawthorne was dismissed from the position in June of 1849, after Zachary Taylor became president.

Shortly after he lost his position, his mother died; jobless and distraught, with a family to support and no means to do so, Hawthorne was desperate. Numerous friends and literary acquaintances contributed funds to his family, while he apparently wrote furiously. According to his wife, he spent the fall of 1849 writing nearly nine hours each day (Wineapple, 208). Despite this remarkable period of productivity, when James T. Fields, a young editor at Ticknor, Reed & Fields, visited Hawthorne personally to request to see some of his work, Hawthorne denied that he had written anything. Hawthorne eventually relented and gave Fields a draft of a story that would become *The Scarlet Letter.* Fields was thrilled with it and promised to publish it.

As he was completing work on *The Scarlet Letter*, Hawthorne still had his doubts about how it would be received. In a letter to his friend Horatio Bridge in February of 1850 (during which time the first part of the book was at the printer's while he was revising the second half), he wrote: "Some portions of the book are powerfully written; but my writings do not, nor ever will, appeal to the broadest class of sympathies, and therefore will not attain a very wide popularity. Some like them very much; others care nothing for them, and see nothing in them" (228). Despite the encouragement of his editor and friends, Hawthorne could not shake his fears about the reading public, which had not been kind to him in his previous publishing.

But *The Scarlet Letter* would in fact be warmly received by critics and readers. The first edition of the novel, in March of 1850, was 2,500 copies; another 2,000 were being printed within two weeks of the first (Wineapple, 216); the momentum of the book's sales was impressive: "fifteen hundred copies of the second edition sold in three days" (216). Brisk sales were matched (and perhaps encouraged) by positive reviews. The opening of a review in *Graham's Magazine* was effusive in its praise: "In this beautiful and touching romance Hawthorne has produced something really worthy of the fine and deep genius which lies within him" (239). The word "genius" was used in more than one review. Orestes Brownson, in *Brownson's Quarterly*, explained "the work before us is the largest and most elaborate of the romances he has as yet published, and no one can read half a dozen pages of it without feeling that none but a man of true genius and a highly cultivated mind could have written it. It is a work of rare, we may say of fearful power" (250). Both reviews and sales were encouraging, and Hawthorne finally began to enjoy some of the pleasures of his profession.

By 1851, his fame had increased remarkably. In his preface to the 1851 reissue of *Twice-Told Tales*, he referred again to his former claim that he had felt himself to be "the obscurest man of letters in America" during his years of publishing in magazines and annuals, but he also acknowledged that he had finally gained some measure of fame. Still he felt that his early writings were not encouraged, which added to the burden of his life as an author. He claimed that for almost twelve years of his early writing career, "he had no incitement to literary effort in a reasonable prospect of reputation or profit; nothing but the pleasure itself of composition—an enjoyment not at all amiss in its way, and perhaps essential to the merit of the work in hand, but which, in the long run, will hardly keep the chill out of a writer's heart, or the numbness out of his fingers" (289). The lack of fame or fortune for his toils clearly led to disappointment, as he increasingly turned toward money-making opportunities outside of the writing life.

At this time, Hawthorne also developed a friendship with another important literary voice of his time, Herman Melville. Melville dedicated *Moby-Dick* to Hawthorne. In his essay, "Hawthorne and His Mosses," published in 1850, Melville saw Hawthorne as underappreciated. He wrote, "Let America, then, prize and cherish her writers' yea, let her glorify them. They are not so many in number as to exhaust her goodwill" (261). He feared that Hawthorne's writing would only be appreciated too late for the writer to enjoy his own acclaim. He believed Hawthorne "one of the new, and far better generation of your writers" and exhorted Americans to "Give not over to future generations the glad duty of acknowledging him for what he is. Take that joy to yourself, in your own generation" (263). He clearly believed that Hawthorne's lack of fame was because he was only an American. Speaking of *Twice-Told Tales* and *The Scarlet Letter*, Melville claimed "there are things in those two books which, had they been written in England a century ago, Nathaniel Hawthorne had utterly displaced many of the bright names we now revere on authority" (263). Melville closed his review claiming that Hawthorne's books "should be sold by the hundred thousand; and read by the million; and admired by every one who is capable of admiration" (268). Melville and Hawthorne exchanged warm letters and visited one another, developing a literary friendship valuable to both parties. Hawthorne it seems was also a fan of Melville's writing: he had already written a positive review of *Typee* in the *Salem Advertiser* in 1846.

Edgar Allan Poe also reviewed Hawthorne, though somewhat less glowingly than Melville. Poe wrote in his review, "I have not been wrong, perhaps, in citing him as *the* example, *par excellence*, in this country, of the privately-admired and publicly-unappreciated man of genius" (241, emphasis in original). Poe claimed that Hawthorne was not better known because "he is neither a man of wealth nor a quack" and because of "the very marked idiosyncrasy of Mr. Hawthorne himself" (242). But not all of Poe's praise was glowing; he commented that Hawthorne's "books afford strong internal evidence of having been written to himself and his particular friends alone" (246). Much of the praise he did write about Hawthorne was tempered by reservations. Reviewing *Twice-Told Tales*, Poe explains that the sketches included in the collection are "the product of a truly imaginative intellect, restrained, and in some measure repressed, by fastidiousness of taste, by constitutional melancholy, and by indolence" (247). Nonetheless, he did see value in Hawthorne's use of local scenes and admired his artistry, insisting that Hawthorne's *Tales* "belong to the highest region of Art" (250). "We know of few compositions which the critic can more honestly commend than these *Twice-Told Tales*. As Americans, we feel proud of the book" (250). This claim to Americanness was indeed part of the appeal of Hawthorne's work.

Hawthorne's improved outlook in his literary life was matched by an upturn in his nonliterary life as well. Despite his numerous early setbacks in nonliterary jobs achieved through political appointments, his engagement in politics finally paid off in 1853, when President Franklin Pierce appointed him to a position as United States Consul in Liverpool. The previous year, he had completed a biography of Franklin Pierce (also a Bowdoin classmate), which brought about the favorable appointment. Unfortunately, when it became clear that Pierce would not be reelected for a second term, it was clear that Hawthorne's position would once again be subject to politics, so he left the job to travel with his family, before eventually returning to New England, where he continued to write stories and novels.

Despite the rather positive reception he had from the literary lights of his day, Hawthorne did not gain the kind of popularity that he sometimes sought. Whether out of frustration or a sense of his own superiority, Hawthorne was disdainful of many of his contemporary writers (particularly women) and often dismissed the American readership. He wrote a letter to his publisher, William Ticknor, in January of 1855 that

America is now wholly given over to a d—d mob of scribbling women, and I should have no chance of success while the public taste is occupied with their trash—and should be ashamed of myself if I did succeed. What is the mystery of these innumerable editions of the *Lamplighter*, and other books neither better nor worse?—worse they could not be, and better they need not be, when they sell by 100,000 (304).

This quote is often used to show Hawthorne's attitude toward American readers and authors alike, particularly women. Hawthorne had expressed similar disdain years before; in writing in his 1830 biographical sketch of religious dissenter Anne Hutchinson, he likened her to "the ink-stained Amazons [that] will expel their [male] rivals" (218). Women writers, in Hawthorne's eye, threatened his own finances, and further debased the tastes of readers. Herman Melville was also aware of Hawthorne's disdain for the reading public. He wrote "men like Hawthorne, in many things, deem the plaudits of the public such strong presumptive evidence of mediocrity in the object of them, that it would in some degree render them doubtful of their own powers did they hear much and vociferous braying concerning them in public pastures" (265). Although readers began to give him more respect, Hawthorne did not particularly relish his reading public.

Hawthorne was a harsh critic of the reading public, but he often turned his harshest criticism toward himself. Hawthorne frequently indicated that he was dissatisfied by his own production, in both the kind and volume of writing he managed to complete. In the preface to his 1846 *Mosses from an Old Manse*, he lamented that he had produced "No profound treatise of ethics—no philosophic history—no novel, even, that could stand, unsupported, on its edges. All that I had to show, as a man of letters, were these few tales and essays, which had blossomed out like flowers in the calm summer of my heart and mind" (288). Indeed, he claimed that "such trifles, I truly feel, afford no solid basis for a literary reputation" (288). Although he clearly longed for that "literary reputation," it seems that he at times felt it was beyond the reach of his own abilities and performances. He was so dissatisfied by his first novel, *Fanshawe: A Tale*, which he had published anonymously and at his own expense in 1828, that he tried to destroy all copies of it. It seems he was somewhat successful in disavowing the work, since even his own wife didn't discover the existence of the novel until after he died (Wineapple, 78). He was known for destroying all drafts of his work, and admitted in his preface to the 1851 edition of *Twice-Told Tales* that he had burned these items "without mercy or remorse, and, moreover, without any subsequent regret" (289). In June of 1853, he wrote in his journal (published posthumously as *The American Notebooks*): "I burned great heaps of old letters and other papers, a little while ago, preparatory to going to England. Among them were hundreds of Sophia's maiden letters" (280). Satisfied to see them destroyed, he wrote, "What a trustful guardian of secret matters fire is!" (280).

Hawthorne's reputation, particularly among other authors, continued to grow. After Hawthorne's death in 1864, Longfellow wrote a poem in tribute to him. The last two stanzas evoke the loss that Longfellow felt:

> There in seclusion and remote from men
> The wizard hand lies cold,
> Which at its topmost speed let fall the pen,
> And left the tale half told.
>
> Ah! who shall lift that wand of magic power,
> And the lost clew regain?
> The unfinished window in Aladdin's tower
> Unfinished must remain!
>
> (qtd. in Norton, 89)

After his death, Hawthorne's reputation increased as generations discovered his stories and novels, particularly *The Scarlet Letter* and *The*

House of the Seven Gables. Both novels have been reprinted numerous times, and the former was even made into a popular film in 1995. One indicator of Hawthorne's popularity in contemporary American culture is surely indicated by the growth of the Hawthorne tourism industry. Numerous places associated with Hawthorne himself and his novels have become tourist attractions, with substantial restoration budgets and admission fees for tours. The Old Manse in Concord, where Hawthorne and his wife lived, and where Hawthorne wrote *Mosses from an Old Manse,* has been declared a National Historic Landmark, currently administered by the Trustees of Reservations. The Wayside in Concord, where Hawthorne spent the last four years of his life, and the only home Hawthorne actually owned, is also a National Historic Landmark and is now part of Minute Man National Historical Park. A group of historic homes and museums in Salem, known collectively as "The House of Seven Gables," includes Nathaniel Hawthorne's birthplace and the seven-gabled house (Turner-Ingersoll Mansion, built in 1668) that Hawthorne made famous with his novel. According to a *New York Times* article, "Nearly 150,000 people visit the House of Seven Gables in Salem every year" (Driscoll).

Recently the Hawthorne family was in the spotlight again, when, on June 26, 2006, the bodies of Hawthorne's wife, Sophia Peabody, and daughter Una, were reinterred in Sleepy Hollow Cemetery (where Hawthorne himself was buried). The two were moved at great expense from their original resting places in Kensal Green Cemetery in London. The event was widely reported in the popular press, with local papers reporting that "the town of Concord turned out in force, in respect for the Hawthornes. It was standing-room only on the lawn of the Old Manse, the Hawthorne family's first home, where some two hundred gathered under a tent for a service after the private interment" (Lobron). Despite his sometimes negative portrayal of New Englanders in his stories, Hawthorne has been embraced as a literary master and native son of Massachusetts.

Henry James wrote in 1879 that

Hawthorne's career was probably as tranquil and strikingly deficient in incident, in what may be called the dramatic quality. Few men of equal genius and of equal eminence can have led on the whole a simpler life. [. . .] Hawthorne's career had few vicissitudes or variations; it was passed for the most part in a small and homogeneous society, in a provincial, rural community; it had few perceptible points of contact with what is called the world, with public events, with the manners of his time, even with the life of his neighbors. (268)

This has certainly been the opinion of many critics and biographers of Hawthorne over the years. Yet despite what might be seen as shortcomings, Hawthorne's writing and reputation has lived on through countless reevaluations. As James wrote, "in the field of letters, Hawthorne is the most valuable example of the American genius" (268). After his lifelong struggles to be an author, he has long since been held in the highest esteem among the judges of American literature.

Works Cited

Bank, Stanley. *American Romanticism: A Shape for Fiction*. New York: G. P. Putnam's Sons, 1969.

Bridge, Horatio. *Personal Recollections of Hawthorne*. 1893. New York: Haskell House Publishers, Ltd. 1968.

Brownson, Orestes. "Literary Notices and Criticisms: *Brownson's Quarterly* 4 (October 1850) 528–32." Reprinted in *The Scarlet Letter and Other Writings*. Ed. Leland S. Person. New York: W. W. Norton, 2005: 250–253.

Driscoll, Anne. "Beneath Hawthorne's Gables, Tourism Aids Needy." *New York Times* (May 8, 1988). NewYorkTimes.com.

Hawthorne, Nathaniel. *The American Notebooks*. Ed. Randall Stewart. New Haven: Yale University Press, 1932.

_____. "From *Graham's Magazine* [Edwin Percy Whipple] 36 no. 5 (May 1850) 345–46." Reprinted in *The Scarlet Letter and Other Writings*. Ed. Leland S. Person. New York: W. W. Norton, 2005: 239–241.

_____. "Letter to Elizabeth C. Hathorne, Raymond. March 13th 1821." Reprinted in *Nathaniel Hawthorne's Tales*. Ed. James McIntosh. New York: W. W. Norton, 1987: 295–296.

_____. "Letter to G. S. Hillard, Boston. March 5th, 1849." Reprinted in *The Scarlet Letter and Other Writings*. Ed. Leland S. Person. New York: W.W. Norton, 2005: 220–221.

_____. "Letter to H. W. Longfellow, Cambridge. 4 June 1837." Reprinted in *Nathaniel Hawthorne's Tales*. Ed. James McIntosh. New York: W. W. Norton, 1987: 296–298.

_____. "Letter to H. W. Longfellow, Cambridge. 11 November 1847." Reprinted in *The Scarlet Letter and Other Writings*. Ed. Leland S. Person. New York: W. W. Norton, 2005: 219–220.

_____. "Letter to Horatio Bridge, Portsmouth. Feb. 4th 1850." Reprinted in *The Scarlet Letter and Other Writings*. Ed. Leland S. Person. New York: W.W. Norton, 2005: 228–229.

_____. "Letter to William D. Ticknor, January 19, 1855." Reprinted in *Nathaniel Hawthorne, The Letters, 1853–1856*, ed. Thomas Woodson et al., *The Centenary Edition of the Works of Nathaniel Hawthorne*, vol. 16. Columbus: Ohio State Univ. Press, 1987: 304.

_____. "Mrs. Hutchinson." In *Tales, Sketches, and other Papers by Nathaniel Hawthorne, with a Biographical Sketch by George Parsons Lathrop*. Boston: Houghton, Mifflin and Co., 1889: 217–226.

_____. "The Old Manse: The Author Makes the Reader Acquainted with His Abode." Preface. Reprinted in *Nathaniel Hawthorne's Tales*. Ed. James McIntosh. New York: W. W. Norton, 1987: 268–288.

_____. "Preface to the 1851 Edition of *Twice-Told Tales*." Preface. Reprinted in *Nathaniel Hawthorne's Tales*. Ed. James McIntosh. New York: W. W. Norton, 1987: 289–292.

James, Henry. "Hawthorne." In *A Casebook on the Hawthorne Question*. Ed. Agnes McNeill Donohue. New York: Thomas Y. Crowell Co., 1963: 268–283.

Lobron, Alison. "Hawthorne Revisited: Author's Kin are Reinterred." *The Boston Globe* (June 27, 2006). Online through Boston.com.

Longfellow, Henry Wadsworth. "Twice-told Tales." *North American Review* 45, no. 96 (July, 1837): 59–73. Reprinted in *Nathaniel Hawthorne: The Contemporary Reviews*. Ed. John L. Idol, Jr., and Buford Jones. Cambridge, Cambridge UP: 1994. 23–24.

Mellow, James R. *Nathaniel Hawthorne in His Times*. Baltimore: The Johns Hopkins University Press, 1980.

Melville, Herman. "Hawthorne and His Mosses." In *A Casebook on the Hawthorne Question*. Ed. Agnes McNeill Donohue. New York: Thomas Y. Crowell Co., 1963: 253–268.

Norton, Charles Eliot. *Henry Wadsworth Longfellow: A Sketch of His Life*. New York: Houghton, Mifflin & Co., 1907: 87–89.

Poe, Edgar Allan. "Nathaniel Hawthorne." In *A Casebook on the Hawthorne Question*. Ed. Agnes McNeill Donohue. New York: Thomas Y. Crowell Co., 1963: 241–253.

Wineapple, Brenda. *Hawthorne: A Life*. New York: Alfred A. Knopf, 2003.

Nathaniel Hawthorne's Critical Reception_____

Matthew J. Bolton

Some great writers toiled in obscurity until their deaths, to be discovered only decades after they were in their graves. Others achieved great fame during their lifetimes, only to be forgotten by subsequent generations. Hawthorne, though, managed to find widespread popularity at the height of his powers, and has never lost a dedicated readership. In this essay Matthew Bolton charts the rises and falls of Hawthorne's literary stock value from his first fame in the 1850s through today. Along the way he discusses different schools of criticism and what they've made of him. Bolton's article, by describing the shapes of Hawthorne criticism as a whole, provides a useful guide to the rest of this volume.   — J.L.

A decade and a half after Nathaniel Hawthorne's death, Henry James published a long essay in praise of his literary predecessor. James recalls the excitement which greeted the publication of Hawthorne's *The Scarlet Letter* in 1850:

> The book was the finest piece of imaginative writing yet put forth in the country. There was a consciousness of this in the welcome that was given it—a satisfaction in the idea of America having produced a novel that belonged to literature, and to the forefront of it. Something might at last be sent to Europe as exquisite in quality as anything that had been received. (James, 108)

The Scarlet Letter was immediately recognized as a great novel, and has never gone out of print in the hundred and fifty some-odd years since it was first issued. Such instant and sustained recognition of literary greatness is rarer than one might think. Herman Melville's *Moby-Dick*, for example, published a year after *The Scarlet Letter* and dedicated to Hawthorne, met with a very different sort of reception. The book sold poorly, was reviewed harshly, and virtually disappeared from public consciousness until it was rediscovered by literary critics of the 1920s. As a third model of literary reception, one might place alongside *The Scarlet Letter* and *Moby-Dick* any number of novels published to great acclaim in the 1850s that now lie forgotten. Hawthorne's was not an overnight success, for he had been publishing novels and stories under his own name and various pseudonyms from 1828 onward. Yet when widespread recognition came at last, it was to be lasting. The reading public and critical establishment very rarely get it as right as they did with Nathaniel Hawthorne.

In contrast to many of his mid-nineteenth-century contemporaries, whose reputations waxed and waned over the generations, Hawthorne has always held a place in critical formulations of the American literary tradition. Because Hawthorne never faded into obscurity or fell out of favor, his critical reception across the nineteenth, twentieth, and twenty-first centuries reads like a précis of changing modes of literary criticism and scholarship itself. The phases of Hawthorne criticism reflect the evolution of literary theory itself: from the biographical and historical focus of the first half of the twentieth century, to the textual explication of the mid-century New Critics, to the feminist, Marxist, and deconstructionist readings of the 1970s and 1980s, and finally to the disparate approaches that mark the present "post-theory" era. *The Scarlet Letter* and a handful of tales, notably "The Minister's Black Veil" and "Young Goodman Brown"—as well as, to a lesser extent, novels such as *The House of the Seven Gables*—have been constant placeholders in a shifting canon and in a shifting theoretical landscape. *The Scarlet Letter*'s long-standing inclusion in high school and college American literature syllabi (among its many other merits, the novel's brevity certainly has helped to hold its place on reading lists) has ensured that new generations continue to encounter the novelist. Hawthorne's work continues to be read, even if the ways in which it is read have changed.

Those wishing to study the course of Hawthorne's life and career may refer to several fine biographies, including those of James Mellow, Arlin Turner, T. Walter Herbert, and, most recently, Brenda Wineapple. Larry Reynolds's *A Historical Guide to Nathaniel Hawthorne* provides much in the way of background information on the author. Hawthorne's letters, available in four volumes as well as in the more compact *Selected Letters*, provide a window into the poet's daily life. Bibliographies are another important tool for any student of Hawthorne. Nina E. Browne's bibliography from the turn of the century lists all of Hawthorne's works in chronological order, while Scharnhorst's *Nathaniel Hawthorne: An Annotated Bibliography of Comment and Criticism before 1900* can point readers to several thousand nineteenth-century responses to the novelist. Jeanetta Boswell's *Nathaniel Hawthorne and the Critics: A Checklist of Criticism, 1900–1978* serves a comparable function for twentieth-century criticism. *The Nathaniel Hawthorne Review* publishes annual bibliographies of new work on the author. By accessing the Modern Language Association's International Bibliography, available through the Web sites of most colleges and universities, a student may readily search for Hawthorne criticism within any given time period.

There are many good compilations of Hawthorne criticism. J. Donald Crowley's *Hawthorne: The Critical Heritage* is an invaluable guide to the reactions of Hawthorne's contemporaries to his work. Gary Scharnhorst edited a collection of critical responses to *The Scarlet Letter*, while Bernard Rosenthal edited a comparable collection focusing on *The House of the Seven Gables*. Each volume excerpts a number of contemporary and modern responses to its respective book. Rosenthal's annotated bibliography, divided by era, is particularly helpful to a reader looking to scan the field of Hawthorne criticism. The Norton Critical Edition of *The Scarlet Letter* supplements the full text of the novel with a series of contemporary and modern responses to it. Colacurcio's *New Essays on "The Scarlet Letter"* is an excellent collection of contemporary criticism, as are the several essay collections that Millicent Bell has edited. Cady and Budd's *On Hawthorne:*

The Best from American Literature reprints two dozen representative twentieth-century journal essays on Hawthorne, paying particular attention to the New Critical writers of the 1950s and 1960s. *The Cambridge Companion to Nathaniel Hawthorne*, edited by Richard H. Millington, contains essays on Hawthorne by twelve modern scholars. The book, which is one volume in Cambridge University Press's series of guides to major authors, includes ancillary materials such as a chronology of the author's life and an annotated bibliography of criticism.

*   *   *

Nathaniel Hawthorne was born on July 4, 1804, in Salem, Massachusetts. He was descended from a line of prominent Puritans; a Judge Hathorne (the "w" was Nathaniel's addition to the family name) had been one of the presiding officials at the Salem witch trials. Hawthorne's father died when Hawthorne was a boy, so he and his two sisters were raised by their widowed mother. He attended Bowdoin College, where his classmates included the poet Henry Wadsworth Longfellow and future president Franklin Pierce, whose authorized biography Hawthorne would later write. After college, Hawthorne returned to his family's home in Salem, where he spent the next ten years writing fiction. He produced an anonymous, self-published novel, *Fanshawe*, that seems to have been based on his experiences at Bowdoin. Hawthorne later took great pains to disown the work and to destroy extant copies of it. After *Fanshawe*, Hawthorne turned to writing short stories and tales, which he published anonymously in an annual called *The Token*. By the middle of the decade, he had written the "The Minister's Black Veil" and "Young Goodman Brown," which he published in *New England Magazine* under his own name. In 1837 these and other previously published stories were collected in the volume *Twice-Told Tales*. Many of the short stories related to Puritanism and its legacy. Hawthorne's old classmate Longfellow reviewed the volume, praising "the exceeding beauty of his style" and contrasting Hawthorne's clarity of expression favorably with the Gothic style that had come into vogue (Crowley, 58). Longfellow would similarly praise the expanded version of *Twice-Told Tales* that Hawthorne published five years later. In this later review, the poet identifies Hawthorne as a distinctly American writer, one who "gives us no poor copies of poor originals in English magazines," but who rather "seeks and finds his subjects at home, among his own people, in the characters, the events, and the traditions of his own country" (Crowley, 81).

Shortly before publishing *Twice-Told Tales*, Hawthorne ended his decade of seclusion. He would be as busy and active for the next few years as he had been reclusive and withdrawn for the past ten. He served as an editor for a monthly magazine, wrote a series of children's books, worked in the Boston Custom House, became engaged, and spent a disastrous half-a-year living in a utopian collective called Brook Farm. This last experience would be the basis of his 1853 novel *The Blithedale Romance*. In 1842 he married his fiancée, Sophia Peabody, and moved with her to Concord, Massachusetts, where they settled into Emerson's former residence, the Old Manse. Sophia and her sister Elizabeth, who had been one of the Brook Farm contingent, knew Emerson and other Transcendentalists. Concord was the unofficial center of the American Transcendental movement, the site of a remarkable confluence of intellectuals, artists, and abolitionists. Through his wife and his sister-in-law, Hawthorne become friends with Ralph Waldo Emerson, Henry David Thoreau, Margaret Fuller, and other members of the Transcendentalist circle. In Concord, Hawthorne wrote a series of short stories which he would later publish as *Mosses from an Old Manse*. The book was favorably received; it certainly did not hurt his reputation that Hawthorne, through his Concord associates, now had friends who moved in literary circles. Margaret Fuller praised the volume in the *New York Daily Tribune*. Melville and Edgar Allan Poe both reviewed the work, and each touched on the question of why Hawthorne had not yet attained the wide audience he deserved. Poe speculated that Hawthorne was capable of greater things than he had yet accomplished, arguing that other writers "estimate an author, not as do the public, altogether by what he does, but in great measure—indeed, even in the greatest measure—by what he evinces a capability of doing" (Crowley, 146). Melville's brilliant, bizarre, and rambling review, published in 1850, argues that the reading public and its critics have simply failed to plumb Hawthorne's depths. He argues, "The world is mistaken in this Nathaniel Hawthorne. He himself must often have smiled at its absurd misconceptions of him. He is immeasurably deeper than the plummet of the mere critic" (Crowley, 116). Melville goes on the compare Hawthorne to Shakespeare, arguing that Americans are blind to a Shakespeare among them.

In the same year that *Mosses from an Old Manse* was published, 1846, Hawthorne was appointed surveyor in the Salem Custom House. It was his Democratic sympathies and his connection to Franklin Pierce that got him the position, and when the Democrats lost the White House three years later, Hawthorne lost his job. He would reflect on his time in this role in "The Custom House," the prologue to *The Scarlet Letter.* In 1850, he published *The Scarlet Letter* to great and immediate claim. A review in *The Boston Post* read, "The whole is a prose poem, and must be regarded as such, and judged by poetical standards" (Scharnhorst, 18). *Literary World* proclaimed, "Our literature has given to the world no truer product of the American soil, though of a peculiar culture, than Nathaniel Hawthorne" (Scharnhorst, 23). Yet the reviews were not entirely praiseworthy, for some of Hawthorne's contemporaries objected to the work on moral grounds. The *Christian Register* voiced objections both to Hawthorne's parodying of his former associates in "The Custom House" and to the lack of forgiveness that characterizes the Christian characters in the novel itself. While acknowledging that *The Scarlet Letter* is "unquestionably a work of genius," the editors argued that "as a Christian narrative . . . it is utterly and entirely a failure" (Scharnhorst, 27). This failure stems from the portrayal of the Puritans as unforgiving and Hester as unrepentant. They argue, "The author nowhere recognizes the transforming and redeeming power of that Christian faith through which the most sinful may be converted and leave their sins behind" (28). This is a critique that would continue to manifest itself, in one guise or another, for several decades: that Hawthorne's vision of society was too bleak, static, and unrelenting to make for a dramatically satisfying story.

After losing his position at the customhouse and publishing *The Scarlet Letter*, Hawthorne moved to Lenox, Massachusetts, where he began his friendship with Herman Melville. He entered a remarkably prolific period, publishing in 1851 a collection for children, an expanded version of *Twice-Told Tales*, and *The House of the Seven Gables*. Hawthorne's second book was well-received, on the whole, but it was often compared unfavorably to *The Scarlet Letter*. A typical review, this one from *Peterson's Magazine*, reads: "When we had read the first twenty pages of this romance, we felt inclined to dissent from the prevalent opinion of the press, that it was inferior to *The Scarlet Letter*. As we proceeded, however, we were forced to acknowledge that our contemporaries were correct" (Rosenthal, 36). The following year saw Hawthorne publish his third novel, *The Blithedale Romance*. Again the response was positive but qualified: good, but no *Scarlet Letter*. In 1852 Hawthorne also published an official biography of his former classmate Franklin Pierce, who was running for president. It was an act which Pierce would recompense, upon taking office, by appointing Hawthorne as United States Consul to Liverpool, England. The period of prolific writing would come to an end, and Hawthorne was only to publish one more novel: *The Marble Faun*, in 1860. The book was based on his experience living in Rome and Florence, after the conclusion of his consulship, and is the only of Hawthorne's novels to have a European setting. Its story of Americans abroad in Italy touches on some of the themes and plots that would animate Henry James's novels and stories. Hawthorne would produce four fragments of novels, one published as a tale and three published posthumously as fragments, but no more finished masterpieces. He died in 1864, while touring New England with Franklin Pierce.

In the two or three decades following Hawthorne's death, his reputation as one of America's preeminent writers was solidified. The three fragments of novels were widely reviewed and generally praised. Retrospective assessments of the novelist's body of work were overwhelmingly positive. Henry James, Anthony Trollope, and Leslie Stephen (who may be best known now as the father of Virginia Woolf, but who was himself an important writer) all wrote retrospectives on Hawthorne's work. James's assessment is the most thoroughgoing and insightful, though both Trollope and Stephen draw interesting contrasts between American and English literature. More important, perhaps, than the conclusions that Trollope and Stephen draw about the two bodies of literature is their readiness to accept Hawthorne's novels as representative of American literature *in toto*. According to Trollope, American literature is characterized not by the "broad humor" of Mark Twain but by "an undercurrent of melancholy, in which pathos and satire are intermingled" (Crowley, 520). A melancholy that one might attribute to Hawthorne alone is instead identified as the definitively American temperament. Stephen is more critical of Hawthorne than is Trollope, taking issue with his lack of directness: he has "sought refuge from the hard facts of commonplace life by retiring into a visionary world" (Crowley, 495). Stephen is one of many who will associate Hawthorne less with his own era than with that of the Puritans about whom he wrote. "Hawthorne's mind," Stephen writes, "amidst the obvious differences, had still an affinity to his remote forefathers. Their bugbears had become his playthings; but the witches, though they have no reality, have still a fascination for him" (497).

Leslie Stephen's attitude toward Hawthorne prefigures a fin-de-siècle decline in the author's popularity. While Hawthorne's own contemporaries and the generation that followed him had little but praise for the novelist, early twentieth-century audiences regarded his work more coolly. Two or three generations after his death, Hawthorne was widely considered to be rather morose and primitive. Summing up this strain of turn-of-the-century criticism, Gary Scharnhorst writes, "The author had become, according to this critical estimate, the very type of character he had depicted in such tales as 'The Minister's Black Veil'" (xix). Hawthorne's own Puritan heritage tended to count against him during this period, for critics made few distinctions between Hawthorne, a man of the nineteenth century, and the seventeenth-century characters he had created. This falling off of popularity had predictable results for the field of Hawthorne research; Rosenthal characterizes the first half of the twentieth century as "a lull in Hawthorne Studies" (167). While *The Scarlet Letter* was still widely read and still regarded as an American classic, the general tenor of critical discourse treated the book as being exceptional among Hawthorne's novels rather than representative of them. Scholars in the first half of the century tended to view Hawthorne's work through a historical lens rather than a more literary one, and perhaps the most valuable contributions of the period explore Hawthorne's source materials. Chandler, Drake, Griffiths, Herron, and Turner identify locations, family names, and incidents from New England history that Hawthorne may have appropriated in his novels and short stories. T. S. Eliot saw Hawthorne's interest in history as being a reaction to the narrowness of nineteenth-century American life, suggesting, "The only dimension in which Hawthorne could expand was the past, his present being so narrowly barren. It is a great pity, with his remarkable gift of observation, that the present did not offer him more to observe" (Eliot). In addition to the historical focus of the era, critics and researchers ushered original Hawthorne materials into print. Among the most valuable contributions of the period are the author's American and English notebooks, edited by Randall Stewart and published in the 1930s and 1940s, respectively.

At the end of the 1930s and beginning of the 1940s, several of the most important critics of the day published books or essays that read Hawthorne through a decidedly more literary lens than their predecessors had possessed. In *Maule's Curse: Seven Studies in the History of American Obscurantism*, Yvor Winters considers allegory and morality in Hawthorne's *The House of the Seven Gables*. Carl Van Doren includes a chapter on Hawthorne in his *The American Novel, 1789–1939*. Van Doren identifies Hawthorne's great strength as a pictorial one, the crafting of settings that sometimes threaten to overshadow his plots and characters. F. O. Matthiessen likewise devoted a chapter to Hawthorne in *The American Renaissance*, a book that would recast the landscape of American literature and help to legitimize American studies. In 1949, Mark Van Doren (brother of Carl) wrote *Nathaniel Hawthorne: A Critical Biography*, a study of the author's life and work.

The post-war period would bring a wealth of new readings and research to Hawthorne's work. In the 1950s, the New Criticism was in its ascendancy. With their interest in hermeneutical readings of the text, critics such as R. W. B. Lewis, Millicent Bell, and Grace Wellborn focused on the literary structures of Hawthorne's novels and short stories. New Criticism served as a necessary corrective to the overly determined biographical readings that had marked the preceding century of criticism. It was a school of criticism that lent itself particularly well to the appreciation and explication of Hawthorne, an author whose work is highly structured and allegorical. One of the approaches of the period was to trace patterns across the novels and stories, identifying and explaining recurrent images, settings, or types of characters. Adams, for example, writes about Hawthorne's gardens, pools, and trees. Wellborn's series of articles address the significance of numbers (three and seven) and plants in *The Scarlet Letter*. Lewis identifies Hawthorne's use of the Adamic figure and the trope of the fortunate fall. By attending to patterns of meaning, symbolism, and diction that animate and inform the novels, the New Critics restored Hawthorne to literary grounds, reading his work as literature rather than as artifacts of Puritan or colonial thought.

Another sea change in Hawthorne studies came in the 1970s and 1980s with the rise of post-structuralist literary theories. Psychoanalytic readings, such as Crews's *The Sins of the Fathers: Hawthorne's Psychological Themes*, took a Freudian approach to the author's fiction. Feminist theory emerged as a particularly important lens through which to view Hawthorne. Critics challenged and refined traditional readings of Hester Prynne, Phoebe Pyncheon, and other of Hawthorne's women. Nina Baym's article "Thwarted Nature: Nathaniel Hawthorne as Feminist" as well as her subsequent book on *The Scarlet Letter* identifies feminist themes and sympathies in Hawthorne's work. More recently, James Wallace and Jamie Barlowe have taken up the same issue, both taking as their point of departure Hawthorne's complaint that he was writing in competition with a "mob of scribbling women." Emily Budick takes a different approach by studying women writers, from 1850 to the present, who have worked in what she identifies as the Hawthorne tradition. Idol and Ponder's *Hawthorne and Women: Engendering and Expanding the Hawthorne Tradition* is a collection of feminist readings of Hawthorne. Finally, Robert K. Martin's "Hester Prynne, *C'est Moi*: Nathaniel Hawthorne and the Anxieties of Gender" examines some of the issues that arise when men, be they novelists or critics, write about women.

The post-structuralist era saw critics bringing other theoretical approaches, including deconstruction, queer theory, and narratology, to bear on Hawthorne's work. J. Hillis Miller's slim *Hawthorne and History: Defacing It* deconstructs traditional understandings of Hawthorne's historical fiction and of the notion of the historical itself. Karen Kilcup's "'Ourself behind Ourself, Concealed—'" explores the homoerotics of reading in *The Scarlet Letter.* In the field of narratology, Thomas Moore has made a study of Hawthorne's prologues and frame devices, while Richard Millington examines the narrative conventions of the romance as reworked by Hawthorne.

It would be an oversimplification to imagine that each new period or school of criticism brings an end to the one that preceded it. These critical approaches intermingle, and critics may borrow whatever approaches best lend themselves to Hawthorne's texts. Structuralism, for example, remains an important lens through which to read Hawthorne, in part, no doubt, because Hawthorne himself paid such attention to structural issues. His tendency toward allegory continues to reward critics whose interest lies with symbolic or thematic patterning. By the same token, historicism has gone into and out of fashion, yet remains a strong current in Hawthorne studies precisely because Hawthorne himself was a historian. In every generation, therefore, scholars have considered Hawthorne's source materials and his historical analogues. Finally, biographical and contextual approaches to the author continue to thrive. McFarland's *Hawthorne in Concord*, Margaret Moore's *The Salem World of Nathaniel Hawthorne*, and Cheever's *American Bloomsbury* are a few of the many recent biographical or contextual studies. Today, the field of Hawthorne studies is a wide one in which scholars from a range of backgrounds are doing critical work.

Yet the output of literary critics and scholars is not the only measure of a given author's significance. One ought to take stock of the response not only of academic writers to a given novelist but also of other artists and novelists. Hawthorne's work has been adapted into operas, stage plays, and films. Perhaps more important, Hawthorne was central to the creative development of several great American writers across several generations, including Herman Melville and Emily Dickinson in his own time, Henry James in the next generation, and such disparate talents as William Faulkner and Margaret Atwood in the twentieth century. Hawthorne's legacy lies not only in the lasting power of his own work but also in the influence he had on the course of American literature as a whole.

Works Cited

Adams, John F. "Hawthorne's Symbolic Gardens." *Texas Studies in Language and Literature* 5, no. 2 (1963): 242–54.

Barlowe, Jamie. *The Scarlet Mob of Scribblers: Rereading Hester Prynne*. Carbondale: Southern Illinois University Press, 2000.

Baym, Nina. *The Scarlet Letter: A Reading*. Boston: Twayne, 1986.

_____. "Thwarted Nature: Nathaniel Hawthorne as Feminist." In *American Novelists Revisited: Essays in Feminist Criticism*, ed. Fritz Fleishmann, pp. 58–72. Boston: G. K. Hall, 1982.

Bell, Millicent. *Hawthorne's View of the Artist*. New York: State University of New York Press, 1962.

_____, ed. *Hawthorne and the Real: Bicentennial Essays*. Columbus: Ohio State University Press, 2005.

_____, ed. *New Essays on Hawthorne's Major Tales*. New York: Cambridge University Press, 1993.

Brodhead, Richard, H. *Hawthorne, Melville, and the Novel*. Chicago: University of Chicago Press, 1976.

_____. *The School of Hawthorne*. New York: Oxford University Press, 1986.

Budick, Emily Miller. *Engendering Romance: Women Writers and the Hawthorne Tradition, 1850–1990*. New Haven: Yale University Press, 1994.

Cady, Edwin H., and Louis Budd, eds. *On Hawthorne: The Best from American Literature*. Durham: Duke University Press, 1990.

Chandler, Elizabeth Lathrop. "A Study of the Sources of the Tales and Romances Written by Nathaniel Hawthorne before 1853." *Smith College Studies in Modern Language* 7, no. 4 (July, 1926): 1–64. Reprint. Darby, PA: Arden Library, 1978.

Cheever, Susan. *American Bloomsbury: Louisa May Alcott, Ralph Waldo Emerson, Margaret Fuller, Nathaniel Hawthorne, and Henry David Thoreau: Their Lives, Their Loves, Their Work*. New York: Simon & Schuster, 2006.

Colacurcio, Michael J., ed. *New Essays on "The Scarlet Letter."* Cambridge: Cambridge University Press, 1985.

Crews, Frederick C. *The Sins of the Fathers : Hawthorne's Psychological Themes*. 1966. Berkeley : University of California Press, 1989.

Crowley, J. Donald. *Hawthorne: The Critical Heritage*. New York: Routledge, 1970.

Drake, Samuel Adams. "Salem Legends." In *A Book of New England Legends and Folk Lore in Prose and Poetry*, pp. 167–201. Boston, Little, Brown, 1901. Reprint. Detroit, Singing Tree, 1969.

Dunne, Michael. *Hawthorne's Narrative Strategies*. Jackson: University Press of Mississippi, 1995.

Elbert, Monica M. *Encoding the Letter "A": Gender and Authority in Hawthorne's Early Fiction*. Frankfurt, Germany: Haag & Herchen, 1990.

Eliot, T. S. "The Hawthorne Aspect." In *The Question of Henry James*, ed. F. W. Dupree, pp. 108–119. New York: Henry Holt, 1948.

Gale, Robert L. *A Nathaniel Hawthorne Encyclopedia*. Boston: G. K. Hall, 1991.

Griffiths, Thomas Morgan. *Maine Sources in "The House of the Seven Gables."* Waterville, ME: Thomas Morgan Griffiths, 1945.

Hawthorne, Nathaniel. *The American Notebooks*. New Haven, CT: Yale University Press, 1932.

_____. *The English Notebooks*. Ed. Randall Stewart. New York: MLA, 1941.

_____. *The House of the Seven Gables*. New York: Penguin, 1986.

_____. *The Letters*. 4 vols. Ed. Thomas Woodson, L. Neal Smith, and

Norman Holmes Pearson. The Centenary Edition of the Works of Nathaniel Hawthorne. Columbus: Ohio State University Press, 1985–8.

_____. *The Scarlet Letter: A Norton Critical Edition.* Eds. Seymour Gross, Sculley Bradley, Richmond Croom Beatty, and E. Hudson Long. New York: W.W. Norton & Co., 1988.

Herron, Ima Honaker. "The New England Village in Literature." In *The Small Town in American Literature*, pp. 28–69. Durham, NC: Duke University Press, 1939. Reprint. New York: Pageant, 1959.

Idol, John L., Jr., and Melinda Ponder, eds. *Hawthorne and Women: Engendering and Expanding the Hawthorne Tradition.* Amherst: University of Massachusetts Press, 1999.

James, Henry. *Hawthorne.* English Men of Letters Series. London: Macmillan, 1879.

Kilcup, Karen L. "'Ourself behind Ourself, Concealed—': The Homoerotics of Reading in *The Scarlet Letter.*" *ESQ: A Journal of the American Renaissance* 42 (1996): 1–28.

Lewis, R. W. B. *The American Adam: Innocence, Tragedy, and Tradition in the Nineteenth Century.* Chicago: University of Chicago Press, 1955. Reprint, 1971.

McCall, Dan. *Citizens of Somewhere Else: Nathaniel Hawthorne and Henry James.* New York: Cornell University Press, 1999.

McFarland, Philip James. *Hawthorne in Concord.* New York: Grove Press, 2004.

Martin, Robert K. "Hester Prynne, *C'est Moi*: Nathaniel Hawthorne and the Anxieties of Gender." In *Engendering Men: The Question of Male Feminist Criticism.* Eds. Joseph A. Boone and Michael Cadden, pp. 122–39. New York: Routledge, 1990.

Matthiessen, F. O. *The American Renaissance: Art and Expression in the Age of Emerson and Whitman.* New York: Oxford University Press, 1941.

Mellow, James R. *Hawthorne in His Times.* Boston: Houghton Mifflin, 1980.

Meyerson, Joel, ed. *Selected Letters of Nathaniel Hawthorne.* Columbus: Ohio State University Press, 2002.

Miller, J. Hillis. *Hawthorne and History: Defacing It.* Cambridge: Basil Blackwell, 1991.

Millington, Richard H. *The Cambridge Companion to Nathaniel Hawthorne.* Cambridge: Cambridge University Press, 2004.

_____. *Practicing Romance: Narrative Form and Cultural Engagement in Hawthorne's Fiction.* Princeton: Princeton University Press, 1992.

Moore, Margaret B. *The Salem World of Nathaniel Hawthorne.* Columbia: University of Missouri Press, 1998.

Moore, Thomas R. *A Thick and Darksome Veil: The Rhetoric of Hawthorne's Sketches, Prefaces, and Essays.* Boston: Northeastern University Press, 1994.

Pearce, Roy Harvey, ed. *Hawthorne Centenary Essays.* Columbus: Ohio State University Press, 1964.

Pfister, Joel. *The Production of Personal Life: Class, Gender, and the Psychological in Hawthorne's Fiction.* Stanford: Stanford University Press, 1991.

Reynolds, Larry J., ed. *A Historical Guide to Nathaniel Hawthorne.* New York: Oxford University Press, 2001.

Rosenthal, Bernard. *Critical Essays on Hawthorne's "The House of the Seven Gables."* New York: G. K. Hall, 1995.

Scharnhorst, Gary. *The Critical Response to Nathaniel Hawthorne's "The Scarlet Letter."* New York: Greenwood Press, 1992.

Turner, Arlin. "Hawthorne's Literary Borrowings." *PMLA* 51 (June, 1936): 543–62.

_____. *Nathaniel Hawthorne: A Biography.* New York: Oxford University Press, 1980.

Van Doren, Carl. "Nathaniel Hawthorne." In *The American Novel, 1789–1939.* New York: Macmillan, 1940.

Van Doren, Mark. *Nathaniel Hawthorne: A Criticial Biography.* New York: William Sloane, 1949.

Wallace, James D. "Hawthorne and the Scribbling Women Reconsidered." *American Literature* 62 (1991): 201–22.

Wellborn, Grace Pleasant. "The Mystic Seven in *The Scarlet Letter.*" *South Central Bulletin* 23 (1963): 23–31.

_____. "Plant Lore and *The Scarlet Letter.*" *Southern Folklore Quarterly* 27 (1963): 160–67.

_____. "The Symbolic Three in *The Scarlet Letter.*" *South Central Bulletin* 23 (1963): 10–17.

Winters, Yvor. *Maule's Curse: Seven Studies in the History of American Obscurantism.* Norfolk, CT: New Directions, 1938.

The Burden of Secret Sin:
Nathaniel Hawthorne's Fiction_____

Margarita Georgieva

If there is a single theme that runs through all of Hawthorne's fiction, it must be sin—the same theme that so occupied the seventeenth-century Puritans who figure prominently in Hawthorne's works. Herman Melville wrote that "this great power of blackness in him derives its force from its appeals to that Calvinistic sense of Innate Depravity and Original Sin, from whose visitations . . . no deeply thinking mind is always and wholly free" (Melville, 243). "It is that blackness in Hawthorne," he added, "that so fixes and fascinates me" (Melville, 244).

That blackness has fascinated many readers since, and Georgieva here outlines some of the more important forms sin can take in Hawthorne's works. Sin can be etched on the body in physical form; it can be a curse stretching across the generations; it can be lurking behind a veil. It is never obvious, though, never visible on the surface. And Hawthorne, while he was asking some very old questions about the nature of sin, was not content with the old answers. He repeatedly challenges religious orthodoxy, as, for instance, when he questions the old notion of Original Sin.

Georgieva teases out the varieties of sin from a wide selection of Hawthorne's fiction, both the major short tales and long romances, and she reminds us that the expulsion from Eden was the result of eating from the Tree of Knowledge of Good and Evil: to know the nature of sin is to be sinful.   — J.L.

The fiction of Nathaniel Hawthorne has frequently been defined in musical terms on account of the recurring themes it contains. Very much like the leitmotifs of a symphony or an opera, these themes possess "a slight, delicate, and evanescent flavor," yet they frequently carry "some definite moral purpose" (Pearson, 243). Sin is one of them. References to sin can be found throughout Hawthorne's writings, in his earliest as well as in his latest. It is *The Scarlet Letter* (1850)[1] that is the most quoted and the most frequently associated with the thematic of sin. However, *The House of the Seven Gables* (1851) and a great number of Hawthorne's shorter works address the same problem. His fiction explores the weight of the Puritan conception of sin at a time when the Transcendentalist idea of the goodness of man saw light. Thus, Hawthorne's writings offer a relatively dark view of human nature, oftentimes alleviated by cautious optimism. A number of critics have agreed that Hawthorne's fiction shows signs of the disappearance of the doctrine of original sin which was to gradually become "backwater theology" (Barna, 325) and which left room for something more positive and hopeful. This is exactly what happens with *The Scarlet Letter*, which "ceased to be a stigma which attracted the world's scorn and bitterness, and became a type of something to be sorrowed over, and looked upon with awe, yet with reverence too" (Pearson, 240).

Kane Egan in his article "The Adulteress in the Market-Place" (1995) believes that "Hawthorne comes before the public to condemn the sins of his generation" (Egan, 1) and then moves on to something more constructive, suggesting future change and evolution. These statements seem to contradict the general impression of gloom, which is regularly attributed to Hawthorne's fictional world. However, most of his works contain elements of novelty that soften the sin-obsessed Puritan worldview. His distinction between "knowledge as sin" and "secret sin" is the key to the problem.

Sin in Hawthorne: Toward a Definition

In 1759, the influential and eloquent Puritan minister Jonathan Edwards wrote that humankind was "born into the world with a tendency to sin" (Edwards, 228). Humanity was entitled to "misery and ruin for their sin, which actually will be the consequence unless mere grace steps in and prevents it" (Edwards, 228). In his defense of original sin,

Edwards proposes nothing bright and offers a somber, dismal view of the human character. Nathaniel Hawthorne's paternal ancestors were all Puritan. A great part of his fiction is indisputably anchored in this heritage and is concerned with the concept of "sin."

But what is the exact meaning to be applied to "sin" in Hawthorne's fiction? In 2003, in his article "Hawthorne and Sin," Denis Donoghue proposed to explain the notion of sin as it is used by Hawthorne. Donoghue attempted a definition but he justly remarked that in Hawthorne, the notion of sin seems "all general and vague" at first, while "none of the characters has a convinced sense of sin" in total accordance with the Biblical canon (Donoghue, 1, 2). Donoghue explains that when Hawthorne "referred to sin, he seemed to assume a force of evil so pervasive that it did not need to be embodied in anyone or in any particular action" (Donoghue, 3). There is a lot of truth in this remark, and it can be applied to the quasi-totality of Hawthorne's fiction. For example, Hester Prynne's sin is rarely talked of openly and except for the frequent allusions to adulteration, the text of *The Scarlet Letter* is more concerned with "a kind of fetishistic fascination with the 'nameless'" (Egan, 26), which seems to have more universal value than the simple reference to a definable sin. Hawthorne is only slightly more explicit in *The House of the Seven Gables*, where the seven gables manifestly stand for the seven capital sins and evoke the principle of their hereditary transmission. Was Hawthorne abiding by the Bible when he wrote of sin? The definition of sin in Genesis 4:7, for example, is not less obscure: "[. . .] if you do not what is right, sin is crouching at your door [. . .]".[2] But what is right? In Hawthorne's fiction, the word "sin" itself is only sparsely used. A variety of expressions and synonyms are used (such as "evil," "mischief," "vice," "fall," "disobedience"). For example, the author explains that he has

[. . .] provided himself with a moral [. . .] namely, that the *wrong-doing*[3] of one generation lives into the successive ones, and [. . .] becomes a pure and uncontrollable *mischief* [. . .] (Pearson, 243)

This is where the main difficulty of defining sin in Hawthorne arises. "Wrong-doing" and "mischief" seem to replace "sin" here, as if the word itself was not meant to be put down in writing. To define something that is only implicitly referred to and rarely plainly stated may prove a difficult task.

Indeed, there is a certain complexity in the concept of sin as we find it in Hawthorne's fiction. The reader is confronted with several categories of sin, some more obvious than others. Many of these are fused together into a larger whole, creating an atmosphere, or rather, a pervasive mood of gloom and guilt. In some of Hawthorne's short stories, the characters' unconscious awareness of the original sin is transferred to a visible, physical burden. Such is the case in "The Minister's Black Veil" (1836) and "The Birth-Mark" (1843), where sin is perceived as unavoidable. The characters' bodies are maimed. They carry the indelible traces of sin. This is exactly what Chillingworth means when he explains to Dimmesdale that "he to whom only the outward and physical evil is laid open, knoweth, oftentimes, but half the evil which he is called upon to cure" (Pearson, 164). In that case, all attempts to cure (that is, to obtain an absolution) are apparently unpardonable. This is the burden of most sinners in Hawthorne's fiction. Rev. Hooper covers his face with a black veil to hide his sins and the veil is not to be removed even after his death, while the removal of Georgiana's birthmark rapidly kills her. The fact that Dimmesdale is "standing on the scaffold, in this vain show of expiation" (Pearson, 171) does not help him overthrow the burden. His sin shows on his face and body as a mysterious ailment. Death is his only relief.

On the other hand, sin in Hawthorne is explicitly connected to sexuality. "John Inglefield's Thanksgiving" (1840), for example, tells the story of the fallen Prudence, conscious of her sins but unaware of her sleepwalking attempts to seek forgiveness from her father. Both "The Wedding Knell" (1836) and *The Scarlet Letter* explore the various transformations of sexual sin, stressing its omnipresence regardless of the nature of the relationship. The lawful as well as the adulterous union is condemned as corrupt, the former by a higher power and the latter by society. In addition, in some of Hawthorne's fictions, sin is transmitted to younger generations by sinful parents and/or family members. In some cases, it is further aggravated by cruelty, murder, and witchcraft (such as in *The House of the Seven Gables*). In others, it is society that perpetrates sinful practices and these become unpardonable sins. The child in "The Gentle Boy" (1832) dies in expiation of Quaker mass killings and of a host of nameless crimes. The weight of "an indelible stain of blood" and of "a large share of the awful responsibility" (Pearson, 890–891) is too heavy for him. The gentle boy is a Christ-like figure, unconsciously aware of humanity's evils, of religious "extravagancies, and [. . .] persecution" (Pearson, 890). He is the recipient of both the original and the unpardonable sin. In "Young Goodman Brown" (1835), the eponymous hero does not know if what he has seen is true but nevertheless dies a cynical and disillusioned man. The contact with the darker side of his townsfolk and with their sins is the reason for his death, Hawthorne implicitly suggests.

Another interesting example is *The Scarlet Letter*, which is built upon a series of sins. All characters carry their share of the original sin. The adultery committed by Hester Prynne and Dimmesdale aggravates their situation. Chillingworth, on the other hand, is to be held responsible for committing the sin of abandonment. The moral abuse and social ostracizing practiced on Hester Prynne are collective sins. Simultaneously, *The Scarlet Letter* seems to follow the Biblical "Judge not, that ye be not judged" (Matthew 7:1), meaning that since all humans are sinners, judging in God's place is yet another unpardonable sin. The repetitive violations of the Biblical law indicate that Hawthorne's paramount concern was to actually solve the problem of defining sin.

Knowledge as Sin

Many of the examples we mentioned are obviously related to the concept of knowledge. Much in line with the Biblical canon, Hawthorne's earliest interpretation of the original sin is connected to the sin of forbidden knowledge acquisition. The original sin of the first human beings was knowledge—Adam and Eve conquered their independence by taking the decision to consume the fruit of the Tree of Knowledge of Good and Evil. The first sin they became guilty of was the acquisition of knowledge. In spite of the understanding humanity now possessed, the fratricide committed by Cain demonstrated a conscious predisposition to perpetrating evil. Therefore, evil formed the darker, burdensome, hidden part of humanity's complex identity which was to be revealed only through man's direct relationship with God. This is what happens to both Rev. Hooper and Dimmesdale, who deal with sin on their own, thus becoming men "of awful power over souls that were in agony for sin" (Pearson, 879). That is also why Dimmesdale whispers of "the great judgment day" (Pearson, 175). "Then, and there," says he to Pearl, "before the judgment-seat, thy mother, and thou, and I must stand together. But the daylight of this world shall not see our meeting!" (Pearson, 175).

According to some Puritan doctrines, the guilt of the first humans was handed down from one generation to another. Hence, every child was to carry the burden of the original sin, the weight of which was more often than not increased by the addition of the sins of his own parents. Indeed, the beginning of *The Scarlet Letter* informs the reader that "the past [is] not dead" (Pearson, 100). Indeed, it is because of that persistent past that Hawthorne himself had changed his name. Actually, his statement globally refers to the common Puritan past and to its collective guilt. This statement indicates that the story Hawthorne is about to tell explores the characters' desire to discover the hushed secret that lies hidden beneath the complex symbols and taboos of "the Puritan instinct" (Pearson, x). The deepest desire of many of these characters is to find out the exact nature of sin. In fact, a close inspection of Hawthorne's texts reveals a recurrent usage of the words "know," "aware," "penetrate," "reveal." In addition, the plots are based on a succession of repeated sins. Jac Tharpe interprets these repetitions in terms of a relentless search for identity, "[. . .] the search for identity and individuality is original sin, while the unpardonable sin is tyranny over the identity of another" (Tharpe, 80). In Hawthorne, both types of sin are superposed and their accumulation is the greatest imaginable burden to be placed upon the human soul. Many of his characters know or are aware of this impalpable, obscure burden and their "concerns involve knowledge [and] the study of human origins and purpose" (Tharpe, 10). Pearl cannot answer when she is asked the question "Canst thou tell me, my child, who made thee?" (Pearson, 149). Her ignorance is revealing and her silence addresses the central issue in Hawthorne's work. Knowledge of parentage, origins and identity is forbidden. It is one of the fundamental taboos, and its purpose is to prevent the revelation of secrets that are not meant for mortal eyes. Goodman Brown becomes the witness of sacrilege and this, in part, leads him to perdition. Goodman Brown possesses a secret. He has discovered and knows the nature of man. He knows himself. This awareness is godlike and it is precisely what God forbade to Adam.

In "Ethan Brand" (1850), Hawthorne remarks that "there was something in the man's face which he was afraid to look at" (Pearson, 32). Ethan Brand is actually possessed with a fanatical desire to discover the nature of sin. He possesses knowledge and this is what terrifies those who look at his face and into his eyes. Flames dance in Ethan Brand's eyes, reminding the reader of the utmost evil and of the fires of Hell. Upon his return after a long absence, Ethan Brand watches a dog chase its tail, the symbol of the futility of his vain quest of self-knowledge. Hawthorne remarks that Ethan Brand has indulged in the "*sin of intellect* that triumphed over the sense of brotherhood with man and reverence for God and sacrificed everything to its own mighty claims" (Hawthorne, 232). In the "The Minister's Black Veil," most of the characters find it difficult to look at Mr. Hooper's veil, most probably because it hides his awareness and understanding of a multitude of sins. As a minister, he is the immediate recipient of the sins of an entire congregation. The veil shields them from the knowledge the minister carries. However, his own existence becomes increasingly dependent on that knowledge and this is also what prevents him from taking off the veil. His burden is heavier not because of the pressure exercised on him to remove the veil but because of the accumulation of knowledge about sin. But does Hawthorne really depict knowledge as sinful? Does he claim that ignorance preserves the soul of his characters from sinking into "blacker depths of sin" (Pearson, 151)?

Secret Sin

The plots of the works we cited examine the implications of knowledge on the spiritual life of the individual. Undeniably, Hawthorne's fiction is mostly about knowing the unknown and many of his characters are obsessed with the idea of discovering a secret. For example, the acquaintances, friends and family of Rev. Hooper want "to penetrate the *mystery* of the black veil" and "to reveal the mystery of so many years" (Pearson, 679, 881). Hester Prynne speaks of the "sin here so awfully *revealed*" (Pearson, 236) as if "sin" were synonymous to "secret." Much in the same fashion, Rev. Hooper's congregation "whispers that [he] hide[s] [his] face under the consciousness of secret sin" (Pearson, 878). This is one of the few instances when Hawthorne uses both "secret" and "sin" to specify the nature of Rev. Hooper's sin. The example illustrates what is probably one of the most intriguing particularities of Hawthorne's conception of sin. In reality, knowledge is a secondary preoccupation to him. What everyone wants to know is the secret. The secret drives the story forward and it is also related to sin. The secret is frequently likened to untruth and from there, to a lie. In the preface of *The House of the Seven Gables*, Hawthorne explains that every piece of fiction, "as a work of art," must "rigidly subject itself to laws, and [. . .] it sins unpardonably so far as it may swerve aside from the truth of the human heart" (Pearson, 243).

All types of sin in Hawthorne involve a secret, a mystery. The black veil of the minister, that piece of crape, to their [the congregation's] imagination, seemed to hang down before his heart, the symbol of a fearful *secret* between him and them. (Pearson, 877)

When he preaches, the subject of Rev. Hooper's sermon

had reference to *secret sin*, and those sad *mysteries* which we hide from our nearest and dearest, and would fain conceal from our own consciousness, even forgetting that the Omniscient can detect them. (Pearson, 874)

This secrecy generates a series of double-binds where Hawthorne's characters have to choose between two unsatisfactory alternatives. On the one hand, they can accept to share the secret and reveal the truth in an attempt to expiate the sin. In that case, however, they are condemned by the community and this is what happens to Hester Prynne in *The Scarlet Letter.* On the other, they can choose to move on, without an open confession of the secret sin, and are haunted by that knowledge forever. Both "The Minister's Black Veil" and "Young Goodman Brown" are cases in point. At any rate, they will have to bear the burden of their guilt to their death even though they do not seem to believe that what they have done is sin. Rather, it was a "consecration" in Hester's own words. However, Hester Prynne realizes that she will never be delivered of her burden, of the secret she keeps about herself. "Here had been her sin [. . .] She had returned, therefore, and resumed [. . .] the symbol of which we have related so dark a tale" (Pearson, 239).

Secret sin gradually becomes an idée fixe with a large scope of implications. The sinful characters struggle with the inability to communicate effectively and their incapacity to contribute to a collective moral effort bars the way to compassion. They become withdrawn and distant and the fact that they preserve their secret sin damages their body and soul. Accordingly, many of Hawthorne's secret sinners appear as socially ostracized individuals or as solitary wanderers. Hester Prynne lives on the margin of society and the eponymous hero of

"Ethan Brand" embarks on a long twenty-year search for the Unpardonable Sin only never to find it. Hawthorne remarked that "never was seen such headlong eagerness in pursuit of an object that could not possibly be attained" (Hawthorne, 231). His only sin is his own secret obsession with sin. Not focusing on his life outside of sin is his major error.

*   *   *

The plots of Hawthorne's stories introduce large numbers of prying, secondary, background characters. They are inquiring and intrusive. They are intriguing. Most of them are built on the assumption that they could become counterparts of the reader and as such, they are fascinated by secrets and will attempt to solve the mysteries. Critics have remarked that such narratives operate a twist on the prevailing interpretation of sin within the Puritan religious doctrine. In fact, Hawthorne was cautiously "remolding the old Puritan sense of the burden of sin with an artistic delicacy" (Gorman, 19). Beyond the first reading and under the surface of the text lies the idea that knowledge should no longer be considered a sin. To Hawthorne knowing is not a sin but keeping burdensome knowledge for oneself *is* sin. The fact that Rev. Hooper keeps his awareness of sin to himself is sinful toward those who love him and toward the members of his congregation. The fact that Dimmesdale confesses only partially is sinful too because of the implications the secret has on the lives of Hester and Pearl. In fact, Hawthorne seems to say that the value of the original sin lessens progressively, while the burden of the unpardonable sins grows. This is due to the suffering the sinners inflict on others. In "Earth's Holocaust" (1844), Hawthorne tells us that "this wide world had become so overburthened with an accumulation of worn-out trumpery, that the inhabitants determined to rid themselves of it by a general bonfire." This story epitomizes Hawthorne's conception of secret sin as a joint responsibility. Contrary to what it appears, the burden of secret sin is not something personal. Actually, secret sin is a shared responsibility. It is a collective burden. The yoke of secret sin is heavier than that of the original sin because our immediate ancestors are to be held accountable for it. There is nothing humanity could have done about expiating the original sin. However, Hawthorne seems to say, humanity is directly blamable for the wrongs it commits. Hushing the wrongs, dissimulating the sin only aggravates the crime.

Notes

1. Years in parentheses indicate publication dates.
2. Also cited by Herbert Gorman in *Hawthorne: A Study in Solitude* (1927).
3. The italics are mine.

Works Cited

Barna, Mark Richard. "Nathaniel Hawthorne and the Unpardonable Sin." *World and I* 13 (March 1998).

Donoghue, Denis. "Hawthorne and Sin." *Christianity and Literature* 52 (2003).

Edwards, Jonathan. "Christian Doctrine of Original Sin Defended." In *Basic Writings*. Ed. Ola Elizabeth Winslow. New York: Penguin Books, 1966.

Egan, Kane, Jr. "The Adulteress in the Market-Place: Hawthorne and the Scarlet Letter." *Studies in the Novel* 27 (1995).

Gorman, Herbert. *Hawthorne: A Study in Solitude*. New York: George H. Doran Company on Murray Hill, 1927.

Hawthorne, Nathaniel. *Selected Short Stories.* Greenwich, CT: Fawcett Publishing, 1983.

Pearson, Norman Holmes, ed. *The Hawthorne Treasury: The Complete Novels and Selected Tales of Nathaniel Hawthorne.* New York: The Modern Library, 1999.

Tharpe, Jac. *Nathaniel Hawthorne: Identity and Knowledge.* Carbondale: Southern Illinois University Press, 1967.

Nathaniel Hawthorne and American Romanticism

Jennifer Banach Palladino

> We've grown so accustomed to thinking of Hawthorne as a commentator on the Puritan seventeenth century that it's easy to forget that he was a man of his own century as well. But Hawthorne came of age in America's Romantic era, and his works, which began appearing in the 1820s and continued until his death in 1864, show the marks of his own intellectual and cultural milieu.
>
> Jennifer Banach Palladino here gives an overview of international Romanticisms, especially the variety that flourished in America in the middle of the nineteenth century. She draws attention to the age's passion for nature—often with a capital *N*—and the fascination with individual psychology. She also relates these larger concerns to literary movements like the Gothic, and literary techniques like symbolism, that figure so prominently in Hawthorne's major works.   — J.L.

Nathaniel Hawthorne is commonly recognized as one of the most significant writers in the history of American literature, and yet, regardless of such unity on the subject of the author's importance, books and articles on Hawthorne contain a dizzying array of conflicting opinions regarding the proper classification of his work. Despite arguments that Hawthorne's tales and romances display elements of Victorianism, realism, and even devices that could be considered precursors to modernism and post-modernism, Hawthorne's work is most commonly placed within the context of Romanticism alongside the great majority of the nation's most revered writers: Washington Irving, James Fenimore Cooper, Herman Melville, Walt Whitman, Emily Dickinson and many others. He wrote from the early 1820s to 1864, the year of his death, penning his major works—four romances (*The Scarlet Letter*, *The House of the Seven Gables*, *The Blithedale Romance* and *The Mar-*

ble Faun) and numerous short stories (or "tales" as he preferred that they be called)—between 1850 and 1860. Hawthorne was acquainted with a young, rapidly evolving America, caught between revolutions and on the brink of civil war. Westward expansion was in full force, and American citizens were faced with tough issues such as slavery, women's rights, and immigration. Additionally, America was experiencing a boom in industrialism and, subsequently, a swift transition to urbanization as cities became the new centers of commerce. The combination of political unease and rapid economic change created an explosive cultural atmosphere that was not far removed from the atmosphere of those European countries that had emerged from war and revolution not long before. They too had experienced industrial revolutions and were teetering on the brink of modernity, now facing the more difficult side-effects of industrial advancement. In Europe and in America, people were faced with the threat of extinction of those ways of the past worth carrying on, those most human aspects of life which were now being lost in the drive for progress and economic growth. In response, artists, musicians, writers, and philosophers began producing works that centered on humanity's most distinct elements—elements which could not be reproduced by machines and which dealt not in the realm of economic prosperity but in the realm of the prosperity of the human spirit. Collectively their efforts gave way to an international cultural movement which had profound effects on society, and which is still exhibiting its effects and influence today.

While elements of Romanticism have certainly been evident in works created prior to the mid- or late-eighteenth century, it is typically acknowledged that Romanticism gained full momentum as a cultural movement in England around the time of the publication of William Wordsworth's and Samuel Taylor Coleridge's collection of poems *Lyrical Ballads* circa 1798. Following the Age of Enlightenment and in the midst of scientific and industrial revolutions, a rational view of the world had become commonplace, and as the economy shifted from agricultural to industrial, there was less attention paid to the individual.

As the more humanizing elements of society seemed to be falling into the background, artists, musicians, writers, politicians, and philosophers reacted swiftly, hoping to speak out against those cultural changes that they felt were ultimately socially and morally detrimental. They found their voice in the realization of their art, which became a tool for social change while serving as the embodiment of those creative faculties that they thought ought to be preserved and celebrated.

The Romantics reacted to their surroundings while also addressing the internal and spiritual effects of the societal changes to which they bore witness. As trees began disappearing with the clearing of land for industry, and as chimneystacks and factories became more commonplace scenery, Romantics began to feature nature as a primary subject in their work, exalting it as a wellspring for emotion and placing it at the center of spirituality. Romantics also placed greater emphasis on the potential of the individual and the idea of the common man as hero, as machines began to replace human workers. They illuminated in their works the significance and power of emotion, freedom, and imagination.

With the desire to speak about these issues and express them appropriately, Romantics often turned to reflection on the past, drawing from those works which took humanity and its deepest, most distinct elements, as its core subject. This fueled a revival of heroic narratives, or romances as they were known, previously popular in medieval times. In England, for instance, readers were exposed to the Byronic hero, idealized but flawed characters such as Percy Bysshe Shelley's resurrected Prometheus, Emily Brontë's Heathcliff, and Charlotte Brontë's Jane Eyre. A revival of new Gothic tales also emerged, producing literature which included ghosts, haunted castles, and those mysterious objects which would allow an author to represent the most powerful of human emotions such as horror and awe. In Britain readers enjoyed the terror-filled *Frankenstein* of Mary Shelley, the ghostly romance of Emily Brontë's *Wuthering Heights*, and Samuel Taylor Coleridge's supernatural poem *The Rime of the Ancient Mariner.*

Romantics also addressed religion through their works, shifting the focus from popular, organized religions such as Puritanism and Calvinism to a more general spirituality tied in with nature and the experience of God's presence via the sublime. The spirituality proposed by Romantics was devoid of the strict system of sin and guilt evident in organized religion and created an accessible view of salvation which was now attainable to the everyman through his communing with nature and through his experience of imagination and emotion. These new ideals were promoted in the hopes of overcoming the predominant systems based upon logic and reason which seemed to be negating a true sense of spirit following the Enlightenment.

Among other changes, women and children began to attain a more significant role in art of the day, as the traditional role of women was questioned in literature. The creation of art and literature by women also further enhanced the view that women were equally immersed in the process of intellect and spirituality. Furthermore, nationalism was proposed as a formal philosophy by Jean-Jacques Rousseau and Georg Wilhelm Friedrich Hegel, and a distinct sense of nationalism grew as citizens found strength in maintaining their country's traditions via literature, oral history, and folklore.

While all of these themes were commonly linked to the period of time during the mid- to late-eighteenth century in England, related concerns and the themes they gave birth to in the arts were certainly not limited to any one geographic area or to any single genre. They were concerns shared by the citizens of many European countries, evidenced in multiple genres from music to art, philosophy, and politics. As America underwent its own economic, political, and cultural transformation in the nineteenth century, Romantic themes surfaced in literature, art, and philosophy there as well. Writers such as Herman Melville, Emily Dickinson, and James Fenimore Cooper took to the styles and themes which had been evident in British Romantic works. Hawthorne's own stories also corresponded thematically to their British counterparts and exhibited countless literary devices present in British

Romantic works. In order to delve deeper into the psychological realm of the characters, he utilized symbolism, a key device in works of the period. Hawthorne's symbols, such as the scarlet letter *A*, the minister's black veil, and Rappaccini's garden, elevated the use of symbolism, transforming it from a clever supporting device to a key element in the very formation of the core of the work. The employment of symbolism also granted readers some distance from the close confines of reality, allowing them greater freedom in their individual interpretations. Hawthorne's use of symbols had a distinct social applicability as well. Literary scholar Elissa Greenwald notes, "Precisely through symbolism, romance may provide insight into character and social conditions. . . . Symbolic representation may also provide social analysis, especially of a society that depends on symbols for its very constitution, like that of the Puritans in *The Scarlet Letter*" (5).

Also typical of Romantic works, Hawthorne's characters were psychologically complex, allowed to exhibit the full range of human emotions and suggest the extent of human potential. Women and children especially were allowed a key place in his stories. One could contend that this preference was due to Hawthorne's own involvement with women, including his predominantly female family and the influence of his wife Sophia Peabody. Hester Prynne and the precocious Pearl of *The Scarlet Letter* have become two of the most memorable characters in all of American literature, and literary critic Harold Bloom has gone so far as to propose that Hawthorne actually preferred these characters to Dimmesdale and Chillingworth, assigning them greater significance (Bloom, 6). If one considers the whole of Hawthorne's work, it seems probable that the female characters are indeed bestowed with a deeper self, an antidote to self-repression and, as such, represent a new modern way of living filled with possibility. Indeed many scholars have drawn this conclusion. Many of the female characters are also representative of selfless love. There is Georgiana of "The Birth-Mark" who is willing to do anything in devotion to her husband, and Beatrice of "Rappaccini's Daughter" who dies in her movement toward love. If one has any reservations about the preference given to Hawthorne's female characters, they might only consider the male counterparts—for instance, the now-repressed Dimmesdale and the obsessed Chillingworth. Or one might consider Hester's offspring, Pearl, a child who embodies freedom; despite her origin, which is troubling to all else, she seems to be free of the self-imposed restrictions of her forbears.

Hawthorne also frequently featured the artist/poet in many of his works, allowing him to deal with issues of the conflict of the artist in society. Owen Warland of Hawthorne's tale "The Artist of the Beautiful" embodied this struggle between artist and society, a timely issue and a personal one for Hawthorne. Through characters like Owen, Hawthorne could also examine the relevance and reliability of human imagination, a key concept in Romantic works. Scholar Sheldon W. Liebman makes the apt observation that Owen "is not just an artist but a *Romantic* artist, caught between the antitheses of ideal and real, spirit and matter, imagination and understanding, and art and criticism" (128).

As it was with many British works (the most obvious comparison being the aforementioned *Frankenstein* by Mary Shelley), many of Hawthorne's tales and romances also seemed to indicate an unease regarding the impact of scientific advancements on the human spirit. Hawthorne's characters are enraptured by the possibilities of science but often lack moral concern—unselfish concern—regarding its proper and noble application. The characters are, rather, divorced from humanity, caught up in the idea of self and the possibility of attaining perfection. In "The Birth-Mark," Aylmer's attempt to remove a birthmark from his wife's face results in her death. Hawthorne's Rappaccini of "Rappaccini's Daughter" is also blinded by science, specializing in raising poisonous plants, a pastime which ultimately results in the death of his daughter. Even Dr. Heidegger's interest in science in "Dr. Heidegger's Experiment" has tragic implications, as the consequences of the misuse of science lie not just with the scientist or creator but with those who are given access to the scientist's discoveries as well. Hawthorne carried these metaphors to the extreme. The stories were dark, verging on the bizarre, and had the potential to elicit an overwhelming emotional response from readers.

Like other American authors of this time period such as Edgar Allan Poe and Washington Irving, Hawthorne believed in empowering his works by emphasizing the psychological and the aesthetic, and thought that this could best be accomplished by setting works within a Gothic framework, which included ghosts, witchcraft, and other mysterious scepters. Scholar Donald A. Ringe summarizes these instances succinctly, giving us a sense of the prevalence of this device in Hawthorne's works:

> His earliest stories are filled with Gothic devices. "The Hollow of the Three Hills" (1830) is an effective tale of witchcraft with a chilling conclusion, and such well-known stories of the period as "My Kinsman, Major Molineux" (1832) and "Young Goodman Brown" (1835) are steeped in Gothic atmosphere and contain strong intimations of the demonic. In "Howe's Masquerade" (1838) we find the ghostly procession of Royal Governors who glide down the stairs and out the door of the Province House on the night of the British evacuation of Boston; and in "Edward Randolph's Portrait" (1838) the well known Gothic device of the mysterious painting. Indeed, in "The Prophetic Pictures" (1837) Hawthorne combines two such Gothic elements, the mysterious painting and the prophetic warning. (153)

Gothic elements were not just a symptom of Hawthorne's tales, however. They pervaded Hawthorne's romances as well:

> In "The Custom House", the long introduction to *The Scarlet Letter* (1850), Hawthorne uses a number of such devices: the dusty manuscript found in the garret . . .and the strange relic of cloth. . . .In *The House of the Seven Gables* (1851) he includes an ancestral curse . . .And in *The Marble Faun* (1860), he even employs so traditional an element as the sinister monk . . . (153–154)

Hawthorne had read Gothic tales voraciously as a child, and now, through the use of Gothic elements in his own work, he could elaborate on concerns of his own time including the dangers of abandoning one's humanity, of failing to accept imperfection, and of aligning oneself too closely to a single idea. We find these concerns evidenced in many of his characters: again we find Rappaccini, and Aylmer of "The Birth-Mark" who align themselves with science; Chillingworth and the cast of *The Scarlet Letter* who adhere blindly to dogmas, Ethan Brand, of the tale by the same name, who adheres to his pride and his self, abandoning all else.

Hawthorne crafted the atmosphere of each story carefully, as settings were also crucial to creating a truly emotional experience for the reader. The American wilderness, which was now being conquered and cleared in real life, appeared as a key setting in works like *The Scarlet Letter* and "Young Goodman Brown," functioning as a kind of haunted castle of the new world. It was presented to readers as a powerful and mysterious place of revelation. Hawthorne worked carefully in his descriptions, paying careful attention to his depictions of light and dark and his use of symbolism.

Some scholars have contended that Hawthorne's use of Gothic elements was due to America's brief and, therefore, inadequate history, which left a lack of dramatic information for writers to cultivate. While this may be true, it does not seem to be Hawthorne's fundamental motivation behind his employment of the Gothic, nor was use of the Gothic simply a device for heightened entertainment. As Ringe further elaborates, "The Gothic world of Hawthorne's fiction serves . . . an important thematic purpose. It provides the appropriate vehicle for expressing the somber truths which Hawthorne believed Americans of his generation needed most to know" (176). Like many Romantic authors, Hawthorne concerned himself with the past. He explored it literally, but also used it as a metaphor within which he could explore ideas of guilt, sin, and atonement. The primary example of this is his romance *The House of the Seven Gables*. The use of ghosts and their counterparts allowed Hawthorne to manifest the past, a key topic throughout his oeuvre, while the highly charged atmospheres allowed the author to create an evocative, emotional setting.

And yet, despite the presence of otherworldly ghosts and the darkness that pervaded his tales, Hawthorne's work always remained tethered to the plight of humanity. Herein was his primary concern. If there is any doubt, readers have only to examine the scene in *The House of the Seven Gables* whereby Clifford attempts to jump out a window in order to join a mass of people processing by. He is restrained by Phoebe and Hepzibah. Perhaps speaking for all of Hawthorne's characters, if not for the author himself, he acknowledges the profound effect it would have had on him if he could have jumped and survived. He would have, after all, rejoined humanity. As scholar Terence Martin points out "to lose touch with humanity is to destroy a necessary moral, emotional, and psychological balance. The great danger is abstraction, the indulgence of a preference for idea, which cuts one off—be it in pride, egotism, vengeance, or suffering—from humanity" (68). It is not only Clifford who presents this warning. Hawthorne's characters are all, in some way, bearers of this message.

While all of these elements helped to bind Hawthorne to the current of international Romantic work, his own work was unique in its particular attention paid to the American spirit. As it was for the British Romantics, American Romantics were concerned with the state of their nation and the effect the changes were having on the individual. For Hawthorne, the changes taking place in America were of the utmost concern. He sensed the division among American citizens, the movement away from tradition. He was sensitive to the shift away from those noble ideals brought about by the revolution. Hawthorne's son, Julian, later spoke of his father's concerns, revealing that ". . . the prospect of the dissolution of that mighty nation which had embodied the best hopes of mankind was a deep pain to him; it seemed likely to be the death of that old spirit of patriotism which had come down to us from the Revolution" (Hawthorne, 270). However, it was not just the threat of the death of the spirit of patriotism, but the threat of the death of the spirit itself which Hawthorne took as the true subject of each of his works. Here he realized the necessity of reflecting upon one's past, recognizing that confronting the present circumstances of his nation made revisiting his country's history, as well as his own familial history, a necessity. He worked to expose those elements which were detrimental in an effort to truly preserve those noble elements on which the country was founded. As such, Hawthorne chose to address the colonial history of America in his writings. He utilized New England settings and created allegories based around the ideas of Puritanism, allowing him to deal with information that was of a very personal nature. Hawthorne was born in Salem, Massachusetts on July 4, 1804. His relatives, emigrants from England, had been involved in the persecution of Quakers in the seventeenth century and were also involved in the judging at the Salem witch trials. It was a source of shame for the author, who changed the spelling of his last name from Hathorne to Hawthorne in order to disassociate himself from the troubling past of his ancestors. He found the ideas of Puritanism, with its strict denial of emotion and sexuality and system of sin and guilt, hypocritical and troubling. For this reason, stories like *The Scarlet Letter*, "Young Goodman Brown," and "The Maypole of Merry Mount" exposed the hypocrisies of Puritanism and dealt with the issue of good and evil as they are manifested in both the public and private realms. *The House of the Seven Gables* further explored the Puritan concepts of guilt and atonement through the Pyncheon family, who carried their burden not for years, but for centuries.

In light of the author's life work, he was never able to truly separate himself from his Puritan heritage. Literary critic Henry Seidel Canby observed that "Though he freed himself from its precepts, he never escaped from the brooding upon sin and the moral life that was the cause of Puritanism and its legacy. . . . Spiritual failures, moral failures, were for him, as for the Puritans, the great theme" (56). Indeed, for Hawthorne the concepts of spirituality and American citizenship were intertwined. Hawthorne, who indicated that he preferred that his lengthier works be recognized as romances and not novels, seemed to understand that the romance and the composition of the definition of America were congruous. The power of Hawthorne's work lay then in his "perception and exploitation of the parallels between the course of romance and the course of history—of the shared tension between inspiration and expression, sentiments and words" (Bell, 181). Certainly, it was this vision which made Hawthorne's version of American Romanticism so unique. In his book *The Development of American Romance*, scholar Michael Davitt Bell recognized this concept, namely that "American actuality had lost touch with America's supposed ideals. . . . the 'ideals' with which Hawthorne concerns himself are not political values like 'justice' and 'equality'. They are, rather, 'spiritual', experiential" (192).

Finally, any discussions of Hawthorne as a Romantic should not dismiss those scholars who would argue that the author was, in fact, something other than a Romantic. The author has perhaps attained such a secure place within the canon of American literature precisely due to the versatility of his work and the breadth of his style, which displays elements of various periods, styles, and genres. Any contrary differences of opinion might serve as an important reminder that Romanticism is a category which has allowed its authors a large degree of flexibility and the potential for individualism despite congruencies in theme, overlap in the employment of particular stylistic devices, or even shared intentions. The arms of Romanticism hold a tremendous variety of work including the music of Franz Schubert, Frédéric Chopin, and even Ludwig van Beethoven; the art of the Hudson River School; the philosophy of Jean-Jacques Rousseau and Johann Wolfgang von Goethe; the poetry of John Keats, Lord Byron, and Percy Bysshe Shelley; the Gothic tales of Washington Irving, Edgar Allan Poe, and Hawthorne to name only a few. Furthermore, traces of Romanticism exist in the works of our time just as they were evident in works prior to the formal recognition of Romanticism as a movement. Scholar Greenwald reminds us that, as literary critic Northrop Frye has previously observed, "Romance persists even in the form of the nineteenth-century novel" (Greenwald, 3). It was "not repudiated by the end of the nineteenth century, but formed the very basis of modernism" (Greenwald, 158).

We can be fairly certain that Hawthorne himself would have argued against particular and confining distinctions or boundaries in literature. Hawthorne managed to work in line with the cultural context of the time in which he lived and wrote, while bridging the past through the use of Victorian styles and themes, a concern with colonial history, and an examination of Puritanism and history, with futuristic styles and devices such as tendencies toward realism, a concern with the psychological, and a penchant for mixing genres which has now become a standard component of post-modern works. All the while Hawthorne has displayed a unique individualism that is truly characteristic of the same American spirit the author sought to defend. It is perhaps for this reason that Hawthorne's work has sometimes been characterized as the pinnacle of American Romanticism and which has made Hawthorne such an important figure in the history of literature. Perhaps the most important observation about Hawthorne and his work is revealed in his skepticism. In his skepticism he left room for possibility. Unlike many Romantic works, Hawthorne's works indicated that he was actually skeptical of traditional notions of revolution. While they are certainly dramatic, his own works are not a revolutionary sounding call, but rather a precursor to the modern democratic ideal, the call to change through the empowerment of the individual. This is the American romance. As scholar Michael Davitt Bell puts it, "the American romancer was to function as etymologist for that most mystic of words, 'America'" (172). Hawthorne functioned then as the supreme romantic etymologist, defining America through the romance born of its individualism and its spirit.

Works Cited

Bell, Michael Davitt. *The Development of American Romance: The Sacrifice of Relation*. Chicago: The University of Chicago Press, 1980.

Bloom, Harold, ed. *Nathaniel Hawthorne*. Modern Critical Views. New York: Chelsea House Publishers, 1986.

Canby, Henry Seidel. *Classic Americans: A Study of Eminent American Writers from Irving to Whitman*. New York: Russell and Russell, 1959.

Greenwald, Elissa. *Realism and Romance: Nathaniel Hawthorne, Henry James, and American Fiction*. Ann Arbor, MI: UMI Research Press, 1989.

Hawthorne, Julian. *Nathaniel Hawthorne and His Wife: A Biography*. Vol. 2. Boston: Houghton Mifflin, 1884.

Liebman, Sheldon W. "Hawthorne's Romanticism: 'The Artist of the Beautiful.'" *ESQ: A Journal of the American Renaissance* 22, no. 2 (1976).

Martin, Terence. *Nathaniel Hawthorne*. New York: Twayne Publishers, 1965.

Ringe, Donald A. *American Gothic: Imagination and Reason in Nineteenth-Century Fiction*. Lexington: University Press of Kentucky, 1982.

Bibliography and Further Reading

Barbour, Scott, Bruno Leone, and Clarice Swisher, eds. *Readings on Nathaniel Hawthorne*. San Diego, CA: Greenhaven Press, 1996.

Berlin, Isaiah. *Roots of Romanticism*. Princeton: Princeton University Press, 2001.

_____, ed. *Nathaniel Hawthorne's "The Scarlet Letter."* Modern Critical Interpretations. New York: Chelsea House Publishers, 1986.

Bosco, Ronald A., and Jillmarie Murphy, eds. *Hawthorne in His Own Time: A Biographical Chronicle of His Life, Drawn from Recollections, Interviews, and Memoirs by Family, Friends, and Associates*. Iowa City: University of Iowa Press, 2007.

Budick, Emily Miller. *American Romance Fiction: The Nineteenth Century*. New York: Macmillan, 1996.

Colacurcio, Michael J. *The Province of Piety: Moral History in Hawthorne's Early Tales*. Durham: Duke University Press, 1995.

Dekker, George. *The American Historical Romance*. Cambridge: Cambridge University Press, 1990.

Frye, Northrop. *Anatomy of Criticism*. Princeton, NJ: Princeton University Press, 1957.

Gamer, Michael. *Romanticism and the Gothic*. Cambridge: Cambridge University Press, 2000.

Gerber, John C. *Twentieth Century Interpretations of "The Scarlet Letter."* Englewood Cliffs, NJ: Prentice-Hall, Inc., 1968.

Goodman, Russell B. *American Philosophy and the Romantic Tradition*. Cambridge: Cambridge University Press, 2008.

Hawthorne, Nathaniel. *Collected Novels*. New York: Library of America, 1983.

_____. *Tales and Sketches*. New York: Library of America, 1982.

Heath, Duncan. *Introducing Romanticism*. New York: Totem Books, 2006.

James, Henry. *Hawthorne*. Ithaca, NY: Cornell University Press, 1998.

Levine, Robert S. *Conspiracy and Romance: Studies in Brockden Brown, Cooper, Hawthorne, and Melville*. Cambridge: Cambridge University Press, 1989.

McCall, Dan. *Citizens of Somewhere Else: Nathaniel Hawthorne and Henry James*. Ithaca, NY: Cornell University, 1999.

McIntosh, James, ed. *Nathaniel Hawthorne's Tales: Authoritative Texts, Backgrounds, Criticism*. New York: W.W. Norton & Company, 1987.

Mellow, James R. *Nathaniel Hawthorne in His Times*. Boston: Houghton Mifflin Company, 1980.

Miller, Edwin Haviland. *Salem Is My Dwelling Place: A Life of Nathaniel Hawthorne*. Iowa City: University of Iowa Press, 1991.

Millington, Richard H., ed. *The Cambridge Companion to Nathaniel Hawthorne*. Cambridge: Cambridge University Press, 2004.

_____. *Practicing Romance: Narrative Form and Cultural Engagement in Hawthorne's Fiction*. Princeton: Princeton University Press, 1992.

Morse, David. *American Romanticism: Volume 1—From Cooper to Hawthorne, Excessive America*. Basingstoke, Hampshire: Palgrave Macmillan, 1987.

Reynolds, Larry J. *A Historical Guide to Nathaniel Hawthorne*. Oxford: Oxford University Press, 2001.

Roe, Nicholas. *Romanticism: An Oxford Guide*. Oxford: Oxford University Press, 2005.

Scharnhorst, Gary. *Nathaniel Hawthorne: An Annotated Bibliography of Comment and Criticism Before 1900*. Metuchen, NJ: Scarecrow Press, 1988.

Swann, Charles. *Nathaniel Hawthorne: Tradition and Revolution*. Cambridge: Cambridge University Press, 1991.

Wagenknecht, Edward. *Nathaniel Hawthorne: The Man, His Tales and Romances*. New York: Continuum Publishing Company, 1989.

Wineapple, Brenda. *Hawthorne: A Life*. New York: Alfred A. Knopf, 2003.

CRITICAL
READINGS

The Scarlet Letter_____

Hugo McPherson

> In the two decades after Northrop Frye published his momentous *Anatomy of Criticism* (1957), a school of "myth criticism" flourished in North American universities. Although it attracted many of the best critical minds in the 1960s and '70s, much of that criticism has not stood the test of time: in reducing works of literature to collections of archetypes, myth criticism stripped them of everything that made them distinctive.
>
> Hugo McPherson, though, reminds us that Hawthorne's work often responds well to modes of criticism ill suited to other fiction. Myth criticism is well suited to Hawthorne's works, for Hawthorne himself thought in terms of archetypes and symbols. McPherson draws attention to Hawthorne's eternal and universal character types; in his reading, *The Scarlet Letter* is "less about sin than an account of the plight of the Dark Lady and the mercurial hero, menaced by a tyrannical old man of reason." And in examining the underlying structures of Hawthorne's masterpiece, he gives us a new way to think about the tensions between England and America, between reason and passion. The essay works up to a meditation on the meaning of the famous *A*, for McPherson an "ambivalent symbol" that "becomes Hawthorne's emblem of the human heart."   — J.L.

The point has perhaps been made that Hawthorne's mythological tales, 'these old baby stories,' are closer to the heart of his artistic vision than criticism has generally allowed. The iron men, Dark Ladies, mercurial heroes, and frail princesses of his idealized mythology have their sad relatives in the worlds of American and European experience. What, we must now ask, is their significance for Hawthorne's masterpiece, *The Scarlet Letter*? And what is their relation to those abortive romances with which Hawthorne struggled in the melancholy afterlight of his career?

So much has been written about *The Scarlet Letter* that there can now be no question of dealing in detail with what criticism has said. The chief difficulty with many readings is that they fail to get beyond the explicit moral and psychological issues of the tale to see it as expressive action. A second difficulty is that critics do not always keep in mind that Hawthorne is studying the fate of the self in *Puritan* America; that the book is his analysis and critique of the colonial society which evolved, finally, into the stifling narrowness of 'The Custom-House.' In one important sense the critics who focus on ideas and moral concepts are right: viewed as a moralized tale, the book does read as a definition of the Christian pattern of sin, its consequences and its expiation. But there are several problems which such analyses fail to resolve. First, if the book is simply a moral tale, then Pearl appears as an improbable and even fantastic creation whose final flight to Europe seems irrelevant. Second, Hawthorne's handling of the central symbol, the *A*, appears fanciful and over-elaborate. Third, the role of the Puritan community and its leaders receives little attention. Fourth, the last chapter appears weak—a polite tying up of ends, and a provokingly ambivalent commentary on the tale's meanings. And finally, the introductory sketch, 'The Custom-House,' seems to have no more than a tenuous connection with the romance itself.

Seen in relation to the mythology of the tales and romances discussed above, however, *The Scarlet Letter* would appear to be less about sin than an account of the plight of the Dark Lady and the mercurial hero, menaced by a tyrannical old man of reason in a community which reveres law above all else, sees human nature as depraved, and fears passion and imagination equally. It would also appear to be a quest for the meaning of *A* or Pearl—a meaning which the action of the tale gradually unfolds. These themes are congruent with the themes of the later romances and myths; and the imagery of this tale, which carries much of the burden of meaning, is similarly the imagery of the later work. Without for a moment rejecting the discursive moral aspects of the story, we may observe its shape as myth by reviewing the action chronologically, keeping the images in clear focus, and allowing the protagonists of Hawthorne's later tales to assert their kinship to Hester, Dimmesdale, and the others.

The chronological action of *The Scarlet Letter* begins in Europe. Hester, a beautiful and innocent English maiden, marries a decaying scholar, Chillingworth. Their union, apparently, is a failure, for Hester later reflects that Chillingworth's foulest offence was that 'in the time when her heart knew no better, he had persuaded her to fancy herself happy by his side.' Hers was a 'marble image of happiness' which had been 'imposed upon her as the warm reality' (C, I, 177). Thus at the root of the action we have the Dark Lady-Black Man situation which Hawthorne was later to develop in Zenobia and Westervelt, in Miriam and her model, and Proserpina and Pluto. But Chillingworth, in contrast with his later incarnations, is neither a quack nor a demon-priest; he is, in Europe at least, a kindly enough man, and a great scientific scholar.

Unhappily, reason has so dominated Chillingworth's career that it has cut him off from feeling, from the delights of the heart and the flesh which he sees imaged in Hester. When he first meets Hester in New England he is able to admit that it was the obsession with knowledge that made him an impotent husband: '"I,—a man of thought,—the book-worm of great libraries,—a man already in decay, having given my best years to feed the hungry dream of knowledge,—what had I to do with youth and beauty like thine own! Misshapen from my birth-hour, how could I delude myself with the idea that intellectual gifts might veil physical deformity in a young girl's fantasy!'" (C, I, 74). As a 'type' of reason, he is disproportioned from the beginning; and when he learns that he cannot rule the lush beauty, passion, and domestic creativity typified by Hester, he becomes vengeful. In a second interview with Hester he describes his relation with Dimmesdale: 'A mortal man, with once a human heart, has become a fiend for his especial torment' (C, I, 172). And Hester expresses her pity for 'the hatred that has transformed a wise and just man to a fiend!'

Hawthorne does not explain why Chillingworth decides to emigrate to America, but it is clear that the Puritan reliance on law and reason are agreeable to his temper, and that the community needs his talents. His tragedy is that, when he fails to establish a true bond with Hester, he (like the Puritans) condemns her passion as demonic, and vows to destroy the person or 'type' that was capable of winning her. As his interest turns from healing to vengeance, he becomes wizened and begrimed by the smoke of his furnace. At length he tells Hester that he recalls his old faith; that their situation is 'a kind of typical illusion' which he is powerless to change. He has become the darkest, most deterministic Puritan of them all.

The third figure of this 'typical illusion' is Arthur Dimmesdale, a brilliant young scholar whose fame has re-echoed at Oxford. His name, Arthur, suggests a great hero (students of Kenneth Burke might pun the name into Arthur-Author, or Art for short) whose role in the community is purely spiritual; he will unendingly battle the powers of blackness as defined by scriptural and civil law. But Arthur is irresistibly attracted to Hester. Where he is pale and ethereal, she is rich and voluptuous; where he is intellectual and imaginative, she is earthy and material—skilled in domestic arts. In secret this couple conceive a child—a Pearl—who unites in herself their two natures.

Arthur resembles the moonlight-mirror types of Hawthorne's mythological tales; in Chillingworth's words, 'the Creator never made another being so sensitive as this' (C, I, 171). But, for all his mercurial ability, Dimmesdale is neither a demi-god nor champion; far from the virile questing Bellerophon, he wanders in the dim dale of a world which his faith assures him is depraved, bearing the burden of a nature which he believes to be evil. As a type of spirit or imagination, his place in Puritan society is the pulpit, and he feels a piercing guilt over the part of his nature which draws him to the things of this world.

At the beginning of the romance, then, we have not a bipolar conflict between Head and Heart, but a situation in which a fecund, richly creative Dark Lady is 'wedded' to two men, neither of whom, in Puritan

New England, will admit his connection with her. The minister lacks the courage to admit that his nature has a passionate side; the scientist reviles the lady and swears her to secrecy so that he can pursue an inhuman revenge. And the righteous community brands the lady with a scarlet letter that has 'the effect of a spell, taking her out of the ordinary relations with humanity, and enclosing her in a sphere by herself' (C, I, 54).

As Gordon Roper and John Gerber have argued,[12] the subsequent course of the story proceeds in a kind of chain reaction in which one character or type dominates, expends its energy, and ignites the fuse that sets a new force in motion. At first the Calvinist community dominates in punishing Hester: then Chillingworth, recognizing Dimmesdale as his victim, begins to torture him; next Hester acts to free her lover from his suffering; and finally the delicate hero, Dimmesdale, takes control, makes his confession, and with a kiss sets Pearl free of the spell that enthralled her. This, in a sentence, is the story of the Puritan-American quest. We must consider each phase of it in detail, for Hawthorne's rendering is so rich that no incident or image is superfluous.

The first force, the Puritan community, provides the theatre for the drama; its ethos is a major target of Hawthorne's criticism. With its stern and drearily unimaginative denial of so much that is rich and warm in human nature, this community would become, in the nineteenth century, the stuffy 'custom' house of Hawthorne's introductory sketch. It believes above all in empirical fact and in law; when feeling or passion, sensual or artistic, go beyond orthodox limits, they are consistently related to the dark—to the Black Man. The sea-captain who witnesses the Puritan holiday at the end of *The Scarlet Letter* calls the rulers 'those sour old Puritans.' Hawthorne's own reflection on their magistrates is: 'They were, doubtless, good men, just, and sage. But, out of the whole human family, it would not have been easy to select the same number of wise and virtuous persons, who should be *less capable* of sitting in judgment on an erring woman's heart, and disentangling its mesh of good and evil, than the sages of rigid aspect towards whom Hester Prynne now turned her face' (italics mine, C, I, 64).

The fathers of this community (like the twin fathers, Minos-Aegeus, of the Theseus story) are the ageing soldier, Governor Bellingham, and the benign Rev. Mr. Wilson (who, in turn, is related to 'the holy Apostle Eliot' and that 'half-mythological personage,' the Rev. Mr. Blackstone).[13] The chatelaine of the community is Mistress Hibbins, a 'sour-tempered' hag who is 'wedded' in sterile spinsterhood to her domineering brother, the Governor.

In his account of Hester's visit to the Governor's Hall, Hawthorne brings into close dramatic relation all of the forces at work in the Puritan community. The 'chances of popular election' have caused the arch-English Governor 'to descend a step or two from the highest rank' (C, I, 108). Nevertheless, he is still powerful and respected, although his head, separated from his body by a Jacobean ruff, reminds Hawthorne of 'that of John the Baptist on a charger.' Q. D. Leavis has pointed out the relevance of this image to the Puritan separation of mind and body. Governor Bellingham's brilliantly polished armour, the iron facade of the Puritans, is prominently displayed in his hall, where it reflects, greatly magnified, Hester's scarlet letter, the symbol which rouses the iron man's rage.

The composite impression that we get of the Governor's mansion combines gold, sun, iron, splendour, and power—the images of the tyrant. Governor Bellingham, as his garden reveals, has not reproduced in New England the culture of the Old Country. The most prominent products of his tillage are cabbages and pumpkins, 'lumps of vegetable gold.' The few rose bushes and apple trees, the flower of English culture, have descended from the Rev. Mr. Blackstone's importation.

The forces which flank the Governor are: the Rev. Mr. Wilson, the saintly but aged gentleman who hopes that 'pears and peaches might yet be naturalized in the New England climate'; Roger Chillingworth, whose empirical 'medical' knowledge has been welcomed by the Puritans, though they fear that he may be in league with the Devil; and Arthur Dimmesdale, the ethereal young minister whose duties in the town, fighting the powers of night, have apparently made him frail and ill. The figures who complete this caste are Mistress Hibbins and Hester. Mistress Hibbins, though the colony's first lady, does not appear in the sunshine, but remains in a shuttered upstairs room. Her daylight role is so empty that she has long since turned vengeful and entered the devil's service. Hester, her New England sister, still appears in public, though condemned to wear the ignominious *A*. But the New England scene has wrought a great change upon her: she dresses in drab gray; her luxuriant hair is concealed; and when she meets the sunny Governor, 'the shadow of the curtain' falls on her and partially conceals her (C, I, 109). New England womanhood, that is, unless it descends to the brutal, 'man-like' callousness of the Boston goodwives, is forced out of the sunshine. Hester, in her New England life, has become like Minerva—a goddess of needle and loom, an intellectual who voyages boldly in the dusky region of mind. She has lost what are, for Hawthorne, the warmest qualities of womanhood (C, I, ch. 13).

The occasion of Hester's visit to Governor Bellingham is the report that Pearl is to be taken away from her—a proposal which Hawthorne places in perspective by suggesting that the Puritan government often meddles in affairs over which it should have no real jurisdiction—affairs as trivial as a quarrel over a pig. On this occasion—the community's second attempt to punish Hester—the erring mother is saved by Wilson and Dimmesdale who, unlike Governor Bellingham, feel great sympathy for the child who personifies the scarlet *A*.

Chillingworth, the second activating force of the story, cares nothing for Pearl's fate. On hearing Dimmesdale's plea for Pearl and Hester, he recognizes his victim, and proceeds with the greatest subtlety to play upon the minister's sense of sin and guilt. He has indeed chosen 'to withdraw his name from the roll of mankind' (C, I, 118). But Hawthorne makes it clear that Chillingworth's power to tyrannize over Dimmesdale results from the Puritan fear of imagination and instinct—the night side of experience. Puritan society cannot recognize these powers as essentially human rather than Satanic. Chillingworth candidly explains Dimmesdale's weakness to Hester: "'With the superstition common to his brotherhood, he fancied himself given over to a fiend, to be tortured with frightful dreams, and desperate thoughts, the sting of remorse, and despair of pardon; as a foretaste of what awaits him beyond the grave. But it was the constant shadow of my presence!—the closest propinquity of the man whom he had most vilely wronged!'" (C, I, 171–72)

In literal terms there is no question that Dimmesdale has 'vilely wronged' the scientist by expressing his love for Hester. But in 'typical' terms he has wronged himself by denying the true nature of his powers. Similarly, Chillingworth has wronged Hester by concealing his relation to her—by failing to be a benign 'father.' Small wonder that Dimmesdale and Hester—the types of passionate, imaginative men and women—suffer in Calvinist society!

Hawthorne's rejection of the Calvinist view of human nature, however, does not lead him to espouse the cause of man's 'natural goodness,' the Transcendental view. For him there is an ideal, perfect realm, and an imperfect, human realm. Human nature is inevitably imperfect. But the fatal error of the Puritans is their failure to recognize all of man's gifts—to achieve an integration of all of man's forces. The Puritan life is a half-life, and its outcome is likely to be tragic.

Hester, the third activating force in this 'typical' drama, follows a long, tortuous, and erroneous path before she is able to act decisively, and even then she takes the wrong course. Isolated by the brand she must wear, she discovers at the Governor's Hall, and later in the forest, that even the sunshine now flees from her. She does not share the sin-centred view of man's nature that obsesses her husband and lover, and indeed the whole Puritan community; and 'through seven long years' she rejects the view that her act of love was depraved: 'She was patient—a martyr, indeed—but she forbore to pray for her enemies; lest, in spite of her forgiving aspirations, the words of the blessing should stubbornly twist themselves into a curse' (C, I, 85). Robbed of her glamour and denied her fecundity, she assumes a 'marble coldness'; 'her life had turned, in a great measure, from passion and feeling, to thought' (C, I, 164), and she speculates with a boldness that 'our forefathers . . .would have held to be a deadlier crime than that stigmatized by the scarlet letter.' Mistress Hibbins, recognizing Hester's alienation from the community of iron men, tempts her to hold rendezvous with the Black Man, but she is saved by her responsibility to her 'Pearl.'

The line which her thinking takes is Transcendental, and leads her to assert that her transgression with Dimmesdale 'had a consecration of its own.' But Hawthorne does not agree. He describes her speculations as wanderings in a 'dismal labyrinth' of thought, a moral wilderness. If the Puritan obsession with evil is extreme, Hester goes too far in the opposite direction and begins to think of human nature as 'naturally good.' Her wanderings had taught her 'much amiss'; the scarlet *A* had indeed 'not done its office.'

Hester finds her power to act when Dimmesdale—equally isolated and helpless—mounts the scaffold like a somnambulist in the dead of night to make a desperate and ineffectual admission of his guilt. Hester and Pearl, who have been 'watching at a death-bed,' join him, and as he takes the hands of his wife and child he feels 'a tumultuous rush of new life . . . pouring like a torrent into his heart, and hurrying through all his veins, as if the mother and child were communicating their vital warmth to his half-torpid system. The three formed an electric chain' (C, I, 153). Like Theseus, clutching the thread of sympathy that joined him to Ariadne, Dimmesdale experiences a resurgence of power, but he is still unable to act, for he still fails to understand that Reason is the force that tortures him with guilt. When the leering Chillingworth is revealed across the square, he asks: 'Who is that man, Hester? . . . I hate him' (C, I, 156). Still a Puritan, Dimmesdale cannot challenge the tyranny of the force that is held in such honour in New England. He evades Pearl's charge, 'Thou wast not bold!—thou wast not true!' with the assurance that he will appear publicly with her and Hester 'at the great judgment day.' He is then led away by his familiar fiend, who still triumphs. Ironically, the sexton later finds Dimmesdale's glove on the scaffold and warns him: "'Since Satan saw fit to steal it, your reverence must needs handle him without gloves, henceforward'" (C, I, 158).

In this 'black' confessional Dimmesdale has found the secret of his eventual triumph—the identity of his persecutor, and the human bond which will give him the power to act. But Hester has found immediate power to act on her 'speculations.' She informs Chillingworth that she will no longer keep the secret that he is 'wedded' to the scarlet woman. And she meets Dimmesdale in the natural setting of the forest to persuade him that they should escape from the cruel austerities of New England. For a brief time Dimmesdale enjoys this 'natural' setting. He recognizes that Chillingworth's cold and logical investigation of the human heart is an unpardonable sin. Reunited with his lover and their child, he exclaims that this relation—with Hester restored to her original beauty—is indeed 'the better life!' (C, I, 202). And in Pearl he recognizes 'the oneness of their being . . .at once the material union, and the spiritual idea, in whom they met, and were to dwell immortally together' (C, I, 207).

But as the minister walks home from the forest his mind wanders in a 'maze' of blasphemous and lustful images—as dangerous as the maze of thought in which Hester had wandered. He realizes that Hester's thrilling plan of escape to a state of nature where there are no formal restraints will be no real escape but rather a second betrayal of himself: 'Tempted by a dream of happiness, he had [momentarily] yielded himself, with deliberate choice, as he had never done before, to what he knew was deadly sin.' The only solution to his problem, then, is to make a 'deliberate choice' which is his own, not Hester's: he must publicly assert his true nature—the nature of the human condition. At this point Dimmesdale finds both his heroism and his humanity. Like Hamlet at the conclusion of Shakespeare's tragedy, he becomes the tragic witness of man's imperfection—'The readiness is all.' Having gained this insight he is able to write a new election sermon. Thus his last night speeds away 'as if it were a winged steed, and he [like

Bellerophon] careering on it' (C, I, 225). And on the next morning he makes his grand confession—proclaims his true self. Tragic 'recognition' has occurred; heroic death ensues. Like Hamlet, Dimmesdale dies for truth.

To say, however, that in his expiring moment Dimmesdale renounces the Puritan faith, would be a distortion of Hawthorne's statement. Dimmesdale is a Puritan to the end. His triumph is his recognition that the dark experience which his brethren regard as demonic is an integral part of man's full nature; as a Puritan he thinks of it as 'the worst,' but he knows that it must be acknowledged, for by repressing it man makes it a source of unending torture. Thus his act of self-recognition and self-assertion—the public reunion with Hester—releases Pearl from the 'spell' which had made her seem a demon child. For Hester and Dimmesdale, the types of passion and imagination in Puritan society, there can be no conventional happy ending. But Pearl, through their fortitude, becomes a complete woman instead of a Puritan half-woman—the first representative of a new breed, the first *complete* American.

Given this understanding of Dimmesdale's drama, we may now interpret fully the meaning of that meteor-like *A* in the sky—the portent which many of Hawthorne's critics have thought merely fanciful. When Dimmesdale is reunited upon the scaffold with his lover and child, the 'great vault' of the sky

> brightened, like the dome of an immense lamp. It showed the familiar scene of the street, with the distinctness of mid-day, but also with the awfulness that is always imparted to familiar objects by an unaccustomed light . . .[Every detail became sharply visible] but with a singularity of aspect that seemed to give another moral interpretation to the things of this world than they had ever borne before . . .They [the family] stood in the noon of that strange and solemn splendor, as if it were the light that is to reveal all secrets, and the daybreak that shall unite all who belong to one another. (C, I, 154)

This clear moment, that is, is the moment of vision: it reveals the deep truth of nature that 'all who belong to one another' should be united. But Dimmesdale, still shackled like the 'others of his superstitious brotherhood,' can understand this clear light only as a portent of doom. Having 'extended his egotism over the whole expanse of nature,' he misses the meaning of the revelation; 'the disease in his own eye and heart' lead him to see a vast letter A, the universal witness that he (and this whole night realm of experience) is depraved (C, I, 155). The beauty of the vision is quenched in his obsessive awareness of sin. Only after the final forest scene will he grasp the real meaning of the A, and find the power to proclaim it.

This brings us finally to the centre of the romance—to Pearl and to the meaning of the scarlet A, Hawthorne's richest symbol. Hawthorne discovered the A in the Custom-House, that deadening institution whose rigid commitment to routine, mechanical measurement, and rules, threatened the complete annihilation of his imagination. As a man 'who felt it to be the best definition of happiness to live throughout the whole range of his faculties and sensibilities' (C, I, 40), Hawthorne re-garded the A as a bright point of hope—a release from the latter-day Puritan 'custom' house of his age, and a promise of imaginative fulfil-ment.

From the outset the A is an ambivalent symbol. Its 'scarlet woman' meaning for the Puritans is clear but by the last line of the story when we see it as an heraldic A *Gules* on Hester's and Dimmesdale's com-mon tombstone, it has assumed a meaning that is beyond the philoso-phy of any Puritan. All of the meanings with which Hawthorne invests it are relevant; and all are united organically in Pearl, the 'living em-bodiment' of the A. The scarlet letter, finally, becomes Hawthorne's emblem of the human heart—of its imperfection, and its labyrinthine mixture of good and evil. The letter is blood red (*gules*) rather than scarlet, for it betokens 'our common nature.'

From the Puritan point of view, the A stands specifically for adultery and, in general terms, for sin—for the fallen aspects of man's nature which must be brutally suppressed: sexual knowledge; sensory indulgence, and the broad area of fancy and intuition which Puritanism labelled 'witchcraft.' Man has only the law of Scripture and reason to guide him, and even reason may deceive him in his study of God's providence. The *A* is thus further associated with the sin of Adam, with hell, infernal fire, Satan, demons, fairies, and so on. The magistrates' intention in branding Hester with this lurid mark is to make her a living warning to others who are tempted to give in to unlawful impulses. Its corrective function will be to reduce Hester's rich femininity to the drab, un-sexed coarseness of the community goodwives (C, I, 50); to make her colourless, submissive, and unthinking—denying her nature on earth to gain life eternal.

But the effect of the scarlet brand on Hester is not at all what her male judges expected. She clings stubbornly to the belief that her sin 'had a consecration of its own,' and the whole seven years of her torment fail to convince her that her natural impulse is depraved. Puritanical men are the people who fear her gifts. She tells Pearl that 'Once in my life I met the Black Man! . . .This scarlet letter is his mark!' (C, I, 185). Hawthorne underlines in various ways Hester's failure either to accept the Puritan meaning of the *A* or to arrive at an adequate personal understanding of it. At one moment she speaks of being 'disciplined to truth' by the *A*, and at the next she confesses that she is lost in a 'dismal maze' of thought (C, I, 166). Her bitterness over Chillingworth's attempt to kindle a 'household fire' (C, I, 74) in his heart by marrying her leads Hawthorne to remark: 'But Hester ought long ago to have done with this injustice . . . Had seven long years, under the torture of the scarlet letter, inflicted so much of misery, and wrought out no repentance?' (C, I, 177) She does feel a throb of pain whenever another sinner's eyes fall on her badge, as though other people understand her guilt, and themselves wear the *A* secretly. And she does understand that a green *A*, which Pearl makes out of seaweed, 'has no purport'; the *A* is an emblem that speaks of mankind and his moral dilemmas, not of Nature. But a genuine understanding and acceptance of the *A* will come only after Dimmesdale's heroic revelation and death. Then, having witnessed in Europe the fulfilment of Pearl's womanhood, Hester will return to New England and do what she can to prove that the *A* is not a demonic badge: 'Here had been her sin; here, her sorrow, and here was yet to be her penitence. She had returned, therefore, and resumed—of her own free will . . . the symbol of which we have related so dark a tale.' (C, I, 263)

Hester's understanding of her scarlet emblem comes slowly and painfully, but Hawthorne's treatment of the *A* leads the reader fairly quickly to question its Puritan meaning and consider other possibilities. The sympathy which the Madonna-like young mother of the first scaffold scene feels for Hester suggests that the emotions of motherhood are perhaps closer to the truth of human nature than the stern legality of 'the righteous Colony of the Massachusetts, where iniquity is dragged out into the sunshine!' (C, I, 54). If Governor Bellingham's hollow steel armour reflects only glaring sun, an enormously exaggerated *A*, and Pearl's impish smile, the simple Puritan 'folk,' guided more by human feeling than doctrine and law, sometimes think of Hester's *A* as meaning able or angel. The *A*, it is rumoured, looks like 'a nun's cross'; it repels the devilish arrows of the Indians (C, I, 163); as embroidered by Hester, it is a work of art; it is a portent in the sky which the 'disease' in the minister's 'own heart and eye' (the Puritan ethos) makes him see as a cosmic revelation of his depravity, but which Hawthorne sees as a sign of 'the daybreak that shall unite all who belong to one another' (C, I, 154). The point to be made here is that Hawthorne, however 'tasteless' his critics find his symbolism, is not merely fanciful. Every *A*-image that he uses adds a new shade of meaning to the symbol. The *A* becomes the centre towards which all extremes tend. And it is a living centre, for Pearl represents it in the flesh.

The traditional meaning of 'pearl' as the soul or self is surely Hawthorne's meaning. We have already noted that Dimmesdale sees the child as the 'material union, and the spiritual idea' of himself and Hester. But Hawthorne's elaboration of Pearl, *A*, and crimson images serves the serious purpose of deepening and expanding the meaning of his symbol. To the Puritans Pearl is an imp, a demonic child, or a witch; she is outside the law; unrestrained, apparently, by any of the strictures which shape little Puritans. Hester, in her defiance of the Puritan interpretation, deliberately dresses Pearl in scarlet fashions, as if to underline the absurdity of regarding as evil an infant who 'was worthy to have been brought forth in Eden; worthy to have been left there, to be the plaything of the angels, after the world's first parents were driven out' (C, I, 90). This costume, however, reminds the Rev. Mr. Wilson of 'one of those naughty elfs or fairies' who, in pre-Reformation England, were benignly regarded. In Old England, that is, such magical qualities were valued rather than feared; people believed in *good* fairies.

The scarlet or crimson colour also links Pearl to roses, the traditional symbol of beauty and love. She claims to have been plucked from the native rosebush which blooms bravely at the prison door; and she imperiously demands to have the sunshine reflected from the Governor's house, and the English roses in his garden. But the Governor's light and flowers are not hers; the young American, as Hester expresses it, must 'gather . . . [her] own sunshine' (C, I, 103). In Boston, the flower which overshadows the wild rose is 'the black flower of civilized society, a prison.' Pearl combines in herself the attributes of the sturdy native rose and its cultivated English sister; she does not recognize the 'black flower.'

This rose imagery helps us to understand why Pearl must go to Europe at the end of the romance. She cannot thrive in the black-flowering garden of New England where English roses flourish but feebly and native roses are unregarded. When Pearl pelts the scarlet *A* with roses, Hester feels only pain, but the child understands intuitively that it is her mother's true badge. She seems to know, too, that this is the mark on her father's breast; and, however inappropriate in terms of realistic fiction, she embraces the full legacy of the *A* by kissing it (C, I, 212).

Through love, the force which binds her father and mother, Pearl has learned an intuitive acceptance of the *A*. But her integration of the gifts of Hester and Dimmesdale has no place in Puritan America. She must therefore find her fulfilment in Europe as the first representative of a new breed—the figure who presages James's immaculate heroines, 'the heiress of all the ages.' Pearl, moreover, looks forward to Phoebe Pyncheon and Priscilla. One might safely say that she is the first genuine Miss America.

Thus, though the Puritan phase of the American quest ended darkly, the picture was not overwhelmingly black. 'In the spiritual world,' the 'mutual victims,' Chillingworth and Dimmesdale, may find their hatred transmuted into 'golden love.' And even in America the full self—the forces of reason, feeling, and imagination or spirit—may yet be recognized. If Hester's foresight can be trusted, 'at some brighter period, when the world should have grown ripe for it, in Heaven's own time, a new truth would be revealed, in order to establish the whole relation between man and woman on a surer ground of mutual happiness' (C, I, 263). America, that is, will accept fully the bright, creative powers of its womanhood, and the imaginative gifts of its men. Pearl has even inherited Roger Chillingworth's wealth, the greatest thing that the Puritans created—so great, indeed, that the witch-child, had she wished, 'might have mingled her wild blood with the lineage of the devoutest Puritan among them all.'

The story of Hester's and Dimmesdale's struggle through 'seven long years' to learn the meaning of *A* is Hawthorne's central theme. In the mythological tales the hero and the Dark Lady surmounted their difficulties happily enough, but in the world of experience they seldom triumph. Man is fallen; his characteristic atmosphere is that dusky area in which warm hearthlight and clear moonlight mingle; or, in nature, the 'cool brown light' of sun and shadow. This is the realm of the integrated self. The statement of *The Scarlet Letter* is basically what Hawthorne has said elsewhere. The 'seven long years' of Hester's torture are like the seven generations, or Seven Gables, of the Pyncheon-Maule conflict, and the seven years of Hollingsworth's quest to establish an institution for criminal reform. In the same way, the embroidered scarlet *A* is a 'talisman' or token of 'our common nature'; it is the talisman which later appears in *Blithedale* as Zenobia's exotic flower (handed on to Priscilla) and in *The Marble Faun* as the seven stones in the bracelet which Miriam presents as a wedding gift to Hilda. But Hawthorne will not have his New World inherit the guilt of the Christian tradition. Pearl is surely the luminous prophecy of the coming of Phoebe Pyncheon and Holgrave—a prophecy upon whose fulfilment we have, in Blithedale's Priscilla and Coverdale, Hawthorne's later, less sanguine comments, and in Hilda and Kenyon, his qualified hope.

Notes

12. Gordon H. Roper, ed., 'Introduction,' to *The Scarlet Letter and Selected Prose Works* (New York, 1949); John Gerber, 'Form and Content in *The Scarlet Letter*,' *New England Quarterly*, XVII (March 1944), 25–55.

13. The birth of America was, for Hawthorne, associated with the myth of Europa and Cadmus: 'The Dragon's Teeth.' The Rev. Mr. Blackstone, he records, was 'the first settler of the peninsula; that half-mythological personage who rides through our early annals, seated on the back of a bull' (C, I, 107).

Chiefly about Coverdale:
The Blithedale Romance

Clark Davis

Henry James wrote in 1879 that Hawthorne's life "had few perceptible points of contact with what is called the world, with public events," but Hawthorne was in fact deeply involved in politics. Among Hawthorne's less-read works is a *Life of Franklin Pierce* (1852), a campaign biography of his friend from Bowdoin College who, later that year, would go on to win the United States presidency.

It's another kind of politics, however, that interests Clark Davis, who sees *The Blithedale Romance* as "the most brilliant example of Hawthorne's work as a political writer." Davis redefines *political*, using it not in the obvious sense but to refer to a way of addressing otherness—"engaging a topic with clear political implications . . . through the disengaged point of view made possible through fiction." Davis's work is informed by Emmanuel Levinas and other ethical philosophers, and he uses the notion of "self-limitation" and "radical humility" to understand Hawthorne's ethics. He situates Hawthorne's depiction of Coverdale—"clearly the most controversial of Hawthorne's central characters"—between "the realist impulse" and "the fantasist impulse," which Hawthorne combines "as a way of demonstrating the limitations of each." Davis is therefore able to read *The Blithedale Romance* as a "critique of socialism, of any large-scale political reform," because "the political must begin with the ethical."   — J.L.

The most brilliant example of Hawthorne's work as a political writer is clearly *The Blithedale Romance*. By "political" I mean of course his sense of himself as a romancer engaging a topic with clear political implications but doing so through the disengaged point of view made possible through fiction. For someone who has expressed anxiety about the effects of partisan politics on his artistic voice,

Blithedale offers an astonishing recovery of that voice through a reexamination of Hawthorne's own artistic strategies. The result is perhaps the most dramatic example of the extent to which Hawthorne was willing to go to establish an ethical position based upon self-limitation.

He begins in his usual way, with a preface that argues quite seriously for the book's generic identity. Though clearly concerned about realist critiques of his unrealistic stories, Hawthorne chose a remarkably real-world, remarkably political topic for a work published the same year as the Pierce biography. And yet, as though in defiance of the obvious, he continues to argue for the separation between the fictional and the real: "He begs it to be understood, however, that he has considered the Institution itself as not less fairly the subject of fictitious handling, than the imaginary personages whom he has introduced there. His whole treatment of the affair is altogether incidental to the main purpose of the Romance; nor does he put forward the slightest pretensions to illustrate a theory, or elicit a conclusion, favorable or otherwise, in respect to Socialism" (*CE*, 3:1). Again, how are we to read such statements? If it is obvious to us that a writer who sets his story in a socialist community cannot avoid commenting on socialism, there is no reason to believe it was less obvious to Hawthorne. So, if we wish to understand his purpose, we can take this claim as yet another preemptive apology, an artful dodge away from a range of critical comments, or we can take it as an enactment of shyness and another demonstration—bolder, more brazen—of the "sort of politician" Hawthorne hoped to be.

The key appears in the following sentence: "In short, his present concern with the Socialist Community is merely to establish a theatre, a little removed from the highway of ordinary travel, where the creatures of his brain may play their phantasmagorical antics, without exposing them to too close a comparison with the actual events of real lives" (*CE*, 3:1). This "removal," this disengagement from the real, is more than just a defense of the imagination; it establishes an ethical space, a space of self-consciousness and self-limitation that allows Hawthorne precisely the sort of statement he has just offered. In other words, he can offer a position on socialism, but only through his denial of such a purpose. Such a deliberate separation does not imply that he has escaped the broad range of the political, but it does suggest that his goal is to avoid the narrow limitations of overtly political language. For that sort of argument we can turn to "some one of the many cultivated and philosophic minds" Hawthorne lists at the end of his preface, those who can write a "history" of the experiment and adumbrate its "lessons."

Without such an opening maneuver, paradoxical though it is, a writer of political fiction might not escape the set patterns of opinion, the overt politics, that already dominated this type of topic. In the case of the Pierce biography these constraints were clearly in place, and their power to reduce any comment to the simplistic binaries of partisan debate clearly troubled Hawthorne, despite his Democratic sympathies. By announcing his separation from such debates he does not propose a formalist isolation, an artistic immunity from the political; he hopes to combine artistic vision with material reality to produce an involvement with the "real" *by means of* imaginative distance: "The Author has ventured to make free with his old, and affectionately remembered home, at Brook Farm, as being, certainly, the most romantic episode of his own life—essentially a daydream, and yet a fact—and thus offering an available foothold between fiction and reality" (*CE*, 3:2). Hawthorne usually couches such explanations in terms of artistic defensiveness. He needs this "foothold" to avoid exposing the "paint and pasteboard" (*CE*, 3:2) of his characters. But the union of fact and dream also establishes a double critique, a twofold vision that anticipates his deliberate self-limitation in "War-Matters." The realist impulse demands a commitment to the real, an immersion in the moment and in the epistemology of the material. The fantasist impulse demands a similar allegiance to the supernatural, the possibility of strangeness. Hawthorne insists on combining these opposing commitments as a way of demonstrating the limitations of each. It is a strategy of checks and balances meant to isolate the individual as an inherently limited subject.

What separates *Blithedale* from Hawthorne's earlier romances is its dramatic presentation of precisely this double critique in the form of its narrator, Coverdale. Clearly the most controversial of Hawthorne's central characters, Coverdale has provoked a variety of responses both as a narrator (or narrative device) and as a potentially autobiographical figure. He has been described as unreliable, crazy, self-absorbed to the point of blindness, ineffectual, and/or a deluded but cunning murderer. But in terms of Hawthorne's position as an artist within/against politics, there are really only two significant questions to ask about Coverdale: How close is he to Hawthorne? and What is the purpose of his limitations as a narrator?

The relationship between *Blithedale*'s author and its narrator has been the subject of extensive comment. For those interested in portraying Coverdale as partially or totally unreliable the space tends to be sharply defined. Beverly Hume, for instance, finds "a distance which enables [Hawthorne] not only to manipulate Coverdale's conflicting perceptions but also Coverdale's authorial manipulation of those perceptions."[1] Likewise, Harvey L. Gable Jr. notes that "Hawthorne is able to reveal simultaneously the ideology motivating Coverdale's actions, his feelings as he suffers the consequences, and his later reflections upon the experience."[2] Other critics have been less sure of this divide, preferring a more subtle appreciation of Hawthorne's potential for self-masking. Richard Brodhead, for instance, senses that "Hawthorne's distance from Coverdale is not a consistent one. In his evaluations of *Blithedale* Coverdale's judgments often have a sane balance, suggesting that they have his author's approval, whereas at other points he exhibits a moral obtuseness that makes him seem to be the object of Hawthorne's scorn."[3] In a similar vein, Irving Howe calls Coverdale a "highly distorted and mocking self-portrait," while Edgar Dryden sees the narrator as a "veil or disguise Hawthorne wears" that is both "manifestation" and "distortion."[4]

Most important for the present discussion, however, is the general agreement among *Blithedale*'s readers that Coverdale is a notably self-conscious device. Brodhead, for instance, calls the novel "the most self-conscious of all Hawthorne's fictional exercises," which Charles Swann extends to "the most successful skeptical examination of the authority of the author and his narrative."[5] But what specific form does this self-consciousness take? And what is its purpose? It would be possible to argue, for instance, that Hawthorne's strategy is to give a political critique of utopianism the air of objectivity by intentionally criticizing the book's narrative voice. In this sense his skepticism of reform could be disguised, and rendered more powerful, through self-deference. To make such an argument, however, it is also necessary to believe that Hawthorne's career-long investigation of the self's epistemological limits was a sham, conscious or not, nothing more than a rhetorical strategy. That is, Hawthorne either naively offered self-critique as a form of truth when it was nothing more than a politically interested maneuver, or he knowingly employed self-deference as a form of ingratiation in the service of his political position.

These conclusions seem to me equally off the mark, both arrogant and absurdly cynical. That Hawthorne is a notably crafty author is undeniable, as are his awareness of craft and his ability to integrate rhetorical strategy into his thematic interests. But the question to ask is not what political purpose underlies the disposition of craft but in what ways rhetoric or style embodies the philosophical goals of the work. Take, for instance, this passage from late in *Blithedale*, in which Coverdale offers what sounds very much like a Hawthornian position:

> This is always true of those men who have surrendered themselves to an over-ruling purpose. It does not so much impel them from without, nor even operate as a motive power within, but grows incorporate with all that they think and feel, and finally converts them into little else save that one principle. When such begins to be the predicament, it is not cowardice, but wisdom, to avoid these victims. They have no heart, no sympathy, no reason, no conscience. They will keep no friend, unless he make himself the mirror of their purpose; they will smite and slay you, and trample your

dead corpse under foot, all the more readily, if you take the first step with them, and cannot take the second, and the third, and every other step on their terribly straight path. (*CE*, 3:70)

As Brodhead points out, one of the difficulties of seeing Coverdale as an entirely unreliable narrator is the presence of just such passages. Here Coverdale sounds very much like Hawthorne, rehearsing the familiar criticism of blind idealism and its ethical toll on friendship. The comment might just as well apply to Melville or Elizabeth Peabody as to Hollingsworth, reenacting the Hawthornian withdrawal from a well-meaning but aggressive personal invasion. In an otherwise positive portrayal, we might well attribute such a voice to the author himself and designate Coverdale as Hawthorne's genuine alter ego.

But by this point in the book we have already seen several of Coverdale's weaknesses: his narcissism, his passive-aggressive voyeurism, and his tendency to favor fantasy over reality. Though it might be said that the passage above is the reflection of the older and wiser narrator rather than the Coverdale within the narrative, such a separation is highly questionable. We have only to look to his infamous "confession" (itself a product of the retrospective voice) to determine that the lessons Coverdale may have learned exist side by side with those traits present from the novel's beginning. In fact, it is questionable whether Coverdale learns anything in the course of the narrative; he does not noticeably "develop" as a character, nor does he show convincing signs of distance from his former self.[6] In this sense opinions offered late in the book tend to have the same status as those offered near the beginning. Even more important, these opinions exist on the same plane, in the same vocal space, as Coverdale's absurd speculations and fantastic self-indulgences. In other words, this is a character who speaks both sense and folly, who mouths Hawthorne's cherished ideas and, at the same time, shows himself to be ineffectual and foolish.

The challenge posed, then, is to read the passage above not simply as a Hawthornian "moment" in the narrative but as a Hawthornian position taken up by a foolish, self-centered character. "I will give you my position on idealism," Hawthorne seems to say, "but I will give it to you from the mouth of a sneaky, self-deluded poet, a silly man who hides in trees, ogles women, and fantasizes about what's under their clothes." For what purpose? If this is a rhetorical strategy meant to strengthen the offered argument, it is not very effective. If anything, Coverdale is a poor spokesman for any position Hawthorne might want to promote. Instead of disarming critics, this maneuver is more likely to arm them with precisely the sort of weapon they require—namely, proof that anti-idealism produces an ineffectual, overly aesthetic self-concern.

Given Hawthorne's skepticism, however, his sense that everyone "squints," it seems much more likely that he is attempting to tell his audience something about the nature of point of view. In other words, he offers a position and exposes its limits simultaneously, neither to strip the statement of meaning nor to disarm opposition but to demonstrate what it means to engage not in spite of but *by means of* disengagement. As he will do in "War-Matters," he emphasizes conversation over monologue, listening over conflict. For if conversation requires both commitment and listening, engagement and distance, then Hawthorne has hit upon a fictional method for demonstrating that necessary combination. He has created in Coverdale a type of narrative voice that makes room for and even solicits response and critique, that intentionally opens itself to his readers' alternative "voices."

This approach is evident in Hawthorne's obvious self-parody in chapter twelve, where Coverdale in his "bower" serves to ridicule not only Hawthorne's earlier work—"Sights from a Steeple," especially— but also his cherished historical perspective, his "hundred years" vision: "It may have been the cause, in part, that I suddenly found myself possessed by a mood of disbelief in moral beauty or heroism, and a conviction of the folly of attempting to benefit the world. Our especial scheme of reform, which, from my observatory, I could take in with the bodily eye, looked so ridiculous that it was impossible not to laugh aloud" (*CE*, 3:101). To take such a passage as purely a product of Hawthorne's position we would have to believe not only that Hawthorne is suspicious of reform (which he is) but that he is similarly suspicious of "moral beauty and heroism" (which he clearly is not). In fact, the entire episode in the bower is so much the product of self-scrutiny that even Coverdale senses its potential absurdity. That his distance above the world makes "the whole matter look ridiculous" says as much about the potential distortions of such a perspective as it does about its access to historical truth.[7] But this self-critique does not imply the complete vacancy of the position; it simply shows that all perspectives, both near and far, are inherently limited by their very status as perspectives. Such positions can be held with conviction but should not be held to the exclusion of response, to the point, that is, of monologue or, in the Melvillian sense, monomania.

This fundamental position is implied in the principle of "responsibility" cited by Coverdale late in the text in reaction to the "pale man in blue spectacles" (*CE*, 3:198): "He cited instances of the miraculous power of one human being over the will and passions of another; insomuch that settled grief was but a shadow, beneath the influence of a man possessing this potency, and the strong love of years melted away like a vapor" (*CE*, 3:198). The mesmeric hold here duplicates both totalitarian politics and deterministic models of human behavior. The "wizard" is in some respects a tyrant and a "scientist" of the Rappaccini variety, able to deprive the "maiden" of free will and to strip any subject of ethical possibility: "Human character was but soft wax in his hands; and guilt, or virtue, only the forms into which he should see fit to mould it. The religious sentiment was a flame which he could blow up with his breath, or a spark that he could utterly extinguish. It is unutterable, the horror and disgust with which I listened, and saw, that, if these things were to be believed, the individual soul was virtually annihilated, and all that is sweet and pure, in our present life, debased, and that the idea of man's eternal responsibility was made ridiculous, and immortality rendered, at once, impossible, and not worth acceptance" (*CE*, 3:198).

Again, the passage appears to duplicate Hawthorne's typical rhetoric, but it does so from within a demonstration of its own compromised position. Hawthorne has created a flawed, obviously limited character as the spokesman for a philosophy of self-restraint, thereby presenting his argument at the same time that he shows us what it means. No one is immune from the fundamental position of Coverdale's speech; that is, we cannot escape the "eternal responsibility" of the ethical subject, no matter how strongly we may believe in the truth of our position. In this sense the passage offers more than a recovery of sin or guilt from a pseudo-scientific determinism. It registers the fundamental relationship of human beings in terms of "response." Responsibility implies interaction, the formal structure of conversation. In order to respond we must listen; in order to be responsible we must understand our relation to the rest of the world, our responsibility to see our actions within the context of human relationships. The mesmerist thus duplicates the nonethical position of the monomaniacal idealist: He sees the world as an extension of the self and others as creatures of his own mind. There is no response from the world outside the mesmerists's self because he recognizes no limits to his own dominion. He is therefore capable of the greatest atrocities because there is no one to "answer to."

This notion of responsibility can be applied broadly, as an antitotalitarian political model, or narrowly, as a structure for personal relationships. Its fundamental position within friendship or love seems the likely focus of Zenobia's veiled lady story, which itself can serve to scrutinize the book's personal relationships. The story's climactic moment, in fact, replays the similarly significant scene from "The Minister's Black Veil" in which the Reverend Mr. Hooper refuses to lift his veil for his fiancee, Elizabeth. In Zenobia's version, however, there is no promise of an apocalyptic unveiling within the historical structure of Christianity. This Calvinist teleology has been replaced by the promise of an earthly revelation as an immediate reward for a faith that transcends the material. Where the two scenes meet is on the issue of social or human faith. Hooper demands a faith in Christian history; the Veiled Lady demands a faith in human relationships. In both cases, the men involved wish to maintain a type of certainty that will reduce or eliminate risk or surprise. Hooper refuses to place himself in the epistemologically limited position of equality with another human being. Theodore likewise cannot relinquish that "natural tendency toward scepticism" (*CE*, 3:113) that otherwise protects him from the risks associated with belief. In the terms of Coverdale's later defense of responsibility, neither Hooper nor Theodore is able to relinquish a controlling interest in the situation sufficiently to escape comparison to the mesmerist. Each wishes to control the situation, philosophically if not physically. And for Hawthorne it seems but a small step from such egoistic rigidity to the "power of one human being over the will and passions of another" attributed to Westervelt. It is even arguable that the refusal to acknowledge limitation of the self, the refusal of responsibility, necessarily creates a battle of wills that cannot help but produce one-sided control within a relationship. In other words, the model of political conflict, when applied to friendship, can render nothing more than the total victory of one self over another.

Blithedale's other relationships bear out this central notion. Each appears to offer pessimistic comment on the realistic possibility of an ideal friendship. The aggressive demands of Hollingsworth on Coverdale, Zenobia, and Priscilla are so clearly the object of critique that they merit little specific comment. Hollingsworth, like his predecessor Chillingworth, is a relatively flat character used to exemplify the specific, local damage caused by absolutism. But his lack of dimension or depth also functions as a representation of the limits of his vision. In this light we should resist the temptation to identify such characters in Hawthorne's work as little more than the quasi-allegorical tools of rhetoric. They are, in addition to their rhetorical function, expressionist distortions meant to communicate the character's inner limitations. Thus Hollingsworth, when compared with the book's other characters, seems the thinnest because he is the thinnest; each of his relationships to specific others serves to highlight his failure to interact, to engage in the richness of human "response."

Coverdale might be thought to be similarly limited, by his own self-concern if nothing else. What separates him from Hollingsworth, however, is his admittedly occasional critique of absolutism—a self-consciousness within self-absorption. As a result we get a much more complex, shifting character, one who attempts to dominate relationships in certain ways but who also withdraws, who manipulates the distance between himself and others as a partially conscious form of self-restraint. He may value privacy for all the wrong reasons, for the opportunities it offers for voyeurism, escapism, or lack of commitment, but he also reveals how privacy can help obviate Hollingsworth's mistakes. In this sense he is both a spokesman for withdrawal and, remarkably, a walking critique of the self in isolation.

Zenobia, by contrast, seems remarkably engaged, both personally and politically. It is only her ultimate commitment to Hollingsworth, her willingness to sacrifice her independence for love, that places her within the range of the book's interrogation of personal relationships. Generally speaking, it is her elevation of love over political purpose that is thought to drive Hawthorne's critique of utopian reform; as this argument goes, even the strongest woman is not immune from the power of the heart and will sacrifice everything when that power calls. But it seems just as likely that she functions primarily as a warning against self-sacrifice, against losing the self inside someone else—the sacrifice of distance. She is willing to give herself totally to Hollingsworth, and this, more than anything, is the cause of her downfall, not because she surrenders her feminism but because she surrenders her self, like Georgiana in "The Birth-Mark." Her death can then be seen as a symbolic necessity, a way of representing the death of the self through the sacrifice of distance.

Priscilla, on other hand, seems strangely immune from such losses, despite her long sufferance at the hands of Westervelt. She emerges from the veil into a paradoxical figure of "happiness," the curiously powerful helpmeet of the morally wrecked Hollingsworth: "I did meet them, accordingly. As they approached me, I observed in Hollingsworth's face a depressed and melancholy look, that seemed habitual; the powerfully built man showed a self-distrustful weakness, and a childlike, or childish, tendency to press close, and closer still, to the side of the slender woman whose arm was within his. In Priscilla's manner, there was a protective and watchful quality, as if she felt herself the guardian of her companion, but, likewise, a deep, submissive, unquestioning reverence, and also a veiled happiness in her fair and quiet countenance" (*CE*, 3:242).

It is difficult to tell, at first glance, what such a relationship is meant to suggest. Hollingsworth's failures are easy enough to understand, but Priscilla's "submissive" triumph, her "veiled happiness" mixed with "reverence" seems strangely contradictory. Is this the ethical happiness of self-limitation, the "slender woman" who finds joy in helping others, who has emerged from the veil with a clearer sense of her relationship to the world? Or is there, within her "watchful" protection, an air of victory, of having changed places with the "powerfully built" but now powerless man who once enthralled her? It is difficult to see what sort of happiness she can have in this situation, except a sense of self-worth brought on by a version of maternal power. This is certainly not an ideal relationship in Hawthorne's terms; it is just as one-sided, just as monologic as any controlled by Westervelt or the dreaded mesmerists of Hawthorne's imagination. Hollingsworth's "self-distrust," after all, has little in common with a Hawthornian sense of self-limitation. Hollingsworth has moved from blind egotism to complete loss of self, and the pattern of his fall explains the dangers of his type of monomania. Deprived of his only idea, his single meaning, he is now nothing more than a dependent soul, a "veiled lady" of sorts, who can do little more than lean against his "guardian."

On the whole, then, *The Blithedale Romance* has little to offer in the way of ideal relationships. Its critique of socialism, of any large-scale political reform, rests on the primary contention that the political must begin with the ethical, that personal relationships are the foundation and model for societal action. As we saw in his arguments with Elizabeth Peabody, Hawthorne refused to consider ideas about social change without considering their origin within the context of one-to-one human interaction, and he was skeptical of the tendency of activists to elide the often resistant, perplexing aspects of human individuality in the name of a progress of ideas. Such a position can at times produce the quietism with which Hawthorne has been variously charged. However, it also creates a type of engagement that refuses to see the self as separate from the relationships out of which it was formed, an engagement that insists upon the constant self-scrutiny of ethical distance.

The Child's Mission: *Our Old Home*

Two important examples of just such a self-positioning appear in *Our Old Home*, the public version of Hawthorne's *English Notebooks* and the ostensible record of his term as consul to Liverpool. In the first, Hawthorne offers an account of his relationship with Delia Bacon, the American scholar obsessed with demonstrating that a secret society led by Francis Bacon was responsible for writing the plays of William Shakespeare. This tonally complex retrospective includes descriptions of their initial meeting, Hawthorne's imaginative reconstruction of Bacon's attempt to exhume Shakespeare's gravestone, an account of the critical reception of her book, and a brief mention of their falling out. Throughout, Hawthorne presents the eccentric and self-absorbed Bacon as he would one of his fictional characters. Indeed, it is arguable that she interested him precisely because of her resemblance to those isolated, obsessed figures that populate his fiction. And yet this is more than a simple case of artistic voyeurism. Hawthorne is, in a very real sense, involved in Bacon's life, even if for a short time, and his willingness to become involved, combined with his habit of detached observation, produces an interesting model for the type of engagement he prefers. Specifically, it allows us to see how he understood the limitations that exist between human beings and the ways those limitations, if acknowledged, establish ethical boundaries to thought and action. During the initial meeting, for instance, Hawthorne quickly decides that Bacon is a "monomaniac," completely dependent for her identity and place in the world upon her all-consuming "theory" (CE, 5:106–7). He considers debating the matter with her, offering an "explanation for this theory," but understands that dialogue is impossible: "She had as princely a spirit as Queen Elizabeth herself, and would at once have motioned me from the room" (CE, 5:107). Instead he takes up his usual position of observer, curious to see the effects of so dominant an idea, ready to help where possible but conscious of the limits of her attention. What he does not do, somewhat surprisingly, is dismiss her as a crank.[8] Nor does he take offense at her imperious egotism. Even after she dismisses him for some less-than-loyal comment, he maintains a sort of distant fidelity to her uniqueness of character: "In consequence of some advice which I fancied it my duty to tender, as being the only confidant whom she now had in the world, I fell under Miss Bacon's most severe and passionate displeasure, and was cast off by her in the twinkling of an eye. It was a misfortune to which her friends were always particularly liable; but I think that none of them ever loved, or even respected, her most ingenuous and noble, but likewise most sensitive and tumultuous character, the less for it" (CE, 5:114).

It is possible, of course, that Hawthorne's sympathy here is merely ironic, revealing Bacon's faults while pretending to overlook them.[9] But such a reading misses a crucial attitude shared by Hawthorne with romanticism in general—the admiration for the self's integrity, the ability to be true to oneself. As Isaiah Berlin explains, "The fact that there is admiration, from the 1820s onwards, for minorities as such, for defiance as such, for failure as being nobler in certain respects than success, for every kind of opposition to reality, for taking up positions on principle where the principle itself may be absurd . . .—this is significant. What romanticism did was to undermine the notion that in matters of values, politics, morals, aesthetics there are such things as objective criteria which operate between human beings, such that anyone who does not use these criteria is simply either a liar or a madman, which is true of mathematics or of physics."[10]

The celebration of the failed but true character similarly informs Hawthorne's descriptions of Pierce, who likewise inspires his loyalty despite, or perhaps because of, Pierce's political losses. In both cases, the celebration of integrity arises not from a desire to avoid action; in fact, in Bacon's case it is Hawthorne's potential overreaching that ends the relationship and effectively precludes any further assistance he might offer. Instead, the appreciation for the truth of character arises out of a sense of the limits of understanding, out of the pluralist impulse that is based, certainly for Hawthorne, upon the problematic nature of truth and epistemology. If indeed there are limits to understanding others, then there should also be limits to action with respect to others. Such a position does not produce political paralysis; Hawthorne has been able to help Bacon, for instance, in certain ways but not beyond the boundaries of her own, perhaps deluded, self-conception.[11] But what separates Hawthorne's sympathy, in this sense, from the more robust activism of someone like Melville is his unwillingness to sacrifice the autonomy of an individual like Bacon for social action that, no matter how productive, would strip her of her self-determination.

We have already seen the difficulties of such an approach within the context of partisan politics. Its limitations within actual relationships, particularly in light of Hawthorne's personal reticence, appear most forcefully later in *Our Old Home* in a passage recounting a visit to the West Derby workhouse: "By-and-by we came to the ward where the children were kept. . . . And here a singular incommodity befell one member of our party. Among the children was a wretched, pale, half-torpid little thing, (about six years old, perhaps, but I know not whether a girl or a boy), with a humor in its eyes and face, which the governor said was the scurvy, and which appeared to bedim its powers of vision, so that it toddled about gropingly, as if in quest of it did not precisely know what" (*CE*, 5:300). As we know from the matching pages in *The English Notebooks*, the "member of our party" is Hawthorne himself, the shy consul who seems more horrified than amused that this "sickly, wretched, humor-eaten infant" has taken "an unaccountable fancy" to him (*CE*, 5:300): "It said not a word, being perhaps underwitted and incapable of prattle. But it smiled up in his face—a sort of woeful gleam was that smile, through the sickly blotches that covered its features—and found means to express such a perfect confidence that it was going to be fondled and made much of, that there was no possibility in a human heart of balking its expectation. It was as if God had promised the poor child this favor on behalf of that individual, and he was bound to fulfil the contract, or else no longer call himself a man among men" (*CE*, 5:300).

It may be difficult to read this passage without judging it to be a piece of overt sentimentality, a Dickensian moment of middle-class redemption in the embrace of the wretched poor. But two important elements alter the conventional tone. First, there is the very serious claim of human otherness, embodied in this case by a child whose alienating features Hawthorne clearly emphasizes. There is, in other words, a face—silent, smiling, but, most importantly—looking at another face. This look, which does nothing to minimize Hawthorne's revulsion, does produce a remarkably candid moment for this notably cagey writer: "Nevertheless, it could be no easy thing for him to do, he being a person burthened with more than an Englishman's customary reserve, shy of actual contact with human beings, afflicted with a peculiar distaste for whatever was ugly, and, furthermore, accustomed to that habit of observation from an insulated standpoint which is said (but, I hope, erroneously) to have the tendency of putting ice into the blood" (*CE*, 5:300–301).

This stark self-portrait, though lightly disguised, undercuts the surge of sentimentality that might otherwise overtake this episode. It is a remarkable moment. Hawthorne is telling us not only that he understands the limitations of his own personality but that in the face of a particular human demand, the disengagement of the shy observer must yield, even if it is never fully relinquished. Whatever ideas may be in place prior to this demand simply do not function. The "struggle" Hawthorne describes before he picks up "the loathesome child" can only be emotional or, at any rate, nonintellectual, to be symbolized and rationalized in retrospect but not at the moment of decision: "No doubt, the child's mission in reference to our friend was to remind him that he was responsible, in his degree, for all the sufferings and misdemeanors of the world in which he lived, and was not entitled to look upon a particle of its dark calamity as if it were none of his concern; the offspring of a brother's iniquity being his own blood-relation, and the guilt, likewise, a burthen on him, unless he expiated it by better deeds" (*CE*, 5:301).

Readers of *The House of the Seven Gables* will recognize Hawthorne's attitude to historical guilt, the transference of responsibility from one generation to the next. But just as important is the conjunction of basic human responsibility with the question of individual "concern." For all of Hawthorne's heightened sense of privacy, for all his interest in the limitations and sanctity of the individual self, he here describes the self as both detached and engaged, inherently separate *and* inherently connected, free to make choices, yes, but bound by "blood-relation" to respond, to answer.

From *Hawthorne's Shyness: Ethics, Politics, and the Question of Engagement* (Baltimore: The Johns Hopkins University Press, 2005): 105-117. Copyright © 2005 by The Johns Hopkins University Press. Reprinted by permission of The Johns Hopkins University Press.

Notes

1. Beverly Hume, "Restructuring the Case against Hawthorne's Coverdale," *Nineteenth-Century Fiction* 40, no. 4 (1986): 399.

2. Harvey L. Gable Jr., "Inappeasable Longings: Hawthorne, Romance, and the Disintegration of Coverdale's Self in *The Blithedale Romance*," *New England Quarterly* 67, no. 2 (1994): 258.

3. Richard Brodhead, *Hawthorne, Melville, and the Novel* (1976), 100.

4. Irving Howe, *Politics and the Novel* (1957), 170, and Edgar A. Dryden, *Nathaniel Hawthorne: The Poetics of Enchantment* (1977), 106.

5. Brodhead, *Hawthorne*, 108, and Charles Swann, *Nathaniel Hawthorne: Tradition and Revolution* (1991), 239.

6. I disagree in this respect with Kenneth Marc Harris, who argues that "Coverdale is neither a hypocrite nor a self-deceiver at the time he is actually telling his story, although he may now regard himself as having been either or both at the time of the events he is describing." *Hypocrisy and Self-Deception in Hawthorne's Fiction* (1988), 129.

7. See the discussion of Hilda from *The Marble Faun* in Part 3.

8. One precedent might have been his treatment of the equally eccentric Jones Very: "Hawthorne received it [Very's 'mission'] in the loveliest manner—with the same abandonment with which it was given—for he has that confidence in truth—which delivers him from all mean fears—and it was curious to see the respect of Very for him—and the reverence with which he treated his genius. There is a petulance about Hawthorne generally—when truth is taken out of the forms of nature . . . though the happiest and healthiest physical nature tempers it—so that it only expresses itself on that one occasion. But in this instance he repressed it and talked with him beautifully." Elizabeth Peabody to Emerson, December 3, 1838, quoted in Edwin Gittelman, *Jones Very: The Effective Years 1833–1840* (1967), 282–83.

9. Brenda Wineapple suggests that Bacon is less of a threat to Hawthorne than other women writers because she wrote nonfiction. *Hawthorne: A Life* (2003), 290. The example of Margaret Fuller might suggest otherwise. Indeed, Hawthorne's complex relationship with Fuller provides a balance of sorts both to his infamous attacks on "scribbling women" and to his more tolerant encounter with Bacon. Fuller clearly provoked equal measures of intimate sympathy and vengeful misreading. She is perhaps the one person with respect to whom Hawthorne had difficulty maintaining his own ethical distance. See Thomas Mitchell, *Hawthorne's Fuller Mystery* (1998).

10. Isaiah Berlin, *The Roots of Romanticism* (1999), 140.

11. "Hawthorne would neither cast Bacon off nor take credit when he secured a publishing contract [for her] from Parker and Son. Nor would he balk at assuming financial responsibility for her book, which Parker required as a condition. (To cover his investment, Hawthorne demanded that Ticknor bring out half the agreed-on copies—five hundred in all—doubtless hoping to offset inevitable losses.) He also consented to write a preface for the book, another crucial item for the negotiations with Parker." Wineapple, *Hawthorne*, 292–93.

Re-figuring Revelations:
Nathaniel Hawthorne's *The Scarlet Letter*_____

Evans Lansing Smith

The Greek word is *apokalypsis*; the Latin is *reuelatio*. Both mean "uncovering" or "revealing," and they lend their name to the final book of the Christian Bible, the Revelation to John of Patmos, in which the secrets of the end of the world are revealed.

Hawthorne lived in an avowedly apocalyptic age. He came to maturity at the height of the Second Great Awakening, when preachers throughout New England invoked the Book of Revelation daily, convinced that the end times were at hand. Evans Lansing Smith admits that Hawthorne was "very likely suspicious" of this millenarian vision, but he highlights the importance of apocalyptic themes and images in his works, especially in *The Scarlet Letter.* That work, as Smith points out, "is impelled from the beginning by the need to uncover what has been concealed." But it is not merely literal uncovering that makes *The Scarlet Letter* an apocalyptic work. Smith turns to typology, a mode of interpretation in which events in the past prefigure events in sacred history, to make the link between revelation and Revelations, between uncovering and "universal cataclysm," in "a peculiarly American breed of apocalypse."

At the center of his study is the hieroglyph, the writing system that was first decoded, thanks to the parallel passages on the famous Rosetta Stone, in 1822, when Hawthorne was at Bowdoin. Well into the nineteenth century hieroglyphics retained their association with mysticism and ancient wisdom, as Hawthorne knew when he depicted Pearl as a "living hieroglyph."   — J.L.

The theme of apocalypse is one of the most enduring and central in all of American literature, from Michael Wigglesworth to Thomas Pynchon. Along the way, its development engaged the great figures of the American Renaissance—Emerson, Melville, Poe, and Hawthorne.

In *The Scarlet Letter*, allusions to the Book of Revelation determine the basis of the novel's theme and structure to an extent not fully recognized by most critics of the novel, who have failed to note that Hawthorne attempts in this work a comprehensive refiguration of the Biblical apocalypse. By focusing on the root meaning of "apocalypse" as an uncovering of hidden or buried secrets, Hawthorne raises hermeneutical and epistemological questions relevant to the debates about Emersonian transcendentalism and its relation to theology raging during his time.[1]

Visions of the end derived from Scripture were, as is well known, a standard concern of the intellectual community of Hawthorne's New England, particularly so in the context of the so-called Second Great Awakening, which emphasized the necessity of religious reform as a means of millennial hope. David Bjelajac has charted the apocalyptic visions in the sermons of the time with reference to Boston's rejection of Jacksonian democracy, its internal debate regarding Emersonian transcendentalism, and the painting of *Belshazzar's Feast* by Washington Allston. The painting, left unfinished at the artist's death, depicts the prophet Daniel, who points to the mystical writing on the wall that interrupts the King's feast and predicts the fall of Babylon and the liberation of the Jews. The subject was traditionally interpreted as "an Old Testament type for the Last Judgement" and as one of those "apocalyptic texts prophesying the end of time" and the building of the New Jerusalem (Bjelajac 22). This millennialism "pervaded nearly every social and religious group in America during Allston's life" (23), particularly among those New Englanders alarmed by the materialist secularism of Jacksonian democracy. The subject had previously been treated in Benjamin West's painting of 1776, in which the painter may well have intended a reference to King George and the fall of the British Empire (Bjelajac 45). West's painting illuminates the mystical letters on the wall with a supernatural aura much like Hawthorne's lighting effects used to describe the letter in the sky during the second scaffold scene in *The Scarlet Letter*.

Hawthorne saw Washington Allston's painting sometime after 1844, when it was first exhibited in the Boston Athenaeum. He remarked that the "imperfect beauty" of its unfinished state demonstrated "that the deeds of the earth, however etherealized by piety or genius, are without value, except as exercises and manifestations of the spirit" (quoted by Bjelajac 16). Elizabeth Palmer Peabody, Hawthorne's sister-in-law, believed that Allston's scriptural painting "could function in the same direct manner as the handwriting on the wall" as a warning to prepare "for the more spiritual revelation of Christ" (148–149). She also argued that the Old Testament should be taught in Unitarian Sunday schools (which had decided not to) because if it was interpreted "spiritually or symbolically then it retained its usefulness as a moral guide for both the individual and the nation" (156).[2] This notion was common to New England Federalists who accepted the Puritan notion that American history "would lead the way to the second coming of Christ" (157), and who also found themselves at odds with both Jacksonian democratic secularism and Emersonian transcendentalism, which suggested that "it was unnecessary to introduce God's supernatural grace or the Holy Spirit into the formula of religious conversion" because of the inherent divinity of man (180).

Such issues and such an approach to scripture are of central importance to an understanding of *The Scarlet Letter.* Hawthorne was indeed very likely suspicious of American millennialism, as Foreman and others suggest, but I will argue below that he shared the suspicions regarding transcendentalism expressed by the painter Washington Allston, who may well also have been, along with Elizabeth Peabody, influential in his decision to employ the apocalyptic typology of the Bible in *The Scarlet Letter.* In addition to the image of the end of the old world and the creation of the new, there are four other Biblical themes derived from Revelation which play crucial roles in the novel: the notion of unveiling, prophecy, the last battle, resurrection and judgment. These five aspects of Revelation, often mixed together, form the basis of the novel's structure and theme, as is most clearly evident in the famous scaffold scenes, which are the skeleton of the plot.

In the first of these scenes, Hester Prynne stands before the Puritan fathers of Boston in order to accept their Judgment regarding her sin of adultery. While she stands alone upon the scaffold, holding the infant Pearl beneath the scarlet letter on her breast, the Puritan fathers look down on her from the balcony above and plead with her to reveal the name of the child's father, her partner in sin. They call upon Arthur Dimmesdale, the charismatic young minister and concealed father of the child to persuade Hester to uncover the secret betokened by the scarlet letter, but she remains silent. Hence, the novel begins shortly after the commission of the original sin, which is covered over by a second sin, Hester's concealing of the identity of the father, and Dimmesdale's reluctance to reveal himself as such. The word *apocalypse*, of course, means literally "to uncover" or "reveal" that which has been veiled or covered over. In the New Testament, the word for "to cover" (*katakalypto*) is logically related to the word for "to uncover" (*apokalypto*), and is occasionally linked with the notion of "the covering of sin by loving action" (Bromiley 406). Hence, the plot of *The Scarlet Letter* is impelled from the beginning by the need to uncover what has been concealed by Hester's loving protection of Dimmesdale, a need evidenced most obviously by Roger Chillingworth's efforts to discover the identity of the child's father.

It is during the second scene on the scaffold that the explicitly apocalyptic basis of the novel's plot is clearly related to the Book of Revelation. Compelled by the maddening burden of his guilt, Dimmesdale leaves his study one night and goes to climb the scaffold where Hester had hidden his sins from the world seven years earlier. During "this vain show of expiation" (148), Dimmesdale feels that "the doom of his existence was stealing onward" and that the lantern he sees being carried toward the scaffold would soon "reveal his long hidden secret" (150). He feels a "great horror of mind, as if the universe were gazing at a scarlet token on his naked breast, right over his heart" (148). It is the "uncovering" or "revelation" (an apocalypsis) of this "long hidden secret" that Dimmesdale both fears and desires at this point. Hester and

Pearl are then seen walking home from the death-bed of the Governor, and Dimmesdale invites them to climb up onto the scaffold with him. When Pearl asks him when they will all stand there together again, Dimmesdale, as yet unwilling to undergo a public exposure at noontide, says, "At the great judgment day! Then, and there, before the judgment-seat, thy mother, and thou, and I, must stand together! But the day light of this world shall not see our meeting" (153).

Immediately after this explicit allusion to the Last Judgment of the Book of Revelation, a meteor sheds an awful and "unaccustomed light" that illuminates all visible things "with a singularity of aspects that seemed to give another moral interpretation to the things of this world than they had ever borne before" (154). Such supernatural celestial phenomena announcing the universal judgment are of course common signs of the Last Day (in Matthew 24:30 Jesus says "then shall appear the sign of the Son of man in heaven . . . and they shall see the Son of man coming in the clouds of heaven"), which Hawthorne sees in this scene as an unveiling of hidden things: "They stood in the noon of that strange and solemn splendor, as if it were the light that is to reveal all secrets, and the daybreak that shall unite all who belong to one another" (154). The meteor, then, prefigures revelation, judgment, and the reunion of the dead after the general resurrection. Hawthorne tells us that such "meteoric appearances" were interpreted "as so many revelations from a supernatural source" betokening the "doom" or "destiny of nations" (154–155). The word "doom" here carries the dual sense of an end and a destiny, of annihilation and revelation as two sides of the same coin (a symbolon). Shortly afterwards, Hester and Arthur see Chillingworth "at no great distance from the scaffold" and notice the "malevolence" of his expression, here fully revealed, or uncovered for the first time in the novel: "Certainly, if the meteor kindled up the sky, and disclosed the earth, with an awfulness that admonished Hester Prynne and the clergyman of the day of judgement, then might Roger Chillingworth have passed with them for the arch-fiend" (156). After this vision of Chillingworth as the Anti-Christ from Revelation, the meteor vanishes, "with an effect as if the street and all things else were at once annihilated" (156).

Here then is the sense of a universal cataclysm ("all things else were at once annihilated") combined with the notions of the revelation of hidden secrets, of death and Judgment, of the final battle with the "archfiend," and a hint of resurrection which characterizes Hawthorne's allusions to the Apocalypse throughout the novel. Dimmesdale feels "a tumultuous rush of new Life" when he takes Hester's hand on the scaffold (153).

Hawthorne's primary concern in this scene, however, is not metaphysical or theological: in the attempt to decipher "the awful hieroglyphics" inscribed upon the veil of clouds by the meteor (155), Hawthorne delves deeply into the epistemological issues central to the novel's treatment of the theme of revelation. His focus is on the hermeneutic problem raised by the hieroglyphical letter in the sky "Nothing was more common, in those days," Hawthorne writes, "than to interpret all meteoric appearances . . . as so many revelations from a supernatural source" (154). The task of interpretation, however, often fell upon

> some lonely eyewitness who beheld the wonder through the colored, magnifying and distorting medium of his imagination, and shaped it more distinctly in his afterthought. It was indeed a majestic idea, that the destiny of nations should be revealed, in these awful hieroglyphics, on the cope of heaven. A scroll so wide might not be deemed too expansive for Providence to write a people's doom upon. . . . But what shall we say, when an individual discovers revelation, addressed to himself alone, on the same vast sheet of record! In such a case, it could only be the symptom of a highly disordered mental state, when a man, rendered morbidly self-contemplative by long, intense, and secret pain, has extended his egotism over the whole expanse of nature, until the firmament itself should appear no more than a fitting page for his soul's history and fate. (155)

This passage emphasizes the shaping power of the subjective imagination in the hermeneutic task, raising the post-Kantian dilemma "that what a man knows is not an objective external world but simply the internal structure of his own mind projected upon an essentially indeterminate ground" (Irwin 241). Hence, Hawthorne attributes Dimmesdale's perception of the meteoric "A" as a token of his sin to

> the disease in his own eye and heart. . . . Not but the meteor may have shown iself at that point, burning duskily through a veil of cloud; but with no such shape as his guilty imagination gave it; or, at least, with so little definiteness, that another's guilt might have seen another symbol in it. (155)

The syntactical twisting here betokens Hawthorne's sense of the epistemological dilemma, complicated later in the chapter when he tells us that the sexton had also seen "A great red letter in the sky,—the letter A,—which we interpret to stand for Angel," since Governor Winthrop had died during that "visionary" night (158). What Providence inscribes upon the "scroll" of the "firmament" is subject to a multiplicity of conflicting and uncertain perceptions, as if the "veil of cloud" has been so partially uncovered as to render any interpretation of the letter suspect and relative. Each reader of the "awful hieroglyphics" deciphers them differently. As John Irwin notes in his book on the symbol of the Egyptian hieroglyphics in American literature, "For Hawthorne and Melville, the ambiguous character of the hieroglyphics was their prime significance. The hieroglyphics were the linguistic analogue of an enigmatic external world whose shape was various enough to sustain almost any interpretation that man projected on it in the act of knowing" (239).

It is important to note here that Hawthorne sees the hermeneutic task as an attempt to decipher the hieroglyphic of nature. Nature, in fact, is imagined during this episode as a Book authored by Providence. The heavens are a "scroll" to "write a people's doom upon," a "vast sheet of record," and a "fitting page for [the] soul's history" (155). Surely these details are significant when seen in the context of the Book of Revelation, in which the world is seen precisely as a book, the seals of which must be broken before it can be read. The "A" in the sky may as well stand for Apocalypse, but it represents only a partial uncovering, the mysterious import of which remains subject to the distortions of a diseased mind. One has the feeling that Hawthorne in fact denies any sort of analysis access to the ultimate revelation, which may be fully uncovered only by grace on the Judgment Day.

Earlier in the novel, Dimmesdale says as much to Roger Chillingworth, his alchemical physician, who, as a natural philosopher, argues that no secrets are inaccessible to analysis. As Hester's betrayed husband, Chillingworth has attached himself to Dimmesdale in order to delve into the secrets of his heart, and uncover the identity of Pearl's father. "Would it be beyond a philosopher's research," Chillingworth asks of Dimmesdale and the other Church fathers, "to analyze the child's nature, and from its make and mould, to give a shrewd guess at the father?" (116). Pearl, in fact, is later termed a "living hieroglyph" who requires "a prophet or magician skilled to read the character of flame" (207). That is to say, she is analogous to the letter "A" on Hester's breast and to the letter "A" in the sky: she is the hieroglyphic signature of her father, whose identity Chillingworth claims to be able to "read" in her "character of flame." The Church fathers, however, reply that such a presumption of the hermeneutic power of profane philosophy "would be sinful. . . . Better to fast and pray upon it [the mystery of Pearl's father]; and still better, it may be, to leave the mystery as we find it, unless Providence reveal it of its own accord" (116).

This dialogue pits philosophy against theology on the hermeneutic question of revelation. Chillingworth represents the agnosticism of modern scientists, and their techniques of empirical analysis. Hawthorne says that these

Skilful men, of the medical and chirurgical profession. . . . seldom . . . partook of the religious zeal that brought other emigrants across the Atlantic. In their researches into the human frame, it may be that the higher and more subtile faculties of such men were materialized, and that they lost the spiritual view of existence amid the intricacies of that wondrous mechanism, which seemed to involve art enough to comprise all of life within itself. (119)

Chillingworth's alchemy is similarly called a "ponderous and imposing machinery" (119), suggesting that Hawthorne intends us to see him as a prototype of the "mechanistic" science just emerging in the seventeenth century when the story is set. This was a science struggling to free itself from the occultism and magic of the Renaissance, and in so doing it laid the foundations for modern scientific method.[3]

Interestingly enough, Chillingworth also anticipates modern psychoanalysis: in his treatment of the ailing Dimmesdale, he assumes that the Reverend's "bodily infirmity" has "its groundwork" in the psyche, Dimmesdale's "thought and imagination" (124). Hawthorne's description of Chillingworth's method might be seen as a prophetic portrait of the psychoanalyst, fifty years before Freud's *Die Traumdeutung*:

> [T]he man of skill, the kind and friendly physician—strove to go deep into his patient's bosom, delving among his principles, prying into his recollections, and probing every thing with a cautious touch, like a treasure seeker in a dark cavern. . . . If [the physician] possess native sagacity, and a nameless something more,—let us call it intuition . . . if he have the power, which must be born with him, to bring his mind into such affinity with his patient's, that this last shall unawares have spoken what he imagines himself only to have thought: if such revelations be received without tumult and acknowledged not so often by an uttered sympathy as by silence, an inarticulate breath, and here and there a word, to indicate that all is understood . . . then, at some moment, will the soul of the sufferer be dissolved, and flow forth in a dark, but transparent stream, bringing all its mysteries into the daylight. (124)

Hawthorne opposes this analytic science. In the novel, Chillingworth is the "arch-fiend" with whom Dimmesdale, as a Christian soldier, does battle on the last day. As Douglas Robinson points out in his study of Apocalypse in American fiction,

> Without opposition, the apocalypse is nothing: spatial (earth–heaven) and temporal (present–future) oppositions are decided eschatologically by the moral opposition between good and evil, between God and Satan—the cosmic battle (polemos) that both precipitates and enacts the end. (10)

Typically, Hawthorne extends the moral and metaphysical implications of the polemos into the epistemological realm. Chillingworth's notion that all hidden secrets can be made accessible to knowledge by the methods of "philosophical" analysis is opposed in the novel by the Reverend Dimmesdale, who, in his ministerial capacity, is Christ's representative on earth. In a private conversation between Chillingworth and Dimmesdale, Hawthorne pursues the conflict. After picking some grotesque weeds from a man's grave in the cemetery, Chillingworth imagines that "They grew out of his heart, and typify, it may be, some hideous secret that was buried with him, and which he had done better to confess during his lifetime" (131). (The weeds, that is to say, are a "type" or emblematic hieroglyph concealing, yet expressing the mysteries of the heart.) Dimmesdale responds by saying the poor sinner was unable to confess in his lifetime, and calls Chillingworth's notion that all hidden secrets should be brought to light by his science a "fantasy" (131). Dimmesdale then counters with the theological perspective on the issue of revelation:

> There can be, if I forebode aright, no power, short of the Divine mercy, to disclose, whether by uttered word, or by type or emblem, the secrets that may be buried with a human heart. The heart, making itself guilty of such secrets, must perforce hold them, until the day when all hidden things be revealed. Nor have I so read or interpreted Holy Writ, as to understand that the disclosure of human thoughts and deeds, then to be made, is intended as a part of the retribution. That surely were a shallow view of it. No; these revelations, unless I greatly err, are meant to promote the intellectual satis-

faction of all intelligent beings, who will stand waiting, on that day, to see the dark problem of this life made plain. A knowledge of men's hearts will be needful to the completest solution of that problem. And I conceive, moreover, that the hearts holding such miserable secrets as you speak of will yield them up, at that last day, not with reluctance, but with joy unutterable. (131–132)

The last day is, of course, described in the Book of Revelation, and here imagined as the day "when all hidden things will be revealed," particularly "the secrets buried with a human heart" (remember the linguistic association of "buried" or "covered" sins mentioned above). Only "Divine mercy" can bestow such knowledge, uncover the sins buried with the heart, and make plain the "dark problem of this life." "For now we see through a glass, darkly," Paul says in I Corinthians 13:12, "but then face to face." The Greek word translated as "darkly" in this passage is *ainigmati*, the root of our "enigma," and this captures exactly the hermeneutic problem at the base of the epistemological debate between Chillingworth and Dimmesdale: as the Reverend's name suggests, to be alive is to be lost in the maze of dark wood (a dim dale), where any effort of interpretation must remain tangled in enigma until the Apocalypse. The notion of apocalypse here focuses on its root meaning of "uncovering," which involves the hermeneutic task of deciphering the hieroglyphic language of the novel.

Other passages from the New Testament correspond to Dimmesdale's sense of a deferred uncovering, available through grace on the last day. Jesus says of the coming of the Kingdom, "there is nothing covered, that shall not be revealed, and hid that shall not be known" (Matthew 10:26). This statement occurs four times in the Gospels (see also Luke 8:16 and 12:2, and Mark 4:22), and clearly prefigures the apocalypse as an uncovering of hidden things. In the verse cited from Matthew, the Greek word translated as "revealed" is *apokalyptical*, literally "will be uncovered." Chillingworth's response to this theological perspective is characteristically scientific: he says of these covered secrets, "Why not reveal them here?" (132). This is a significant statement of his point of view in the epistemological conflict, and a prefiguration of the last scene on the scaffold at the end of the novel. That famous scene involves a literal uncovering of hidden sin, as Dimmesdale removes his shirt, exposing what some parishioners see as a scarlet letter "A" branded on his chest. The context of the verse cited from Matthew may even have informed Hawthorne's conception of this scene: Jesus is enjoining the people not to fear those who may kill the body for speaking the truth, and after the prophecy of a day of uncovering, he says, "What I tell you in darkness, that speak ye in light: and what ye hear in the ear, that preach ye upon the housetops" (Matthew 10:27). In Luke, the remark is a warning to speak out against the "hypocrisy" of the Pharisees by proclaiming the truth spoken in darkness "upon the housetops" (12:3). This is, of course, exactly what Dimmesdale does on the scaffold in the chapter called "The Revelation of the Scarlet Letter." He publicly, at noontide from the elevation of the scaffold, acknowledges the guilt he had seen God revealing to him in the darkness during his "visionary" night on the scaffold. And he does so by a literal apocalypse, an uncovering that reveals his hidden sin, and betokens his hypocrisy.

Just as episodes in the Old Testament were taken by typological criticism as prefiguring their fulfillment in the New Testament, the scenes on the scaffold in *The Scarlet Letter* stand in relation to each other as type and anti-type: the end fulfilling and completing the beginning. What was covered in the first episode of Hester's public punishment— the identity of the father—is uncovered during the last episode, when the unhappy family stands united at last. The end of the novel is prefigured in its beginning, and all along the way through the dark wood: the Alpha and the Omega of Revelation 22:13 have been brought together. Hawthorne sets this scene in the context of the millennial hopes for renewal in the New World so important to the mythologized view of America as the New Jerusalem. It is Election Day, when, as Hester says, "a new man is beginning to rule" and the population rejoices "as if a good and golden year were at length to pass over the poor old world" (229). Dimmesdale's sermon is infused with "a spirit as of prophecy" as "it was his mission to foretell a high and glorious destiny for the newly gathered people of the Lord" (249). Hawthorne contrasts this mission with that of the apocalyptic seers of Israel, who "had denounced judgements and ruin on their country" (249).

After the sermon, Dimmesdale proceeds to the scaffold, but he must fight off Roger Chillingworth before he is able to climb it. Their final conflict is clearly to be seen as the last battle between Christ and Anti-Christ. In this scene, Dimmesdale enacts the role of the Crucified Redeemer, while Chillingworth is seen as the "wretched and wronged old man opposing it with all his might!—with all his own might and the fiend's" (253): "old Roger Chillingworth thrust himself through the crowd,—or perhaps, so dark, disturbed, and evil was his look, he rose up out of some nether region,—to snatch back his victim from what he sought to do" (252). The crowd is stunned into silence, and waits upon "the judgement which Providence seemed about to work" (253): they seem to know that "some deep life matter—which, if full of sin, was full of anguish and repentance likewise—was now to be laid open to them" before the "bar of Eternal Justice" (254). Then Dimmesdale proceeds to uncover the "red stigma" searing his "inmost heart":

> With a convulsive motion he tore away the ministerial band from before his breast. It was revealed! But it were irreverent to describe that revelation. For an instant the gaze of the horror-stricken multitude was concentrated on the ghastly miracle; while the minister stood with a flush of triumph in his face, as one who, in the crisis of acutest pain, had won a victory. (255)

The imagery of the triumphant agony of the crucifixion is unmistakable here, and the immediate effect of the apocalyptic revelation is the defeat of Chillingworth, who kneels down beside Dimmesdale "with a blank, dull countenance, out of which the life seemed to have departed" (255).

After Dimmesdale collapses on the scaffold, Hester "partly raised him, and supported his head against her bosom" (255). While at the beginning of the novel, when proceeding to her own humiliation on the scaffold, she had been seen as a Madonna figure, "with the infant at her bosom" like the "image of Divine Maternity" (56), here she is pictured as the Mater Dolorosa, the Pieta with the crucified one on her lap. In the middle of the novel, of course, she had been seen by the Church Fathers at the Governor's Hall as the "scarlet woman, and a worthy type of her of Babylon" (110), referring of course to the Whore of Babylon from the Book of Revelation. It is therefore certainly true, as Nina Baym says, that Hester is "a kind of archetypal mother-goddess" (19). Specifically, she is an avatar of what Jung called the "mother archetype," a loving and terrible figure combining the opposites of life and death within herself. She is Dimmesdale's "better angel" (201), offering him new life in the forest scene, the temptress leading him into a "world of perverted spirits" (222), and "the angel and apostate of the coming revelation" (263).

The novel in fact ends with Hester's prophetic vision of the future, prophecy being a crucial element of the Apocalypse of St. John, and, as Peter says in Acts 2, a sign of the coming of the end (here both of the novel and of the world): "your young men shall see visions, and your old men dream dreams: And on my servants and on my handmaidens I will pour out in those days of my Spirit; and they shall prophesy" (2:17–18). We should recall that this scriptural prophecy comes just after the description of the descent of the Holy Ghost at Pentecost, that Dimmesdale is endowed with the Pentecostal gift of tongues, "symbolizing the power . . . of addressing the whole human brotherhood in the heart's native language" (142), and that Dimmesdale had "a spirit as of prophecy" come upon him during the Election Day sermon just before his own end (249). Hester's prophetic powers, however, are revisionary, feminist in fact.[4] Although she acknowledges she is not herself the "destined prophetess" she imagined she might be when young, she anticipates a new and better world in her belief

that, at some brighter period, when the world should have grown ripe for it, in Heaven's own time, a new truth would be revealed, in order to establish the whole relation between man and woman on a surer ground of mutual happiness . . .The angel and apostate of the coming revelation must be a woman, indeed, but lofty, pure and beautiful; and wise, moreover, not through dusky grief, but the ethereal medium of Joy . . . (263)

Hence, the ending of *The Scarlet Letter* combines the imagery of judgment and resurrection, the last battle, prophetic visions of the end of an old world and the coming of the new, and the uncovering of hidden secrets associated with the Apocalypse. But it is an open ending, leaving basic questions unanswered. The uncovering of Dimmesdale's shame on the scaffold is itself problematic. Though "Most of the spectators testified to having seen, on the breast of the unhappy minister, a SCARLET LETTER," its origin is explained by "various explanations, all of which must necessarily have been conjectural" (258). Some see it as the product of Dimmesdale's penitential flagellation, others see it as a stigma produced by Chillingworth's necromancy, and others still as the "awful symbol" produced by the "wonderful operation of his spirit upon the body" (258). Others more generously deny there was any mark whatsoever on Dimmesdale's breast, and read his death in Hester's arms as a parable "to express to the world how utterly nugatory is the choicest of man's own righteousness" (259). Hawthorne leaves the reader to choose among as many theories regarding the origin of the letter as there have been throughout the novel regarding its significance. The letter remains to the end a hieroglyphic symbol of mysterious and indeterminate meaning, calling into question our ability objectively to decipher the world around us.

As readers, we are left in the midst of the maze, in the middle of the "dark problem" of life. "For now we see through a glass, darkly" [ainigmati]; alive before the coming of Christ on the Last Day, our vision must necessarily be enigmatic, partial, distorted. Only with the Apocalypse of the end will all hidden things be revealed, so that we may see the truth face to face. Hawthorne's conclusion to the novel is in this sense strictly doctrinal, favoring Dimmesdale's view that Chillingworth's analytical hermeneutic cannot gain access in this life to what will be made known only during the revelation on the Last Day. I think it is quite true to point out, as John Irwin does, that what we see in the nineteenth century is a gradual "movement from an interest in an other world of absolute values to an interest in how the mind knows the physical world to an interest in how symbolization in a sense creates our 'world'" (318). Certainly one sees in *The Scarlet Letter* a mingling of metaphysical and epistemological concerns in the various efforts to interpret the significance of the hieroglyphic letter. Yet Hawthorne's stubborn insistence on the ambiguous and indeterminate nature of his symbols stands strictly in line with theological notions that the true hidden meaning of life can never be known without the intervention of divine grace, without genuine Apocalypse. This notion counters the Emersonian idea that the hieroglyphic emblems of the world are imme-diately accessible to such divinely inspired democrats as the poet, without the mediation of divine grace.

There is no "end" in Hawthorne's novel, no cataclysmic annihila-tion, and no final revelation agreed upon by all. What is missing from his apocalypse is precisely the end-of-the-world scenario so much at the heart of the biblical Book of Revelation. Instead, what Hawthorne seems to imagine is what Douglas Robinson calls "a Protestant dream of historical apocalypse—a dream of a transformation *of* history *in* his-tory that would consummate and so give meaning *to* history" (2). This is most forcefully suggested in Dimmesdale's last Election Day ser-mon, with its vision of a truly blessed New England, one with a "high and glorious destiny" (249). Significantly, Dimmesdale's prophecy lacks those denunciations of judgment and ruin characteristic of the apocalyptic visions of "the old prophets of Israel" (249). Hawthorne seems to want to have it both ways: Apocalypse as a secular image of the American Dream of transformation of history within history by his-tory, and Apocalypse as the sacred revelation of hidden mysteries achieved through divine grace on the Last Day. The former secularized view is represented by Chillingworth, who argues that hidden secrets should be revealed now, "here" in this life (132), as indeed they are on the scaffold at the end of the novel. The latter sacramental view is represented by Dimmesdale; his "revelation" of the scarlet letter at the end of the novel is left ambiguous, with the sense that its significance will only be made plain by the final revelation of which it is but the type. In this respect also, *The Scarlet Letter* seems a peculiarly American breed of apocalypse, which, as Robinson argues, characteristically has it both ways: "American iconoclasm is iconically mediatory; images of nature are negated apocalyptically not in order that they might be thrown out, but that the writer might incorporate and transform them into the mediate ground for visionary contact" (8). This tendency yields what Robinson calls a "ternary logic of intercession, in place of Hegel's binary logic of supersession. . . . to allow writer and reader to perceive the opposites (earth and new earth, present and future) in opposition without subsuming or supplanting them" (8). Hence, in the American breed of apocalypse as Robinson sees it, this world may in fact obstruct our access to ultimate revelation: it is not, however, "destroyed by fire but is itself converted into the mediatory icon of Christ, the self-unveiling veil that reveals by standing between" (9). The veil is to be made transparent by a shift in vision effected by art, not to be destroyed by cataclysm.[5]

From this perspective, the uncovering of the scarlet letter in the penultimate chapter is tantalizingly partial, exactly that revelation within history which transforms its witnesses but does not finally, ultimately annihilate or illuminate them. The revelation does not end the world, but neither does it resolve its own enigma. The novel retains the "veil" of the world without destroying it. Its last image is "iconically mediatory." Dimmesdale's sacrificial confession on the scaffold is that "self-unveiling veil that reveals by standing between." It is a revelation within history that momentarily provides us with a glimpse of a more ultimate uncovering: it is a type of Apocalypse.

From *ATQ* 4, no. 2 (June, 1990): 91-104. Copyright © 1990 by University of Rhode Island Press. Reprinted by permission of University of Rhode Island Press.

Notes

1. Douglas Robinson develops an elaborate methodology for the study of the image of the end of the world in our tradition. Oddly enough, the text he chooses as representative of Nathaniel Hawthorne's handling of the theme is *The House of the Seven Gables*, a novel which fits in nicely with his hermeneutic, but which is not Hawthorne's most explicitly apocalyptic novel. The most thorough discussion of Hawthorne's typological use of Revelation in *The Scarlet Letter* is Clifford Foreman's dissertation, which approaches the subject in terms of "two competing typologies. The typology connected with Dimmesdale's three ascents of the scaffold points towards the ultimate 'Revelation' of the last chapter and the last judgement, deflating the Puritan's vision of the enterprise. But Hester's Emersonian typology suggests that the revelation of sin can be escaped" (3427A). Lois Zamora devotes only one paragraph to her discussion of apocalypse in American literature to *The Scarlet Letter*, which she sees as dramatizing a "strongly felt dialectic between millennial and cataclysmic versions" of apocalypse (115). Her article generally, however, is a fine and concise overview of the theme, and her anthology of essays on the subject a useful survey of apocalypse in other arenas of American culture. Henry Lindborg focuses less on St. John's Revelation than on the apocalyptic Book of Enoch. Finally, Charles Swann accurately associates Hester's prophecy at the end of the novel with the Second Coming but does not develop the observation into a thorough study of the novel.

2. Arlin Turner's chapter on "The Peabodys" in his biography of Hawthorne omits any detailed discussion of Elizabeth Peabody's ideas and their possible impact on the novelist. He prefers to see her instead as a kind of infatuated invader of Hawthorne's privacy.

3. The definitive study of alchemical and occult philosophies in the late Renaissance and early 17th century in England is by Frances Yates, who shows how the Rosicrucians provided the foundation for the emergence of modern science. D. H. Lawrence also notes that Chillingworth "belongs to the old medieval school of medicine and alchemy" (148), and that he is "the magician on the verge of modern science, like Francis Bacon, his great prototype" (149).

4. Charles Swann notes that Hester is "more subversive than is usually recognized in that she desires and prophesies a radical subversion of the patriarchal structures of her society" (264), and that "she looks forward to the Second Coming of Christ—only this time as a woman. Angel and Apostate indeed of a coming Revelation!" (266). Clearly, this suggests a feminist Hester, one favoring a "radical (but reasonable) reordering of theological language" (266).

5. For a deconstructive, neo-Freudian discussion of the veiling imagery in Hawthorne, see Irwin (265–270, 274–275, 280–285).

Works Cited

Baym, Nina. 1983. Introduction. *The Scarlet Letter.* Nathaniel Hawthorne. New York: Viking Penguin.

Bjelajac, David. 1988. *Millennial Desire and the Apocalyptic Vision of Washington Allston.* Washington: Smithsonian Institution Press.

Bromiley, Geoffrey W. 1985. *Theological Dictionary of the New Testament.* Grand Rapids: William B. Eerdmans.

Foreman, Clifford William Willis. 1987. "Typology in the Fiction of Nathaniel Hawthorne." *DAI* 47 (March): 3427A.

Hawthorne, Nathaniel. 1962–. *The Scarlet Letter.* Vol. 1 of *The Centenary Edition of the Works of Nathaniel Hawthorne.* Ed. William Charvat et al. 18 vols. to date. Columbus: Ohio State University Press.

Irwin, John T. 1980. *American Hieroglyphics: The Symbol of the Egyptian Hieroglyphics in the American Renaissance.* New Haven: Yale University Press.

Jung, Carl Gustav. 1972. *Four Archetypes: Mother, Rebirth, Spirit, Trickster.* Princeton: Princeton University Press.

Lawrence, D. H. 1964. *The Symbolic Meaning: The Uncollected Versions of Studies in Classic American Literature.* Ed. Armin Arnold. New York: Viking.

Lindborg, Henry J. 1986. "Hawthorne's Enoch: Prophetic Irony in *The Scarlet Letter.*" *Transactions of the Wisconsin Academy of Sciences, Arts, and Letters* 74:122–125.

Robinson, Douglas. 1985. *American Apocalypses: The Image of the End of the World in American Literature.* Baltimore: The Johns Hopkins University Press.

Swann, Charles. 1987. "Hester and the Second Coming: a Note on the Conclusion of *The Scarlet Letter.*" *Journal of American Studies* 21: 264–268.

Turner, Arlin. 1980. *Nathaniel Hawthorne: A Biography.* New York. Oxford University Press.

Westcott, Brooke Foss, and John Anthony Hort. 1969. *The Kingdom Interlinear Translation of the Greek Scriptures.* New York: Watchtower Bible and Tract Society of Pennsylvania.

Yates, Frances A. 1978. *The Rosicrucian Enlightenment.* Boulder, Colorado: Shambhala.

Zamora, Lois Parkinson. 1983. "The Myth of Apocalypse and the American Literary Imagination." *The Apocalyptic Vision in America: Interdisciplinary Essays on Myth and Culture.* Ed. Lois Parkinson Zamora. Bowling Green, Ohio: Bowling Green University Popular Press.

Hawthorne as Essayist:
Our Old Home and
"Chiefly About War Matters"

Thomas R. Moore

Hawthorne was a compulsive note-taker, and he often turned to his notebooks for inspiration for his published works. Sometimes he drew on them directly: he took the pieces collected from his English notebooks and published them in 1863 as *Our Old Home*.

Thomas R. Moore, in his careful rhetorical analysis of that work, argues that Hawthorne "wrote nonfiction within the established tradition of the informal essay," and that *Our Old Home* should be read as a "collection of informal travel essays." He is acutely aware of what's at stake in a reader's conception of the genre of the work: by treating Hawthorne as a travel essayist, he places him in a tradition that begins with Michel de Montaigne, William Hazlitt, and Thomas De Quincey, and continues into the twentieth century with Paul Theroux, William Least Heat Moon, and John McPhee. This long view allows him to tease out some of the hidden meanings of *Our Old Home*, including one of Hawthorne's perennial themes, the tensions between England and America.   — J.L.

No American, complexly speaking, finds himself in England for the first time, unless he is one of those many Americans who are not of English extraction. It is probable, rather, that on his arrival, if he has not yet visited the country, he has that sense of having been there before. . . . His English ancestors who really were once there stir within him, and his American forefathers, who were nourished on the history and literature of England, and were therefore intellectually English, join forces in creating an English consciousness in him.

—William Dean Howells, *Certain Delightful English Towns*, 1906

Conduct, on the other hand, the soul
"Which the highest cultures have nourished"
To Fleet St. where
Dr. Johnson flourished. . . .
                    —Ezra Pound, "Hugh Selwyn Mauberly," 1920

Labeling Hawthorne's short nonfiction—with the consequent as-signment to a literary genre—has presented difficulties to his critics and reviewers from the outset. Hawthorne himself, in response perhaps to Irving's successful *The Sketch Book of Geoffrey Crayon, Gent.*, fa-vored the term "sketch" for his early nonfictional pieces—with the ex-ception of "The Old Manse" which he called an essay. Poe, in his April and May 1842 reviews of *Twice-Told Tales* in *Graham's Magazine*, in-sisted upon "essay."[1] Henry James, in discussing *Our Old Home* in his 1879 *Hawthorne*, is uncomfortable with categorization, moving from "papers" to "articles" to "chapters" to "sketches," fastidiously avoid-ing the more solid "essays" (117–122). Modern critics have been equally tentative in labeling the contents of *Our Old Home*, Raymona Hull calling "Leamington Spa" a "sketch" (83) in a 1984 article, and James A. Hijiya in 1974 using the improbable "chapters" (364) to iden-tify the twelve essays.

Distinctions between "sketch" and "essay" are blurry at best. We could hazard that while the essay tends toward the argumentative, the sketch tends toward the autobiographical or descriptive, and while the essay favors definition and seeks closure, the sketch favors exploration and deflects closure. A succinct definition notwithstanding, I will ar-gue here that throughout his career Hawthorne wrote nonfiction within the established tradition of the informal essay; accordingly, Poe's early designation of Hawthorne as essayist is accurate: *Our Old Home*, pub-lished the year before Hawthorne died, is a commonly mislabeled and critically undervalued collection of informal travel essays.

In his 1990 *The Rhetoric of the "Other" Literature*, W. Ross Win-terowd—his title indicating the continuing difficulty of categorizing belletristic nonfiction—distinguishes between the formal and the informal essay. Citing Mark Twain, James Thurber, and E. B. White as American practitioners of the form, he writes that the informal essay "is personal and not as highly structured as the formal"; further, the informal essay is "anecdotal" and "the author has no obligation to assume a disinterested stance toward issues" (96). Emerson, who in 1856 had published his *English Traits*, a collection of nineteen essays drawing on his visits to England in 1833 and 1847, is cited as a practitioner of the formal essay. Winterowd also places the American essayists— omitting mention of Hawthorne, a common critical oversight—in the tradition of English and French essay writing, citing Montaigne, Swift, Hazlitt, and DeQuincey as informal essayists, and Addison, Johnson, Arnold, Mill, Newman, and Pater as formal essayists (96). As a writer of informal travel essays in *Our Old Home*, Hawthorne may also be positioned with twentieth-century travel writers and essayists such as Paul Theroux, William Least Heat Moon, John McPhee, and E. B. White.

Both Robert Atwan in the "Foreword" and Justin Kaplan in the "Introduction" of *The Best American Essays 1990* attempt—without success—to define the form. In exploring the difference between "article" and "essay," Atwan writes that "it is impossible to come up with an airtight definition of an essay" (ix). Kaplan notes the "hermetic, self-referential quality" of essayists such as Bacon, Lamb, and Stevenson, and says that "their covert subject matter, no matter what their title said, was the act of writing itself" (xiii). But he also capitulates, writing that

> attempts at genre definition and subclassification in the end simply tell you how like an eel this essay creature is. It wriggles between narcissism and detachment, opinion and fact, the private party and the public meeting, omphalos and brain, analysis and polemics, confession and reportage, persuasion and provocation. All you can safely say is that it's not poetry and it's not fiction. (xiv)

The following rhetorical analysis of the essays of *Our Old Home* will, I hope, help to demonstrate that Hawthorne is an essayist of stature. The nineteenth-century term "sketch," which carries with it suggestions of incompletion and resistance to closure, does not fairly evaluate Hawthorne's personal/reflective/travel essays such as "Chiefly About War Matters" and those which make up *Our Old Home*.

Hawthorne's interest in travel and travel writing dated from the years in Salem following his graduation from Bowdoin. In a letter to Franklin Pierce on June 28, 1832, he mentions his "story-teller" project, a proposed series of tales and sketches united by a traveling storyteller; the project, we know, was never to prove successful (CE XV 224).[2] His reading during these Salem years included much travel literature. Beth L. Lueck (with help from Marion Kesselring's careful tallying of books charged to Mary Manning, Hawthorne's aunt, from the Salem Athenaeum) writes that he read widely in the genre, "ranging from travels in Great Britain, Germany, Turkey, and Africa to those in his native land, including *Bartram's Travels*, and to his compatriot Washington Irving's *Tales of a Traveller*" (156). In 1856, Hawthorne had high praise for Emerson's *English Traits*, writing to the author from Liverpool on September 10 that "undoubtedly, these are the truest pages that have yet been written, about this country" (CE XVII 540).

With characteristic self-deprecation Hawthorne told his publisher James T. Fields on October 18, 1863, that *Our Old Home* was "not a good or weighty book" and that it didn't "deserve any great amount either of praise or censure" (CE XVIII 603). A hundred and thirty years later, however, we may easily disagree with Hawthorne's cautious estimation of his work. These essays on English and American manners are pungent and prickly, still displaying the "beauty and delicacy" and "the appearance of a triumph" that Henry James hailed in 1879 (117). Readers in the intervening years have for the most part overlooked Hawthorne's essays; shadowed by the popularity of his novels and short stories, the essays have drawn little critical and even less popular attention. With the resurgence of interest in the personal essay and travel essay in our own age, Hawthorne's contributions deserve a fresh critical evaluation.

The essays are characterized by a dialectical rhetoric—America is contrasted with England—and they become, for Hawthorne's American audience, an assessment of the meaning of America, a theme echoing a subtext of the prefaces to *The House of the Seven Gables*, *The Blithedale Romance*, and *The Marble Faun*. The essays are drawn from Hawthorne's *English Notebooks*, compiled during his consulship in Liverpool and travels in England from 1853 through 1857, and as Judy Schaaf Anhorn writes in "Literary Reputation and the Essays of *Our Old Home*," they are "episodic and descriptive but related in subject and theme" with "the motif of literary pilgrimage" unifying the book (157). Upon his return to Concord and the Wayside in 1860, Hawthorne reshaped and distilled the notebook entries, creating twelve essays, ten of which were published in the *Atlantic Monthly* before all were assembled into one volume in 1863. The opening essay, "Consular Experiences," was printed in *Our Old Home* without prior magazine publication, and a segment of "Lichfield and Uttoxeter," entitled simply "Uttoxeter," was published in the *English Keepsake* in 1857 and also in the April 1857 *Harper's New Monthly Magazine* (CE V lvi).[3] "To a Friend," Hawthorne's staunch and unpopular pledge of allegiance to Franklin Pierce, serves as the preface for the collection.

One rhetorical configuration of the essays is the continuation of the debate on aesthetics begun in the prefaces, where Hawthorne poses "the Actual" against "the Imaginary," how things really are against the artist's perception and transmission of images of things. Hawthorne's aesthetic objectives in the composition of fiction and of nonfiction merge here; in both genres he must create an impression of reality. His objectives as romance writer—as expressed in *The House of the Seven Gables* preface—is how to disguise reality since "the Reader may perhaps choose to assign an actual locality to the imaginary events of this narrative" (CE II 3). Similarly, the objective as essay writer is how to enhance empirical reality, as Hawthorne writes in "Up the Thames," how to give "creative truth to my sketch, so that it might produce such pictures in the reader's mind as would cause the original scenes to appear familiar, when afterwards beheld" (CE V 258). Although these aesthetics and rhetorical purposes may appear to be at cross purposes—the first disguising a scene, the second enhancing a scene—they may also be viewed as similar in that both are concerned with creating images beyond mundane reality to move the reader. In both, in the fiction as well as in the nonfiction, the task for the writer is to create an impression of reality.

Hawthorne's discussion in "Up the Thames" of "the futility of the effort to give any creative truth" (CE V 258) to his essays serves as an important gloss in the preface-centered debate on the aesthetic and rhetorical issues at play in his discourse. Hawthorne writes, in *The House of the Seven Gables* preface, that "it has been no part of his object . . . to describe local manners," and that his romance has "a great deal more to do with the clouds overhead, than with any portion of the actual soil of the County of Essex" (CE II 3). In the same ironic vein he writes in *The Blithedale Romance* preface that his concern is "to establish a theatre, a little removed from the highway of ordinary travel, where the creatures of his brain may play their phantasmagorical antics, without exposing them to too close a comparison with actual events of their real lives" (CE III 1).

Just as the romance writer must displace the "actual soil" and create a "theatre" in order to work his craft through impressions of reality, the essayist, Hawthorne writes, must work his craft by creating similar impressions of reality. For Hawthorne the aesthetic and rhetorical issues of fiction and nonfiction come together in the creation of scene: both the essayist and the romance writer insist upon a distancing from the actual. He writes in "Up the Thames":

> Impressions . . . states of mind produced by interesting and remarkable objects, these, if truthfully and vividly recorded, may work a genuine effect, and, though but the result of what we see, go further towards representing

the actual scene than any direct effort to paint it. Give the emotions that cluster about it, and, without being able to analyze the spell by which it is summoned up, you get something like a simulacrum of the object in the midst of them. (CE V 259)

Thus the "actual" scene—eschewed by the romance writer, as Hawthorne writes in "The Custom-House," who seeks a "dim coal-fire," a "fair-land, where the Actual and the Imaginary may meet" (CE I 36)— is here in the essay created by impressions, by an effect, by a similar distancing from the "actual."

The paragraph in "Up the Thames" quoted from above, functioning as an aside on aesthetics, is inspired by a single notation in *The English Notebooks*. On September 10, 1855, Hawthorne wrote—in a line framed by prosaic recordings of the details of Westminster Abbey— that "impressions, states of mind, produced by noble spectacles of whatever kind, are all that it seems worth while to attempt reproducing with the pen" (212). In "Up the Thames" he amplifies this idea by asserting that the travel essay is a particularly appropriate vehicle for "simulacrums" of the actual. He writes that he draws the "comfortable inference, that the longer and better known a thing may be, so much the more eligible is it as the subject of a descriptive search" (CE V 259). In "Civic Banquets" he reiterates this rhetorical objective of the essay, stating, with the familiar self-deprecating tone, that: "After all my pains, I fear that I have made but a poor hand at the description, as regards a transference of the scene from my own mind to the reader's" (CE V 315). After visiting the scene of Samuel Johnson's penance— Johnson returned fifty years after disobeying his father to do penance (CE V 132)—in the square at Uttoxeter, Hawthorne again suggests that the "actual" is better communicated by an *impression* of the factual rather than by a literal recording of "the sad and lovely story" in "the absurd little town" (CE V 138). "Sublime, and beautiful facts," he writes, "are best understood when etherealized by distance" (CE V 138).

How the writer may perceive scene and character, and how the writer may communicate those perceptions of the actual, serve as one rhetorical configuration for *Our Old Home*, just as a shifting perception of truth serves as one rhetorical configuration in "The Custom-House." What is noticeably different about the rhetorical make-up of *Our Old Home* is the more flexible and less defensive narrative voice in the later essays. Hawthorne assumes a more confident and relaxed posture in *Our Old Home*, and this induces the narrator to makes discoveries as he writes. The discourse of the essays is epistemic, rather than simply conveying what he saw in the English scene and the English character, Hawthorne shows us how the act of writing fosters discovery. In "Leamington Spa" Hawthorne notes that "the article which [he is] writing has taken its own course"; he had set out to write about "the many old towns—Warwick, Coventry, Kenilworth, Stratford-on-Avon," but finds he is writing about "country churches" instead (CE V 61).

A loosening of the determined narrative control of such earlier sketches as "Sights from a Steeple" or "Sunday at Home" is evident in "Leamington Spa." The narrator feels "a singular sense of having been there before" when he views the "ivy-grown English churches (CE V 63). He is reminded of the wooden Salem meeting-houses that "on wintry Sabbaths" were "the frozen purgatory" of his childhood (CE V 63). This sense of déjà vu triggers a

> delightful emotion, fluttering about me like a faint summer-wind, and filling my imagination with a thousand half-remembrances, which looked as vivid as sunshine, at a side-glance, but faded quite away whenever I attempted to grasp and define them. (CE V 63)

The relaxed narrative voice that organizes by free association reminds us of the voice of an earlier essay, "The Old Manse," where a similar associative consciousness mediates the discourse. In "The Old Manse" Hawthorne and Ellery Channing floated "from depth to depth" along the Concord River watching the changing shapes of clouds "couched above the house" (CE X 23, 25). When Hawthorne was happiest—as a young husband or traveling dignitary—his nonfiction style was imbued with a relaxed self-confidence.

Claude M. Simpson comments on this aspect of the discourse of *Our Old Home*, writing that Hawthorne showed "a willingness to let patterns of association govern the order of parts" in the essays (CE V xl). It is this reliance on impressions—and the subsequent departure from a more formulaic and less spontaneous organizing principle— that allows us to read the essays today with as much sense of discovery as readers did in the 1860s. Hawthorne eschewed the sentimental and hackneyed descriptions of country houses and cathedrals—expectations for readers of the travel essay—and relied instead on metaphor and image to communicate his vision. The solid Englishwoman of "Leamington Spa," whose description stirred up Hawthorne's English reviewers, is "massive with solid beef and streaky tallow" and "has the effect of a seventy-four gun ship" (CE V 48–49).[4] In "Outside Glimpses of English Poverty" Hawthorne visits the laundry room of an almshouse. The "hot and vaporous" atmosphere becomes a democratic breath, inhaled by the paupers, the American visitors, and even Victoria, "had the Queen been there."

> What an intimate brotherhood is this in which we dwell, do what we may to put an artificial remoteness between the high creature and the low one! A poor man's breath, borne on the vehicle of tobacco-smoke, floats into a palace window and reaches the nostrils of a monarch. It is but an example, obvious to the sense, of the innumerable and secret channels by which at every moment of our lives, the flow and reflux of a common humanity pervade us all. (CE V 299)

The "transference of the scene" (315) to the reader's mind is enabled by the relaxed narrative voice extemporizing on the image of the laundry vapor.

How things are perceived and communicated is a recurrent rhetorical configuration of the twelve essays. As the narrator leaves Manchester on the Sheffield and Lincoln railway in "Pilgrimage to Old Boston," he notes that "on a railway . . .what little we do see of the country is seen quite amiss, because it was never intended to be looked at from any point of view in that straight line." It is, he continues, "like looking at the wrong side of a piece of tapestry" (CE V 140). He is more concerned with how it was, with "the old highways and foot-paths." The "brooks and rivulets," which require all objects to adhere to their "curves and undulations," are compared to the "perfectly artificial" line of the railway (CE V 140). Henry A. Tuckerman, a contemporary American travel writer whom Hawthorne admired, wrote in a similar vein about the difficulty of viewing the past from the railway. In *A Month in England* Tuckerman writes that "the private and carriage-like cars" and "the telegraph-wires running parallel to the tracks" are "features of modern science . . .which do not suggest an inkling of the antiquated towns we are about to enter" (16).

In "Up the Thames" Hawthorne commented that Tuckerman's *Month in England* was "a fine example of the way in which a refined and cultivated American looks at the Old Country, the things that he naturally seeks there, and the modes of feeling and reflection which they excite" (CE V 259). Both Tuckerman and Hawthorne seek a literary-imbued past before—or despite—the inconveniences of modern technology. What they discover often does not fulfill their expectations. As Hawthorne enters Uttoxeter, his literary expectation—what he remembers from his reading—of the scene of Johnson's penance is altered by the actual view. Where Boswell had described Johnson's father's book-stall "as standing in the market-place, close beside the sacred edifice" (CE V 133), Hawthorne finds that the church and the market-place are well separated. Tuckerman, to discover the past beneath the glitter of the present, explores the "subterranean chapel at the rear of a modern store . . . to decipher half-legible inscriptions, or the sculptures used by the early Christians" (20).

On occasion the discoveries beneath the facade, beneath the mask, are problematical. A curious scene of unveiling at the Cathedral of

Lichfield has a "sinister effect" on Hawthorne; and he feels afterwards "at odds with the proper influences of the Cathedral" (CE V 129). He has observed a group of boy choristers in white robes who look "like a peculiar order of beings, created on purpose to hover between the roof and pavement of that dim, consecrated edifice" (129). As one of the choristers pulls off his gown after the service, the boy is transformed into "a common-place youth of the day, in modern frock-coat and trowsers of a decidedly provincial cut" (129). The unveiling is an uncomfortable, un-Hawthornian gesture, reminding us of Father Hooper who was carried "a veiled corpse . . . to the grave" (CE IX 52), and the amiable narrator of "The Old Manse" who, though a gracious host to Channing, says: "So far as I am a man of really individual attributes, I veil my face" (CE X 33). Even if the removal of the chorister's robe in Lichfield Cathedral reveals only the drab reality of the present and not some secret sin or individual foible, the unveiling is unsettling to Hawthorne.

While perception of scene and the creation of images constitute one rhetorical configuration of *Our Old Home*, a less confrontive—and less coy—narrative voice constitutes another. In "Consular Experiences," which describes the "shabby and smoke-stained edifice" where Hawthorne as consul "impart[ed] both advice and assistance in multifarious affairs that did not personally concern [him]" (CE 6, 31), the narrator is humorous and direct, distinctly more at ease than the shifting and evasive persona of "The Custom-House." The first person narrative voice is confident. Hawthorne no longer has to don disguises (M. de l'Aubepine, the "decapitated surveyor," Eustace Bright) or masquerade as "the obscurest man of letters in America"; he is now the political emissary and famous author who has successfully opened an "intercourse with the world." But he is still the observer of humanity, "a man with a natural tendency to meddle with other people's business," and he finds that the Liverpool Consulate "could not possibly be a more congenial sphere" for such observations (CE V 30). In "About Warwick," in a scene reminiscent of "Sights from a Steeple," Hawthorne ascends the tower of the chapel and looks down from a hundred feet to observe, not the secret sins of his Salem townsfolk, but "a rich and lovely English landscape, with many a church-spire and noble country-seat" (CE V 79). The memories—and scars—of Salem quietly persist, however. After descending the "winding tower-stair," Hawthorne sees the old men in the chapel garden and is reminded of "the Salem Custom-House, and the venerable personages whom I found so quietly at anchor there" (CE V 81).

Confident control of the narrative in the essays replaces the coyness and vindictiveness of the prefaces; the defiant tone of "To a Friend" remains isolated in the preface to *Our Old Home* and does not infect the essays. In "Recollections of a Gifted Woman," the narrator feels "not the slightest emotion . . . nor any quickening of the imagination" while viewing Shakespeare's house (CE V 99). With Hawthornian reserve and control, the narrator draws back, reflecting that "whatever pretty and apposite reflections [he] may have made upon the subject had either occurred to [him] before [he] ever saw Stratford, or have been elaborated since" (99). The scene echoes earlier visits to public places. In "My Visit to Niagara" (*The Snow Image*), the narrator, instead of running "like a madman, to the falls" (CE XI 281), "alighted with perfect decency and composure," commenting that "such has been [his] apathy, when objects, long sought, and earnestly desired, were placed within [his] reach" (282). In "Old Ticonderoga" (*Uncollected Tales*), the narrator again pulls back, preferring his own fancy to the young lieutenant's dry description, "as accurate as a geometrical theorem, and as barren of the poetry that has clustered round its decay" (CE XI 187).

In "Leamington Spa," the narrator comments that he carries to any public monument the accumulated perceptions of "history, poetry, and fiction, books of travel, and the talk of tourists" (CE V 63). Such perceptions confuse "the images of things actually seen" (63), and, in a passage which explains the psychological as well as the historical resonance of the volume's title, Hawthorne speculates on the "hereditary haunts" of our old home. His "pretty accurate preconceptions" mingle with "images of things actually seen":

> the illusion was often so powerful, that I almost doubted whether such airy remembrances might not be a sort of innate idea, the print of a recollection in some ancestral mind, transmitted with fainter and fainter impress through several descents, to my own. I felt, indeed, like the stalwart progenitor in person, returning to the hereditary haunts after more than two hundred years, and finding the church, the hall, the farmhouse, the cottage, hardly changed during his long absence—the same shady by-paths and hedge-lanes—the same veiled sky, and green lustre of the lawns and fields—while his own affinities for these things, a little obscured by disuse, were reviving at every step. (CE V 63–64)

We are reminded of Hester Prynne's return, first to England where Pearl has been bequeathed "a very considerable amount of property" (CE I 261), and then of Hester's reappearance in New England where "there was a more real life . . .than in that unknown region where Pearl had found a home" (CE I 262–263). Pulled by "hereditary haunts" on both continents, Hester in the end chooses the place of "her sin . . . her sorrow . . . [and] her penitence" (263).

The confident narrator in the essays of *Our Old Home* on occasion ducks behind a veil of modesty when the author of "The Red Letter A" is recognized in his English travels. In "Pilgrimage to Old Boston," a bookseller had "heard the name of one member of our party," and the visitors are thus accorded "great courtesy and kindness" (CE V 158). Inside the bookshop, "veiled behind the unostentatious front," are two upstairs rooms, one of which contains "a counterpane of fine linen, elaborately embroidered with silk . . . in a most delicate style of needle-work" (158). In a scene echoing the fictitious discovery in "The Custom-House" of the "certain affair of fine red cloth" that shows a "wonderful skill of needle-work" (CE I 31), the counterpane in the upstairs room in Boston, England, carries "the cypher, M. S." and "was embroidered by the hands of Mary Queen of Scots" (CE V 158). In "Near Oxford" the narrator, recognized, again slips behind a veil. Here the narrator comments that the famous American author is "a friend of mine" who, when asked if he had written "The Red Letter A," responds "doubtfully" that he "believed so" (181–182).

In "Outside Glimpses of English Poverty" Hawthorne becomes "one member of our party" when an uncomfortable incident occurs in the almshouse (CE V 300). A "sickly, wretched, humor-eaten" foundling clings to "that individual, and he was bound to fulfill the contract [to fondle the child], or else no longer call himself a man among men" (300). The passage which follows in the text serves as a brief and revealing self-analysis: Hawthorne stepping back to observe Hawthorne as a member of the party of Americans:

> it could be no easy thing for him to do, he being a person burthened with more than an Englishman's customary reserve, shy of actual contact with human beings, afflicted with a peculiar distaste for whatever was ugly, and, furthermore, accustomed to that habit of observation from an insulated stand-point which is said (but, I hope, erroneously) to have the tendency of putting ice into the blood. (CE V 300–301)

It is characteristic of the Hawthorne in the prefaces—though atypical of the usually straightforward voice of the essays—to include such a narrative gesture of distance and masquerade. Without revealing to the reader that he is engaging in self-analysis, Hawthorne first veils his fame and then his awkwardness in the almshouse encounter. Arlin Turner comments on the passage, writing that "it would not be easy to compose a better succinct statement of the way he saw himself—or the way he appears in the light of full biographical evidence" (291).

Another rhetorical configuration of the volume is the interplay of opposites, with frequent use of parentheses and dashes emphasizing the dialectical substructure of the pieces. The essays comprise an international debate on manners, morals, and physiognomies, with American vision and voice set in opposition to English vision and voice. The "elephantine" English matron of "Leamington Spa" composed of "steaks and sirloins" and "streaky tallow" (CE V 48–49), is contrasted with the "trim little damsels" of America described in "A London Suburb" (CE V 240). England produces "feminine beauty as rarely as . . . delicate fruit" (240); the "maiden blossom" matures into "an overblown cabbage-rose" or "an outrageously developed peony" (49–50). While the American male, in his "dry atmosphere," is becoming "too nervous, haggard, dyspeptic, extenuated, unsubstantial, [and] theoretic," John Bull, "has grown bulbous, long-bodied, short-legged, heavy-witted, material, and, in a word, too intensely English" (64). And whereas the English farmer respects the ancient paths where "the footsteps of the aboriginal Britons first wore away the grass," the American farmer would "plough across any such path, and obliterate it with his hills of potatoes and Indian corn" (51).

In "Recollection of a Gifted Woman," the account of Hawthorne's visit to Delia Bacon and Stratford, the English trees and landscape invite comparison with the New England countryside. New England's landscape, "even the tamest, has a more striking outline" than the "Old Country" which is "utterly destitute" of "lakelets" or "the wayside brooks that vanish under a low stone-arch, on one side of the road, and sparkle out again on the other" (CE V 90). The trees in England "have nothing wild about them"; an American tree would be "the more picturesque of the two" (91). The English oak has "a certain John Bullism in its figure, a compact rotundity of foliage, a lack of irregular and variant outline, that make it look wonderfully like gigantic cauliflower" (91). In Stratford, the narrator is impressed with the great number of old people, more "than you could assemble on our side of the water by sounding a trumpet and proclaiming a reward for the most venerable" (96). In explanation he suggests—in a list uncomfortably close to the television ads saturating our own nightly newscasts—that "hair-dyes, false teeth, modern arts of dress, and other contrivances of a skin-deep youthfulness, have not yet crept into these antiquated English towns"

(96). The English "grow old without the weary necessity of seeming younger than they are" (96).

In "Outside Glimpses of English Poverty," the next to last essay in the volume, the oppositional tone is replaced by a tone of compassion. The ironically titled essay, compelling in its vigorous and unrelenting description of English slums and an almshouse, shows Hawthorne again looking beneath the facade, turning away from "the prosperous thoroughfares" to observe "precincts that reminded [him] of some of Dickens's grimiest pages" (CE V 277). He wanders the back streets with their gin-shops and pawn-broker establishments; he records the meager offerings in shop windows in Gogol-like details: "half-a-dozen wizened herrings, some eggs in a basket . . . fly-speckled biscuits, segments of a hungry cheese, pipes and papers of tobacco" (CE V 280). He writes that he is drawn to the "sombre phantasmagoric spectacle, exceedingly undelightful to behold, yet involving a singular interest and even fascination in its ugliness" (277). Here he is not a dispassionate Chillingworth nor a "cold observer, looking on mankind as the subject of his experiment" (CE XI 99) like Ethan Brand, but the essayist intent on looking within his subject to discover his own moral position.

Arlin Turner comments that "Outside Glimpses of English Poverty" shows "how persistently the subject [of poverty] occupied his mind" (266). Visiting another room in the almshouse, after the episode of the foundling clinging to him, the narrator sees "a woman holding a baby, which beyond all reach of comparison, was the most horrible object that ever afflicted my sight" (CE V 302). The baby

> was all covered with blotches, and preternaturally dark and discolored; it was withered away, quite shrunken and fleshless; it breathed only amid pantings and gaspings, and moaned painfully at every gasp. . . . Young as the poor little creature was, its pain and misery had endowed it with a premature intelligence, insomuch that its eyes seemed to stare at the bystanders out of their sunken sockets knowingly and appealingly, as if summoning us one and all to witness the deadly wrong of its evidence (303).

Although he had commented earlier in the essay, in the passage of Hawthorne describing Hawthorne, that he had the tendency to observe from an "insulated stand-point" and to put "ice into the blood" (300–301), clearly his compassion, and moral judgment, are evident here. "Outside Glimpses of English Poverty" ends by juxtaposing a luxurious English wedding, one the narrator had earlier observed, against the almshouse scenes. It is an affair of "joyful bells," "white drapery," and "shaven lawns" (308–309), and the narrator asks: "Is, or is not, the system wrong that gives one married pair so immense a superfluity of luxurious home, and shuts out a million others from any home whatever?" (309).

Hawthorne's compassion and his genuine fascination with the underside of human life is also evident in an essay depicting the American scene, "Chiefly About War Matters," subtitled, "By a Peaceable Man," published in the *Atlantic* in July, 1862. In March of that year, in response to an invitation from Horatio Bridge, Hawthorne visited Washington, called on President Lincoln, went aboard the *Monitor*, watched General McClellan review his troops, and at Harper's Ferry visited the "old engine-house, rusty and shabby," that John Brown had used as a fortress ("War Matters" 327). Just as he had focused on the "horrible objects" in the English almshouse, here he focuses on a group of Confederate captives in "that dreary hole" of a fortress (330). Earlier, on the battlefield, one of them had "trampled the soul out of [the] body" of "a wounded Union soldier [who] had crept on hands and knees to his feet, and besought his assistance" (330). The Confederate was a "wild-beast of a man"; his face was "horribly ugly"; he "met nobody's eye, but kept staring upward into the smoky vacancy towards the ceiling, where, it might be, he beheld a continual portraiture of his victim's horror-stricken agonies" (330).

The scene echoes the description in "The Old Manse" of the boy at the Battle of Concord who "uplifted his axe, and dealt . . . a fatal blow" to the wounded British soldier "who raised himself painfully upon his hands and knees, and gave a ghastly stare" (CE X 9–10). In "Chiefly About War Matters," Hawthorne confronts not only the enormous issue of the morality and justification of the Civil War, but also the issue of the underside of the conflict, the sufferings of individuals caught up in it. In discussing "Chiefly About War Matters," Arlin Turner comments that the essay is "among the most helpful of his writings" in showing how Hawthorne's "mind worked and how he adapted the materials of observation to literary use" (364–365).

"Chiefly About War Matters" and the essays of *Our Old Home* were both written with the readership of the *Atlantic Monthly* as a shaping authority on Hawthorne, and here, in contrast to the earlier publishing in *The Token*, a gift book annual, market forces are a positive influence. The *Atlantic*, founded in 1857, was purchased by Ticknor and Fields in 1859 while James Russell Lowell was still editor (Charvat 170). It presented a more worldly audience than had the readership of *The Token*, for whom Hawthorne had shaped several earlier sketches, and it published the contemporary literary elite, including Oliver Wendell Holmes, Thoreau, Edward Everett Hale, Whitman, Longfellow, and Henry Tuckerman, whose travel essays Hawthorne had praised in "Up the Thames." Hawthorne was addressing a sophisticated audience, in much the same way that modern essayists E. B. White and John McPhee speak to the literate, wealthy, eastern, upper middle-class readership of *The New Yorker*.

The audience Hawthorne addressed when he published essays in the *Atlantic Monthly* was—in political terms at least—his adversary. In 1903 M. A. DeWolfe Howe, in *Boston: The Place and the People*, wrote that the "function of the *Atlantic*" was to "provide a full and free opportunity for the expression" of three "strangely powerful forces": "the spiritual cause of Transcendentalism," "the politico-moral causes of antislavery," and "the intellectual and artistic interest of purely creative writing" (242). Hawthorne was well aware that his unsympathetic attitude toward the war would antagonize the *Atlantic*'s Northern readership, and this awareness helps account for the dialectical nature of the discourse and satirical tone of the essay. The pro-Union position of Hawthorne's fellow authors in the *Atlantic* is illustrated by Longfellow's patriotic poem about the sinking of the Union sloop-of-war *Cumberland* by "the iron ship of our foes" in the December 1862 issue (669–670), and by Whittier's "The Battle Autumn of 1862" in the October issue of the same year (510–511). Recognition of this historical context of "Chiefly About War Matters" is helpful in analyzing the controversial discourse.

The rhetoric of "Chiefly About War Matters" refocuses our attention on Hawthorne's shifting relationship with his text. Just as the introductory paragraphs to "The Custom-House" present a polyphonic conversation among "author," "reader," "some authors," "the inmost me," "editor," and several other speakers and listeners, so "Chiefly About War Matters" presents a multi-vocal text. Here Hawthorne uses footnotes—and undercuts the convention of the footnote as legitimate textual commentary or citation—to comment, as if in another persona, against his own text: narrative voice (Hawthorne) against footnote commentary (Hawthorne). In discussing John Brown after the visit to Harper's Ferry, Hawthorne writes that "nobody was ever more justly hanged" (327). He continues:

> any common sensible man, looking at the matter unsentimentally, must have felt a certain intellectual satisfaction in seeing him hanged, if it were only in requital of his preposterous miscalculation of possibilities. (328)

Anticipating the outcry from the North—and from his Concord friends in particular—for his unpopular stance, Hawthorne footnotes the passage quoted above with the following comment—humorous or sarcastic depending upon the reader: "Can it be a son of old Massachusetts who utters this abominable sentiment? For shame" (328). A year later Emerson would cut out the preface—the dedicatory letter to Pierce— in his copy of *Our Old Home* (Howe *Hostess* 15), and after Hawthorne's funeral would write in his journal, on May 24, 1864, of "the painful solitude of the man" and of his "unwillingness and caprice" (*Journals* 306).[5]

Hawthorne glosses himself again in "Chiefly About War Matters." After observing the Confederate prisoners, he writes that it is "an immense absurdity that they should fancy us their enemies"; he continues, asserting that

> no human effort, on a grand scale, has ever yet resulted according to the purpose of its projectors. The advantages are always incidental. Man's accidents are God's purposes. We miss the good we sought, and do the good we little cared for. (331–332)

The passage is footnoted, with the editorial "we" (Hawthorne) addressing "the author" (Hawthorne), and the footnote carries the ambiguous prediction that "the present war" will "illustrate our remark":

> The author seems to imagine that he has compressed a great deal of meaning into these little, hard, dry pellets of aphoristic wisdom. We disagree with him. The counsels of wise and good men are often coincident with the purposes of Providence; and the present war promises to illustrate our remark. (332)

Eight footnotes create a recurrent tension in the discourse of the essay, the contradictory voice from the bottom of the page in discord with the provocative analysis in the main text. In response to the narrator's comment that "it is so odd, when we measure our advances from barbarism, and find ourselves just here!" the debunking footnote voice retorts: "We hardly expected this outbreak in favor of war from the Peaceable Man; but the justice of our cause makes us all soldiers at heart, however quiet in our outward life" (321). And in reaction to the editorial excision of the portrait of Lincoln—whom Hawthorne referred to as "Uncle Abe," with hair that had seen "neither brush nor comb that morning" (310)—Hawthorne wrote in a letter to Fields: "What a terrible thing it is to try to let off a little bit of truth into this miserable humbug of a world!" (CE XVIII 461).

Henry James, along with many others, read the footnotes as additions by Hawthorne's editor at the *Atlantic*, noting only "the questionable taste of the editorial commentary, with which it is strange that Hawthorne should have allowed his article to be encumbered" (138–139). After consideration of the various manuscripts and letters involved in "Chiefly About War Matters," James Bense argues convincingly in "Nathaniel Hawthorne's Intention in 'Chiefly About War Matters'" (1989) that Hawthorne had conceived of the essay "as a censorship hoax" (200). "As a result of the constraints [Hawthorne] felt while trying to write honestly about the war," Bense says, "he created a satirical dialectic between his narrator and an imaginary editor" (200). Bense extends his observation of the dialectical nature of this essay, asserting that "the opposition within the essay is a corollary to the dialectical habit that probes for truth in much of [Hawthorne's] writing" (214). Bense's assertion congenially supports my own observations regarding the function of the oppositional rhetoric of the essays.

"Leamington Spa," published in the October 1862 *Atlantic*, three months after "Chiefly About War Matters," includes a headnote addressed to "My Dear Editor" signed by "A Peaceable Man" which is omitted from *The Centenary Edition* of the essays. Humor, irony, and ambiguity form a Hawthornian stew in the discourse of the headnote. The Peaceable Man, whose identity must have been clear to the *Atlantic* readership even though authorship in the magazine was only identified in a semi-annual "Contents," refers to the editor's "cruel and terrible notes upon [his] harmless article in the July Number" (451). Thus Hawthorne assumes yet another persona, commenting upon his own editorial comments in the July issue. In the headnote the Peaceable Man, fully anticipating but seeming to relish the controversy he would create over his description of English womanhood in "Leamington Spa," concludes ironically:

I cannot lose so good an opportunity of showing the world the placability and sweetness that adorn my character, and therefore send you another article, in which, I trust, you will find nothing to strike out,—unless, peradventure, you think that I may disturb the tranquility of nations by my plan of annexing Great Britain, or my attempted adumbration of a fat English dowager! (451)

Perhaps a real anger at Ticknor and Fields's excision of the Uncle Abe profile—a well as the fundamental difference in Hawthorne's political views from his editors'—led to the inclusion of the "steaks and sirloins," a gratuitous and bizarre addition which diminishes the otherwise tasteful—if prickly—*Our Old Home*.

The closing lines of "Civic Banquets," the concluding essay of *Our Old Home*, serve as one of the last instances of Hawthorne consciously addressing his readership, and the scene plays upon the usual ambiguity about the composition of that audience. The English dignitaries who are gathered around the table to hear his after-dinner-speech are an audience within the text, and the reader of the essay—in the shadows of the room/text—strains to hear the speech as well. The reader is maneuvered into the role of perpetual listener—perhaps one of "the few who will understand him, better than most of his schoolmates and lifemates" (CE 13)—since he must imagine the words that do not follow in the text. Hawthorne stands, the audience applauds, silences, and waits for him to begin. The final lines of this last essay read:

bidding my three friends bury me honorably, I got upon my legs to save both countries, or perish in the attempt. The tables roared and thundered at me, and suddenly they were silent again. But, as I have never happened to stand in a position of greater dignity and peril, I deem it a stratagem of sage policy here to close these Sketches, leaving myself still erect in so heroic an attitude. (CE V 345)

In "Some of the Haunts of Burns," Hawthorne ends the essay by suggesting that, after the visit to the places Burns knew, "there will be a personal warmth for us in everything that he wrote," that "we shall know him in a kind of personal way, as if we had shaken hands with him, and felt the thrill of his actual voice" (CE V 212). Hawthorne's own "actual voice"—distant, ambiguous, and slippery—is more difficult to isolate.

Notes

1. Poe, in a review of *Twice-told Tales* in the April 1842 *Graham's Magazine*, wrote that "most of them are essays properly so called. It would have been wise in their author to have modified his title, so as to have reference to all included" (85). In the May 1842 issue of *Graham's Magazine*, he wrote that "many of them are pure essays; for example, 'Sights from a Steeple,' 'Sunday at Home,' 'Little Annie's Ramble,' 'A Rill from the Town-Pump,' 'The Toll-Gatherer's Day,' 'The Haunted Mind,' 'The Sister Years,' 'Snow-Flakes,' 'Night Sketches,' and 'Foot-Prints on the Sea-Shore'" (87). Poe adds that the "predominant feature" of the essays is "repose. There is no attempt at effect. All is quiet, thoughtful, subdued" (88).

2. Quotations are from the *Centenary Edition of the Works of Nathaniel Hawthorne*, William Charvat, Roy Harvey Pearce, Claude M. Simpson, and Thomas Woodson, general editors. References are indicated in parentheses in the text by edition, volume number, and page number.

3. "Leamington Spa" was published in the *Atlantic Monthly* VII (October 1862): 451–62; "About Warwick" was published in the *Atlantic Monthly* X (December 1862): 708–20; "Recollections of a Gifted Woman" was published in the *Atlantic Monthly* XI (January 1863): 43–58; "Pilgrimage to Old Boston" was published in the *Atlantic Monthly* IX (January 1862): 88–101; "Near Oxford" was published in the *Atlantic Monthly* VIII (October 1861): 385–97; "Some of the Haunts of Burns" was published in the *Atlantic Monthly* VI (October 1860): 385–95; "A London Suburb" was published in the *Atlantic Monthly* XI (March 1863): 306–21; "Up the Thames" was published in the *Atlantic Monthly* XI (May 1863): 598–614; "Outside Glimpses of English Poverty" was published in the *Atlantic Monthly* XII (July 1863): 36–51; and "Civic Banquets" was published in the *Atlantic Monthly* XII (August 1863): 195–212 (*CE* V liv–lviii).

4. In an unsigned essay on *Our Old Home*, "A Handful of Hawthorne," in *Punch* 79 (October 1863), the reviewer noted: "You have written a book about England, and into this book you have put all the caricatures and libels upon English folk, which you collected while enjoying our hospitality" (392). In the same essay Hawthorne's description of English matrons was termed "calmly terrible" (394). Henry Bright in the *Examiner* (October 1863) wrote that Hawthorne's characterizations of the English were

"cynical and contemptuous" (396). The anonymous reviewer in *Blackwood's Magazine* 94 (November 1863) responded to *Our Old Home* by writing, in "Hawthorne on England," that the English "shall not be more bulbous, longer-bodied, or shorter-legged, in consequence of the publication of his book—and that our women will still charm our purblind race though they have not the stamp of Mr. Hawthorne's approbation" (402).

5. Ticknor and Fields deleted, before publication in the *Atlantic*, several paragraphs of "Chiefly About War Matters" that gave an unflattering portrait of Lincoln to the abolitionist northern readership. Hawthorne wrote to Fields on May 23, 1862, complaining that Fields was omitting "the only part of the article really worth publishing" (*CE* XVIII 461). Hawthorne was, as we have seen, at political cross-purposes with the abolitionist stance of the *Atlantic*; his ambiguous footnotes in "Chiefly About War Matters" and the preface to *Our Old Home* further provoked his readers.

Works Cited

Anhorn, Judy Schaaf. "Literary Reputation and the Essays of *Our Old Home*." *Studies in the Novel* 23 (1991): 152–166.

Atwan, Robert. Foreword. *The Best American Essays 1990*. Ed. Justin Kaplan. New York: Ticknor & Fields, 1990. ix–xii.

Bense, James. "Nathaniel Hawthorne's Intention in 'Chiefly About War Matters.'" *American Literature* 61 (1989): 200–214.

Bright, Henry. *Examiner* (17 October 1863): 662–663. Rpt. in J. Donald Crowley. *Hawthorne: The Critical Heritage*. New York: Barnes and Noble, 1970. 395–398.

Charvat, William. *The Profession of Authorship in America, 1800–1870: The Papers of William Charvat*. Ed. Matthew J. Bruccoli. Columbus: Ohio State University Press, 1968.

Emerson, Ralph Waldo. *The Heart of Emerson's Journals*. Ed. Bliss Perry. New York: Dover, 1958.

"A Handful of Hawthorne." *Punch* 79 (17 October 1863): 339–340. Rpt. in J. Donald Crowley. *Hawthorne: The Critical Heritage*. New York: Barnes and Noble, 1970. 392–398.

Hawthorne, Nathaniel. *The Centenary Edition of the Works of Nathaniel Hawthorne*. Ed. William Charvat et al. 20 vols. Columbus: Ohio State University Press, 1962–88.

———. "Chiefly About War Matters." *The Complete Works of Nathaniel Hawthorne*. Ed. George Parsons Lathrop. Vol. XII. Boston: Houghton Mifflin, 1883. 229–345.

———. *The English Notebooks*. Ed. Randall Stewart. New York: MLA of America, 1941.

———. "Leamington Spa." *Atlantic Monthly* 10 (1862): 451–462.

"Hawthorne on England." *Blackwood's Magazine* 94 (November 1863): 610–623.

Rpt. in J. Donald Crowley. *Hawthorne: The Critical Heritage*. New York: Barnes and Noble, 1970. 398–404.

Hijiya, James A. "Nathaniel Hawthorne's *Our Old Home*." *American Literature* 46 (1974): 363–373.

Howe, M. A. DeWolfe. *Boston: The Places and the People*. New York: Macmillan, 1903.

———. *Memories of a Hostess*. Boston: The Atlantic Monthly Press, 1922.

Howells, William Dean. *Certain Delightful English Towns*. New York: Harper & Brothers, 1906.

Hull, Raymona E. "Nathaniel Hawthorne's 'Old Home.'" *The American Transcendental Quarterly: A Journal of New England Writers* 50 (1981): 83–91.

James, Henry. *Hawthorne*. 1879. Ithaca: Cornell University Press, 1956.

Kaplan, Justin. Introduction. *The Best American Essays 1990*. Ed. Kaplan. New York: Ticknor & Fields, 1990. xii–xix.

Kesselring, Marion L. *Hawthorne's Reading, 1828–1850: A Transcription and Identification of Titles Recorded in the Charge Books of the Salem Athenaeum*. 1949. Rpt. n. p.: Norwood Editions, 1976.

Longfellow, Henry Wadsworth. "The Cumberland." *Atlantic Monthly* 10 (1862): 669–670.

Lueck, Beth I. "Hawthorne's Ironic Traveler and the Picturesque Tour." *Hawthorne's American Travel Sketches*. Hanover, New Hampshire: University Press of New England, 1989. 153–180.

Poe, Edgar Allan. "Review in *Graham's Magazine*" 1842 (20): 254. Rpt. in *Hawthorne: The Critical Heritage*. Ed. J. Donald Crowley. New York: Barnes and Noble, 1970. 84–85.

———. "Review in *Graham's Magazine*" 1842 (20): 298–300. Rpt. in *Hawthorne: The Critical Heritage*. Ed. J. Donald Crowley. New York: Barnes and Noble, 1970. 87–94.

Pound, Ezra. *The Selected Poems of Ezra Pound*. New York: New Directions, 1949.

Tuckerman, Henry T. *A Month in England*. 1853. Gloucester: Alan Sutton, 1982.

Turner, Arlin. *Nathaniel Hawthorne: A Biography*. New York: Oxford University Press, 1980.

Whittier, John G. "The Battle Autumn of 1862." *Atlantic Monthly* 10 (1862): 510–11.

Winterowd, W. Ross. *The Rhetoric of the "Other" Literature*. Carbondale: Southern Illinois University Press, 1990.

"A Small Heap of Glittering Fragments":
Hawthorne's Discontent with the Short Story Form_____

Kathryn B. McKee

Literary careers rarely fall into neatly demarcated sections. Most writers jump from short works to long and back again, moving willy-nilly between fiction and nonfiction, poetry and prose. But Hawthorne is different. Apart from his early book-length Gothic romance *Fanshawe* (1828)—a work he later disavowed and sought to suppress—all his early fiction was short. In 1846, though, he wrote to a friend, "I never mean to write any more stories," and he kept his word. Beginning with *The Scarlet Letter* in 1850, all the fiction he wrote in his late career was long. Such a sharp turn in a literary career demands an explanation.

In this essay Kathryn B. McKee examines the reasons that led Hawthorne to abandon the short forms, focusing especially on the tales written in the 1840s. She also gives us an opportunity to rethink the longer works in a new context, reminding us, for instance, that *The Scarlet Letter* was originally conceived as a collection of short stories. In exposing the "personal doubts about the tale as suitable vehicle for his creativity," McKee sees *The Scarlet Letter*—especially its central symbol, the famous letter *A*—as a culmination of his efforts to find an answer to his generic problems. In that work, McKee argues, Hawthorne "is at last able to describe the moment of artistic creation that eludes him in the earlier tales."   — J.L.

Between the spring of 1844 and the winter of 1848/1849, Hawthorne wrote three tales that reflect his growing dissatisfaction with the short story as a genre and his consequent movement toward adopting the full-length romantic novel as his preferred artistic form. "The Artist of the Beautiful" and "Drowne's Wooden Image" (both written in early 1844) and "The Snow-Image" (likely written in late 1848 or early

1849) each comment on Hawthorne's view of the artist and on his perception of his own suitability to fill that role. They also work together to reveal Hawthorne's view of art itself, and in so doing reflect his personal doubts about the tale as suitable vehicle for his creativity. Artistic productions in Hawthorne's earlier works, "The Prophetic Pictures," and "Edward Randolph's Portrait," for instance, become more powerful with the passage of time. But in "The Artist of the Beautiful," "Drowne's Wooden Image," and "The Snow-Image," forces the creator cannot control destroy the progressively transient medium of artistic creation—metal, wood, and finally snow. The fragile articles at the center of the latter three tales mirror the limitations Hawthorne had come to see as inherent in the short story genre.

Interestingly, Hawthorne composed "The Artist of the Beautiful," "Drowne's Wooden Image," and "The Snow-Image" during a period in which he was acquiring more worldly responsibilities. He married Sophia Peabody in 1842, his daughter Una was born in 1844, and his son Julian in 1846. Consequently, he began to question the financial gain short stories could yield. Simultaneously, he came to doubt the ability of that genre to earn for him an enduring literary reputation. In "The Old Manse," Hawthorne reveals that upon moving into his Concord home (where he lived when writing both "The Artist of the Beautiful" and "Drowne's Wooden Image") he resolved to "achieve a novel, that should evolve some deep lesson, and should possess physical substance enough to stand alone" (5). Yet not until *The Scarlet Letter* in 1850 did he find that "physical substance"—in the "authenticity of the outline" of the letter "A" ("The Custom-House" 33). The study of "The Artist of the Beautiful," "Drowne's Wooden Image," and "The Snow-Image," then, provides valuable insight into the literary ambitions and conceptions of art espoused, not only by a writer of short stories, but by an aspiring novelist as well. Hawthorne indicates in "The Custom-House" that he initially conceived of his novel as forming the centerpiece of yet another collection of short stories. He was at first reluctant to accept the advice of publisher James T. Fields and release *The Scar-*

let Letter as an independent volume, as Edwin Haviland Miller points out in *Salem Is My Dwelling Place* (280). Yet the final decision to publish in that genre reflects more than the heeding of editorial advice; it also reveals Hawthorne's desire to employ his literary talents in a different form. Most of the work belonging to the "Old Manse Period Canon," as John J. MacDonald argues, attempts to discover a literary means of "processing the immediate experience of external reality" (15). Part of Hawthorne's "external reality" at this time was certainly financial insecurity. Of equal importance was the reality of his literary ambition.

Although Hawthorne never earned extraordinary amounts of money from his writing, the financial difficulties he and Sophia faced from the time of their marriage until the publication of *The Scarlet Letter* were particularly severe and are well-documented in various Hawthorne biographies. His marriage and his decision to devote himself primarily to magazine writing coincided, resulting in increased financial difficulty for a family rather than for an individual. In November of 1843, he wrote to E. A. Duyckinck with a fairly good-natured attitude toward his paucity of funds: "in short, I have nothing to wish for—except, perhaps, that Providence would make it somewhat more plain to my apprehension how I am to earn my bread, after a year or two. But it will be time enough for that, when the necessity comes" (*Letters* 9–10). Magazine writing was then his primary source of income, but he received erratic payment because the publications themselves were often nearly insolvent. Thus Hawthorne anticipated a need to change either the scope of his present employment or its nature all together.

With the birth of his daughter Una in 1844, the tone of Hawthorne's financial discussions changed dramatically. His March 24, 1844, letter to G. S. Hillard, his lawyer, is particularly telling, not only of his financial state, but also of his attitude toward his current occupation:

> I find it necessary at last to come out of my cloud-region, and allow myself
> to be woven into the somber texture of humanity. There is no escaping it

any longer. I have business on earth now, and must look about me for the means of doing it. It will never do for me to continue merely a writer of stories for the magazines—the most unprofitable business in the world. . . . (*Letters* 23)

The sense of urgency underlying Hawthorne's words is unmistakable. Directly linked to his financial crisis during this period was an artistic crisis. Because, as Nina Baym observes, magazine work required Hawthorne to write quickly and often, he "had no time for fantasizing, for waiting until an idea ripened, for picking, choosing, and discarding" (98). Baym continues by pointing out that even if Hawthorne had wanted to undertake a novel-length project at this point, he simply could not have done so; the magazine work was too demanding (116). In as early as June 1843, Hawthorne, in a notebook entry, expresses uneasiness about the quality of his stories and sketches: "the necessity of keeping my brain at work eats into my comfort. . . . I keep myself uneasy, and produce little, and almost nothing that is worth producing" (Simpson 388). Although *Mosses from an Old Manse* appeared in 1846 and included many tales written between 1843 and 1845, Edwin Miller argues that Hawthorne "dried up creatively" as his financial anxiety increased (246). Hawthorne's reflections about the difficulty he found in writing "The Old Manse," the work he crafted as the introductory sketch to *Mosses from an Old Manse*, are particularly telling of his doubts about himself as a writer and the short work he had produced to date. In July of 1845 he wrote to Duyckinck that "my story ["The Old Manse"] makes no good progress. There are many matters that thrust themselves between, and hinder my mind from any close approximation of the subject" (*Letters* 105). These "matters" no doubt included financial pressure to finish the collection. In December the sketch was still not complete, and he confessed to Duyckinck: "I write continually—but am conscious, even at the moment, that I am not writing the true thing" (*Letters* 136). Most revealing of Hawthorne's state of mind is a January 1846 letter to Duyckinck in which he decrees:

I never mean to write any more stories . . . . It is rather a sad idea—not that I am to write no more of this kind, but that I cannot better justify myself for having written at all. As the first essays and tentatives of a young author, they would be well enough—but it seems to me absurd to look upon them as conveying any claim to a settled literary reputation. . . . If they were merely Spring blossoms, we might look for good fruit hereafter; but I have done nothing but blossom all through the summer. (*Letters* 139–140)

Thus at this crucial juncture, Hawthorne debated more than the financial wisdom of pursuing a literary career; he also questioned the artistic value of what he had already produced and doubted his ability to achieve a more far-reaching success. Tom Quirk, in an article examining the relationship between Hawthorne's late tales and "The Custom-House," acknowledges that Hawthorne's notions of art underwent a change before he wrote *The Scarlet Letter*, but he finds that "those decisions and adjustments, when they came, came in a flurry. It was during the last two years before the publication of *The Scarlet Letter* that Hawthorne reached . . . the 'crossroads' of his development as a writer" (220). Indeed the "crossroads" may have come as late as 1848, but Hawthorne was philosophically approaching that turning point several years earlier.

The stories composed in the eight years between Hawthorne's marriage and the publication of *The Scarlet Letter* are uneven in quality; "The Artist of the Beautiful," "Drowne's Wooden Image," and "The Snow-Image" reflect that range. "The Artist of the Beautiful" is superior to both of the other tales, largely because Hawthorne had long nurtured the ideas he presents to us in Owen Warland's career. Notebook entries from as early as 1837 point to Owen's dilemma.[1] There are no notebook entries suggestive of "Drowne's Wooden Image," hinting that Hawthorne composed that story quickly, probably to be sold almost immediately. A snow image resembling Violet and Peony's playmate surfaces in the notebooks as early as 1836 but in a very different form from the snow girl readers finally meet in "The Snow-Image."

Hawthorne does not again mention such a creature until an 1849 entry that also differs markedly from the final product.[2] Because, as Darrel Abel points out in *The Moral Picturesque*, an "'image' invariably tells as much about the person who imagines or sees it as it does about the person seen in the image" (150), these three stories and the artwork at their centers reveal a great deal about Hawthorne. The created objects symbolically reflect his dissatisfaction with the short story genre, and the stories themselves literally illustrate in their varied quality the consequences of adopting magazine writing as a profession.

"The Artist of the Beautiful" reflects Hawthorne's growing uneasiness about the value and the quality of his work. The narrator tells us that Owen Warland, the story's artist figure, exhibited from childhood a penchant for whittling small, useless objects. The adult Owen is equally impractical in the eyes of the community, creating a series of minute mechanisms that culminate in the artificial butterfly he presents to the Danforths as a wedding present. "'[G]ive me the worker in iron. . . . He spends his labor upon a reality,'" declares Peter Hovenden, Owen's former employer, as he compares Owen to Danforth the blacksmith (449). Later, writing in "The Custom-House," Hawthorne hears much the same thing that Owen does, but his reproaches come from those "stern and black-browed Puritans" of his ancestry; "'What is he?' murmurs one gray shadow . . . to the other. 'A writer of story-books! What kind of a business in life. . . . Why, the degenerate fellow might as well have been a fiddler!'" (10). Unable to make a satisfactory living at his writing, Hawthorne repeatedly analyzed the usefulness of "the kind of business in life" he had chosen. His sympathies do not rest entirely with the story's artist figure. When Owen releases the mechanical butterfly in the Danforth home, Annie "admir[ed] her own infant, and with good reason, far more than the artistic butterfly" (474). Her sensibilities distinguish the authentic from the imitative.

Yet like Owen Warland, Hawthorne had discovered the impossibility of shielding his inner vision from external reality. After Owen destroys his mechanism following Danforth's visit, the narrator reflects:

"thus it is that ideas which grow up within the imagination, and appear so lovely to it . . . are exposed to be shattered and annihilated by contact with the Practical" (454). By 1844, the year he wrote "The Artist of the Beautiful," Hawthorne could no longer ignore the power of the practical world; the reality of financial obligation was undeniable. The artist explains to Annie that the butterfly "'may well be said to possess life, for it absorbed my own being into itself'" (471). Thus Owen's existence becomes indistinguishable from the form he creates. At this period of Hawthorne's life, his life too was literally indistinguishable from his creations. Financially he felt compelled to write stories and to sell them. Hawthorne did not always share Owen's luxury of destroying his project and reconstructing it later, and so Owen mimics a composition process that Hawthorne may well have admired in its allowance for gradual evolution. Certainly "The Artist of the Beautiful" is a tale that evolved, but hastily-constructed pieces like "Drowne's Wooden Image" were too literally Hawthorne's fate to allow for much revision.

Owen Warland's minute productions also reveal Hawthorne's artistic misgivings about the short story genre. Millicent Bell finds the "association of tinyness [with Owen] . . . restricting" (104), and Nina Baym concludes that the "miniature . . . he produces represents the belittling of imagination" (110–111). The narrator explains that the size of Owen's creations contributes significantly to the public's inability to appreciate his genius. Likewise Hawthorne doubted his ability to acquire "a settled literary reputation" based solely on his short fiction. Hovenden speculates that Owen "would turn the sun out of its orbit, and derange the whole course of time, if . . . his ingenuity could ever grasp anything bigger than a child's toy" (448). In Hovenden's eyes, and at moments in Hawthorne's, Owen misuses his talent. Short stories, as Hawthorne wrote to Duyckinck, "were merely Spring blossoms"; the story of Owen Warland suggests that even in 1844 Hawthorne wanted to accomplish something that he perceived as more noteworthy than the mere composition of tales. The butterfly's demise does not shock Owen. It "'is not now to me what it was when I beheld it afar off, in the day-dreams of my youth,'" he tells Annie as his creation floats about the room (471). For this reason, perhaps, he does not cry out when the Danforth child crushes the butterfly, leaving only "a small heap of glittering fragments, whence the Mystery of Beauty had fled for ever" (475). Owen had ceased to look for the mystery in so finite an object. Likewise, Hawthorne had discovered that short stories were just so many fragments, incapable of sustaining him financially or artistically. As Owen recognized his butterfly to be merely imitative of nature, so Hawthorne perceived his short stories as inadequate when compared with the more substantial form of the novel.

"Drowne's Wooden Image" also includes an artist figure, but he is in many respects Owen's antithesis. Unlike Owen and his youthful genius, Drowne the wood carver has never displayed any particular talent. Rather "[f]rom his earliest boyhood, he had exhibited a knack," although his creations (pump-heads and gatepost urns) are of no more practical value than so many of Owen's "whirligigs" (307–308). Like Owen, Drowne submits his greatest creation to the public eye, but he meets with dramatically different results than does the "Artist of the Beautiful." Because Drowne is one of the ordinary townspeople, rather than a man hopelessly removed from their sphere as is Owen, his work attracts much attention from the town's citizens. When he invites them to view the completed figure of a woman, "most persons, at their first entrance, felt impelled to remove their hats, and pay such reverence as was due to the richly dressed and beautiful young lady" (314). Instead of reaching out to touch her as Hovenden and the Danforths touch the butterfly, these spectators feel "a sensation of fear; as if, not being actually human, yet so like humanity, [the figurehead] must therefore be something preternatural" (314). And although the "inhabitants visited it so universally, that, after a few days of exhibition, there was hardly an old man or a child who had not become minutely familiar with its aspect" (315), they become familiar with Drowne's wooden image by gazing at it, not by touching it. In "The Artist of the Beautiful," the artist removed from the sphere of humanity creates an object that shatters upon contact with the practical world; here the practical man creates an artistic object that the practical world is afraid to touch. Thus this symbol interacts no more successfully with its viewers than does the butterfly. Although the story does not conclude with the figurehead's demise, Drowne's wooden image is impractical and certain to rot. It is of no value to Drowne or to the townspeople or even to the ship's crew, who will not even be able to see it, fastened to the front of the vessel.

Yet certainly we can understand "Drowne's Wooden Image" as affirming the power of art, and many critics and readers have done so. "Drowne's wooden image has come to life!" rings through the streets when Captain Hunnewell appears with a lovely maiden on his arm who would seem to be the ship's figurehead endowed with life (316). Hawthorne gives us a way to explain this episode. He alludes to a Portuguese woman who had been sheltering herself in the care of Captain Hunnewell, and thus we intuit that likely she, and not the figurehead herself, walks down the street. Drowne falls in love, then, with the model whom he uses for the figurehead, and by his love becomes empowered to create one truly lifelike work of art. By demystifying the figurehead's apparent endowment with life, Hawthorne does not necessarily undercut Drowne's powers. Even if the carved woman never walks through the town, she does capture with remarkable accuracy the features of this living woman. Thus Bell understands the story to be Hawthorne's assertion that love for a "human reality" rather than for "a cold ideal" promotes the greatest art (134). Drowne has loved not just the statue, but the woman.

Yet finally Hawthorne suggests that Drowne exercises little actual power in the creation of the figurehead and in so doing returns to nagging questions about the artist and his work. The narrator's account of the creative process renders it almost magical; the woman appears to have sheltered herself within the wood, and so the wood worker releases rather than creates her. And even if Drowne does carve away one masterpiece, he does not remain an artist. When Copley, the sculptor, enters the shop after seeing Captain Hunnewell and the exotic maiden,

Drowne casts upon him a mournful expression drained of imaginative sensibility. Looking at the beautiful figurehead, Drowne exclaims, "this image! Can it have been my work? Well—I have wrought it in a kind of a dream" (9). Drowne loses the two authentic things in his life: the exotic woman and the power to capture the essence of humanity he sees in her face. All that remains is the wooden image that likewise will sail away on the front of Hunnewell's ship.

What remained for Hawthorne was also the wooden image at the story's center, symbolic of concerns about his ability to sustain his artistic achievement. Hawthorne had recently married, and he may well be affirming in this story love's ability to influence artistic production. But Drowne does not retain his creative powers, and Hawthorne suggests that even his one noteworthy production came about less by his skill than by some indefinable quality inherent in the wood. Even shortly after his marriage, Hawthorne was dissatisfied with the quality of his work; as economic pressure came to bear, he was clearly concerned about maintaining the imaginative stamina required to produce magazine stories at a lucrative rate. Drowne, then, is what Hawthorne feared becoming—a man surrounded by his own lifeless, wooden creations, with the capability to produce nothing better and only a fleeting recollection of a skill once exercised. If Owen's butterfly comes to symbolize the artist's crushed aspirations, the figurehead points to the loss of creative power itself. Hawthorne confronted both misgivings in his artistic life.

"The Snow-Image" is the sort of tale such a wooden artist would produce and further illustrates Hawthorne's fears about his compromised career. Again he comments on the predicament of the artist and the durability of his art. If, as Darrel Abel concludes in *The Moral Picturesque*, "snow-images" are Hawthorne's "favorite symbolism for imaginative power" (142), then this tale, one of the last Hawthorne wrote before shifting to the novel form, speaks powerfully about his view of art at a crucial stage in his artistic development.

In this story Hawthorne again undercuts the power of art and the power of the artist. The artist figures are children, a fact that in itself signals their limitations in dealing with the external world. These children, Violet and Peony, employ a creative process reminiscent of Drowne's. The snow girl they fashion "seemed . . . not so much to be made by the children, as to grow up under their hands" (10). Throughout the story, Hawthorne further minimizes the power of both of the artist figures by causing them to appear as insubstantial images. After her brother tumbles into a drift, Violet observes, "you look exactly like a snow-image, Peony" (9). While constructing the snow child, Violet is more "a cheerful Thought . . . than a physical reality" (9). Thus the creators themselves seem to have no more staying power than their production. The neighbors, in fact, see no snow-images at all, only Mr. Lindsey, the children's father, "running about his garden in pursuit of a snow-drift" (21). In maintaining that the snow image is a human child, Mr. Lindsey, like the insistent practical concerns nagging at Hawthorne, completely undermines the imaginative creation. The puddle that results after he forces the snow girl to sit in front of the stove, at least in Mr. Lindsey's eyes, is simply snow from the children's shoes. He consistently denies the existence of the snow-image, the artistic creation at the tale's center. And his words end the story. Here, in one of Hawthorne's most stunning indictments of the power of art, the world not only fails to see any wonder in an artistic work, but fails to see the work at all.

Although the existence of the snow child remains convincing to her creators, even their interaction with the creature is limited by its form, just as Hawthorne had come to find his relationship with the short story awkward. Here the exchange between the artists and their art is a cold one, both literally and metaphorically. As Mr. Lindsey brings the child into the house, he dismisses the remonstrances of his wife and children by saying, "she is so cold, already, that her hand has almost frozen mine" (22). Likewise, when the children try to hold hands with the snow girl, her touch stings them, and they pull away. The snow image draws the red of its lips from Peony's cheeks, but after that exchange, which rightly should demonstrate some affection, Peony can only exclaim "what a cold kiss!" (14). The artistic creation is not ultimately what its creators had imagined, a snow sister. Instead the image is frigid; it has no sustained power for its viewers or its creators or even for Hawthorne, who felt his own creative powers constricted by the short story form to the production of "a childish miracle," the subtitle of "The Snow-Image."

In 1844, the same year in which he composed "The Artist of the Beautiful" and "Drowne's Wooden Image," Hawthorne discussed the drain of magazine writing in a letter to G. S. Hillard: "I could not spend more than a third of my time in this sort of composition. It requires a continual freshness of mind; else a deterioration in the article will quickly be perceptible" (*Letters* 23). Such is the case in "The Artist of the Beautiful," "Drowne's Wooden Image," and "The Snow-Image": central images in each story reflect "a deterioration in the article" that is "quickly perceptible." The fragility of these artistic objects parallels Hawthorne's view of the tale itself as an art form that could no longer offer him financial or creative sustenance.

In *The Scarlet Letter*, however, Hawthorne found both the symbol and the genre to meet his needs. In contrast to the frigidity of the snow child's cold kiss, the letter "A" sears its way from the past into the present. Hawthorne writes in the "Custom-House": "I happened to place [the letter] on my breast . . . it seemed to me, then, that I experienced a sensation not altogether physical, yet almost so, as of burning heat; and as if the letter were not of red cloth, but red-hot iron" (32). Richard Millington, in *Practicing Romance*, identifies this "moment of sympathetic exchange" as one in which "the external becomes internal" for Hawthorne (61). Yet a transference of the internal to the external also takes place, as Hawthorne's own literary ambitions fasten at last upon an external symbol that will not bow beneath its weight as the butterfly, the wooden figure, and the snow girl have done. The power of the "A" comes in part from its foundation—the desire for a literary career that could not be built on the fragile and powerless artwork at the center of hastily-composed tales like "Drowne's Wooden Image" and "The

Snow-Image." The power of the "A" comes too from the legacy embodied within it, inescapable for Hawthorne and infinitely expansive in terms of its relation to his own life and the lives of his readers. As scholars have consistently argued, most recently Sacvan Bercovitch in his accomplished study *The Office of The Scarlet Letter*, the ambiguity of the "A" is its greatest asset. The richness and the durability of this piece of artwork contrast sharply with the restrictive and powerless forms made of metal, wood, or snow featured in earlier stories.

Significantly, in *The Scarlet Letter*, Hawthorne is at last able to describe the moment of artistic creation that eludes him in the earlier tales. He does not include that moment in "The Artist of the Beautiful"; Owen is locked up in his shop, laboring beyond our eyesight when creating the butterfly. And Hawthorne denies the artist any real creative power in "Drowne's Wooden Image" and "The Snow-Image." Writing in "The Custom-House," however, Hawthorne describes "moonlight" as the "medium . . . most suitable for a romance-writer to get acquainted with his illusive guests" (35). Yet this imaginative world of moonbeams must mingle with the authenticity of the "coal-fire" from an ordinary hearth to communicate "a heart and sensibilities of human tenderness to the forms which fancy summons up. It converts them from snow-images into men and women" (36). His use of the word "snow-images" is not merely coincidental. Hawthorne had recently released his collection of tales called *The Snow-Image*, and so, as F. O. Matthiessen points out, this passage from "The Custom-House" may constitute a pointed acknowledgement of his disappointment in the quality of his recent work (262). In defining the artistic moment that converts "snow-images" into people, Hawthorne likewise defines himself as an artist who no longer deals in the lifeless forms of mechanized butterflies, wooden figureheads, and snow children. Instead, the artistic creation at his novel's center endures beyond the lifetimes of both the fictional Hester Prynne and her creator, supporting an enduring literary reputation that Hawthorne himself believed the glittering fragments of short fiction could never provide.

Notes

1. Lea Newman refers to notebook entries from October 7, 1837, October 16, 1837, and January 4, 1839, as suggestive of the main plot of "The Artist of the Beautiful." On October 7, Hawthorne compared man's "finest workmanship" to Nature's superior craft (*Notebooks* 157–158). On October 16, Hawthorne noted: "a person to spend all his life and splendid talents in trying to achieve something naturally impossible" (*Notebooks* 165). In 1839 Hawthorne was more specific: "to represent a man as spending life and the intensest labor in the accomplishment of some mechanical trifle" (*Notebooks* 185).

2. For this story Newman cites an October 25, 1836, entry and a March 16, 1849, entry (292). In 1836 Hawthorne contemplated "a boyish combat with snowballs, and the victorious leader to have a statue of snow erected to him" (*Notebooks* 29); in 1849 he wrote "the same children who make the little snow-girl shall plant dry sticks etc., and they shall take root and grow; immortal flowers etc." (*Notebooks* 287).

Works Cited

Abel, Darrel. *The Moral Picturesque: Studies in Hawthorne's Fiction*. West Lafayette, Indiana: Purdue University Press, 1988.

Baym, Nina. *The Shape of Hawthorne's Career*. Ithaca: Cornell University Press, 1976.

Bell, Millicent. *Hawthorne's View of the Artist*. New York University Publishers, Inc., 1962.

Bercovitch, Sacvan. *The Office of the Scarlet Letter*. Baltimore: Johns Hopkins Press, 1991.

Charvat, William et al., eds. *Mosses from an Old Manse*. By Nathaniel Hawthorne. *The Centenary Edition of the Works of Nathaniel Hawthorne*. Vol. X. Columbus: Ohio State University Press, 1974.

———. *The Scarlet Letter*. By Nathaniel Hawthorne. *The Centenary Edition of the Works of Nathaniel Hawthorne*. Vol. I. Columbus: Ohio State University Press, 1962.

———. *The Snow-Image and Uncollected Tales*. By Nathaniel Hawthorne. *The Centenary Edition of the Works of Nathaniel Hawthorne*. Vol. XI. Columbus: Ohio State University Press, 1974.

MacDonald, John J. "The Old Manse Period Canon." *Nathaniel Hawthorne Journal* 2 (1972): 13–39.

Matthiessen, F. O. *American Renaissance: Art and Expression in the Age of Emerson and Whitman*. New York: Oxford University Press, 1941.

Miller, Edwin Haviland. *Salem Is My Dwelling Place: A Life of Nathaniel Hawthorne*. Iowa City: University of Iowa Press, 1991.

Millington, Richard. *Practicing Romance: Narrative Form and Cultural Engagement in Hawthorne's Fiction*. Princeton: Princeton University Press, 1992.

Newman, Lea. *A Reader's Guide to the Short Stories of Nathaniel Hawthorne*. Boston: G. K. Hall, 1979.

Quirk, Tom. "Hawthorne's Last Tales and 'The Custom-House.'" *ESQ: A Journal of the American Renaissance* 30.4 (1984): 220–231.

Simpson, Claude M., ed. *The American Notebooks*. By Nathaniel Hawthorne. *The Centenary Edition of the Works of Nathaniel Hawthorne*. Vol. VIII. Columbus: Ohio State University Press, 1972.

Woodson, Thomas et al. *The Letters, 1843–1853*. By Nathaniel Hawthorne. *The Centenary Edition of the Works of Nathaniel Hawthorne*. Vol. XVI. Columbus: Ohio State University Press, 1985.

Hawthorne and Nineteenth-Century Perfectionism

Claudia D. Johnson

A "combination of seventeenth-century Puritanism and nineteenth-century progressivism"—Claudia D. Johnson's short phrase may sum up Hawthorne's central concerns as well as any such formulation. In this essay, Johnson finds the most important point of contact between these two worlds in the doctrine of "perfectionism," a system of religious thought championed by Thomas C. Upham, one of Hawthorne's professors at Bowdoin College.

"Perfectionism" isn't freedom from evil; for Hawthorne, as for most orthodox Christians, humanity is inescapably sinful. But neither does the perfectionist unquestioningly accept the Calvinist conception of predestination, in which human effort has no place. Johnson identifies three aspects to moral perfection, which are summed up in three propositions: love is the motive force; the perfect man lives in this world, rather than the next, and achieves a kind of union with the world; and the perfectionist is active rather than passive. These propositions can be seen in both *The Scarlet Letter* and *The House of the Seven Gables*, but they appear most clearly in Hawthorne's tale "The Haunted Mind."

In love, in engagement with the world, and in active virtue, Johnson argues, Hawthorne finds a way to transcend the gloomy inwardness that so often marked Puritan thought and so often weighed on Hawthorne's own mind. "Only when he faced the awful truth that he was the worst of sinners," Johnson argues, "could he begin to grow in love. Man's ultimate concern, however, could not continue to be his own soul nor his own salvation in the hereafter, but the well-being of his brothers on this earth."   — J.L.

One of the most prominent members of the Bowdoin College faculty at the time of Nathaniel Hawthorne's attendance was a young philosopher-psychologist named Thomas C. Upham. Horatio Bridge, Hawthorne's college classmate and friend, remembered Upham, who was Professor of Moral and Mental Philosophy during their senior year, as "young, scholarly, gentle, and kind to the students, by all of whom he was much beloved."[1] A few critics have speculated about the influence of Upham's theory of trifaculty psychology on Hawthorne,[2] but another of Upham's convictions, on which he wrote a number of books, has received almost no attention. This was the doctrine of Christian perfection for which Upham, in his day, was as well known as for his psychological theories. The very word, "perfection," however, connotes a belief so far removed from the dark vision of Nathaniel Hawthorne as to render absurd any consideration of the writer's relationship to the doctrine.[3] The word leads one to think that the advocates of perfectionism thought that, after having been made "perfect," the heart was free from evil. Nothing, however, could be further from the truth. Thomas Upham, Charles G. Finney, John Humphrey Noyes, and other perfectionists were as thoroughly convinced of the evil of the heart as were their Puritan forebears. The journals and the memoirs of perfectionists disclose that their knowledge of the heart's evil came from painful personal experiences. Like John Humphrey Noyes, they were very much aware of "the labyrinth of iniquity" at the bottom of the heart.[4]

Like the Puritans, perfectionists believed that man is, by nature, sinful and requires regeneration. Unlike those early Calvinists, however, the perfectionists taught that after conversion man could experience a second stage of religious growth when he would, for a second time, be the recipient of God's grace. At this time he was "perfected" by partaking of God's love which "purified" his inclinations. Even after purification, however, evil was a powerful force in the perfect man's heart. Noyes, who had an immense impact on nineteenth-century Protestantism through the circulation of *The Perfectionist*, was convinced that being purified in heart did not exempt one from inner experiences with evil. Evil was a part of the carnal self which would not be lost until the body died, and forces of good and evil would war within even a perfect man until he died. One needed only to look at the tempted Christ to understand this warfare:

> Our theory of Christian life, while it equips the spiritual soldier with a pure heart and a good conscience at the outset, nevertheless does not discharge him from service. To *keep* his heart pure and his conscience good, in the midst of a world of pollution and accusation . . .will cost him many and sore conflicts with his own corrupted propensities, and with "principalities and powers, and spiritual wickedness in high places."[5]

Thomas Upham in *The Interior Life* also warned that evil would be an even greater force within the soul of the perfected man than it was in other men:

> Thou hast contended with Satan, and hast been successful. Thou hast fought with him, and he has fled from thee. But, O, remember his artifices. Do not indulge the belief that his nature is changed. True, indeed, he is now very complacent and is, perhaps, singing thee some syren song; but he was never more a devil than he is now.[6]

Even though evil would continue to fight within his soul, as long as love sustained the perfected man, he had reason to hope that his victories over evil would be assured. In short, the doctrine of perfectionism was in no sense the conviction that the soul could reach a stage in which it was free from the experience of evil.

This clarification of the perfectionists' beliefs about the evil of the heart, which, contrary to what the term may suggest, is not so radically different from Hawthorne's view, may serve to open for consideration the relationship of Hawthorne to this vital and far-reaching nineteenth-century Protestant movement.

Upham and his fellow perfectionists insisted on three essential characteristics of the perfected man which are relevant to Hawthorne's themes: man had to be guided by love, the transforming principle in the life of the perfected man; he had to live in this life rather than for the hereafter; and he had to be active rather than passive. The perfectionist taught that love was the transforming power of the soul, the indwelling principle which caused the old man locked in inwardness to emerge reborn. Love displaced selfish pride and united men. It propelled a perfected man into the world: perfectionism, by definition, meant the state of man in *this life*, not in the hereafter. One of the Methodist perfectionists, William Arthur, goes so far as to label a man's concern for his salvation as a selfish perversion of the gospel.[7]

Just as love drew the good man into this world, it necessarily drew him into fellowship with other men. It made a life of solitude impossible. Introspection was a stage in Christian development, but to prolong seclusion was to be caught in the dead end of selfishness. Asa Mahan, the perfectionist president of Oberlin College, called such inwardness "spiritual paralysis."[8] In Thomas Upham's comments on isolating inwardness one sees the expression of a theme which would be persistently repeated in the works of Nathaniel Hawthorne:

> A being who is supremely selfish is necessarily miserable. . . . Instead of the principle of unity, which tends to oneness of purpose with other beings, and naturally leads to happiness, he has within him the principle of exclusion and of eternal separation. In its ultimate operation, if it is permitted permanently to exist, it necessarily drives him from everything else, and wedges him closer and closer in the compressed circumference of his own personality. . . . This is the true hell and everlasting fire.[9]

The perfect man, therefore, had to ascend from inwardness to union with the world. The man of God who failed in this union abdicated a profound Christian duty, according to Upham:

> The mind, separated from the bonds which link it to others, and falling back upon itself, as both centre and circumference, becomes contracted in the range of its action, and selfish in its tendencies.[10]

Perfectionist doctrine not only insisted upon fellowship in the world, it demanded action in the world. Passivity was a characteristic of the initial religious experience of introspection, but a Christian must move from the passive to an active state. Love, again, was the compelling force. Charles G. Finney, the most prominent evangelist of the second great awakening and an Oberlin perfectionist, wrote of the perfect man:

> ... the intellectual perceptions never sink so low as to leave benevolence to become a stagnant pool. It is never sluggish, never inactive. . . . It is essential activity itself.[11]

Thus, the good man, according to the perfectionist doctrine, followed a definite mythic development. In order to be converted, he descended into the depths of his heart as the Puritans had taught that he must. After having received a clear view of his sins, he was converted. But a man could become entrapped and poisoned in this pious, passive introspection if he were not moved by love. If he were guided by love, he would ascend from inwardness to an active existence on the earth among his fellow human beings. Thomas Upham's student, Nathaniel Hawthorne, saw the perils and possibilities of man in just such terms.

"The Haunted Mind," Hawthorne's sketch of the progress of the mind which descends into inwardness and emerges renewed, mirrors the perfectionists' values as well as their concept of man's spiritual development. In this early sketch, a dreamer in repose isolates himself from the realities of the world in order to descend into his heart, which he subsequently comes to know as an infernal region outside of time, outside of nature, and outside of society, "where the business of life does not intrude" (p. 343).[12] The bed into which the dreamer sinks in "conscious sleep," is no less than a cozy womb until the thought of death breaks in to remind him that the components of this inward world—timelessness, lifelessness, inaction, and isolation—are also the components of death. As he sinks deeper into the tomb of the heart, he is accosted by fiends of his own making and comes to know that to remain forever in this inward inferno is to live forever with fiends. The everyday materials of the real world—book, table, letter—and the influence of love bring the dreamer back to the living world which is now presented in pictures of "gladsomeness and beauty" (p. 348), the last of which is "a brilliant circle of a crowded theatre . . ." (p. 348). Thus the moral history of man's descent and rebirth, as it is portrayed in "The Haunted Mind," is almost identical to that outlined by nineteenth-century perfectionists.

Furthermore, the vision of Hawthorne's major tales and romances is basically perfectionistic in that his characters are measured against the perfectionist possibility. In a few instances his characters reach a greater humanity than they have known before as love displaces self, action displaces inaction, and social concern displaces egoistic isolation. More often, however, his characters fail to ascend from that inwardness which Upham called "a true hell."

Although Hawthorne was strongly convinced that the man who would be regenerated must make a descent into the tomb of the heart, he, like the perfectionists, was just as strongly convinced of the dangers of sustained inwardness. It is not surprising that his characteristic protagonist in the tales is a man who remains in an inner hell, unable to pronounce his brotherhood with other men or to join them in a common struggle. Goodman Brown, the Reverend Hooper, Wakefield, Richard Digby, Adam Coburn, and Roderick Elliston are the protagonists who best exemplify the perfectionist pattern, albeit in Hawthorne's largely negative fashion.

These protagonists are caught in a stage of development which the perfectionists called the descent into the heart. Because each of them meditates within the circle of his own ego, he is removed from the larger world of human society and human passions. The man of adamant physically leaves his village and, shutting himself away in a cave, an image of his own heart, contemplates his righteousness in an evil society. Adam Coburn deserts the village to find shelter in a sect which turns its back on the world and human nature; Wakefield steps aside "from the main business of his life" (p. 163) to seclude himself in disguise; and Goodman Brown leaves his wife and his village not just for a night, but for a lifetime. The Reverend Hooper's veil and Roderick Elliston's bosom serpent are symbolic of the dark obsessive visions which separate them from other men. Neither love nor sympathy touches the Reverend Hooper in his "true hell": "With self-shudderings and outward terrors, he walked continually in its shadow, groping darkly within his own soul . . ." (p. 65). Roderick, too, lives without the love of friends, wife, or God: "Not merely the eye of man was a horror to him; not merely the light of a friend's countenance; but even the blessed sunshine, likewise, which in its universal beneficence typifies the radiance of the Creator's face, expressing his love for all the creatures of his hand" (p. 307). Wakefield, in deserting his wife, loses his place in the universe.

The alternative to gloomy inwardness in each of these tales is the love of a woman who is capable of drawing the self-directed soul back into human society. The Reverend Hooper, however, refuses to lift his veil in order to love Elizabeth. It must always separate him from the world and from love. Richard Digby disregards all of Mary Goffe's pleas that he return with her to the village. Adam Coburn withdraws his hand from Martha's in "satisfied ambition" (p. 476) as he chooses to be a Shaker leader and a brother instead of a lover and father. Although Goodman Brown returns to Faith, he "looked sternly and sadly into her face, and passed on without a greeting" (p. 205). Of these men, only Roderick Elliston is happily reunited with his wife and the society from which he had separated himself.

Like the nineteenth-century perfectionists, Hawthorne often compares the achievement of a higher humanity to growing up, a metaphor which is central to his first two major novels, *The Scarlet Letter* and *The House of the Seven Gables*. The unregenerate man who lingers in inwardness is like a child whose only world is himself, whose primary interest is attending to his own wants, who feels little responsibility for those other than himself, and who, as a stranger in the larger world, sacrifices almost nothing of himself to it.

Indeed, in both of these novels the principal settings suggest the childlike dependency of the characters. The society created by the Puritan elders in *The Scarlet Letter* and the ancestral home place of *The House of the Seven Gables* are both paternalistic shelters from the larger world and reflections of the decay and gloom of the characters who live in them. The most prominent landmarks of the Puritan community are the scaffold, the prison, and the cemetery. The community's most prominent members are stern and somber old men who are incapable of "sitting in judgment on an erring woman's heart and disentangling its mesh of good and evil . . ." (p. 64). The ordinary citizens remain children in this oligarchy.

Dimmesdale is a child not only in his dependence upon the Puritan elders and in his rejection of fatherhood, but in his failure to emerge from the closed circle of his own heart. He is a striking example of the self-centered, unperfected man as he is described on the scaffold under cover of darkness:

> In such a case, it could only be the symptom of a highly disordered mental state when a man, rendered morbidly self-contemplative by long, intense, and secret pain, had extended his egotism over the whole expanse of nature until the firmament itself should appear no more than a fitting page for his soul's history and fate. (p. 155)

Hester also knows years of despairing self-contemplation, pride, and self-deception but, in contrast to Dimmesdale, the love which she feels for him and for Pearl turns her affections outward and enables her not only to endure, but eventually to mature into a stronger and more productive member of human society. After she returns to the place of her ignominy to take up the letter humbly and of her own free will, her acts of charity grow from love rather than from concern for her own salvation:

And, as Hester Prynne had no selfish ends, nor lived in any measure for her own profit and enjoyment, people brought all their sorrows and perplexities, and besought her counsel, as one who had herself gone through a mighty trouble. (p. 263)

In short, despite her inescapable gloom, she comes to possess those traits by which the perfected human being was identified.

A similar pattern discloses the values of perfectionism in *The House of the Seven Gables*, where the inhabitants of the patriarchal shelter remain children, each largely wrapped up in his own world, unacquainted with anything outside that world, and unable to act in it. For all of her life Hepzibah has hidden away in her father's house like a child. Because she has never before "put forth her hand to help herself" (p. 52), she is as clumsy as an infant in setting up her shop, in keeping her house, and in trying to establish a relationship with the everyday world of the street beside her house. Clifford, too, is a child devoid of judgment, overwhelmed by his immature emotions, and absorbed almost entirely in himself. Holgrave, although he does not fit the metaphor of immature child as clearly as Clifford and Hepzibah do, is, nonetheless, unregenerate in that he is largely loveless, egoistic, and ill at ease in the world. He has wandered, homeless, from place to place, from profession to profession, unwilling to become sufficiently involved with his fellow creatures "to help or hinder" (p. 216), but only to observe and analyze them.

Phoebe, on the other hand, lives harmoniously with a world in which she is productive and orderly. Shop-keeping and house-keeping are not mysteries to her, and she is capable of giving her love to the unlovely Hepzibah and Clifford. She represents the agency of love which embodies active commerce with the greater world beyond the self.

The issues which occupied perfectionists continued to be apparent in Hawthorne's last major novels. Miles Coverdale is the chief illustration of the unregenerate or unperfected man in *The Blithedale Romance*. His inaction, his preference for the spiritual, and his obsession with the lives of his friends betray a failure to ascend to the living world. The leafy cave to which he retreats during his Blithedale stay is symbolic of the state of his soul. He is persistently guided by cold curiosity and self-interest rather than by love, and he fittingly ends his life as an unproductive writer and lonely bachelor. Hollingsworth, by contrast, is able to break the circle of his egoistic obsession and to begin reforming himself with the help of Priscilla, his link with the world.

The perfectionistic values which had been the basis for Hawthorne's tales and novels are, in *The Marble Faun*, formulated explicitly as myth in the history of the Monte Benis. The characters in this last major novel are measured against the perfectionist possibility of gaining greater humanity. As the novel opens, each of the four characters is in a state of withdrawal from the active, time-affected world, out of touch with society, and out of sympathy with other people: Donatello in his Arcadia is too animalistic to be called fully human; Hilda lives in an angel's untouchable world; Miriam broods in the dark cave of bitterness; and Kenyon lives in the cold marble world of art. Each must, if he is to reach a higher form of being, first enter a period of self-scrutiny, become fully aware of his own ignominy, and, as Donatello finally does, emerge from inwardness to commit himself in love to other mortals.

After he has committed murder, Donatello begins to brood about the ugliness and mortality of his soul. It is Kenyon who warns him of the dangers of sustained inwardness:

> "Believe me," said he, turning his eyes upon his friend, full of grave and tender sympathy, "you know not what is requisite for your spiritual growth, seeking, as you do, to keep your soul perpetually in the unwholesome region of remorse. It was needful for you to pass through that dark valley, but it is infinitely dangerous to linger there too long; there is poison in the atmosphere, when we sit down and brood in it, instead of girding up our loins to press onward." (p. 273)

In order to grow, the soul must take a new direction. The perfectionist hope of a greater life for a man who dedicates himself in love to humankind is reflected by Kenyon and then by the narrator as they anticipate Donatello's emergence from remorse. Kenyon advises him to avoid the life of seclusion and to make his new life among men:

> "But, for my own part, if I had an insupportable burthen—if, for any cause, I were bent upon sacrificing every earthly hope as a peace-offering towards Heaven—I would make the wide world my cell, and good deeds to mankind my prayer." (p. 267)

Donatello seems to respond to Kenyon's humanism:

> . . . when first the idea was suggested of living for the welfare of his fellow-creatures, the original beauty, which sorrow had partly effaced, came back elevated and spiritualized. In the black depths, the Faun had found a soul, and was struggling with it towards the light of heaven. (p. 268)

That Donatello does eventually achieve what the perfectionists would call a higher humanity is supported by the growth of a mature love for Miriam and by the awakening of a moral sense which leads him to deliver himself up to the world for judgment.

Thus from the earliest published tales to the last major novel, Hawthorne demonstrated that he shared with nineteenth-century perfectionists a timeless moral concern, which had caught the attention of his Puritan ancestors, of how man rises above his natural state to a finer humanity, a greater manhood. Like both Puritan and perfectionist, Hawthorne believed that it was necessary for man to begin by making a journey into his own foul heart. Only when he faced the awful truth that he was the worst of sinners could he begin to grow in love. Man's ultimate concern, however, could not continue to be his own soul nor his own salvation in the hereafter, but the well-being of his brothers on this earth. The arrow of his soul's compass had to be moved outward by love rather than inward, for although contemplation and seclusion were necessary stages in man's development, the complete man had to emerge from seclusion to become an active participant in society. The Hawthornian character who fails to emerge continues to be obsessed and bedeviled. The possibility of regeneration is usually represented by the love of a woman who is invariably a link with society.

Hawthorne found these concerns interesting and useful to the end of his life because he was both Puritan and democrat, convinced of the dangerous inner hell of the soul at the same time that he was caught up in the high possibilities of nineteenth-century society, and because he could not dismiss either the past or the present, either the light or the dark of human nature.

The combination of seventeenth-century Puritanism and nineteenth-century progressivism, which has confused or intrigued Hawthorne's critics, is no other than the religious mind of the age as it was mirrored in the perfectionism of Hawthorne's Bowdoin professor, Thomas C. Upham, and others. Both recognized the dark, forbidden mystery of the soul below, which had to be experienced and transcended in love, and the active, growing world of human relationships above, in which salvation had to be achieved.

From *American Literature* 44, no. 4 (January, 1973): 585-595. Copyright © 1973 by Duke University Press. Reprinted by permission of Duke University Press

Notes

1. Horatio Bridge, *Personal Recollections of Nathaniel Hawthorne* (New York, 1893), p. 53.

2. Marvin Laser, "'Head,' 'Heart,' and 'Will' in Hawthorne's Psychology," *Nineteenth-Century Fiction*, X (Sept., 1955), 130–136; Leon Howard, *Literature and the American Tradition* (New York, 1960), p. 122; Joseph Schwartz, "A Note on Hawthorne's Fatalism," *Modern Language Notes*, LXX (Jan., 1955), 33–36. Laser and Howard cite the influence of Upham's trifaculty psychology on Hawthorne's work. Schwartz makes the point that the insistence of Hawthorne's educators, including Upham, on freedom of the will contributed to his rejection of orthodox fatalism.

3. Merle Curti, "Human Nature in American Thought," *Political Science Quarterly*, LXVIII (Sept., 1953), 354–375; Joseph Schwartz, "Nathaniel Hawthorne, 1804–1864: God and Man in New England," *American Classics Reconsidered*, edited by Harold C. Gardiner, S.J. (New York, 1958), p. 141. These two critics reflect the tendency to ignore or to misrepresent perfectionism. Although Schwartz is aware of Upham's influence, he fails to take perfectionism into account, saying only that Hawthorne had no sympathy with the *Unitarian* idea of "human perfectability." Curti concludes, presumably because Upham was a perfectionist, that he had no sense, as did Hawthorne, of the profound depths of evil in the heart.

The summary of perfectionist doctrine in this paper is made on the basis of primary readings in the following nineteenth-century perfectionist literature: William Arthur, *The Tongue of Fire* (Toronto, 1857); Jeremy Boyton, *Sanctification Practical* (New York, 1867); J. T. Crane, *Holiness* (New York, 1875); Charles G. Finney, *Attributes of Love: A Section From Lectures on Systematic Theology* (Minneapolis, 1963) and *Memoirs* (New York, 1876); R. S. Foster, *Christian Purity* (New York, 1869); Asa Mahan, *Out of Darkness Into Light* (New York, 1876); John Humphrey Noyes, *Religious Experiences of John Humphrey Noyes* (New York, 1923) and *Salvation From Sin* (Wallingford, Conn., 1866); Phoebe Palmer, *Present to My Christian Friend* (New York, 1853); Thomas C. Upham, *Treatise on Divine Union* (Boston, 1857); *Principles of the Interior or Hidden Life* (New York, 1843), and *Life of Faith* (New York, 1845).

4. Noyes, "Journal Entry, July 25," *The Religious Experiences of John Humphrey Noyes*, pp. 47–48.

5. Noyes, *Salvation From Sin*, p. 394.

6. Upham, *The Interior Life*, p. 394.

7. Arthur, p. 129.

8. Mahan, p. 117.

9. Upham, *The Interior Life*, p. 118.

10. Ibid., p. 193.

11. Finney, *Attributes of Love*, pp. 110–111.

12. Quotations from Hawthorne's short stories are taken from *The Complete Works of Nathaniel Hawthorne* (New York, Sully and Kleinteich, 1882, 1883). Quotations from the novels are taken from *The Centenary Edition of the Works of Nathaniel Hawthorne*.

Progress and Providence in
*The House of the Seven Gables*_____

John Gatta, Jr.

The happy ending of *The House of the Seven Gables* has baffled many readers. Did the usually gloomy Hawthorne really see some kind of redemption in the marriage of Pyncheon and Maule? Has the curse been lifted, and have the characters somehow achieved a kind of progress? Or are we meant to read the end ironically, suspicious of the narrator's claims?

In this essay, John Gatta, Jr. argues that our difficulties with the happy ending may be a product of our modern sensibility—we're unable to "understand or appreciate that brighter side of Hawthorne's divided sensibility." He therefore tries to recover nineteenth-century conceptions of progress, and uses them as a background against which to read Hawthorne's romance. Gatta is sensitive to the complexity of the question, aware that progress is no simple matter. He in fact sees three distinct kinds of progress: individual moral and spiritual progress; the public or social progress of the nation; and a kind of religious progress toward apocalypse that "amounts to a teleological drama of redemption."

Behind these notions of progress is the idea of Providence. Noah Webster, Hawthorne's older contemporary and fellow Yankee, defined the word in his *American Dictionary of the English Language* (1828) as "the care and superintendence which God exercises over his creatures," adding that "He that acknowledges a creation and denies a *providence*, involves himself in a palpable contradiction." But Hawthorne knew that accepting Providence could produce just as many contradictions as denying it, and in his works he explores these tensions. Many of Hawthorne's characters, and sometimes Hawthorne himself, question Providence, trying to understand the relationship between the divine plan and human effort.   — J.L.

The prosperous conclusion of *The House of the Seven Gables* would seem to suggest that there is nothing so permanently forbidding about an ancestral curse, or even perhaps about that more ancient human curse of Original Sin, that the combined benefits of money, marriage, and a new house in the country cannot solve. True, it is possible to read Hawthorne's ending ironically—or to recognize, at least, that the monetary fortune bestowed so abruptly on the former tenants of the rusty old house may be an inevitable source of future *mis*fortune. But there can be little doubt that the essential shape of this book is progressive and optimistic. Not only does the marital union between Pyncheon and Maule end a cycle of persecution and retribution that has prolonged itself through a century and a half of New England history, but the spiritual forces of good—in particular, the frankness and rejuvenating sunshine of Phoebe—score in the end a clear if less than total triumph over the forces of evil, represented in the villainy and false smiles of Jaffrey Pyncheon.

Still, it is not easy to say exactly what sort of progress this movement is supposed to imply. What larger prospects for social and historical amelioration might Hawthorne want us to see in the communal regeneration that finally takes place in Salem in 1850, issuing forth symbolically from Maule's Well in the Pyncheon garden? Should we translate the fortunate progression of the story's plot into a statement about the progress of Jeffersonian democracy in America? Or is Hawthorne tracing instead a moral and material progress dictated by the rational secular temper of the Enlightenment, or the social progress of humanity in proto-Darwinian evolutionary terms? Each of these readings has had its proponents;[1] but deciding upon the nature of the progress Hawthorne dramatizes is only part of the problem. Assuming that history is moving somewhere, in some sense, one is still perplexed by the book's contradictory suggestions about the figure that best represents this progress. Is the underlying pattern of history to be understood as a nonprogressive circle, as an ascending straight line, or, as Clifford argues at one point, as an ascending spiral curve? Finally, one is led to ask where Hawthorne located the effective cause of whatever human progress he might have been willing to believe in. Can men and women themselves act as principal or assisting agents, either through social reform movements or other means, to transform the social order they inhabit? Or must any essential improvement in society and its institutions wait upon the decrees of Fate or the providential design of an intelligent deity?

Particularly because of the variety of evidence available on Hawthorne's attitudes toward social-material progress and nineteenth-century social reform, one cannot hope to find a single, comprehensive answer to all of these questions without arriving at something as motley as Uncle Venner's suit of patchwork clothes. But neither is a single answer necessarily in order, for the author of *The House of the Seven Gables* seems to be meditating upon the problem of progress under three different ontological aspects. The romance is concerned, first of all, with charting the moral and spiritual progress of the individual human heart, particularly as the heart seeks to move toward a permanent, life-giving conjunction with "the magnetic chain of humanity." Second, the book implies, within the extended time-frame of its plot, an evaluation of the direction—and progress, if any—of public, social history in America. And finally, on a mythopoeic level that is not always rendered believable, Hawthorne's story amplifies traditional apocalyptic imagery of light, garden, tree, and wedlock to shadow forth what amounts to a teleological drama of redemption. The three sorts of progress to be distinguished, then, have to do, first, with the personal, individual history of the self; second, with social history; and third, with a transhistorical, figurative level of narrative recognizable in traditional Christian terms as sacred or visionary history. If there is any final term of causality linking together all three notions of progress, the word that the romance itself suggests, and a word that occurs often in Hawthorne, is "Providence." A belief in Providence, in the ever mysterious but ultimately benevolent designs of a hidden God, was one of the few points of Christian theology to which Hawthorne himself gave fairly explicit credal assent.[2] But whatever one wants to say about the author's personal religious beliefs, the idea of Providence can explain a good deal about the structure and ordering of his narrative and stands in this book as the final measure against which all progress must be judged.

In relating the moral and spiritual progress of the individual, Hawthorne would inevitably look to a favorite story of his, John Bunyan's classic allegory on the Pilgrim's Progress, for his metaphorical model. Bunyan's tale is alluded to more than once in the romance, as when Clifford marvels in an ironic context over the railroad's ability to eliminate "the toil and dust of pilgrimage." The progress of the pilgrim is associated with a route that, instead of pressing steadily upward or completing a perfect circle to reach its end, leads horizontally through the center of life and its assorted obstacles. Thus Phoebe expresses temporary fears that a marriage with Holgrave might deflect her from a settled path of peregrination, might lead her away from her "own quiet path" to "where it is pathless."[3] But Clifford and Hepzibah are the ones who must travel furthest in their attempts to progress inwardly from isolation and inner desolation to communion and trust.

At least two of Hawthorne's incomplete pilgrims, Holgrave and Hepzibah, show some capacity to take an active part in their own journeys toward self-recovery. Holgrave, despite his inclination toward analytic detachment, consciously resists the temptation to gain psychic control over Phoebe as one of his ancestors had done over Alice Pyncheon. Hepzibah, diminished and physically worn though she is at the start of the romance, still has the strength to resist her cousin Jaffrey and to persevere in her faltering attempts to extend charity within her narrow sphere. Holgrave praises her initiative in opening the cent-shop as "heroic," adding that "if the Pyncheons had always acted so nobly, I doubt whether the old wizard Maule's anathema . . . would have had much weight with Providence against them" (p. 45). But as the daguerreotypist's remark suggests, whatever personal progress the sympathetic characters may make through an individual assertion of will is wholly contingent upon advances made through the larger design of Providence. Phoebe, Hawthorne's practical embodiment of love and redemptive vigor, is obviously the principal agent of that design, particularly in relation to the helplessly passive Clifford. Holgrave explains the apparently chance arrival of Phoebe in other terms when he assures her that "Providence sent you hither to help" (p. 217), a judgment Hawthorne seems to confirm in his own authorial voice when he writes that Phoebe "felt bound to watch over, and be, as it were the Providence of . . . [Clifford's] unconsidered hours" (p. 219).

While it is an unmistakably beneficent Providence that brings Phoebe's sunlight to dispel the darkness of the old Pyncheon mansion, Hawthorne's story also illustrates the more mysterious, paradoxical workings of Providence. At the time Hepzibah has to open her cent shop for lack of funds, she is overcome with shame and trauma at her misfortune; but from a later perspective the incident seems Providentially fortunate, because through it she had first begun to set aside her aristocratic pride, to end her withdrawal from the world, and to join "'the united struggle of mankind'" (p. 45). So too, it is not immediately clear, even to Phoebe, how the recurrence of a bloody death can be anything but lamentable. "'And how,'" she asks, "'could any good come from what is so very dreadful?'" (p. 304). But as Holgrave explains, when the death in question is that of Judge Pyncheon, its peculiarly bloody mode is fortunate because it establishes Clifford's innocence in the previous case of his uncle Jaffrey. And of course the death itself offers kindly release to Clifford and Hepzibah, a release that follows paradoxically upon "five unkindly days" (p. 284) of seasonal storm.

The puzzling ways of Providence also present themselves in Hawthorne's portrayal of the Pyncheon mansion. Built upon greed and injustice, the House of the Seven Gables is in one sense a House of Pride where Clifford and Hepzibah are walled apart from the larger community. But descending into its inner reaches, one finds it is likewise a hopeful symbol suggesting the transformative potential of the human heart. By the same token, the loveliness of the white roses in the

Pyncheon garden arises out of "black, rich soil" produced by years of organic "decay" (p. 86). And though it is ironically true that the greedy schemes of Judge Pyncheon are the immediate cause of his cousin's release from prison, Hepzibah is in a more profound sense right to insist that Clifford owes his freedom not to the judge, but "to God's providence" (p. 233). Hawthorne hints that even Clifford's long imprisonment on false charges was not entirely without Providential benefit to its victim, since otherwise this man might have indulged his unbridled love of the beautiful to the point of becoming quite incapable of loving humanity: "Shall we venture to pronounce, therefore, that his long and black calamity may not have had a redeeming drop of mercy, at the bottom?" (p. 112).

To be sure, there are times when Hepzibah, Holgrave, Clifford, and even the implied author betray serious doubts about the ultimate wisdom and beneficence of Providence. The broken, frustrated life of Clifford provokes the author's most open confession of doubt: ". . . he was an example . . . of that great chaos of people, whom an inexplicable Providence is continually putting at cross-purposes with the world; breaking what seems its own promise in their nature; withholding their proper food, and setting poison before them for a banquet; and thus—when it might so easily, as one would think, have been adjusted otherwise—making their existence a strangeness, a solitude, and torment" (p. 149). Yet Hawthorne qualifies his questionings with phrases like "what seems its own promise" and "as one would think." For while some understanding of the operations of Providence may be gained in retrospect from experience, its inscrutable purpose cannot be identified with certainty at any given moment. Ironically, Hepzibah feels most convinced of the "chill indifference" of Providence toward her "little agonies" (p. 245) at the very moment when Jaffrey's death, as yet unknown to her, has just freed her from these agonies.

In fact, every critical turning point in the providentially ordered spiritual progress of Hawthorne's pilgrims coincides with circumstances of outward failure. Clifford first comes to "a touching recognition . . . of God's care and love towards him" and a "kindly affection for his human brethren" (pp. 167–168) in connection with his completely abortive attempt to escape the house with Hepzibah to attend Sabbath worship, and around the same time as his nearly disastrous attempt to throw himself out of the arched window into the society of the street. Ostensibly, the flight of Hepzibah and Clifford from the dead body of Jaffrey Pyncheon in Chapter 17 likewise accomplishes nothing; their train trip goes nowhere. But the emotionally climactic ending of the episode underscores the psychological and spiritual progress Hepzibah has managed to make to this point. Whereas previously she has tried to pray without success, now, as she kneels on the train platform in a chilly rain, the plea she is able to pour forth indicates her tentative recovery of trust in Providence.

Clearly, then, Hawthorne's romance affirms the reality—indeed, the necessity—of the individual pilgrim's progress. But the attitude it reflects toward the apparent progress of society and of secular history is considerably more ambiguous. Negatively, at least, one can point to certain interpretations of history, certain formulations of the relation between Providence and social-political change, that the author seems to reject. Thus, for the so-called "romantic historians" of the era—one thinks in particular of Hawthorne's sometime friend George Bancroft, whose work he had read—the moral and political progress of humanity as unfolded by Providence (a key term in Bancroft's vocabulary) could be readily observed in history, particularly in American history.[4] Hawthorne appears to endorse this melioristic optimism when he writes of "the great system of human progress, which, with every ascending footstep . . . may be destined gradually to spiritualize us" (p. 121). But the ironic burden of the passage as a whole is simply to point out that the latter-day Judge Pyncheon is slightly less beefy than his Puritan progenitor—while morally speaking, of course, no improvement at all can be traced from one to the other.

On a more serious level, Clifford does propose in his impassioned speech on the train that "all human progress is . . . in an ascending spiral curve" (p. 259), precisely the figure for human advance commonly set forth by the romantic historians.[5] But while we may applaud the flush of enthusiasm, the sense of active engagement with the world, that Clifford feels at the time, his "diseased and transitory" state of mind forbids us from equating his views with the author's. The book indicates some recognition of economic-historical progress as democratic principles advance and aristocratic privilege declines—but nothing like Bancroft's assurance that all history is visibly and irresistibly advancing under the direct influence of Providence. From Hawthorne's standpoint the Puritans, also, tended to make too familiar and direct an association between Providence and the progress of history, however much they may have spoken of "remarkable Providences" and an "inscrutable God."[6] For again, in the present historical dispensation one simply cannot deduce the intentions of Providence toward the City of Man with uniform accuracy, much less presume that those intentions will issue in uniform prosperity. Just so, in the final pages of the book a nameless passerby wonders why his wife only lost money keeping a cent-shop while Old Maid Pyncheon, after her short experiment in trade, is able to ride off with a couple of hundred thousand at least. "'If you choose to call it luck,'" he observes, "'it is all very well; but if we are to take it as the will of Providence, why, I can't exactly fathom it!'" (p. 318).

Yet when we come to the radical's conception of social progress, as reflected especially in the earlier attitudes of Holgrave, we find it no more generally acceptable to Hawthorne than the approaches of Bancroft or the Puritans. Holgrave, a highly sympathetic character by virtue of his integrity and forward-looking energy, is shown to be accurate in his perception of the many evils man inherits from the past, but misguided in his expectation that society can be wholly transformed within the immediate future. According to the author, the main "error" in Holgrave's early ideology "lay, in supposing that this age, more than any past or future one, is destined to see the tattered garments of Antiquity exchanged for a new suit, instead of gradually renewing themselves by patchwork; in applying his own little life-span as the measure of an interminable achievement; and, more than all, in fancying that it mattered anything to the great end in view, whether he himself should contend for it or against it" (p. 180).

So far the argument is simply that social-historical progress, if it exists, is gradual and brought about only by Providence toward some "great end," not at all through human effort. The extremity of the protest reminds us of the author's unpalatable suggestion in his campaign biography of Franklin Pierce (1852) that slavery is an evil that "divine Providence" must remedy "in its own good time," without benefit of "human contrivances."[7] But here he goes on to soften the quietistic tenor of his statement by granting that while Holgrave could do nothing in absolute terms to usher in the new era, "it was well for him to think so." In this way Holgrave could expect to strengthen his character in youth, while in later years "he would still have faith in man's brightening destiny, and perhaps love him all the better, as he should recognize his helplessness in his own behalf; and the haughty faith, with which he began life, would be well bargained for a far humbler one, at its close, in discerning that man's best-directed effort accomplishes a kind of dream, while God is the sole worker of realities" (p. 180).

With this last assertion, which is closely related to Hawthorne's well-known family saying that "Man's accidents are God's purposes,"[8] we arrive at the real heart of the matter. Individual attempts to do good or to carry out social reform cannot contribute in any absolute, autonomous way to remaking the world—least of all can they contribute in precisely the way their altruistic agents intend—and the radical reformers are wrong to imagine otherwise. But if human efforts are powerless in themselves to effect lasting progress, they can assist provisionally in the subtler plan of progress conceived by Providence. In fact, man is distinctly called to participate in realizing the progressive aims of Providence through a power imputed to him, and by his own co-operating yet contingent activity. Despite Hawthorne's fideistic conservatism, then, and the general skepticism toward social reform reflected in sketches like "Earth's Holocaust" and "The Celestial Railroad," his final view is not that of the cynic who would disallow any prospect for future societal reform. In other words, the occasional resemblance he sees between struggling humanity and those pantomime figures on the Italian's barrel-organ, both alike caught in a cycle of meaningless repetition wherein we "all dance to one identical tune, and, in spite of our ridiculous activity, bring nothing finally to pass" (p. 163), is never embraced as a final truth. Yet he is unwilling to specify what shape the collective progress of mankind might now be assuming.

For it is only at the level of sacred or visionary history, what we have indicated as a third level of Hawthorne's narrative, that the teleological progress of the race is assured. Meanwhile, in their experimental attempts to create an ideal society, the communitarian reformers of Hawthorne's day—including his own sister-in-law, Elizabeth Peabody—were proclaiming the imminent realization of the Kingdom of God on earth.[9] But read in the same theological terms, Hawthorne's book insists that the Kingdom cannot be brought visibly to birth in society through deliberate human exertion. Instead its progressive emergence in the world is secret, invisible, coexistent with the seemingly more substantial stuff of fallen human history. For Hawthorne the eternal essence of the spiritual Kingdom is paradoxically here already and not here yet—but it is never to be glimpsed through the unworthy eyes of a Jaffrey Pyncheon.

Accordingly, the visual descriptions in *The House of the Seven Gables* offer a persistent contrast between outer surface and inner substance. Outwardly, Judge Pyncheon embodies strength and solidity while Clifford is shadowy and unsubstantial. Yet as Holgrave's truth-seeking pictures reveal, the hidden spiritual and imaginative capacities of Clifford are ultimately more real, more potent, than the massive pretensions of Jaffrey.[10] An ironic opposition between outward physical appearance and inner truth is likewise implied in the contrast between

Hepzibah's near-sighted frown, which covers a charitable disposition, and the beaming smile of Jaffrey, which masks a malicious intent. But the author grants that perceiving the hidden spiritual "marble" of visionary history amid the more familiar "mud" (p. 41) of secular history can be an awesome challenge, even if one looks to those "higher hopes" (p. 313) beyond earthly woe and tries to maintain "all the deeper trust in a comprehensive sympathy above us" (p. 41).

That Hawthorne did see the underground stream of sacred history progressing toward a final apocalyptic fulfillment is indicated above all, however, in the post-millennial-apocalyptic imagery that threatens to overwhelm the end of his story. Here a "mystic" branch of the Pyncheon elm in Old Salem is transmuted to "bright gold" (p. 285)—reminding us, among other things, of the pure, transparent gold that will constitute the New Jerusalem; while the tree itself whispers "unintelligible prophecies" (p. 319). Alice Pyncheon's posies return to full bloom—"a mystic expression that something within the house was consummated" (p. 286); and the spirit of Alice seems to float heavenward to the accompaniment of musical strains from her harpsichord. But the central sign of an apocalyptic climax, especially when we recall the cosmic marriage celebrated in the Book of Revelation, is the alliance between Holgrave and Phoebe as discussed in almost visionary terms.[11] For one enchanted moment, anyway, the couple is supposedly able to throw off the dead weight of time, which has dominated the judge's "vigil" in Chapter 18, and enter a realized state of eschatology in which "Immortality is revealed anew, and embraces everything" (p. 307). Clearly Hawthorne fastens his attention upon Phoebe in particular as something of a female savior, as the Incarnation of a transcendent religious principle of redemptive love.[12] In contrast to the false spiritualism of the mesmerist, her angelic presence presumably represents man's only true access to "the spiritual world" (p. 206). Hawthorne testifies to the "spiritual force" (p. 137) by which she brings Clifford and Hepzibah back into the "sympathetic chain of human nature," and even goes so far as to call her "a Religion in herself" (p. 168). "She was real!" (p. 141), he declares, and indeed for him she was not only a real tribute to his wife Sophia but a token of all that was most real, beyond the shifting illusions of experience.

But that is not to say she ever becomes quite real for the reader, or that the religious language surrounding Hawthorne's expression of his ideals in this book is ever quite free of pious sentimentality. Unfortunately, Hawthorne did not entirely succeed in his attempt to fuse the visionary dimension of his tale, particularly its favorably apocalyptic conclusion, with a portrayal of present-day life in Salem. Evidently he believed in his ending, as he did in Phoebe, since for him they were a figurative testimony to the reality of Providential involvement in the individual pilgrim's progress as well as in the transhistorical spiritual progress of the human community. Artistically, though, one is troubled by a disparity between the book's figural intention and its fictive execution, a fault too serious to be healed by invoking the special privileges of the symbolic romancer.

Perhaps Hawthorne erred in trying to superimpose an ideal, visionary narrative upon a temporal plot too clumsy and melodramatic to sustain such a purpose. No doubt Shakespeare's *Tempest*, a tragicomedy similarly governed by the superintending influence of "providence divine," reaches closer to artistic perfection, though this work achieves its visionary resolution on an imaginary island, whereas Hawthorne's book is committed in advance to holding its footing in the "actual soil of the County of Essex." But if the modern reader is inclined to scoff at the implausibility of Hawthorne's ending, part of the failure may lie, as some critics have argued, in our own inability *as* moderns to understand or appreciate that brighter side of Hawthorne's divided sensibility which he declared more characteristic of his nature. And still another reason for our perception of failure—this romance of Hawthorne's representing, in any case, a success or failure of the highest significance—probably has to do with limitations inherent in any author's use of language and metaphor. Not even the author of the Book of Revelation, perhaps the most bizarre and influential of all progressive chronicles, could describe the spiritual glories of the New Heaven and New Earth without resorting to pictures of material wealth— appeals far more glittering and opulent than Hawthorne's ingenuous report of the wealth regained by his New England saints at the close of *The House of the Seven Gables.*

From *American Literature* 50, no. 1 (March, 1978): 37-48. Copyright © 1978 by Duke University Press. Reprinted by permission of Duke University Press

Notes

1. A fair representation of the variety of past responses would include Lawrence S. Hall, *Hawthorne: Critic of Society* (New Haven, Conn., 1944), pp. 160–167; Marius Bewley, *The Eccentric Design* (New York, 1959), pp. 175–183; F. O. Matthiessen, *American Renaissance* (New York, 1941), pp. 316–344; and Roy R. Male, *Hawthorne's Tragic Vision* (Austin, Tex., 1957). Probably the most penetrating general analysis of the progress issue written to date, a reading to which mine is much indebted, is Hyatt Waggoner's in *Hawthorne: A Critical Study*, rev. ed. (Cambridge, Mass., 1963), pp. 160–187.

2. See Hubert Hoeltje, *Inward Sky: The Mind and Heart of Nathaniel Hawthorne* (Durham, N.C., 1962), pp. 460–461; supplemented by Leonard J. Fick, *The Light Beyond* (Westminster, Md., 1955); and Hyatt Waggoner, *Hawthorne*, esp. pp. 13–18, 28–29, and 248. Many critics, including Hoeltje, Randall Stewart, W. Stacy Johnson— and, more recently, Joseph Schwartz and Raymond Benoit—have tended to place Hawthorne in or near "the central catholic tradition of Christian humanism" (Waggoner's phrase), though with some disagreement about the specific content of his loosely formulated, presumably neoorthodox, faith. Dissenters from this view (see, for example, the complaints about "theologizing" regularly voiced by Nina Baym, most recently in her book, *The Shape of Hawthorne's Career*, Ithaca, N.Y., 1976, esp. pp. 9, 68–69, and 117–118) find in the imaginative writings a Hawthorne who is much less Christian than skeptic and secularist. One may argue, in any case, that the vocabulary and motivating suppositions of *The House of the Seven Gables* imply an authorial standpoint more openly Christian than that represented in some other Hawthorne works—even if the author's personal investment in credal faith at the time he was writing was no more than tentative or hypothetical.

3. *The House of the Seven Gables*, ed. Seymour L. Gross (New York, 1967), p. 306. All subsequent page references are to this edition, a convenient reprinting of the Ohio State Centenary Text.

4. See David Levin, *History as Romantic Art: Bancroft, Prescott, Motley, and Parkman* (Stanford, Calif., 1959), esp. pp. 25–45, 79–80; and Bancroft's *History of the United States of America*, esp. Vol. 1 (Boston, 1876), p. 3.

5. Levin, p. 28. For a view of Hawthorne's relation to Bancroft that is in some ways contrary to mine, see R. A. Yoder, "Transcendental Conservatism and *The House of the Seven Gables,*" *Georgia Review,* XXVIII (Spring, 1974), 33–52.

6. The spiritual presumption of Hawthorne's Puritans, and their failure to develop a healthy sense of intermediate causality, are illustrated by such things as their aggressive prosecution of "witches"; their complacent historical optimism about the "high and glorious destiny" of God's people in New England is reflected in Dimmesdale's Election Sermon in chapter xxiii of *The Scarlet Letter,* a matter addressed recently by Richard Harter Fogle in "Hawthorne, History, and the Human Heart," *CLIO,* V (Winter, 1976), 175–180. In other respects, of course, Hawthorne sympathized with the Puritans' sense of history, but this larger issue, which has already been developed at length by outstanding critics like Michael Colacurcio, is much too complex to deal with here.

7. *The Complete Works of Nathaniel Hawthorne* in the Riverside Edition, ed. G. P. Lathrop (Boston, 1883), XII, 417.

8. For the fuller context of the saying, see *Works,* XII, 332; similar sentiments are expressed in a letter from Liverpool (cited in Matthiessen, p. 321, n. 4 and in George Woodberry, *Nathaniel Hawthorne,* Boston, 1902, p. 246) where he remarks that God's "instruments have no consciousness of His purpose; if they imagine they have, it is a pretty sure token that they are not *his* instruments . . . God's ways are in nothing more mysterious than in this matter of trying to do good"; but compare his assurance in "Glimpses of English Poverty" (*Works,* VII, 353) that a person "was responsible, in his degree, for all the sufferings and misdemeanors of the world in which he lived, and was not entitled to look upon a particle of its dark calamity as if it were none of his concern."

9. See Elizabeth Palmer Peabody on "Christ's Idea of Society" and the "Plan of the West Roxbury Community." Both pieces appeared in the *Dial,* in 1841 and 1842, and are reprinted in *Selected Writings of the American Transcendentalists,* ed. George Hochfield (New York, 1966), pp. 336–339 and 385–391.

10. These notions are amplified persuasively by Alfred H. Marks, "Who Killed Judge Pyncheon? The Role of the Imagination in *The House of the Seven Gables,*" *PMLA,* LXXI (June, 1956), 355–369; and by Clark Griffith, "Substance and Shadow: Language and Meaning in *The House of the Seven Gables,*" *Modern Philology,* LI (Feb., 1954), 187–195.

11. See Revelation 21–22, which at the same time parallels other aspects of Hawthorne's imagery in its mention of "the fountain of the water of life" (21.6; cf. 22.1), and "the tree of life" (22.2) with its newly burgeoning fruits. Appropriately, Holgrave's earlier premonitions concerning the story's eventual apocalypse (literally, "uncovering") are of "some catastrophe, or consummation" (p. 303), an ambiguity consistent not only with the opposite ends to which Judge Pyncheon and the sympathetic characters are brought but also with the double-expectation of destruction and new creation traditionally associated with the apocalyptic Day of Judgment.

12. This point is developed more fully by Waggoner in *Hawthorne* and, in slightly different terms, by Leo B. Levy in "*The House of Seven Gables*: The Religion of Love," *Nineteenth-Century Fiction,* XVI (Dec., 1961), 189–203. An earlier version of this essay was read initially at a session of the 1976 MLA Convention in New York.

Narrative Techniques and the Oral Tradition in *The Scarlet Letter*

John G. Bayer

Many readers have been taken aback by the apparent contempt for his audience that Hawthorne reveals in "The Custom-House." What was he doing when he opened his most famous work with an assault on his readers? In this essay, John Bayer thinks about Hawthorne's rhetorical postures to find an answer to this relationship between writer and reader.

Bayer notes that Hawthorne relied on Hugh Blair's tremendously influential *Lectures on Rhetoric and Belles Lettres*, a work that first appeared in 1783 and went through many dozens of editions. By paying close attention to the rhetorical situation of Hawthorne's writings, he usefully distinguishes three categories too often lumped together: the *reader*, the *author*, and the *narratee*. This attention to the formal features that define the relation between Hawthorne and the world allows Bayer to describe in detail how "the reader fictionalizes himself."

At the center of his inquiry is orality—the spoken, rather than the written, word—since Bayer finds *The Scarlet Letter* "imbued with the resonance of the spoken word," particularly in Dimmesdale's "oratorical virtuosity" in his sermons. He reminds us that Hawthorne lived during "America's last great age of oratory." Oral tradition, he argues, even shapes the structure of the work as a whole.   — J.L.

Hawthorne's preface to the second edition of *The Scarlet Letter*, dated March 30, 1850, is a brief defense of "The Custom-House" in which he refuses to recant for allegedly indiscreet portrayals of his political enemies. Yet his rebuttal is by no means vociferous; with the first line of the preface, he sets the same disarmingly humble tone that permeates the Custom-House sketch itself:

Much to the author's surprise, and (if he may say so without additional of-fence) considerably to his amusement, he finds that his sketch of official life, introductory to THE SCARLET LETTER, has created an unprecedented excitement in the respectable community immediately around him.[1]

Tonal ambiguity is but one enigma in "The Custom-House." Except for the now classic definition of the romance, the intent of *The Scarlet Letter* "Introductory" has troubled critics, and the tendency has been to ig-nore the remainder—primarily, it would seem, because Hawthorne himself encourages such a dismissal.[2] In the second edition preface he remarks: "The sketch might, perhaps, have been wholly omitted, with-out loss to the public, or detriment to the book . . ." (1). But if the per-sonal essay format surrounding the theory of the romance adds little to our understanding of *The Scarlet Letter* itself, it promises much con-cerning Hawthorne's sensitivity to an assumed audience. In the Cus-tom-House sketch he "speaks" directly to his reader in a familiar, at times jocular, manner as if he were conversing with a friend and confi-dant.[3] That such familiarity is mere pose has been observed, for one, by Jesse Bier, who concludes that Hawthorne's "soft-spoken and unas-suming tone" is "deceptive."[4] This view is borne out by Hawthorne's own comments during the preparations for publishing *The Scarlet Let-ter.* In a letter to his publisher, James T. Fields, he betrays his lack of confidence in the book by proposing that its title be printed in red ink. This, he hoped, would be "attractive to the great gull we are endeavor-ing to circumvent" (xxii). While writing "The Custom-House" Haw-thorne found himself in the awkward position of having to court an au-dience that he assumed to be hostile and for whom he felt contempt. The combative tenor of his comment to Fields seems to be reflected in the decidedly oral-aural cast of the beginning of "The Custom-House," in that oral-rhetorical prescriptions derived from the ancients are po-lemically oriented, directed toward persuasion. Hawthorne refers to himself as a "speaker" and to his reader as a "listener," with whom he must "stand in some true relation" lest "thoughts are frozen and utterance benumbed" (4). He conceives of his audience as an adversary that must be won over and commits himself to finding the proper rhetorical tools of persuasion to render his audience sympathetic. The confusion over the purpose of the Custom-House sketch *in toto* can be allayed once it is understood as an exordium for the romance proper, an atavistic reminder of oral modes of composition.

In the corpus of critical work on Hawthorne, his ties with the oral tradition have received little attention, perhaps because literary romanticism in America has often been defined as a movement pitted against the eighteenth century's preoccupation with classifying the oral-rhetorical prescriptions of antiquity. Hawthorne is ranked among our first great writers precisely because the vision and shape of his works abandoned the static conventionality of the neo-classical period in favor of an original treatment of the short story and the novel-romance. During the first few decades of the nineteenth century, as advances in print technology enabled publishers to widen distribution, the public came to depend less on the spoken word and more on the printed one. Still, the process was gradual, and the oral milieu that spawned the lyceum movement continued to manifest itself, however covertly, in the compositional and thematic concerns of romantic writers.

Hawthorne's anxiety about the audience he projected for *The Scarlet Letter* is one such manifestation. In order to cope with his hostile reader, he apparently relied on Blair's *Rhetoric*, published in 1783, which contained persuasive tactics inherited from a time when oratory dominated writing. Blair's lectures are a typical product of the eighteenth century's drive to regularize the conventions of rhetoric as writing principles and yet are also, paradoxically, a primary source of Hawthorne's familiarity with the oral tradition. From his college years when he read Blair, Hawthorne acquired the habit of keeping commonplace books, a practice also prefigured long before in oral, preliterate societies. He recorded in his notebooks ideas for projected scenes in order to maintain, like his predecessor in the art of narration the oral performer, a storehouse of pre-readied themes that could be shaped into dramatic plot during the act of composition. Moreover, in *The Scarlet Letter* the plot is itself imbued with the resonance of the spoken word, as Hawthorne uses Arthur Dimmesdale's oratorical virtuosity to suggest the evocative power of the sermon in the Puritan community. *The Scarlet Letter* is not only a lasting monument of the romantic movement in American letters, but residual elements from the oral tradition make it a paradigm of America's last great age of oratory.

Although the concepts of audience, reader, and narratee have come to be used interchangeably, it is valuable for purposes of this inquiry to make distinctions among them similar to the accepted distinctions between author and narrator. Thus, *reader* is probably best understood as the counterpart of *author*—that is, the flesh-and-blood being who actually reads the novel, short story, or epic. Similarly, just as the *narrator* is, to use Wayne Booth's phrase, the author's "implied version of 'himself,'" so too is the *narratee* an idealized reader.[5] The term *audience* can best be reserved as a generic concept that denotes listeners or viewers (in whatever special way these terms might pertain to a particular narrative).[6]

In "The Custom-House" Hawthorne manipulates the reader-narratee relationship; and only later, in the romance proper, does he expand his focus to include the more general concept of audience. So excessive is his initial attention to the reader that one is persuaded he was more than a little anxious about "converting" his reader to narratee. From the beginning his tone is apologetic, as he, "the intrusive author," seeks an audience with "the indulgent reader" (3). He seems to presuppose a reader as uncooperative and downright hostile as the pair of spectators in his "Main-Street" (a sketch mentioned later in "The Custom-House"). In that piece an unlucky showman suffers the boorish barbs of two patrons unwilling, or unable, to contribute any of their own imagination to his performances. When the showman suggests to one that he lacks "the proper point of view," he receives the scornful reply: "I have already told you that, it is my business to see things just as they are."[7] The second spectator is no less critical of historical inaccuracies in the skits. A tandem more ill-suited to entertain a Hawthorne romance is probably not to be found, and it is apparently just such a readership Hawthorne addresses in the Custom-House sketch. He conceives of a reader akin to his own ancestors, whom he portrays as specter-critics contemptuous of his craft:

> No aim, that I have ever cherished, would they recognize as laudable; no success of mine—if my life, beyond its domestic scope, had ever been brightened by success—would they deem otherwise than worthless, if not positively disgraceful. "What is he?" murmurs one gray shadow of my forefathers to the other. "A writer of story-books! What kind of business in life,—what mode of glorifying God, or being serviceable to mankind in his day and generation,—may that be? Why, the degenerate fellow might as well have been a fiddler!" (10)

It is clear that Hawthorne assumes a reader in "The Custom-House" whose skepticism and insistence on "reality" are meant to reflect the hard-bitten practicality of many nineteenth-century Americans. How is such a reader won over? Surely Hawthorne's self-imposed burden in this regard is greater than most, and his persuasive strategy will, accordingly, have to be more painstaking. And so it proves to be, as he employs both overt and covert modes of manipulation. His most obvious ploy is outright flattery. Professing great concern lest he violate his "reader's rights" (4), he is patronizing in his use of the conventional appellations "indulgent reader" (3) and "honored reader" (8). As mentioned above, Hawthorne likens his reader to his own forebears in that both parties disdain his profession. Yet at the end of the imagined attack by his Puritan ancestry he includes a qualifier: "And yet, let them scorn me as they will, strong traits of their nature have intertwined themselves with mine" (10). The suggestion is that Hawthorne and his progenitors—and by identification, his reader—are not so estranged after all. There may indeed be some similarity of sentiment in spite of differences in values. What follows this comment are various autobiographical asides, all intended to establish common ground between Hawthorne and his reader. A prime example is Hawthorne's insistence that his children must set down roots somewhere other than Salem because "human nature will not flourish, any more than a potato, if it be planted and replanted for too long a series of generations, in the same worn-out soil" (11–12). This urgent call for change and new growth echoes throughout "The Custom-House." During his tenure as surveyor of the Salem Custom House, Hawthorne had learned this lesson, an especially valuable one for "a man who has dreamed of literary fame" because he will discover "how utterly devoid of significance, beyond his circle, is all that he achieves, and all he aims at" (26–27). Such self-depreciation is hardly incidental. Hawthorne intends his reader to apply this same lesson to his own circumstance, to question whether his own reality-bound preoccupations might not also benefit from exposure to an altogether different perspective.[8] If the reader can be made to sympathize with Hawthorne's personal experience and to see the value of challenging one's stubborn ways—if these effects are managed—the reader will be more receptive to his role as narratee in *The Scarlet Letter.*

Hawthorne seeks his reader's sympathy in yet a third way: by adopting the pose of editor of Surveyor Pue's manuscript. That he includes the romance convention of the found manuscript is once again indicative of his sensitivity to his readership. What has been called quite simply the public's "distrust of fiction" in the nineteenth century is, as already noted, a prejudice shared by Hawthorne's reader.[9] Given this attitude of resistance, Hawthorne places the starting point of his narrative in the public domain; that is, he invites his reader to share in the discovery of the Pue manuscript. He attempts to engender some commonality of experience between the reader and himself in order to prepare for their respective roles in the romance (i.e., narratee and narrator).

All of Hawthorne's devices aimed at enlisting reader sympathy are, furthermore, conscious efforts to build toward closure in the narrative. Hawthorne seems to be aware intuitively that written narrative lacks the immediacy of existential involvement that obtains in an oral performance (as in the case of epic narrative). Early in "The Custom-House" he observes: "as thoughts are frozen and *utterance* benumbed, unless the *speaker* stand in some true relation with his *audience*—it may be pardonable to imagine that a friend, a kind and apprehensive, though not the closest friend, is *listening* to our *talk* . . ." [emphasis added] (4). Hawthorne seems to find the dynamics of oral performance desirable, though only up to a point. Because, as a writer, he must maintain esthetic distance, he is prompted to place himself in what he calls a "true position as editor" (4). The editorial pose functions so as to persuade the reader that Hawthorne himself cannot be held accountable for any discrepancies of historical fact (such as those criticized by the "Main-Street" spectator); the story of Hester Prynne is Surveyor Pue's story, and Hawthorne is simply its editor—a mediator whose sole purpose for "assuming a personal relation with the public" is to reveal the significance of the historical record (4). A reader willing to accept Hawthorne's role as editor is more likely to blame any historical deficiencies on Pue and to respond more willingly to the suggestions of Hawthorne's retelling. By placing the source of his narrative in the public domain, Hawthorne reminds his reader that "real life" events are often ambiguous and unintelligible. The upshot of these tactics will be, if Hawthorne has calculated rightly, to soften his reader's skepticism.[10] Beneath this skeptical veneer Hawthorne ultimately assumes his reader to be "kind and apprehensive," and it is to this latent sympathy that he directs his attention (4). In sum, an essential function of "The Custom-House" is to characterize a composite reader and in turn to prepare that reader for his narratee role in *The Scarlet Letter*. Without such preparation, Hawthorne's artful structuring of his romance would be less evocative. Until the reader steps into the carefully delimited role of narratee, the closure that distinguishes tightly plotted narrative will remain merest potential.

A profile of Hawthorne's reader would include these characteristics: skepticism, discrimination, Yankee practicality. Yet, to be a suitable counterpart to the narrator of *The Scarlet Letter*, he must also display compassion, understanding, imagination. He must cooperate with the writer in spite of the typically American tendency to discredit that which cannot be apprehended through the senses. In order to act as a narratee in a romance, he is required to acknowledge his more sympathetic other half, to consciously sustain an internal counterpoise between tough-mindedness and sensitivity that attunes him to the mixing of reality and ideality in the romance itself. Hawthorne's reader is incapable of entering "a neutral territory, somewhere between the real world and fairy-land" until he can bring with him a mind set that is correspondingly neutral, or balanced (36). It is in this sense that the reader fictionalizes himself. The narratee of *The Scarlet Letter* is a figure of precisely defined proportions who, because of his close identification with the narrator, is privy to knowledge about events in the narrative that eludes both the central characters and the Puritan community at large.

Unlike the oral performer of the epic, who was a perpetual recounter and preserver of historical events, the narrator of *The Scarlet Letter* orchestrates an investigation into the moral implications of events. He is "consistently more interested in meaning and significance than in realism or factual accuracy," and is thus wholly a by-product of the romantic tradition.[11] Robert Scholes and Robert Kellogg trace the origin of this narrator type to the Greeks, whose *histor* "examine[d] the past with an eye toward separating out actuality from myth."[12] Whereas the traditional oral bard had to confine himself to a version of his story formulated through mnemonic device (indeed, he could conceive his role in no other way), the *histor* could present conflicting reports in his search for truth. Similar to this method is what Yvor Winters calls Hawthorne's "formula of alternative possibilities."[13] Hawthorne's editorial function in pivotal scenes in *The Scarlet Letter* frequently consists of summarizing various accounts ostensibly gleaned from wit-

---

nesses. The most striking instance of this technique is the climactic public confession of the Reverend Arthur Dimmesdale, after which the members of the community speculate widely as to the causes for the "letter" that appears on his breast. Here, as elsewhere in the romance, Hawthorne recommends implicitly that the reader exercise his own acumen in choosing from among the suppositions of the crowd. The faceless Puritan community functions as a source of information from which the narrator, the editor, picks and chooses—only to defer final judgment to the reader.

The citizens of Boston function further as a chorus, whose attitudes alternately coincide and stand apart from those shared by the narrator and narratee. The value matrix that establishes the bond between narrator and narratee is centered on sympathy and tolerance. From the beginning of *The Scarlet Letter*, the narrator empathizes with Hester's plight; and the narratee, lest his identification with the narrator after having read "The Custom-House" be incomplete, is encouraged by the callousness of the Puritan community also to side with Hester. The community is in fact an audience in the sense defined earlier: they are viewers and listeners, subject to the innate limitations of sight and hearing. Hawthorne's narrator offers this editorial comment on these limitations:

> When an uninstructed multitude attempts to see with its eyes, it is exceedingly apt to be deceived. When, however, it forms its judgment, as it usually does, on the intuitions of its great and warm heart, the conclusions thus attained are often so profound and so unerring, as to possess the character of truths supernaturally revealed. (127)

The multitude is "uninstructed" in that it lacks the "supernatural" knowledge shared by the narrator and narratee. As a result, its sight (i.e., insight) is distorted. When the crowd relies exclusively on this impaired faculty, as in the scene when Hester's shame is made a "spectacle" on the scaffold, its obsession with guilt precludes compassionate response. Although the members of the community are sometimes equally deceived by what they *hear*, their compassion is nonetheless consistently awakened by the spoken word. When Hester is publicly shamed, she stands quietly, and the heart of the community is hardened. In contrast, when Dimmesdale subsequently entreats Hester to name her partner in sin, his impassioned words "vibrate within all hearts, and [bring] the listeners into one accord of sympathy" (67). At this point the public's view of Dimmesdale is of course still false; they see him as a paragon of moral rectitude. It is only later, in the crucial revelation scene, that sight and sound combine to enhance the people's knowledge and understanding. As Dimmesdale bares his breast, and his soul, the crowd-audience's "great heart [is] thoroughly appalled, yet overflowing with tearful sympathy . . ." (254). They are appalled by what they see and deeply touched by what they hear. As Dimmesdale completes his confession with his dying breath, the Puritan gathering responds with a paroxysm of collective catharsis: "The multitude, silent till then, broke out in a strange, deep voice of awe and wonder, which could not as yet find utterance, save in this murmur that rolled so heavily after the departed spirit" (257). Just as the great heart of the people responds directly to the spoken word, so too are its deepest feelings uttered in spontaneous harmony.

The profound effect of Dimmesdale's dying confession is certainly generated in part by the very fact that he dies. He is revered by his congregation, in spite of his admitted sin, and his untimely death in and of itself leaves them grief-stricken. Yet at the moment of death they no longer stand in mute despair; their voices join in a communal utterance of pity and fear. This spontaneous response can be accounted for only by recognizing the dynamics of the spoken word. Had Dimmesdale died quietly, the crowd would more than likely have remained silent as well. There is a kind of law of inertia that operates in the relationship between speech and silence which states: an absence of speech from a person is usually met with silence from another, but once one speaks the other is obliged to reply. That is, verbal utterance is marked by reciprocity. A discerning examination of "auditory synthesis: word as event" is offered by Walter Ong in *The Presence of the Word*.[14] Father Ong notes that speech evokes reciprocal responses as very few other human activities can. In the absence of oral confession, Dimmesdale's death would have been quite literally a dead event. This is not mere word play, for, as Ong also observes, "sound unites groups of living beings as nothing else does."[15] The Puritans at the scaffold are captivated by the startling admixture of sermon and sin in Dimmesdale's speech. Spellbound by the spectacle, they are totally immersed in a flood of emotion only because Dimmesdale speaks. The rightness of this dramatic scene is confirmed by the fact that "sound situates man in the middle of actuality and in simultaneity, whereas vision situates man in front of things and in sequentiality."[16] The experience of the congregation during Dimmesdale's confession is inclusive, and stands in bold relief when compared with their simply *watching* Hester on the scaffold, an experience of half measure.

Except for the intensifying influence of Dimmesdale's death, the effect of his earlier Election Day sermon is almost identical to that produced by his confession of guilt. It is Dimmesdale's vocal eloquence that causes the similarity of response:

> The eloquent voice, on which the souls of the listening audience had been borne aloft, as on the swelling waves of the sea, at length came to a pause. There was a momentary silence, profound as what should follow the utterance of oracles. Then ensued a murmur and half-hushed tumult; as if the auditors, released from the high spell that had transported them into the region of another's mind, were returning into themselves, with all their awe and wonder still heavy on them. (248)

The congregation sit in respectful silence in the church, but once outside "their rapture broke into speech" (248). Although all speakers anticipate and expect audience recognition, the inspirational influence wielded by Dimmesdale is obviously utterance of a higher order: it is oratory. He is blessed with greater powers than most clerics, for he has received "the gift"—the Pentecostal Tongue of Flame—"symbolizing, it would seem [says Hawthorne], not the power of speech in foreign and unknown languages, but that of addressing the whole human brotherhood in the heart's native language" (141–42). He is all the more unique because his burden of sin has paradoxically enhanced his ability to empathize with his parishioners, such that "his heart vibrate[s] in unison with theirs . . . and sen[ds] its throb of pain through a thousand other hearts, in gushes of sad, persuasive eloquence" (142). A positive sympathy is generated by the bond of sin, and Dimmesdale's affinity with his flock is compounded by a strange blend of saintly breath and wretched flesh.

Not only are the dynamics of plot in *The Scarlet Letter* energized by the power of oratorical display, the structure of the tale has been informed by the oral tradition as well. Hawthorne's composition of his finest romance was guided by entries in his notebooks and journals—commonplace books whose collation very likely grew out of habits engendered while he was a student at Bowdoin College. The curriculum at Bowdoin in 1822, Hawthorne's sophomore year, included classes in Murray's *Grammar* and Blair's *Rhetoric*.[17] The custom of keeping commonplace books for such courses of study can be traced to the proliferation of commonplace collections during the Renaissance, when the print revolution stimulated the urge to catalogue the knowledge of previous, orally dominated generations. The educated among the New England Puritans compiled commonplace books on matters of theological and moral concern, and the efficacy of the practice survived as a pedagogical device in Hawthorne's time, nourished by an oratorical, revivalist spirit. Early nineteenth-century heroes, both secular and orthodox, were often great speakers: Henry Clay, Daniel Webster, John C. Calhoun and Lyman Beecher, William Ellery Channing, Theodore Parker. The age's passion for the spoken word required that declamation remain a part of the college curriculum; and though Hawthorne shied from classroom performance at Bowdoin, he was for a time secretary of the Salem Lyceum, where he maintained good standing by occasionally presenting talks. Temperamentally unsuited for the speaker's platform, he nonetheless benefitted as a writer from his lessons in Blair's *Rhetoric*.

Of particular interest as a probable source for the composition of "The Custom-House" is Lecture XXXI: "Conduct of a Discourse in All Its Parts." It has been demonstrated earlier in this discussion how Hawthorne uses "The Custom-House" in order to prepare his reader for the role of narratee. That he relied on Blair's rhetorical methods to accomplish that task can also be illustrated. From the ancients Blair derived two kinds of exordia for a discourse: *Principium* and *Insinuatio*. The former is a straightforward presentation of the speaker's objective. The latter is used in the special case of a hostile audience. Blair advises: "presuming the disposition of the Audience to be much against the Orator, he must gradually reconcile them to hearing him."[18] Hawthorne appears to have learned this lesson well, for "The Custom-House" shows his masterful ability to, as Blair puts it, "render [the audience] benevolent."[19] Derivative oral-polemical features in "The Custom-House" associate Hawthorne with the Puritan sermon in a manner that sheds new light on his debt to his forebears. Puritan ministers did not think of their congregations as openly hostile, but they were aware that their flock had to be wooed away from the vicissitudes of the workaday world before they would be receptive to the Word. The ancient rhetoric of persuasion served equally well the purposes of Puritan divine and latter-day romancer.

Because Hawthorne found compensatory value in sinfulness, he would seem to stand, on a moral plane, at a far remove from his Puritan ancestors. Yet the matter of sympathy is most certainly a concern shared by Hawthorne and the Puritans. Evidence of this is to be found in their common regard for the efficacy of the spoken word. The preeminent position of the sermon in the life of a Calvinist is well documented, as is the fact that the clergy carefully constructed their sermons to appeal not just to the intellect but also to the heart. Perry Miller contends that in discussing a sermon the Puritans most often dwelt on the manner in which it aroused the affections, or the passions.[20] Appeals to the affections placed the heart in proper sympathy with the doctrinal premise of the sermon. It is about the purpose of exciting the affections that some Puritans and Hawthorne disagree. The extent of this disagreement is made clear when the theme of *The Scarlet Letter* is seen as "the conflict in a soul between the pride which would contract it to harsh and narrow limits and the affections which would reach out and bind it to the natural society of its kind."[21] Hawthorne has romanticized and secularized the notion of affection in such way that its proper purpose is not to serve as a possible aid toward individual salvation but instead to assert one's fellowship in the whole human community. Perhaps the best illustration of Hawthorne's redefining is his description of Hester's alienation from humanity:

> . . .there seemed to be no longer any thing in Hester's face for Love to dwell upon; nothing in Hester's form, though majestic and statue-like, that Passion would ever dream of clasping in its embraces; nothing in Hester's bosom, to make it ever again the pillow of Affection. (163)

Whereas the stirring of the affections was a sermonic strategy for the Puritan clergy, it became in Hawthorne's romance a central theme—needful human sympathy born of the recognition of common sinfulness.

The theme of sympathy is but one among many dramatized in *The Scarlet Letter*. Recent attention to Hawthorne's notebooks has provided a clearer understanding of how these themes were conceived. In the Centenary Edition of Hawthorne's *American Notebooks*, Claude Simpson has briefly outlined Hawthorne's method of working from notes to manuscript:

> During more than a decade before he wrote *The Scarlet Letter* Hawthorne repeatedly recorded notes bearing on the central relationships developed in

that romance and elsewhere in his work: the insidious control of one person by another; the ironic contrast, often hypocritical, between man's social self and his inner anxieties. Other themes similarly treated—the failure of romantic expectations, the zeal for vengeance, the destructiveness of good intentions—suggest the power of ideas, not their translation into dramatic terms.[22]

Hawthorne's method of composition emulates that of Francis Bacon and other Renaissance writers, who augmented the work of encyclopedists by compiling their own commonplace books on various topics of universal concern, called commonplaces. The codification of these *topoi*, or *loci communes*, began with the Sophists, Aristotle, Cicero, Quintilian and others, and found its way to Bacon via the Middle Ages, when scribes worked doggedly to amass the wisdom of the oral past under generic headings. Like Bacon, Hawthorne in turn collected personal bits of insight and stored them to be later filtered through the half-lights of the romance landscape. In the notebook entries related to *The Scarlet Letter*, begun in 1838 and accumulated over the next eleven years, he stressed ideas, not dramatic situations.[23] The notebooks contain the germ for many a scene that blossomed forth in the romance atmosphere, just as the ancient poet's mnemonic storehouse served as a foundation for each new performance. Very early in the history of narrative, oral performers such as Homer used commonplaces as thematic units to be strung together in a loose, rhapsodic approximation of the more tightly plotted written narrative of the novel. Although *The Scarlet Letter* is a strongly unified work, its episodic, highly scenic structure is a reminder of the cumulative drift of oral composition.

The dramatic features of *The Scarlet Letter* have often been noticed, but the relation of Hawthorne's narrative stagecraft to the oral roots of America's native literary tradition has not been accounted for. A close reading of "The Custom-House" and the romance itself reveals that Hawthorne was a writer drawn between America's literary future and her oral past. As shown earlier, the scaffold scenes depicting first

Hester's and later Dimmesdale's guilt are charged with the existential dynamics of speech. Disagreement among critics concerning the purpose of "The Custom-House" has stemmed from the seeming incongruity between it and the romance proper. Once seen as an exordium designed to enlist reader cooperation, its complete function emerges clearly. These oral dimensions are altogether consistent with Hawthorne's rhetorical apprenticeship in college and confirm the judgment that *The Scarlet Letter* is a fictional exemplar of a residually oral age.

From *American Literature* 52, no. 2 (May, 1980): 250-263. Copyright © 1980 by Duke University Press. Reprinted by permission of Duke University Press

Notes

1. Nathaniel Hawthorne, *The Scarlet Letter*, Vol. 1 of *The Centenary Edition of the Works of Nathaniel Hawthorne*, ed. William Charvat et al. (Columbus: Ohio State Univ. Press, 1962), p. 1. All subsequent references are to this edition and are included parenthetically in the text.

2. Critics who have questioned the importance of "The Custom-House" to *The Scarlet Letter* are identified in Sam S. Baskett, "The (Complete) Scarlet Letter," *College English*, 22 (1961), 321. Baskett argues for the relevance of "The Custom-House," as does John E. Becker in *Hawthorne's Historical Allegory* (Port Washington, N.Y.: Kennikat Press, 1971), pp. 61–87.

3. Malcolm Cowley, in his introduction to *The Portable Hawthorne* (New York: Penguin Books, 1977), pp. 6–7, suggests that Hawthorne carried on an "inner monologue" when he conceived his romances, and projected a second part of himself as a participating audience.

4. "Hawthorne on the Romance: His Prefaces Related and Examined," *Modern Philology*, 53 (1955). 17.

5. *The Rhetoric of Fiction* (Chicago: The Univ. of Chicago Press, 1961), p. 70.

6. Three useful analyses of the nature of narrative audience are: Walter J. Ong, "The Writer's Audience Is Always a Fiction" in *Interfaces of the Word* (Ithaca: Cornell Univ. Press, 1977); Gerald Prince, "Notes Toward a Categorization of Fictional 'Narratees,'" *Genre*, 4 (1971), 100–106; Walker Gibson, *Tough, Sweet and Stuffy* (Bloomington: Indiana Univ. Press, 1966), pp. 28–42.

7. "Main-Street," Vol. XI of *Works*, p. 57.

8. A related study is Joseph C. Pattison, "Point of View in Hawthorne," *PMLA*, 82 (1967), 363–69, which argues that dream is the proper "angle of vision" for Hawthorne's reader to adopt.

9. Harry C. West, "Hawthorne's Editorial Pose," *American Literature*, 44 (1972), 211.

10. West, 209.

11. Ibid.

12. *The Nature of Narrative* (London: Oxford Univ. Press, 1966), p. 242.

13. Cited in West, 217.

14. (New Haven: Yale Univ. Press, 1967), p. 111.

15. Ong, *Presence*, p. 122.

16. Ong, *Presence*, p. 128.

17. Randall Stewart, *Nathaniel Hawthorne* (New Haven: Yale Univ. Press, 1948), p. 16.

18. Hugh Blair, *Lectures on Rhetoric and Belles Lettres* (Carbondale, Ill.: Southern Illinois Univ. Press, 1965), II, 159.

19. Blair, p. 158. The art of letter writing, taught in medieval schools and derived from older oratorical structures, included an element called *benevolentiae captatio*, or "the winning of good will." See Walter J. Ong, "Tudor Writings on Rhetoric, Poetic, and Literary Theory" in *Rhetoric, Romance, and Technology* (Ithaca: Cornell Univ. Press, 1970, p. 54.

20. *The New England Mind: The Seventeenth Century* (Boston: Beacon Press, 1961), p. 300.

21. Carl Van Doren, *The American Novel, 1789–1939* (New York: The Macmillan Company, 1940), p. 63.

22. Vol. VIII of *Works*, p. 679.

23. A notebook entry that prefigures the Chillingworth-Dimmesdale relationship reads: "The influence of a peculiar mind, in close communion with another, to drive the latter to insanity" (Vol. VIII of *Works*, p. 170).

Hawthorne and the Sublime_____

Leo B. Levy

Critics have often read Hawthorne's works between the poles of the "picturesque" and the "sublime," two categories of aesthetic thought that became popular in the late eighteenth century and continued to inform discussions of perception well into the nineteenth. The sublime is concerned with the overwhelming, the vast, and the infinite; the picturesque, on the other hand, functions in Hawthorne's works as a kind of regulatory force, keeping the energy of the sublime in check.

In his psychological analysis of the subjective processes that structure perception, Leo B. Levy offers insights into Hawthorne's simultaneous attraction to and repulsion from the sublime, noting that Hawthorne brings to the sublime a doubt and irony rarely seen among Hawthorne's contemporaries. The tales "The Great Stone Face" and "The Great Carbuncle" are the clearest examples of Hawthorne's fascination with sublimity, and show his interest in the relationship between the false sublime (found in the Gothic) and the true sublime (which Hawthorne describes most fully in "My Visit to Niagara"). — J.L.

In the study of Hawthorne's fiction, little attention has been given to the ways in which his work draws upon the traditions of the picturesque and the sublime.[1] In broad terms, these conventions are the poles of Hawthorne's art. The picturesque determines the spatial finiteness that typically governs his form. His subdued landscapes and fanciful imagery are largely derivatives of picturesque style.[2] As a way of looking at landscape, the picturesque views nature through the perspective of the Claude-glass or the aperture, throwing into relief a group of attributes extracted from the whole of nature for aesthetic contemplation. Irregularity of line, roughness and ruggedness of texture, the massing and graduation of light and shade, intricacy and variety of effect—the hallmarks of picturesque style first codified and popularized by William Gilpin—are deeply woven into the fabric of Hawthorne's fiction. Certain classes of objects which become standardized items of picturesque regard, such as fractured rocks, blighted trees, winding streams, and ruined buildings, appear repeatedly in his writings. The thoroughness of Hawthorne's adaptation of this graphic convention to literary art distinguishes him from Irving, Cooper, and Thoreau, among other writers of the romantic period in America, who also responded in a variety of ways to the picturesque tradition. The peculiar value of this mode for Hawthorne seems to have been its power to organize the visual experience of nature in a relatively static pattern.

Historically, as in the paintings of Salvator Rosa and the Gothic novels of Mrs. Radcliffe, the picturesque and the sublime have been convergent modes. In Hawthorne's fiction, as we shall observe, this convergence occurs at points of emotional excitement, when the framed landscape can no longer contain the emotions of awe, wonder, or fear. The contemplation of nature in its elemental or excessive moods, and the vastness and grandeur that these produce, continually implies the idea of the infinite. Hawthorne is at once attracted and repelled by vistas too extended to be readily assimilated by the eye. He shrinks from the infinite, unless he can assimilate it to a framework of familiar ideas. In contrast to most votaries of the sublime, he does not enthusiastically embrace the awful and the immense; he is often circuitous and indirect, doubtful and skeptical, and sometimes defensively ironical. Reflected in these tendencies is a distrust of emotion uncritically experienced; he recoils from the total commitment that the sublime demands. The picturesque, on the other hand, is a regulative principle that suggests a world of tangled boughs and shady thickets, a safe refuge for the mood of unbroken tranquillity. When Hawthorne turns to the description of mountain ranges, precipices, waterfalls, and oceans, or to cataclysmic eruptions such as avalanches and storms, he breaks out of the characteristic moderation of his temperament into an area of unpredictable and often surprising extremes.

In two of his tales, Hawthorne moves from outright rejection of the sublime toward assimilation and acceptance. The earlier tale, "The Great Carbuncle," depicts a quest for a "wondrous gem" that according to legend casts a mysterious light from the remoteness of the Crystal Hills. A group of travelers pass through the luxuriance of a picturesque landscape into the solitary regions of the sublime; the two orders are carefully differentiated:

> A vast extent of wilderness lay between them and the nearest settlement, while scant a mile above their heads was that black verge where the hills throw off their shaggy mantle of forest trees, and either robe themselves in clouds or tower naked into the sky.[3]

The dividing line is the "black verge," but picturesque and sublime are also intermingled. The pilgrims build their camp "on the rugged side of one of the Crystal Hills," constructing "a rude hut of branches, and kindling a great fire of shattered pines" (p. 173). Particularly striking is the blending of picturesque and sublime light:

> As the Cynic spoke, several of the party were startled by a gleam of red splendor, that showed the huge shapes of the surrounding mountains and the rock-bestrewn bed of the turbulent river, with an illumination unlike that of their fire on the trunks and black boughs of the forest trees. (p. 182)

When the travelers reach a higher elevation, they turn in fear from the awesome scene, yearning for the security of the picturesque:

> The innumerable trunks and heavy foliage of the trees had hitherto shut in their thoughts, which now shrank affrighted from the region of wind and cloud and naked rocks and desolate sunshine, that rose immeasurably above them. They gazed back at the obscure wilderness which they had traversed, and longed to be buried again in its depths rather than trust themselves to so vast and visible a solitude. (p. 184)

The central figures in this pilgrimage are a rustic, simple-hearted couple, Matthew and Hannah. They set out alone to find the shrine of the Great Carbuncle, reaching the "bleak realm of upper air" in which "nothing breathed, nothing grew" (p. 185). So desolate is the setting that "Nature herself seemed no longer to keep them company." They pass into regions of gathering mists that finally annihilate "the whole region of visible space" (p. 185). At last, "with a thrill of awful admiration," they behold the radiance of the Carbuncle, "a light that overpowered the moon, and almost matched the sun" (p. 177). Hawthorne makes it clear that simplicity and faith have earned Matthew and Hannah their glimpse of the Great Carbuncle. The Seeker has been struck dead by the sight, and the Cynic blinded. At this point, a puzzling development takes place: Matthew and Hannah decide that they cannot "live by day, or sleep by night, in this awful blaze of the Great Carbuncle" (p. 189). They prefer to dwell in another kind of light—the picturesque light that fills the lower regions of the mountains. Thus Matthew declares:

we will go hence, and return to our humble cottage. The blessed sunshine and the quiet moonlight shall come through our window. We will kindle the cheerful glow of our hearth, at eventide, and be happy in its light. But never again will we desire more light than all the world may share with us. (p. 189)

Some troublesome questions are raised by this resolution. The light, which Hawthorne calls "a ray of glory," is invested with religious significance: it is the dazzling source of an infinite power, before which certain qualities of mind and heart are put to the test. But if simplicity and faith enable Matthew and Hannah to behold the light, why does Hawthorne turn them from it? The other members of the party have undertaken the quest with such dubious motives as greed, intellectual pride, and doubt. They accordingly fail. But the simple couple feels a stronger identity with the spiritual inadequacy of their companions than with the divine light. The cottage and hearth to which they return symbolize not only the domestic virtues but the ties that bind men together in society, in weakness as well as in strength. Hawthorne is making the strange suggestion that the power of faith is at odds with religious illumination. Matthew and Hannah find renewed confidence in "the reality of life and love," not because they have seen the light, but because they have rejected it. Apparently the carbuncle symbolizes not only the Deity but any spiritual principle that puts aside primary human considerations. It is beyond the capacity of humankind to gaze upon sublime light, or even to absorb its radiance. At one point we are told that "that star was throwing its intensest lustre on their hearts" (p. 187), but the luster does not guide Matthew and Hannah in their choice. Light, of course, is the oldest of the symbols of the sublime; its association in "The Great Carbuncle" with a forbidding power suggests the awful splendor of the Hebraic deity—but in Hawthorne's context it more immediately evokes the specter of the terrors and rigors of Puritanism. It is not farfetched to regard this tale as a parable of the faith of Hawthorne's ancestors.

"The Great Carbuncle" suggests transgressions of the kind described in "The Gentle Boy," "The Man of Adamant," "The Shaker Bridal," and other studies of religious zeal and fanaticism. These meanings are inverted in "The Great Stone Face," in which Hawthorne transforms the sublime into a tender and compassionate force. The dazzling light becomes an immense face of benign aspect. The typical imagery of sublime landscape is employed in the description of this face: "It seemed as if an enormous giant, or a Titan, had sculptured his own likeness on the precipice" (III, 414); close up, the face is "only a heap of ponderous and gigantic rocks, piled in chaotic ruin one upon another" (p. 414). Its human features, visible only from a distance, are mild, expressive of "gentle wisdom" and "deep, broad, tender sympathies" (p. 425). Though "grand and awful" in the sublime manner, the face is also "benignant, as if a mighty angel were sitting among the hills . . ." (p. 425). The attempt here is to reconcile the sublime to the human scale of values. "The Great Carbuncle" and "The Great Stone Face" display a remarkable disparity in the act of seeing: the carbuncle repels and blinds, whereas the stone face encourages all who look upon it. The face is believed to be responsible for the rich fertility of the valley upon which it gazes; those who look back upon the face absorb the qualities that radiate from it.

"The Great Stone Face" is a parable of the prophetic Christ, the antithesis of the unapproachable deity of "The Great Carbuncle." Ernest, who resembles Matthew in his simple and humble character, patiently awaits the arrival of a prophet whose features will resemble those of the stone face. After many disappointments, Ernest is at last recognized as "himself the likeness of the Great Stone Face" (p. 438). Years of quiet meditation under the gaze of the face have moved Ernest to become a preacher; his religious vocation is recognized by his neighbors, who had once thought of him as an unimportant person. His thoughts are of the kind "that no other human lips had spoken" (p. 427). The elevation of Ernest to this Christ-like status—and the resemblances to Christ are multiplied—has come about through his contact with the sublime: "he had imbibed the sublimity of [angels'] ideas" (p. 434); and these ideas originate in "the sublimity and stateliness, the grand expression of a divine sympathy, that illuminated the mountain visage and etherealized its ponderous granite into spirit . . ." (p. 430).

This process of spiritualization endows the sublime with a new meaning: the look of "grand beneficence" of the stone face, which finally appears in the face of Ernest, "seemed to embrace the world" (p. 437).[4] Hawthorne has separated the sublime from external nature and fused it with the Christian principle that he typically represents in the redemptive power of many of his women characters. During his courtship of Sophia Peabody, Hawthorne became familiar with the work of Washington Allston; it seems probable that in these two tales Hawthorne is drawing upon Allston, or Allston's sources, for an important distinction between the "moral" and "false" sublime. In *Lectures on Art, and Poems* (New York, 1850), Allston identifies the sublime with "the Infinite Idea . . . either limitless, indefinite, or in some other way beyond the grasp of the mind" (p. 55). The "sublime of thought"—which is the moral sublime—awes the mind with the power of God. The "false" sublime, apparently originating in the debasement of the Gothic, consists of the hideous, the loathsome, and the monstrous.

William Ware, in *Lectures on the Works and Genius of Washington Allston* (Boston, 1852), noted that Allston "sought the sources of the sublime, in almost every case, in states of the human mind, rather than in any outward aspect of nature" (p. 94). Though Allston painted "actual scenes of sublime nature . . . the sources of the moral sublime were those to which he applied for yet higher pleasures, and in which he more frequently sought for subjects for his pencil" (p. 97).[5] Hawthorne's reliance upon this distinction is shown in his insistence upon separating moral sublimity from external circumstances. The "grosser actualities" of facts must be steeped "in a powerful menstruum of thought," if they are to keep the "purely ideal" character of mental activity:

> If this were otherwise,—if the moral sublimity of a great fact depended in any degree on its garb of external circumstances . . . it could not itself be immortal and ubiquitous, and only a brief point of time and a little neighborhood would be spiritually nourished by its grandeur and beauty. (VII, 166)

This is surely a more extreme statement of the position than any painter could in practice accept, and it points to a serious contradiction in Hawthorne's thought. If such a separation were really possible, Hawthorne could not have demonstrated the power of the moral sublime. Without the chaotic jumble of boulders that from a distance projects the benign face—without a dependence upon a descriptive sublimity— the great stone face would have remained an abstract idea, rather than the tangible reality that Hawthorne creates.

In dramatic terms, the moral sublime is a reduction of intensity, a lowering of pitch. The idea that informs "The Great Stone Face" meets the requirements of greatness and vastness, but the meek, semi-divine Ernest is without conflict or turmoil. The bleakness and starkness of the topographical features of "The Great Carbuncle" are absent from "The Great Stone Face." The moral sublime requires an active tragic sense if it is to be sustained, and this sense is not strong in Hawthorne's fiction. Hawthorne's chief mode, in Northrop Frye's terminology, is the low mimetic, or ironic. The optimal standard in his work (with certain notable exceptions) is the pursuit of the ordinary ways that bind men together in society, in dignity to be sure, but in a manner peculiarly unaspiring. Even in embracing the Faust theme, Hawthorne does not emphasize the greatness missed by his Aylmers and Chillingworths and Ethan Brands, but focuses upon the gravity of their errors. His harrowing awareness of man's sinfulness, which Melville mistakenly understood as the index to a great tragic vision, taken alone prevents the emergence of tragedy in the classical or Renaissance sense. The drama of Hawthorne's fiction is in the portrayal of how man falls below the levels that define his essential humanity. Without an exalted sense of man's potentialities, Hawthorne finds few occasions, beyond the unique achievement of "The Great Stone Face," to exemplify the moral sublime. It is no accident that Ernest is modeled upon the character and way of life of Christ, since Hawthorne's rigorously Christian idea of man's limitations permits no other path of life to seem truly heroic.

The logic of Hawthorne's vision forced upon him a variety of "false" sublimity. Allston's term accurately describes the technique that Hawthorne employed to express his apprehension of evil, although he is not guilty of the excesses that Allston condemned. Psychological and moral analysis of perverse states, the excesses arising from the violation of moral law, the consciousness of guilt and the expiation of sin invite dramatization through the emotions cultivated by the false sublime. The monstrous and the terrifying often appear in Hawthorne's climactic scenes. Thus, the upper surface of the lime kiln from which Ethan Brand leaps to his death is described in the imagery of mountain scenery: the top of the kiln is "an immense mass of broken marble"; the "innumerable blocks and fragments of marble" send up "great spouts of blue flame" (III, 495), which cast a "wild and ghastly light" (p. 496) upon Ethan Brand's face. His expression is "that of a fiend on the verge of plunging into his gulf of intensest torment" (p. 496). But nothing in the tale surpasses the terror of Brand's laughter, which is also presented through the mountain imagery of the sublime. Those who hear "the awful laugh, which more than any other token, expressed the condition of his inward being," stand aghast, "dreading lest the inauspicious sound should be reverberated around the horizon, and that mountain would thunder it to mountain, and so the horror be prolonged upon their ears" (pp. 492–493) Sublime emotions are communicated by the setting of "the open space on the hillside . . . set in a vast gloom of forest" (p. 493). This setting is separated by a "darksome verge" (reminiscent of the "black verge" that marks the border of sublime and picturesque in "The Great Carbuncle") from a foreground of picturesque effects:

> Beyond that darksome verge, the firelight glimmered on the stately trunks and almost black foliage of pines, intermixed with the lighter verdure of sapling oaks, maples, and poplars, while here and there lay the gigantic corpses of dead trees, decaying on the leaf-strewn soil. (p. 493)

"Ethan Brand" finds its extraordinary power not in its imagery alone but in the idea that shapes and informs that imagery—in Satan and Ethan Brand together, "each laboring to frame the image of some mode of guilt which could neither be atoned for nor forgiven" (p. 483). It is this idea that leads Hawthorne to the false sublime, that is, to the negative spiritual principle that changes Ethan Brand from a "simple and loving man" (like Matthew and Ernest) into a fiend. The idea of evil, associated with images of vastness and overpowering emotions of terror or fear, is the essence of the Gothic. As a highly structured literary tradition, the Gothic was easily separated from its historical connection with the sublime, and this separation often occurs in Hawthorne's fiction. In *The House of the Seven Gables*, for example, there are a few touches of Gothic *frisson*, but for the most part the Gothic in this romance is dissociated from the extremes that are the concern of the sublime. In general, Hawthorne lowers rather than intensifies the pitch of the gloomy and the terrible. His aim is to spiritualize the Gothic just as he had spiritualized the sublime in "The Great Stone Face." The Gothic becomes another version of the religious sublime, focusing upon the misery and despair of lost souls. Thus, the misanthropist in "The Christmas Banquet," who expounds the philosophy of evil, "wandered about in the darkness, with now and then a gleam of discolored light hovering on ghastly shapes and horrid scenery. . . . And then amid his lore of wretchedness he hid his face and wept" (II, 330).

The awesomeness of the human involvement in evil, the Dantean imagery of fires of hell and flames of torment, the whole apparatus of supernaturalism and ruin, are subjected to the limiting principle that brought about the transition from the intolerable sublimity of "The Great Carbuncle" to the religious sublimity of "The Great Stone Face," in which the power of the infinite is converted into the source of the Christian virtues. The false sublime of the Gothic is placed within the framework of the orthodox Christian drama. The parade of damned souls in Hawthorne's fiction may at times suggest a Manichean view of evil; but the classical and Christian sense of man's limitations, within which he can reasonably exist, balances Hawthorne's view of man's destiny and curtails the extent to which ideas and emotions of unlimited scope can operate.

In some of its appearances the moral or religious sublime is secondary to the aesthetic appeal of vast landscapes or seascapes. These manifestations are typically marginal, but the fascination is there. The narrator of "Footprints on the Sea-Shore" gazes toward the sea, "lost in an unlooked-for and overpowering conception of the majesty and awfulness of the great deep" (I, 507); listening to "the sea's unchanging voice . . . the infinite idea of eternity pervade[s] his soul" (p. 514). In "The Village Uncle," "the illimitable ocean mingling with the sky" (I,

362) again reminds the narrator of "Eternity." In both sketches the sea is primarily represented as friendly and even playful. Sublimity of landscape dominates "The Ambitious Guest" and two sketches, "The Notch of the White Mountains" and "Our Evening Party Among the Mountains." The setting of "The Ambitious Guest" is picturesque as well as sublime: a "lowly cottage," with a hearth "piled high with the driftwood of mountain streams" and "the splintered ruins of great trees" (I, 364), is surrounded by a towering mountain that threatens the inhabitants of the cottage with an avalanche. The "unutterable horror of the catastrophe" breaks upon the family and their guest "in a cataract of ruin" (pp. 373, 374). The Notch of the White Mountains, in the sketch so titled, becomes "one of those symbolic scenes which lead the mind to the sentiment, though not to the conception, of Omnipotence" (II, 477). These mountains "are majestic, and even awful, when contemplated in a proper mood . . ." (p. 478). The related sketch, "Our Evening Party Among the Mountains," features "a picturesque group" of tourists at Ethan Crawford's inn that prepares to set out in search of the Great Carbuncle. The poet, who in the previous sketch had quoted "from some of Byron's rhapsodies on mountain scenery" (p. 478), is identified as the author of a "Sonnet to the Snow on Mount Washington." Its lines are in the sublime style, which Hawthorne rejects as "elegant and full of fancy, but too remote from familiar sentiment . . ." (p. 481).

The most comprehensive treatment of the sublime is in "My Visit to Niagara." The waterfall was a standard object of sublime veneration, and Hawthorne's reactions differ from those of other sight-seers only in his insistence upon being honest about his feelings and in his difficulty in experiencing the prescribed emotions. In another sketch, "Rochester," Hawthorne expresses his disappointment with the Genesee Falls, complaining that "the good people of Rochester had abstracted a part of the unprofitable sublimity of the cascade" (XII, 17). He ironically regrets that the canals and milldams have reduced the roar of the water and diminished the pomp of the water at the approaches to the precipice. The problem of coping with the vastness of Niagara is incidentally noted in "The Prophetic Pictures," in which the painter acknowledges his helplessness in the presence of a great spectacle. He "had flung his hopeless pencil down the precipice, feeling that he could as soon paint the roar, as aught else that goes to make up the wondrous cataract" (I, 205). In "My Visit to Niagara," these difficulties are made the subject of psychological analysis. This sketch is more than an essay in the romantic appreciation of vastness; it examines the subjective processes that make possible an authentic experience of the wild and the natural.

On first viewing the falls, Hawthorne is baffled by his inability to experience the appropriate emotions. His explanation documents the point made earlier in this paper—that the sublime of nature lies beyond the normal range of his powers of perception:

> I had come thither, haunted with a vision of foam and fury, and dizzy cliffs, and an ocean tumbling out of the sky,—a scene, in short, which nature had too much good taste and calm simplicity to realize. My mind had struggled to adapt these false conceptions to the reality, and finding the effort vain, a wretched sense of disappointment weighed me down. (XII, 45)

Nevertheless, by a circuitous route, Hawthorne at last puts himself in possession of the desired aesthetic experience. Much of "My Visit to Niagara" dramatizes the complexities that intervene between anticipation and fulfillment. When he first approaches the falls as a stagecoach passenger, he listens for the roar of the cataract and trembles "with a sensation like dread" (p. 42). His mood is broken when a fellow passenger expresses "loud admiration," and Hawthorne, "by a sudden impulse," throws himself back and closes his eyes. At the falls, his mind has grown benumbed, his spirits apathetic, his enthusiasm fallen "in a deathlike slumber" (p. 43). At the inn he lingers over dinner with "perverse epicurism," minutely inspects the village, and visits the museum at the tollhouse. These evasive rituals completed, he once again tries to put himself in touch with the vastness of the scene, but after an hour inquires, "Were my long desires fulfilled? And had I seen Niagara?" (p. 45). He enviously recalls the early travelers who stumbled unexpectedly upon the scene: "Had its own mysterious voice been the first to warn me of its existence, then, indeed, I might have knelt down and worshipped" (p. 45). After having slept all night with the roar of the waters mingling with his dreams, he feels his "former awe and enthusiasm" reviving. Gradually, after much contemplation, his own feelings tell him that "Niagara is indeed a wonder of the world" (p. 46). He concludes that the experience of the sublime comes only when one stands beside the falls "in the simplicity of his heart, suffering the mighty scene to work its own impression" (p. 46). His mind now finds perfect unison with the scene.[6]

The inclination to kneel down and worship, and the necessity of viewing the falls in an attitude of simplicity of heart, suggest that for Hawthorne aesthetic experience of this kind depends in part upon the religious qualifications that he described in his characters Matthew, Hannah, and Ernest. But "My Visit to Niagara" most strongly emphasizes the inadequacy of conventional attitudes toward the sublime; stereotyped expectations only stand in the way of a rare and difficult experience. Accordingly, much attention is given in the sketch to an ironical dismissal of those who find the experience easy. Hawthorne describes two adventurers and a guide behind the falls; they make what only appears to be a perilous movement toward a rock. A hat blows away, and they emerge, "children of the mist," to receive, "I presume, a certificate of their achievement, with three verses of sublime poetry on the back" (p. 48). One can justly conclude that Hawthorne did not allow himself to be deceived by counterfeit emotions; his account of the sublime is distinguished by its emotional genuineness. For this achievement, who would deny him a certificate?

From *American Literature* 37, no. 4 (January, 1966): 391-402. Copyright © 1965 by Duke University Press. Reprinted by permission of Duke University Press

Notes

1. There are no studies of Hawthorne's interest in the sublime. In "The Machine in the Garden," *New England Quarterly*, XXIX, 27–42 (March, 1956), Leo Marx discusses Hawthorne's use of the picturesque convention as an obstacle to a direct response to the rapidly changing American landscape. Another view, which sees Hawthorne's use of the picturesque as a technique that assists rather than hinders him in coming to terms with technological change, is presented in my note, "Hawthorne's 'The Canal Boat': An Experiment in Landscape," *American Quarterly*, XVI, 211–215 (Summer, 1964).

2. Henry James regards Hawthorne's "relish of gloomy subjects" as synonymous with a taste for the picturesque. "What interested him in such subjects was their picturesqueness, their rich duskiness of colour, their chiaroscuro . . ." (*Hawthorne* [1879], Ithaca, N. Y., 1956, p. 47).

3. *The Complete Works of Nathaniel Hawthorne*, ed. George Parsons Lathrop, Riverside edition (Boston and New York, 1882), I, 173–174. All quotations from Hawthorne are from this edition.

4. The standard work by Samuel H. Monk, *The Sublime: A Study of Critical Theories in XVIII-Century England* [1935] (Ann Arbor, 1961), has been followed by two studies of the religious ramifications of the sublime: Marjorie Hope Nicolson's *Mountain Gloom and Mountain Glory: The Development of the Aesthetics of the Infinite* (New York, 1959), and Ernest Lee Tuveson's *The Imagination as a Means of Grace: Locke and the Aesthetics of Romanticism* (Berkeley, 1960).

5. Charles L. Sanford notes that Allston's lectures departed from Edmund Burke's concept of the sublime chiefly in "the insistence that the passions released into art by the sublime be harnessed to lofty spiritual ends commensurate with a land of virtue whose highest genius was dedicated to the redemption of mankind" (*The Quest for Paradise: Europe and the American Moral Imagination*, Urbana, Ill., 1961, p. 138). Allston's "moral" or "true" sublime enables Americans to reject the morally unsound sublime of the chief English poets. Behind Allston's distinction lies the modification of Burke undertaken by Kames, Blair, and Alison, a change "which united sentiments of the sublime to a great moral idea assumed to exist in and behind nature" (p. 143). Sanford discusses William Cullen Bryant and Thomas Cole but does not mention Hawthorne in this connection. Hawthorne had almost certainly read the three eighteenth-century aestheticians, who among others developed Burke's idea of the sublime.

6. For Henry James, Niagara Falls was entirely a picturesque (in the sense of forming a picture) rather than a sublime phenomenon. "It is not in the least monstrous; it is thoroughly artistic and, as the phrase is, thought out" ("Niagara," reprinted in *The Art of Travel*, ed. Morton D. Zabel, New York, 1962, p. 80). So completely had the sublime lost its force by James's day that he was able to view the falls in classical rather than romantic terms: "the genius who invented it was certainly the first author of the idea that order, proportion, and symmetry are the conditions of perfect beauty" (pp. 81–82).

Hawthorne, the Fall, and the Psychology of Maturity____

Melvin W. Askew

Although Hawthorne's spiritual dramas are resonant with theological implications, Melvin W. Askew argues, Hawthorne had little interest in "the fall as a theological concept with its ramifications in heaven or hell"; for him, "the fall is intimate and personal," and the Christian drama becomes only a trope or a myth that Hawthorne uses to his own purposes.

In Hawthorne's hands, the fall from innocence to experience is a fortunate fall, a *felix culpa*. Hawthorne explores these themes of innocence lost in many of his works, both short and long—"Young Goodman Brown," "The Minister's Black Veil," "Rappaccini's Daughter," "The Birthmark," and *The Marble Faun*—but Askew sees only three characters in Hawthorne's works who successfully manage the transition from innocence to maturity: Edgar in "The Maypole of Merrymount," Josiah in "The Canterbury Pilgrims," and Donatello in *The Marble Faun*. They all succeed by "rejecting the pastoral, false Edens of innocence and inexperience and . . . willingly embracing the conditions of the world." — J.L.

Hawthorne's psychological insights have formed the basis of so many excellent studies that his reputation for psychological sophistication in such areas as psychosomatics and psychoanalysis is now but little short of notorious.[1] Curiously, however, one of the most frequent narrative configurations in his fiction, the fall of man, has not yet been studied in terms of its psychological implications. Nevertheless, in a great number of his best short stories and tales—"The Maypole of Merry Mount," "Young Goodman Brown," "Rappaccini's Daughter," "The Birth-Mark," and "The Minister's Black Veil," as well as his last romance, *The Marble Faun*—Hawthorne deals with a man who stands on the threshold of loss of innocence, not only in the Adamic, moral, and characterological sense explored by R. W. B. Lewis and Leslie Fiedler,[2] but also in a specific psychological sense.

When the protagonist appears in each of these stories, he has just begun to love, or he is soon to be married, or he has only recently been married. Each character, then, is faced with the prospect of assuming mature responsibilities, and each story is an account of how he responds to this crucial psychological situation. And in these stories only three characters accept responsibility and grow into maturity: Edgar in "The Maypole of Merry Mount," Josiah in "The Canterbury Pilgrims," and Donatello in *The Marble Faun*. The remainder try to modify the conditions of acceptance or the conditions of responsibility either by temporizing, like Parson Hooper, or by tampering, like Aylmer and Giovanni, or by straightforward rejection, like Young Goodman Brown. Failing to accept mature responsibility, then, these destroy or reject love and the woman, and simultaneously fail to become human and happy in maturity.

Now the fall of man occurs in each of these stories. The circumstances of Eden are frequently and deliberately contrived, the characteristics of Adam and the fall from grace, the "damnation" or "salvation," is consciously conceptualized. But unlike Dante, Milton, and Bunyan, whose influence helped to give this particular shape to Hawthorne's fiction, Hawthorne himself apparently did not value the fall as a theological concept with its ramifications in heaven or hell. His vision, that is to say, both of man and his fall, stopped sharply on this side of eternity. Pre-eminently, then, the fall is intimate and personal, and its ramifications are worked out in the personal life-experience and existence of the fallen. And its greatest significance is the influence it exerts in the conduct and quality of that specific, individual life. The fall of man, then, freed from theology, becomes a figure of speech, a trope, a myth in Hawthorne's fiction for a universal human circumstance: the profound, psychological complex of experience and knowledge that leads to maturity of mind and heart.

The clearest indication that the fall is psychological and human rather than theological and spiritual is furnished by "The Maypole of Merry Mount." The circumstances of Eden are here closely imitated (even to the detail of a central tree), and the whole is involved in a context of "atheism" (the Merrymounters) and "theism" (the Puritans). None of these figures, however, furnishes the medium by which Edith's and Edgar's fall is accomplished. Strikingly and pointedly they fall through the force of love. Thus Hawthorne writes:

> Just then, as if a spell had loosened them, down came a little shower of withering rose leaves from the Maypole. Alas, for the young lovers! No sooner had their hearts glowed with real passion than they were sensible of something vague and unsubstantial in their former pleasures, and felt a dreary presentiment of inevitable change. From the moment that they truly loved, they had subjected themselves to earth's doom of care and sorrow, and troubled *joy*, and had no more a home at Merry Mount. That was Edith's mystery.[3]

The fall, then, is an earthly one, a fall into "*earth's* doom of care and sorrow, and troubled joy," into humanity, sympathy, responsibility, and maturity.

The condition of the fall in "The Maypole of Merry Mount" also indicates that those who have "truly loved" and fallen accept one another and full responsibility for their love and union. Thus Hawthorne writes of the pair:

> There they stood, pale, downcast, and apprehensive. Yet there was an air of mutual support and of pure affection, seeking aid and giving it, that showed them to be man and wife, with the sanction of a priest upon their love.[4]

Thus, too, the lovers understand that their individual well-being, their self-fulfilment, is inextricably united with the welfare of the loved one. When they are threatened, then, by Endicott, Edgar replies, "Do with me as thou wilt, but let Edith go untouched!" Similarly, Edith answers, "Let [our punishment] be death, and lay it all on me!" There can be no happiness for one without the other.

Now the psychological fall of man is correlated with the theological fall at two levels. First, it is a fortunate fall, a *felix culpa*. Thus at the end of the tale, Hawthorne outlines the fate and life of Edith and Edgar together: they are married by having the "wreath of roses" cast over them by the "gauntleted hand" of Endicott, the symbolic equivalent of the "troubled joy" they earn, since the rose is analogous to the joy in flowery Merry Mount—*felix*—and the gauntlet, to the troubled and dismal Puritan community with its insistence on man's culpability—*culpa*. Thus,

> It was a deed of prophecy. As the moral gloom of the world overpowers all systematic gayety, even so was their home of wild mirth made desolate amid the sad forest. They returned to it no more. But as their flowery garland was wreathed of the brightest roses that had grown there, so, in the tie that united them, were intertwined all the purest and best of their early joys. They went heavenward, supporting each other along the difficult path which it was their lot to tread, and never wasted one regretful thought on the vanities of Merry Mount.[5]

A second correlation is that in both conceptions the fall shatters the organization and circumstances of Eden; or, more accurately, both falls make one "unfit" for Eden. Therefore, as Adam and Eve were driven from the Garden after their sin, so, after they loved, Edith and Edgar "had no more a home at Merry Mount." In both cases, however, both pairs of human beings grow beyond the confines of Eden, Adam and Eve by knowledge, Edith and Edgar by love.

But abstracted from theological meanings suggested by its allegorical framework, "The Maypole of Merry Mount" becomes a deeply humanistic and a profoundly psychological document, one which yields the mythic and narrative formulation of the quality of love, the mechanics of maturity, and, in Hawthorne's view, the inevitable conduct of life. Reduced to concepts, the terms of the myth are these: Love, Maturity-acceptance-responsibility, Life: Love (the fall from innocence); Acceptance ("seeking aid and giving it"); Maturity (the assumption of responsibility; the realization that one's happiness rests in part with the happiness of others, that apparent self-sacrifice is no sacrifice at last, but rather the discovery and fulfilment of one's self) ; and finally, Life (with "troubled joy" as the greatest—and realistically— the only joy or salvation that one finds).

Transcribing this pattern into more narrow psychological terms, note, first, that innocence is not a state of guiltlessness, but rather a state of inexperience and ignorance. Thus a child is innocent, as any Freudian or parent knows, not by virtue of guiltlessness or "sinlessness," but by virtue of ignorance and inexperience. He believes, for instance, that all his narcissistic aspirations can come true, and he does not hesitate to act upon them. The innocent or immature person, then, approaches the world as if it were raw material dedicated solely to his personal gratification. People are to him plastic counters to be manipulated and modified for his personal pleasure. Now this approach to the world has obvious Edenic features: it is whole, integrated, and monolithic; it "organizes" an otherwise apparently chaotic and inscrutable world. And it appears to offer not only total gratification but total security as well. The world, however, does not long tolerate this narcissism, and the innocent tries to manipulate it at his peril.

Paradoxically, love is both the cause of this fall from a narcissistic and infantile Eden and the forgiveness for that fall. By its very nature, love predicates one's own happiness, serenity, and well-being upon the maintenance of those same qualities in the loved one; it doubles, then, the reference of happiness, making it simultaneously inner-directed and outer-directed. Thus the walls and limits of the unified, integrated, and innocent "Eden" are demolished by love, which breaks the narcissistic shell. Simultaneously, love discovers that narcissism is neither practical nor wholesome, that the new world of love must be accepted willingly if, indeed, not eagerly on *its* own terms.

So love itself, then, is the only forgiveness, for it involves the desire to give as well as to take ("seeking aid and giving it"); it involves the realization that happiness for one's self must provide happiness for the loved one. Narcissistic action, therefore, is modified into responsible behavior to assure happiness for others so that part may answer to part and the complements join into new wholeness, a new, though fallen, "Eden."

And under these circumstances the world seems more uncertain and at times unpredictable and threatening, and one must search out his way with some confusion and pain. But respect, sympathy, and love, earn the best that earth can give: life in a "fallen" world with the disillusionment and knowledge that perfect happiness, security, and dreams are never to be found, but with a love and joy which, at certain levels, is inevitably troubled. And this is to be mature and responsible, both in the sense of being able to respond to others, to keep alive one's sensibilities and heart (or in Hawthorne's terms, to preserve sympathy), and in the sense of living in the full awareness that one is answerable for his very existence.

The fall, then, from Merry Mount to maturity is very real in psychological terms, and it entails a painful view of the undecorated, actual condition of mankind. And this fall, again like the theological fall, is fortunate, for it is only through this psychological development that one finds any joy or fulfilment. And though the joy may be "troubled," it is infinitely preferable to the disaster which befalls those of Hawthorne's characters (as well as those people in life) who do not succeed to the vision and the growth. Moreover, if this fall into humanity is accepted, it leads to a new psychological organization, which allows the incorporation and respectful use of the real world (now substituted for the fantastic, narcissistic Eden). And though the new organization is freighted with care and uncertainty, it provides the only medium through which man may exercise most fully those virtues which constitute his humanness and which constitute him man.

II

From this psychological point of view, typical Hawthorne characters accumulate new degrees of freshness and poignancy. For if they are seen as psychologically realistic studies of the various ways in which man may fall and what he may fall into (humanity or inhumanity, love and maturity or narcissism and irresponsibility), then they become delicately shaded but profound variations on the matter of Adam rather than simple repetitions of it.

Of the many characters who appear in "The Maypole of Merry Mount," "Young Goodman Brown," "The Minister's Black Veil," "The Canterbury Pilgrims," "Rappaccini's Daughter," "The Birth-Mark," and *The Marble Faun*, all of which are centrally involved in the myth of maturity, only a small group of the fallen arrive at a new wholeness; only a selected few, that is to say, find integrity, maturity, and responsibility in a fallen and shattered world. Few, indeed, both in Hawthorne's fiction and in life! But each seems to arrive at this coveted psychological and human situation by rejecting the pastoral, false Edens of innocence and inexperience and by willingly embracing the conditions of the world in order to fulfil themselves and their love. Thus Josiah and Miriam in "The Canterbury Pilgrims" reject the Shaker community, embrace one another, and accept the conditions of the real world, in spite of the eloquent descriptions the Pilgrims give of the pitfalls, dangers, and deceits of that world. Thus, too, Edith and Edgar reject their former vanities, embrace one another and the world. So also does Donatello reject the pastoral purity of Monte Beni in order to return to time, responsibility, and Miriam.

But these few (with the possible exception of Beatrice in "Rappaccini's Daughter") are the only ones in the fiction discussed here who reconstruct a new integrity out of shattered fragments of dreams *and* the circumstances of reality, who embrace their humanity, their wholeness for good and evil, and thus claim the stature of manhood or humanness. The others, for various reasons, but with similar disaster, fail. Young Goodman Brown, for instance, unable to accept the patent fact that Faith with the pink ribbons is no angel and that there is no one-to-one correspondence between the circumstances of reality and the circumstances of the catechism taught him by Goody Cloyse, never recognizes the true proportions of Faith's character, the true character of the people in his community, or the true and total potential within himself. He rejects the actual and real, clings to the dream of perfection and security, and lives by that disastrously. He loses sympathy (responsibility and maturity), fails to love, and dies in gloom.

Likewise, the principal characters in "Rappaccini's Daughter" cling to the narcissistic fantasy of remaking the world. Rappaccini intends to reconstruct the world even as he has created the new Garden, and he will set the poisonous but all-powerful Beatrice and Giovanni to rule over it. In pursuit of this dream, however, he loses sympathy and responsibility, and late in life he watches the structure of his dream and false, unrealistic Eden collapse about him. Giovanni, like Aylmer in "The Birth-Mark," confuses perfection of love with perfection of the woman, and in tampering with her, in an attempt to modify and re-create her, he destroys not only the woman but also all his possibilities of happiness. Indeed, both Aylmer and Giovanni are fundamentally unable to love and therefore cannot fall into humanity and maturity. Thus in "Rappaccini's Daughter" Hawthorne writes:

> It was not love, although her rich beauty was a madness to him; nor horror, even while he fancied her spirit to be imbued with the same baneful essence that seemed to pervade her physical frame; but a wild offspring of both love and horror that had each parent in it, and burned like one and shivered like the other.[6]

And again:

> Oh, how stubbornly does love,—or even that cunning semblance of love which flourishes in the imagination, but strikes no depth of root into the heart,—how stubbornly does it hold its faith until the moment comes when it is doomed to vanish into thin mist![7]

The Reverend Mr. Hooper, in a similar pattern of failure, accepts neither Elizabeth nor the world on its own terms. She would have him without the interposed veil, and he would have all the world if it wore a veil. In something little short, then, of a personal narcissistic orgy, Mr. Hooper, in spite of partial success in his ministry, fails at life. He distinguishes himself from the common heart of humanity with his black veil and waits for the world to come round to him. He waits in vain.

Other characters suffer from the same narcissistic impulse, although they do not always appear in such clear circumstances of the fall of man as those discussed here. Note, however, the nameless youth in "The Ambitious Guest," who spends his life in an attempt to build a barren monument to himself, even at the expense of joy and the maiden's hand by the fireside. He ends disastrously. Or note, too, Ethan Brand, who narcissistically, recklessly, and irresponsibly probes into the hearts of others (while he loses his own) in his search for the gratification of finding and confirming his *idée fixe*. Or again, notice Richard Digby, who, in "The Man of Adamant," is represented as turning to stone because he could not love Mary Goffe or tolerate the world; for dabbling in his own lonely salvation, he left his heart, his responsibility, and the world undiscovered.

III

Although the fall is the central theme in Hawthorne's fiction, even in most of those works which do not precisely imitate the matter of Eden and Adam, Hawthorne's characters obviously do not fall from God's grace, or into a theologically conceived hell or heaven. Nor is their "sin" always a theological sin, or their "guilt" theologically construed. They fall, rather, into the worldly, humanistic, and realistic equivalent of these; that is to say, they fall into inhumanity or humanity. If they do not accept the conditions of their fall, the facts of the fallen world, or the knowledge by which their fall was accomplished, they live disoriented in a temporal, dark, and human hell, like Goodman Brown. If, however, they do accept, if they love and arrive at maturity, they find a human salvation and a troubled heaven like that accorded to Edith and Edgar; they live with the troubled joy that earth with its doom of care and sorrow gives as reward. Thus the fall is internal and psychological—where the meanings are; it is neither theological nor, strictly speaking, social.

What occurs after the accepted fall, after the accomplishment of human maturity, Hawthorne does not define in explicit detail. However, in those stories in which maturity is achieved, he discovers enough to indicate that mature life is essentially pathetic. But, again, like his later and perhaps greatest student, Henry James, Hawthorne's principal concern was with the crucial conditions of the fall itself and the individual responses to it—the moral growth or personal disaster that followed. And just as James ended his chronicles of Isabel Archer and Lambert Strether after their discovery and acceptance of the world, just so did Hawthorne leave his characters.

It would be a great violation of both, however, but especially of Hawthorne, to suggest that the psychological pattern of maturity which emerges from his fiction constitutes either its total significance or the fullness of its meaning. Certainly it does not. However, this psychological pattern of Love, Acceptance-responsibility-maturity, and Life, as it is figured forth in the myth of the fall in Hawthorne, adds a new dimension to the other readings to which the dense texture of his fiction so readily lends itself. It adds a dimension which casts other readings into deeper perspective and illuminates anew both the patterns of fiction and the configurations of human existence that appear in much of his work.

From *American Literature* 34, no. 3 (November, 1962): 335 -343. Copyright ©1962 by Duke University Press. Reprinted by permission of Duke University Press

Notes

1. See, for example, any of the following: C. P. Oberndorff, M.D., "The Psychoanalytic Insight of Nathaniel Hawthorne," *Psychoanalytic Review*, XXIX, 373–385 (October, 1942); Vladimir Astrov, "Hawthorne and Dostoievski as Explorers of the Human Conscience," *New England Quarterly*, XV, 296–319 (June, 1942); Lois Atkins, "Psychological Symbolism of Guilt and Isolation in Hawthorne," *American Imago*, XI, 417–425 (Winter, 1954); Howard Brand, "Hawthorne on the Therapeutic Role," *Journal of Abnormal and Social Psychology*, XLVII, 856–868 (October, 1952).

2. R. W. B. Lewis, *The American Adam: Innocence, Tragedy, and Tradition in the Nineteenth Century* (Chicago, 1955); Leslie A. Fiedler, *Love and Death in the American Novel* (New York, 1960).

3. Nathaniel Hawthorne, *Selected Tales and Sketches* (New York, 1958), p. 142. "Edith's mystery" in this passage deserves some special comment, for it is a parallel to Beatrice Rappaccini's "poison," Georgiana's birthmark or blemish, Faith's veil worn at the witches meeting, and the terrible secret Miriam in *The Marble Faun* lives with, the secret embodied in the inscrutable and ambiguous model. Each apparent failing, threat, or blemish appears to be symbolic of the painful fall promised by love and the woman. It is always, however, counterpointed by the woman's remarkable beauty or desirability which appears to symbolize the promise of future joy and fulfilment. Together and in the same woman, the combination of threat and/or blemish with arresting beauty appears to be equivalent to the phrase "troubled joy" and thus analogous to the marriage ceremony in the "Maypole of Merry Mount," which is performed by uniting the lovers in a wreath of roses thrown by a gauntleted hand. In the figure of the woman, then, is prefigured the pain of the fall from innocence and the joy of the assumption of humanity.

4. *Ibid.*, p. 147.

5. *Ibid.*, p. 149.

6. *Ibid.*, p. 279.

7. *Ibid.*, p. 287.

Nathaniel Hawthorne and His Mother:
A Biographical Speculation_____

Nina Baym

Biography can be dangerous stuff, and critics are advised to handle it with care. It is far too easy to explain away literary complexity with casual references to an author's life. Once we begin explaining characters, plots, and turns of phrase with reference to trivia excavated from an author's biography, we run the risk of ignoring everything that makes literature worth reading.

Nina Baym, though, while acknowledging that "*The Scarlet Letter* obviously cannot be called a work of autobiography," offers a more sophisticated biographical reading of that work, focusing on the nearly invisible role of Hawthorne's mother. Hawthorne was raised without a father—Nathaniel Hathorne, Sr., a ship's captain, died when his son was only four—and yet the place of his mother in Hawthorne's life has been strangely neglected. We all remember that he began writing *The Scarlet Letter* shortly after being dismissed from the Custom House; we too often forget that, at exactly the same time, Hawthorne watched his mother die.

Baym goes so far as to argue that "It is not inaccurate to describe *The Scarlet Letter* as Hawthorne's response to his mother's death." It's an odd kind of response, though, for it left very few textual traces. Hawthorne worked to exclude every reference to her from his writing. For Baym, this "representation of the mother as absent actually masks an oppressive sense of her presence in his psychic world." Baym sees elements of Elizabeth Manning Hawthorne in Hester, the "angry and defiant heroine" of *The Scarlet Letter.* "The search for the lost *mother,*" she argues, "rather than the lost father, underlies much of the story patterning in his mature fiction. . . . The idea of matriarchy retained a powerful hold on his imagination."   — J.L.

Every student of Nathaniel Hawthorne's work and life knows that he wrote *The Scarlet Letter* because he lost his job at the Salem Custom House. He told the world so in his autobiographical preface to the story, "The Custom-House," and all later biographers have followed his lead while filling out the details.[1] But the sequence of events Hawthorne chronicles in the preface explains no more than how he came to be free to write, and offers no factual basis for understanding what he wrote. To be sure, his angry and defiant heroine might express some of his own humiliation and rage. To write a story which favored the outcast so heavily against the establishment might have been an act of sweet revenge on the author's powerful enemies.

But such connections are remote. The essence of Hester's character and story (not to mention Dimmesdale's) is untouched. Why did Hawthorne pick a woman protagonist? Why a lone woman? Why a mother? To the extent that we seek biographical explanations for such choices we are probably always limited to surmise rather than certain knowledge. But it seems fair to say that the biographical accounts we now have do not offer hypotheses which engage with these questions.

Another event occurred in Hawthorne's life at the same time, exactly, that he was dismissed from the Custom House. On 30 July 1849, only six days after the new surveyor was appointed, his mother died. Her health had long been fragile, but she had lived to be sixty-nine years old. She was residing in Hawthorne's house (as were his two sisters, both unmarried) when she succumbed to a sudden, relatively brief illness which took the author by surprise. He was greatly affected by her death, coming near to a "brain fever" after her burial on 2 August. Six days later he was writing for the first time of leaving Salem, "this abominable city," forever, as indeed he was to do after finishing *The Scarlet Letter.* By early September he had recovered from his illness and begun *The Scarlet Letter*, working with an intensity that almost frightened his wife, and with a speed that brought the book to completion before the year ended. He was inspired as he had never been before, or was to be again.[2]

Common sense suggests that a work following so immediately on the death of a mother, featuring a heroine who is a mother (and whose status as a mother is absolutely central to her situation), might very likely be inspired by that death and consist, in its autobiographical substance, of a complex memorial to that mother. But one looks virtually in vain for a biographical analysis of *The Scarlet Letter* which pursues such a suggestion.[3] One looks in vain for a reliable, comprehensive account of Hawthorne's mother and his relationship with her. Instead, we have a longstanding and unreliable tradition about her which persists despite a quantity of countervailing evidence. This tradition permits critics to accuse her of a grotesque, pernicious role in his life or, alternatively, to deny her any role at all.

Mark Van Doren, one of the few skeptics, described the situation well: "His mother has long been the subject of a sentimental legend which no evidence supports. She is supposed, soon after her husband's death, to have shut herself away not only from the world but from the Mannings [her natal family] and her own children. There are hints of a darkened room where she takes her meals alone, says nothing, and mourns 'in a Hindoo seclusion' the irreparable sadness of her lot. It appears on the contrary that she was an excellent cook, an attentive mother, and an interesting talker about things past and present. Her son's childhood letters to her, a number of which survive, are addressed to no such awful stranger as the legend suggests."[4] Van Doren could have added that some of her letters also survive, showing an active, outward-looking disposition and betraying no hint of reclusiveness. But despite evidence accumulated and publicized by such scholars as Norman Holmes Pearson, Randall Stewart, Manning Hawthorne, and (recently) Gloria Ehrlich, the legend persists in newer biographies.[5] Thus when we look for Hawthorne's mother we have to make our way past a legend constructed, it seems, to deny access.

It is not hard to understand why the legend has persisted. It has Haw-thorne's own authority behind it, as well as the endorsement of his wife, his sister-in-law, and his son. For those seeking a reason for Haw-thorne's supposed lifelong feelings of gloom and alienation, both the maternal rejection and her example of seclusion seem to provide clues. Such early biographers as George Woodberry, Lloyd Morris, Herbert Gorman, Robert Cantwell, and Newton Arvin depended heavily on the legend to explain the oddities of Hawthorne's imagination and his fic-tion. To other biographers seeking (for various reasons) to connect Hawthorne to the father he never knew and the father's family he had nothing to do with, her alleged absence allowed them to follow their preferences by writing her out of his life altogether. Among such biog-raphers one must include Randall Stewart, Hubert Hoeltje, Arlin Tur-ner, and James R. Mellow.

It is not especially difficult to understand the motives of Haw-thorne's surviving family in transmitting to the public a misrepresenta-tion of his mother. The misrepresentation operated to their advantage, as we shall see; and in any case they would not have been likely to go against a story originating with Hawthorne himself. It is very puzzling, however, to make out Hawthorne's own motives in this case. But it is important to try to do so, for every conscious misrepresentation points to something hidden. Hawthorne seems to have been trying to hide not merely the actual role that his mother had played in his life, but the fact that she had a role at all. Such a denial—completely unnecessary in those innocent pre-Freudian days—only suggests that her role must have been very large indeed.

The legend made its first appearance of record in his early love let-ters to Sophia Peabody, where he writes of his mother's and sisters' ec-centric reclusiveness, and the morbid atmosphere in their house, which he calls "Castle Dismal." (The phrase later became a favorite of Sophia's.) Later he resisted Sophia's urgings that he make their en-gagement known by citing "the strange reserve, in regard to matters of feeling, that has always existed among us. We are conscious of one another's feelings, always; but there seems to be a tacit law, that our deepest heart-concernments are not to be spoken of."[6]

These sentences have carried a good deal of weight with biographers who have taken them at face value instead of observing their highly literary character. They need to be examined for the equivocations of their rhetoric—the unallowable equation of an engagement with deepest, private heart-concernments, for example. And, while asserting the existence of "a strange reserve" these lines imply a group of people deeply attuned to one another's moods and hence, possibly, an understanding beyond the need for speech. In any event, people who are always conscious of one another's feelings must be in more or less constant contact. A particular irony of this letter is the way Hawthorne offers up its obfuscation to Sophia as exemplary of how he can gush out freely to her and to her only.

In fine, what we seem to have here is an instance of a lover's strategy, to claim that nobody understands him and thereby appear both more needy and more interesting in the beloved's eyes, all the while giving her the pleasure of enacting the heroine's role in his romantic drama. "Mine ownest," he wrote her on 4 October 1840, addressing her as though they were already married, "Here sits thy husband in his old accustomed chamber, where he used to sit in years gone by. . . . Sometimes (for I had no wife then to keep my heart warm) it seemed as if I were already in the grave, with only life enough to be chilled and benumbed . . . till at length a certain Dove was revealed to me, in the shadow of a seclusion as deep as my own had been. . . . So now I begin to understand why I was imprisoned so many years in this lonely chamber, and why I could never break through the viewless bolts and bars" (*Love Letters*, I, 223–24).

Sophia's limpid, unsophisticated imagination accepted the lover's hyperbole as literal truth, as Hawthorne expected—for he was aware of, and attracted to, the transparent sensibility which seemed the very opposite of his own. "I tell thee these things," he wrote, "in order that my Dove, into whose infinite depths the sunshine falls continually, may perceive what a cloudy veil stretches over the abyss of my nature" (*Love Letters*, II, 79). Her simple sincerity guaranteed that she would mistake the veil for the abyss. And, as a result of her mistake, she transmitted the legend through conversations and letters until it became an article of family faith.

Sophia was apparently not the only one to whom Hawthorne talked in this vein in the years before his marriage. When Julian Hawthorne was preparing a biography of his parents in the early 1880s he asked Elizabeth Peabody, Sophia's sister, to write up her recollection of Hawthorne during the period of his courtship. (Peabody had sought Hawthorne out after the publication of *Twice-Told Tales* and had introduced him to her sister Sophia.) Her memories can be questioned, since they pertain to a period almost fifty years behind her; but the statements she attributed to Hawthorne resemble those he wrote to Sophia. He is represented as saying, "'We do not live at our house, we only vegetate. Elizabeth [Hawthorne's older sister] never leaves her den; I have mine in the upper story, to which they always bring my meals, setting them down in a waiter at my door, which is always locked.' 'Don't you even see your mother?' said I. 'Yes,' said he, 'in our little parlour. She comes and sits down with me and Louisa [Hawthorne's younger sister] after tea—and sometimes Louisa and I drink tea together. My mother and Elizabeth each take their meals in their rooms. My mother has never sat down to table with anybody, since my father's death.' I said, 'Do you think it is healthy to live so separated?' 'Certainly not—it is no life at all—it is the misfortune of my life. It has produced a morbid consciousness that paralyzes my powers.'"

Peabody then goes on to describe the reclusive widow Hawthorne who, through Julian Hawthorne's biography, found her way into the common understanding of Hawthorne's life. But in the very same description she comments on the widow in a manner that undercuts her own account. "Widow Hawthorne always looked as if she had walked out of an old picture, with her ancient costume, and a face of lovely sensibility, and great brightness—for she did not *seem* at all a victim of morbid sensibility, notwithstanding her all but Hindoo self-devotion to the manes of her husband. She was a person of fine understanding and a very cultivated mind."[7] It takes no great acumen to observe that Elizabeth Peabody could not have known how the widow "always" looked, or characterize her fine and cultivated sensibility if she had seldom left her bedroom. Indeed, the revealing phrase "she did not *seem* at all a victim of morbid sensibility" shows that Peabody's theories of Elizabeth Hathorne did not mesh with her memories.

Julian Hawthorne was a shrewd and tactful man who doubtless perceived discrepancies in the material he had before him. However, given the filial respect which was his announced motive in writing *Nathaniel Hawthorne and His Wife*, he could not contradict views of events maintained by his parents. He transmitted much of Elizabeth Peabody's account, and building from its description of the widow's reclusiveness, he attributed Hawthorne's alienated temperament to the mother's unnatural behavior. Hawthorne "was brought up," Julian wrote, "under what might be considered special disadvantages. His mother, a woman of fine gifts but of extreme sensibility, lost her husband in her twenty-eighth year; and, from an exaggerated, almost Hindoo-like construction of the law of seclusion which the public taste of that day imposed upon widows, she withdrew entirely from society, and permitted the habit of solitude to grow upon her to such a degree that she actually remained a strict hermit to the end of her long life, or for more than forty years after Captain Hawthorne's death. . . . It is saying much for the sanity and healthfulness of the minds of these three children, that their loneliness distorted their judgment, their perception of the relation of things, so little as it did" (*Hawthorne and His Wife*, I, 4–5).

Only a few pages further on, Julian approves Widow Hawthorne's views on education, and credits her with shaping her son's literary sensibilities by encouraging him to read poetry, romance, and allegory. And he prints recollections by other informants which contradict the legend implicitly. But ultimately he fails to engage with the inconsistencies in his narrative. He needs the widow's morbidity for his thesis, which is that Hawthorne was saved as man and artist through his marriage to Sophia. The story that Julian's father had invented as an ardent lover is respectfully promulgated by a dutiful son.

Perhaps the damage done to Elizabeth Hathorne's reputation resulted inadvertently from Hawthorne's campaign to win Sophia. But, unquestionably, there is malice and hostility expressed toward her in the particular legend Hawthorne devised. In some obscure manner she is held accountable for Hawthorne's incarceration in the Castle Dismal. In the fairy-tale structure of the legend (a variant of "Beauty and the Beast," perhaps) she is allocated the role of the enchanter whose evil spell must be undone by the greater power of Sophia's beneficence. While the structure is demonstrably out of keeping with known facts, it might well be an accurate, though necessarily figural, dramatization of Hawthorne's inner reality. If so, then its representation of the mother as absent actually masks an oppressive sense of her presence in his psychic world. But, known facts do not permit us to characterize Elizabeth Hathorne as domineering and possessive. The presence that is symbolized, then, is the presence of Hawthorne's own deep attachment to his mother.

II

Elizabeth Clarke Manning was born in 1780, the third of nine children of Miriam Lord (b. 1748) and Richard Manning (b. 1755). The other children were Mary, b. 1777; William, b. 1778; Richard, b. 1782; Robert, b. 1784; Maria, b. 1786; John, b. 1788; Priscilla, b. 1790; and Samuel, b. 1791: a total of five boys and four girls, all surviving to adulthood. The Mannings were a close-knit and late marrying family who lived together in a large plain wooden house on Herbert Street in Salem. The head of the family, Richard Manning, began his working life as a blacksmith and progressed to owning a stagecoach line. Through this and other enterprises, including land investments, he built a comfortable estate.

Although none of the Manning children attended college (Nathaniel Hawthorne would be the first of the line to do so) there was considerable interest in education among them, and all, including Elizabeth, received some schooling. As adults, they were avid readers. Their religious views inclined toward the liberal, as they belonged to the Unitarian church. (Elizabeth and her sister Mary joined the Congregational Church in 1806, however.) Elizabeth was the first to leave the Manning household, marrying Nathaniel Hathorne—as the name was then spelled—on 2 August 1801, when she was twenty-one years old. Hathorne, a sea captain, was five years older than she, and had probably known her for some time because he lived across the back fence in a house on Union Street, where she moved upon marriage. There is evidence of a courtship of some duration: on a voyage two years earlier Nathaniel had written couplets to his "dear Betsey." The notebook in which these verses were inscribed became in time the property of his son, who copied over one of his father's amatory couplets: "In the Midest of all these dire allarms / I'll think dear Betsey on thy Charms."[8]

The household to which Elizabeth moved was presided over by Nathaniel's mother, a widow; and his two unmarried sisters also lived there. He and his brother Daniel, also a seafaring man, lived at home when they were on shore, which was seldom. He left for sea very shortly after his marriage and was away when Elizabeth bore her first child on 7 March 1802, a daughter also named Elizabeth though commonly called Ebe.

The date of Ebe's birth was barely seven months after that of her parents' marriage. The significance of this seven-month's child has escaped notice, or at least mention, by virtually all of Hawthorne's biographers. But it could hardly have escaped the notice of the three women with whom Elizabeth was now domiciled, nor could it have been insignificant to them. Perhaps they were models for the hostile chorus of women at the beginning of *The Scarlet Letter.* For, as the historian Carl N. Degler reminds us, "bridal pregnancies" in nineteenth-century

America appear to have been quite rare—well under ten percent—and, as evidence of sexual relations outside marriage, led to social stigma which "fell like a hammer" on the errant.[9] Certainly among conservative segments of Salem society, including quite probably the old-fashioned and pious Hathornes, Elizabeth would have been harshly judged. The daughter Ebe grew up into a strikingly independent, only partially socialized woman, much as though she had been exempted from normal social expectations by those entrusted with rearing her. It is not improbable that Hawthorne's depiction of the wild Pearl had as much to do with his memory of Ebe as a child, as it did with his observations of his own daughter Una.

Nathaniel Hathorne Jr. was born on 4 July 1803; his father was again away at sea. A third child, Maria Louisa (called Louisa) arrived on 9 January 1808, barely two weeks after the father had again set sail, this time on what proved to be his last voyage. Early in the spring of that year he died of a fever in Surinam. He left Elizabeth a widow at the age of twenty-eight, with children aged six and four and an infant of a few months. In seven years of married life he had spent little more than seven months in Salem, and had been absent from home at the births of all his children. We need hardly look further for sources of the image of a socially stigmatized woman abandoned to bear and rear her child alone.

However, Elizabeth did not have to deal with her harsh lot alone, although support did not come from the Hathornes. Only a few months after receiving word of her husband's death she returned permanently to the Mannings. It was only prudent for her to do so, since the Hathornes were not well off and she had inherited nothing from Nathaniel. The Mannings were lower on the social scale than the Hathornes but they were prospering, and the family included several vigorous men to look after its interest and conduct its business.

In addition, there is evidence of bad feeling between Elizabeth and her husband's family. Aunt Peabody in her recollection to Julian Hawthorne wrote that Elizabeth "was not happily affected by her husband's family—the Hawthornes being of a very sharp and stern individuality—and when not cultivated, this appeared in oddity of temper."[10] Peabody's syntax is defective here but her intent is to characterize the Hathornes as people who had, through want of cultivation, let a naturally stern individualism turn to oddness and eccentricity. It may well be that they, rather than Hawthorne's mother, went in for solitude. In any event, after she left them Elizabeth Hathorne made little effort to keep up contacts, notwithstanding their continued proximity. Nor is any effort at relationship recorded from their side. On an occasional Sunday young Nathaniel went over and read the Bible in his grandmother's parlour, and the difference between that household of sharp and stern eccentrics, and the cooperative Mannings, must have been imaginatively striking.

The failure of the Hathornes to pursue a relationship with Elizabeth seems stranger than her defection from them, because in losing her they lost grandchildren who bore their name. But perhaps Elizabeth's misstep had disqualified her children as Hathornes in their eyes. Perhaps they viewed her as a social interloper, a female conniver using a woman's age-old trick to entrap a husband. Perhaps their old-fashioned piety led them to perceive her as sinful and fallen. Perhaps the causes of the falling-out were banal. But however it came about, it is impossible that Nathaniel Hawthorne could have absorbed any other perspective on this rift than that of his mother. Through his later readings in New England history he came to associate the early Puritans with the Hathornes, and this association may go far to explain the severity with which he turns their judging natures back on themselves. The Puritans versus a defenseless woman equalled the Hathornes versus his mother. If his mother herself suffered some sense of guilt or shame under the judgment, then her psychological turmoil filtering into her son's consciousness might linger to provide a model for Hester's complex ambivalences. In any event, I should suppose that some heightened response to her situation underlies the poignant depiction of Hester's duress in *The Scarlet Letter.*

Of course much would have been beyond his childish understanding. He would have to be old enough to mesh a knowledge of wedding and birth dates with a knowledge of biological processes before he could relate his mother's guilt, her children, and her separation from the Hathornes in one logical structure. But the aura of mystery—of the uncanny—that accompanies so many "adult doings" in his fiction from "My Kinsman, Major Molineux" to *The Marble Faun* may be an expression of just that deeply-impressed early sense of bewilderment.

As he became more knowing, Hawthorne may have come to feel some guilt himself—guilt over siding with his mother, if she was indeed in the wrong; and guilt over carrying the name of people (perhaps sharing their traits) who had repudiated his mother for the sin of bearing children. *He* was one of those children, and when later in his life he was reading New England history and found a variant spelling of the paternal name—Hawthorne instead of Hathorne—his adoption of that orthography may have been a gesture of counter-repudiation.

Elizabeth's return to the Mannings has been seen as the first step in an intensifying withdrawal, but in fact the Mannings were much more in the world than the Hathornes, and there were enough of them to be a world in themselves. In 1808 the entire clan was intact at Herbert Street. This means that ten people were living there, ranging from Mrs. Manning who was then sixty years old to Samuel who, at age seventeen, was only eleven years older than Hawthorne's sister Ebe. These numbers alone explain Hawthorne's subsequent appetite for solitude; he must have had almost none of it in his boyhood. The addition of Elizabeth and her three children to the Herbert Street group brought the total living in that house to an incredible (by our modern middle-class standards) fourteen.

The three children were apparently regarded as a joint family charge, and their futures were discussed and determined upon by all. After the senior Manning died in 1813, and Richard settled in Raymond, Maine, to manage family property there, the business head of the Mannings became Robert, while Mary ran the household. Given the limited biological understanding of the child, young Hawthorne probably never missed his dead father consciously, and since there were male heads of the Manning household in abundance he probably never grasped, at any level, the fact that he was lacking a father until he was beyond childhood. At the best, this lack could only have been grasped intellectually, for in his emotional world he had several. The evidence is that he missed not one more father, but a home which might be presided over by his *mother* without the intervention of any other adult. For a while this seemed likely: Elizabeth considered settling near Richard in Maine and running her own farm. She actually tried this way of life, on and off, for six years, and though Hawthorne often had to stay behind in Salem for his schooling, he was anxious for her to make Raymond her permanent residence.

"I hope, Dear Mother," he wrote from Salem on 19 June 1821, "that you will not be tempted by any entreaties to return to Salem to live. You can never have so much comfort here as you now enjoy. You are now undisputed mistress of your own House. Here you would have to submit to the authority of Miss Manning. If you remove to Salem, I shall have no Mother to return to during the College vacations. . . . If you remain where you are, think how delightfully the time will pass with all your children around *you*, shut out from the world with nothing to disturb us. It will be a second garden of Eden."[11] Two elements of Hawthorne's imagery are noteworthy. First, Raymond was at that time not a garden but a forest setting (although, perhaps not insignificantly, a rose bush grew before Elizabeth Hathorne's door).[12] Ever after, Hawthorne visualized Eden not as a garden but a forest, albeit that vision was often obscured by subsequent grief and loss in his fiction. Too, the "first" Garden of Eden had no children in it, while Hawthorne's second Eden conspicuously lacks an Adam. If Hawthorne secretly casts himself in Adam's role, then he is his mother's son and lover both. For him, Eden is a benign matriarchy.

A year earlier he had written his mother expressing reluctance to go to college and, more generally, to grow up. "Oh how I wish I was again with you, with nothing to do but go a gunning. But the happiest days of my life are gone. Why was I not a girl that I might have been pinned all my life to my mother's apron."[13] Given the conspicuous gun image, Hawthorne is not complaining about his gender, but about social rules that force a boy out of the Garden of Eden into the cold patriarchal world while permitting a girl to remain enclosed in the maternal paradise. The search for the lost *mother*, rather than the lost father, underlies much of the story patterning in his mature fiction, as does the scheme of flight from the patriarchy. The idea of the matriarchy retained a powerful hold on his imagination throughout life, and he could only view patriarchal social organizations—the only kind he knew, though others could be imagined—with enmity.

The enmity may owe its origins precisely to Elizabeth's return to Salem. Hawthorne may have been hurt and angry that his mother disregarded his wishes in favor of her siblings' entreaties. He may have resented her failure to conform her life to his plans; a residue of bitterness may have indeed affected his relation to her after he graduated from Bowdoin and had to come back to Herbert Street instead of Raymond. But he could fault the Mannings too. Hawthorne was glad enough to leave Herbert Street when he was married, but in fact he never felt at home again.[14] Home was mother.

By 1825 the Manning family had suffered from time and circumstance. Only six were still living at Herbert Street when Hawthorne came back from Bowdoin, although some of the others were domiciled close by. Briefly, the senior Richard Manning had died in 1813, his son Richard had gone to live in Maine, and John had disappeared the same year (presumably lost at sea). Maria died in 1814. Priscilla married in 1817 and Robert in 1824; both moved out but remained in Salem. When Hawthorne was married in 1842 the household had been so far depleted as to consist only of his mother and two sisters. Mrs. Manning died in 1826, William went into bachelor quarters, and Samuel died in 1833. At the time that Hawthorne was stressing his solitude to the Peabody sisters, Mary was still living at Herbert Street, but she died in 1841. Robert died in 1842.

For some reason, the probable cumulative effect of all these deaths on Hawthorne has never been appreciated, possibly because he said and wrote little about them. Whatever effect they had on him, however, they must have been disastrous for Elizabeth, who had made her whole life within the family circle. It is useful to remember that when Hawthorne was married she was mourning for the sister to whom she had been closest, and was soon to lose a brother. If she seemed somewhat reclusive in the years when the Peabody sisters came to know her, it may have been merely because she was sad. Or because she did not change with her changing world—she was approaching the age of sixty, and may have seen no way to fill the void that her departing siblings created. She did remain close to her surviving sister Priscilla (Mrs. Dike) and to Robert's widow, Rebecca.

In the years that Hawthorne was living at Herbert Street after graduation, he may well have been the obscurest man of letters in America (as he poetically characterised himself) but he certainly could not have been the most solitary. He may indeed have had to resort to such devices as taking meals in his room and locking his door in order to get some writing done in that busy house. Still, he walked and visited, went on trips with his uncle Samuel, worked on a magazine in Boston (with help from Ebe). He shared his literary plans and agonized over his failures with his mother and sisters. Ebe selected books for him from the Salem Athenaeum. The three knew about his anonymous first novel *Fanshawe*, although Sophia never learned of it. Ebe was able partly to reconstruct, many years later, the early aborted projects for framed collections of short stories. All three women helped him to collect copies of the pieces printed in *Twice-Told Tales* and to prepare the manuscript for publication.[15] Louisa made him a shirt when he went to Brook Farm, while Elizabeth sewed buttons on his trousers and rejoiced in Osgood's flattering portrait of her son that he had made for her. Louisa, who carried on most of the correspondence with him while he was at the farm, bemoaned the infrequency of his letters and visits in a manner that suggests ordinary family intimacy.[16] That Hawthorne was much petted and greatly adored he implicitly admits (Castle Dismal notwithstanding) in a letter to Sophia gently chiding her for having taken offense at something he had written earlier: "Dearest, I beseech you grant me freedom to be careless and wayward—for I have had such freedom all my life" (*Love Letters*, I, 43).

When Hawthorne fell in love with Sophia Peabody late in 1838 he was thirty-five years old. No evidence survives as to whether his mother and sisters had hoped that he would marry, or wished him to remain single, or simply hoped for his happiness whatever he did. Given their general fondness, the last is the most likely possibility. Certainly, however, they never expected him to *conceal* an attachment, and when he finally announced his engagement a scant month before his wedding, Ebe at least was angered beyond the ability to forgive or to rejoice in his happiness. She wrote to Sophia as follows:

> Your approaching union with my brother makes it incumbent upon me to offer you the assurances of my sincere desire for your mutual happiness. With regard to my sister and myself, I hope nothing will ever occur to render your future intercourse with us other than agreeable, particularly as it need not be so frequent or so close as to require more than reciprocal good will, if we do not happen to suit each other in our new relationship. I write thus plainly, because my brother has desired me to say only what was true; though I do not recognize his right so to speak of truth, after keeping us so long in ignorance of this affair. But I do believe him when he says that this was not in accordance with your wishes, for such concealment must naturally be unpleasant, and besides, what I know of your amiable disposition convinces me that you would not give us unnecessary pain. It was especially due to my mother that she should long ago have been made acquainted with the engagement of her only son.[17]

To some degree, Ebe never forgave her brother for his deviousness. "We were in those [early] days almost absolutely obedient to him," she wrote to Julian. "I do not quite approve of either obedience or concealment" (*Hawthorne and His Wife*, I, 124–25). And, despite her comment about Sophia's amiable disposition, she never warmed to her brother's wife. "I might as well tell you that [Sophia] is the only human being whom I really dislike," a late letter to relatives said. "Though she is dead, that makes no difference. I could have lived with her in apparent peace, but I could not have lived long; the constraint would have killed me."[18] Perhaps Hawthorne's having chosen so timid and conventional a woman caused Ebe to reassess his character.

But Elizabeth responded in a different way, as Hawthorne wrote to Sophia:

> Sweetest, scarcely had I arrived here, when our mother came out of her chamber, looking better and more cheerful than I have seen her this some time, and enquired about the health and well-being of my Dove! Very kindly too. Then was thy husband's heart much lightened; for I knew that almost every agitating circumstance of her life had hitherto cost her a fit of sickness; and I knew not but it might be so now. Foolish me, to doubt that my mother's love would be wise, like all other genuine love! . . . Now I am very happy—happier than my naughtiness deserves. It seems that her heart was troubled, because she knew that much of outward as well as inward fitness was requisite to secure thy foolish husband's peace; but, gradually and quietly, God has taught her that all is good, and so, thou dearest wife, we shall have her fullest blessing and concurrence. (*Love Letters*, II, 93–4)

Despite his mother's loving acceptance, Hawthorne's concealment had done her a great wrong, and he knew it. His little boy's confession of naughtiness refers to more than that concealment, however. He was also confessing the naughtiness of his involvement with Sophia to his mother. And, too (what he did not confess), there was the naughtiness of the way in which he had misrepresented her and his relation with her, to the Peabody sisters (and perhaps to others as well). In fact, I surmise that it was his complex sense of acting in bad faith toward Elizabeth that led him to desire concealment; and then that this concealment became another act of bad faith, in a chain of the sort that Hawthorne's fiction sets out so knowingly. Indeed, for the rest of his life Hawthorne was caught by that act of bad faith since he was never able to rectify it except in the oblique language of his fiction.

And I suspect that there was yet more than the lies about Castle Dismal and solitary meals that burdened Hawthorne's conscience. The constellation of images in which he represented his case to Sophia suggested, as I have said above, that Sophia was to save him from and substitute for his mother. The image of the one woman annihilates the image of the other; on the inner stage, where the image is the person, to let Sophia rescue him is to kill his mother. No evidence exists to suggest that Sophia or Elizabeth regarded each other as rivals; the narrative Hawthorne projected derives (to the extent that it is sincere) from his own emotions and not fact. The narrative suggests—what the belated adolescent quality of his romance with Sophia tends to confirm— that his attachment to Elizabeth was so deep and pervasive that he experienced his love for another woman as doing some kind of violence to her, as a killing infidelity. At the same time, if Hawthorne blamed her for his long years of "enchantment" in the Herbert Street house while the world of adult sexual relationships passed him by, then he must also assuredly have *wanted* to kill her to gain his freedom. And so on, through the complex layers of the heart that Hawthorne knew so well.

Doubtless, Sophia caught no glimmer of these depths in his talk of naughtiness, but we can see that she was not entirely satisfied with his explanations because she later worked out a tale which made Ebe (conveniently) the culprit in the concealment. Obligingly, though in revealing language, Julian transmitted her explanation: Ebe, wishing to come between the two lovers, let Hawthorne know that "news of his relation with Miss Sophia would give [Elizabeth] a shock that might endanger her life." As a loving son, Hawthorne was naturally "not prepared to face the idea of defying and perhaps 'killing' his mother" (*Hawthorne and His Wife*, I, 196–97). This story does not withstand a moment's scrutiny. Ebe could not have forestalled the announcement of an engagement which she didn't know about; her blunt nature was incompatible with concealment; and, of course, Hawthorne knew how his mother was likely to react as well as Ebe did. But, if *Ebe* had not persuaded Hawthorne that his engagement would kill his mother, he had probably persuaded himself.

However, Elizabeth declined to be killed, and hence not even a temporary break in her relations with Hawthorne actually took place. Granted, she did not attend his wedding; but there are other explanations for this than hostility. During his sojourn at the Old Manse he had more than one occasion to return to Salem, and inevitably he stayed at Herbert Street, dining and chatting with his mother and sisters. (See *Love Letters*, II, 107, 114, 120–21, 126–27, 155–56.) When he returned with Sophia and his child Una to Salem upon being appointed to the Custom House, he took up residence in Herbert Street while looking for his own home. He did this as a matter of course. The stay lasted several months—longer than anticipated—and seems to have produced tension. But we must remember that Sophia never became a favorite with the three women, nor did she greatly care for them. For example, we find her writing to her mother in January of 1846 that "on many accounts it would be inconvenient to remain in this house. Madame Hawthorne and Louisa are too much out of health to take care of a child, and I do not like to have Una in the constant presence of unhealthy persons. I have never let her go into Madame Hawthorne's mysterious chamber since November, partly on this account, and partly because it is so much colder than the nursery, and has no carpet on it" (*Hawthorne and His Wife*, I, 307–08). A woman who regarded her husband's closest female relatives only as babysitters, described them as "unhealthy persons," and kept her child out of grand-mamma's room for many weeks because it lacked a carpet, cannot be imagined to have encouraged family intimacy. It seems clear that a major goal on Sophia's part was to preserve the autonomy of her own new family.

Nevertheless, when a house (on Mall Street) that finally suited them was found, it was determined that Elizabeth, Ebe, and Louisa should join them permanently. The house, Sophia wrote to her mother, fortunately had a suite of rooms "wholly distant from ours so that we shall only meet when we choose to do so. Madame Hawthorne is so uninterfering, of so much delicacy, that I shall never know she is near excepting when I wish it; and she has so much kindness and sense and spirit she will be a great resource in emergencies. . . . It is no small satisfaction to know that Mrs. Hawthorne's remainder of life will be glorified by the presence of these children [Julian had been born] and of her own son. I am so glad to win her out of that Castle Dismal, and from the mysterious chamber, into which no mortal ever peeped till Una was born and Julian—for they alone entered the penetralia. Into that chamber the sun never shines. Into these rooms in Mall Street it blazes without stint" (*Hawthorne and His Wife*, I, 314). One wonders how Sophia knew so much about Elizabeth's room if none but the little children had ever entered it, or what opportunities the widow would have had to show her kindness, sense, and spirit if she herself never left it. Indeed, Sophia's obtuseness is equalled only by her complacency (or is some complex defensiveness working itself out here?). What sort of rescue would it be for "Madame Hawthorne" if her lot was to wait in her chamber until called on for help in an emergency?

However, Elizabeth Hathorne had her own kind of spunk, it seems. She made her presence known after all. She began to cook items of food for Hawthorne that he had loved as a boy, and even to carry bowls of coffee to him in his study as he sat writing. Though Sophia was appalled, Hawthorne made no objection. Sophia unbent so far, finally, as to obtain from Elizabeth a recipe for an Indian pudding of which her husband was especially fond.[19]

Hawthorne's feelings about his mother in the years after his marriage are not recoverable, for he spoke of these personal matters only to Sophia and then necessarily in a highly oblique language designed as much to veil as reveal. Sophia regularly read his journal and therefore he had to compose his entries with her expectations in mind. Nevertheless, we can be sure that the threatened loss of his position at the Custom House after the election of 1848 must have been particularly horrifying because he had assumed responsibility for his mother's welfare and undertaken to make a home for her "remainder of life." While he could be sure that the surviving Mannings would provide for her (as they did for Ebe and Louisa after Elizabeth's death), the question was not her physical or even psychological welfare but his own.

Certainly, then, her sudden serious illness and death at just the moment when he became unable to provide for her must have seemed profoundly significant to a man who felt so strongly the force that the inner life exerted on the outer world. It is in the context of a host of like thoughts, which he could not articulate plainly, that we must read his extraordinary journal entry penned the day before his mother died:

> I love my mother; but there has been, ever since my boyhood, a sort of coldness of intercourse between us, such as is apt to come between persons of strong feelings, if they are not managed rightly. I did not expect to be much moved at the time—that is to say, not to feel any overpowering emotion struggling, just then—though I knew that I should deeply remember and regret her. Mrs. Dike was in the chamber. Louisa pointed to a chair near the bed, but I was moved to kneel down close by my mother, and take her hand. She knew me, but could only murmur a few indistinct words— among which I understood an injunction to take care of my sisters. Mrs. Dike left the chamber, and then I found the tears slowly gathering in my eyes. I tried to keep them down; but it would not be—I kept filling up, till, for a few moments, I shook with sobs. For a long time, I knelt there, holding her hand; and surely it is the darkest hour I ever lived. Afterwards, I stood by the open window, and looked through the crevice of the curtain. . . . I saw my little Una of the golden locks, looking very beautiful; and so full of spirit and life, that she was life itself. And then I looked at my poor dying mother; and seemed to see the whole of human existence at once, standing in the dusty midst of it. (*Centenary*, VIII, 429)

Though constrained to repeat the legend of coldness since boyhood (which his boyhood letters so decisively refute), and to finish this entry with an expression of hope in the afterlife suitable for Sophia's eyes, Hawthorne nevertheless permits the depths of his grief to come to light. Connecting Una to his mother through himself, and making this linked chain of three comprise the whole of human existence, he effectively expunges Sophia from the record, makes Una his mother's child, and hence makes his mother both wife and mother to him. But these were not his last words on the subject. His real tribute to her, and to her influence, was to come in *The Scarlet Letter.*

III

The Scarlet Letter obviously cannot be called a work of autobiography or even biography as we use these terms to refer to recognizable literary genres.[20] But this discussion is meant to demonstrate the way in which it, along with "The Custom-House," contains autobiographical and biographical material (his mother's biography) and is engendered specifically by Hawthorne's experience of his mother's death. It is not inaccurate to describe *The Scarlet Letter* as Hawthorne's response to his mother's death. This response is composed of a number of elements difficult to extricate separately from the one dense texture of the romance. The fact that the woman it writes about is dead is paramount, for her death provides the motive for writing and also the freedom to write. The consciously articulated intentions of *The Scarlet Letter*, one might say, are to rescue its heroine from the oblivion of death and to rectify the injustices that were done to her in life, and both of these intentions take death as their starting point.

It is possible, within the elegiac frame of the work, to point to several autobiographical and biographical strands, some pertaining to the mother herself, some to the mother and son, and some to the son alone. First, *The Scarlet Letter* makes a noble attempt to realize the mother as a separate person with an independent existence in her own right; such an attempt represents the son's very belated recognition that his mother was a human being with her own life and consciousness, something more than a figure in his own carpet. As a youth of seventeen begging his mother to live in Maine, Hawthorne had his own Garden of Eden in mind, but he never doubted that his ideal would be hers also, and that a life shut off from the world with her children would content her. Perhaps as a mature man he began to know better.

Yet, in realizing the separate individuality, he must make Hester a mother, for that is what Elizabeth inescapably was, not only as part of his reality but as part of hers also. So he tries to understand what motherhood might mean for a person who does have, as all human beings do, a sense of independent existence. The way in which Pearl both impinges on and defines her mother's selfhood vividly dramatizes the claims that children make on their mothers.

Yet even as he strives to provide Hester with an independent existence as the center of her own world, Hawthorne maintains a double focus. Events in *The Scarlet Letter* never work themselves free of the constant voice of the narrator. We are always aware that the character Hester depends for her reality on the act of narrative generosity which is creating her. Here, Hawthorne reverses the biological relation of mother and child and becomes the creator of his mother. It seems to me that such a reversal not only underlies all representational art, but also responds to a specific set of wishes in the particular author writing at this particular time—the wish to be free of lifelong dependency on maternal power, the wish to have one's mother all to oneself (even if that possession can be attained only after death).

But—another twist in the cable—Hester's instant-by-instant dependence on the narrator-author is reversed again in the testimony of "The Custom-House" where "Hester" is defined as a creative force *outside* the romance which is responsible for his inspiration and his ability to write about her. Thus there is a transcending symbiosis of symbol and artist, mother and son—each created by the other and each dependent on the other for artistic life: the artist dependent on the image which inspires him, and the image dependent on the artist for representation.

There is, finally, an inevitable gap between the image and the being who has inspired it and whom it represents; the image is the refraction of the mother's influence in the son's psychic world. And so the work becomes an ambitious attempt to give his mother her own reality and bring to life her image in his mind as well and somehow to keep these distinct. Mediating between the two intentions of biography and autobiography, Hawthorne as narrator creates a structure in which the identities of the two subjects alternately assert themselves independently and then merge into a larger unity. The unity is best symbolized in the icon of mother and child—Divine Maternity—which is thrust on our attention in the first scaffold scene of *The Scarlet Letter.*

Beyond this complex personal intention, Hawthorne is also concerned to make his romance a public document, and hence much of the work of his text goes into generalizing, extending, and depersonalizing the meaning of his core images. The maternal symbol at the heart of *The Scarlet Letter* is contained within a sophisticated narrative structure, and this structure is distanced from the reader by the prefatory "Custom-House" essay. The personal meanings of the romance are processed through a sequence of narrators (the narrator of "The Custom-House" is not identical to the narrator of *The Scarlet Letter*) who are deeply aware of what, in "The Custom-House," Hawthorne refers to as the reader's right—the reader's right not to have unwanted confidences forced upon him.

Some of the resemblances between Hester's and Elizabeth's stories will, I hope, already be evident from the account provided of her life: the questionable circumstances of their children's births, their repudiation by those assigned society's judging function, the absence of spouse and abandonment of the child entirely to the mother. Facing down Hester's critics and overcoming presumed reader resistance to her, Hawthorne goes beyond forgiveness to complete acquittal. The chief agency of Hester's exoneration is Pearl. Although the narrative perspective is resolutely adult, it silently privileges Pearl's point of view toward her mother over all the others. Her very existence is the narrative's first and last fact, and it legitimizes the act of her mother which engendered her. We cannot doubt that Pearl has a right to be, and hence cannot fault the mother for bringing her into existence. Essentially, too, Pearl is her mother's child only. Though society and Hester are aware that a man participated in the act, Pearl has no sense of this necessity and hers is the view that the reader is forced to adopt. That is, we know that Hester has had a lover but we never really "know" that Pearl has a father. Through Pearl and because of her, then, Hester takes precedence over Dimmesdale and over the society which tries to put him and his cohorts at the organizing center of the fictional world. The world of the romance is organized around her. Matriarchy prevails. Autobiographically speaking, Hawthorne identifies himself once and for all as his *mother's* child.

To be sure, Hester pays a high price for her legitimation, the price of confinement within her motherhood for most of her life. Throughout the romance she is virtually never separated from Pearl; the image she represents, we remember, is inextricably linked to maternity rather than selfhood or even womanhood. The brookside scene in the forest, for all its multiple possibilities of interpretation, dramatizes at some basic level the need of the child to possess the mother all to herself. Pearl recognizes at once through the mother's changed appearance, as Hester blossoms out into relation with Dimmesdale, that the mother is no longer merely and entirely her mother. She cannot abide this. Imperiously she requires that Hester reassume motherhood as her sole reality before she will return to her. The "A" at this point means only maternity: the complex, bewildering, and ambiguous set of events which have set Hester's course for life are ultimately reduced to the "sin" of having given birth to a child.

The tensions between Hester's motherhood and personhood, between the needs of her own life and the needs of her child, between the person herself and the figure in the son's tale, are resolved at a higher level of the story than Pearl's perceptions. The narrator, taking the roles of her prophet, son, and lover simultaneously, creates an image now responsive to its own rhythms and now to the rhythms of the two beings who impinge on her—Pearl, her figured child, and the author-narrator who in many respects is her child grown up. The image to which both subscribe, and within which they enclose Hester, is the Garden of Eden, the benign matriarchy.

One is reminded not only of Hawthorne's adolescent letters but of a lengthy passage from "Main-Street," which is the only tale we are sure that Hawthorne meant to include along with *The Scarlet Letter* in the larger collection he was originally planning. "Main-Street" is a rapid survey of New England history and it begins before the patriarchy comes to impose its civilization on western soil, with the timeless land existing under the rule of a woman:

> You perceive, at a glance, that this is the ancient and primitive wood,—the ever-youthful and venerably old,—verdant with new twigs, yet hoary, as it were, with the snowfall of innumerable years, that have accumulated upon its intermingled branches. The white man's axe has never smitten a single tree; his footstep has never crumpled a single one of the withered leaves, which all the autumns since the flood have been harvesting beneath. Yet, see! along through the vista of impending boughs, there is already a faintly-traced path. . . . What footsteps can have worn this half-seen path? Hark! Do we not hear them now rustling softly over the leaves? We discern an Indian woman—a majestic and queenly woman, or else her spectral image does not represent her truly—for this is the great Squaw Sachem, whose rule, with that of her sons, extends from Mystic to Agawam. That red chief, who stalks by her side, is Wappacowet, her second husband, the priest and magician. (*Centenary*, XI, 50–51)

The white man—adulthood for the race—has arrived, and the happy days of mother-rule retreat to legend and imagination. But within imagination their existence is powerful and pervasive. *The Scarlet Let-*

ter is Hawthorne's testimony to the existence of that inner world ruled over by a woman. The woman in that inner world could never die.

The Scarlet Letter is the only one of Hawthorne's long romances whose origin can be attributed to a specific autobiographical impulse. Alerted by the kinds of concerns it manifests, one can perceive certain biographical implications in the others, however. Although there is not a trace of the Squaw Sachem in *The House of the Seven Gables*, this is a quintessential family story whose deepest meaning resides, ultimately, precisely in her absence. For it tells a tale of the submersion of individual identity and the total loss of happiness and freedom in a male-ruled household. The reason why the alternatives of Pyncheon and Maule can provide no resolution to the excesses of the other is that each remains in essence a patriarchy. Eliminating Pyncheon, the hero Holgrave has nothing to substitute but—himself. One can interpret the families of Pyncheon and Maule as Hathorne and Manning respectively, the run-down aristocrats and the rising laborers, and recall that neither permitted Elizabeth to be mistress in her own house. From another vantage point, the Pyncheon house can be seen as an amalgamation of *both* Hathorne and Manning into a composite figure of hated family oppression, an overwhelming symbol of patriarchal usurpation. In sum, the repudiation of father and fathers imaged forth as a minor point in *The Scarlet Letter* as it defended Hester's priority here becomes the central autobiographical statement.

In this context Phoebe can be only Sophia, as indeed we are asked to understand by other indications (Hawthorne frequently called Sophia Phoebe). Her role in the rescue, or failed rescue, plot is only superficial, however. She is fundamentally unequal to the other powers in the story and at crucial points in the narrative is shown to be susceptible to victimization by them. Hawthorne, I think, is here beginning to realize, or at least to signify, that Sophia was having far less efficacy in his life than he had originally imagined.

That the simplicity of Sophia's imagination was more and more seeming like shallowness rather than infinite depths is more overtly suggested in *The Blithedale Romance* and *The Marble Faun*. In both romances the hated male rulers are abetted, albeit without much awareness, by female figures whose task is to supplant or discredit a more matriarchal or maternal type. (It must be granted that in *The Blithedale Romance* the matriarchal type is badly flawed, and is so to a lesser degree in *The Marble Faun*, so to speak truly no possibility for any restoration of the matriarchy is seriously entertained in either romance.) In *The Blithedale Romance* this dovelike supplanter appears at the beginning as part of the degraded urban complex which the narrator-protagonist wishes to reject for a pastoral ideal. The proper Arcadian values are established at once when the narrator finds Zenobia ruling over Blithedale, but her initial matronly and queenlike authority is systematically undercut and discredited by the collusion of all the other characters until she is driven to suicide. The dove is left in command of the field. But the survivors of the battle are merely the walking wounded, and her lifelong task is to nurse and guard them—a parody of matriarchy, making *Blithedale* in some sense the dark inverse of *The Scarlet Letter.*

Something similar happens in the tortured symbolism and obscure narrative line of *The Marble Faun*, where Kenyon's election of Hilda, the dove transmuted into a steely virgin, is equivalent to retreat from the complexities of an adult world. Hilda's cutting simplifications and platitudes masquerade as a world view which the sculptor, finding himself unable to deal with the implications of adult relations between the sexes, gladly espouses. The babyland to which Kenyon and Hilda are returning at the end of the romance is nothing like the ageless forest presided over by the Indian Queen who, disguised in this romance as Venus, has been rejected by Kenyon on the campagna in favor of Hilda. But Hawthorne does not blame Sophia.

Toward the close of his literary career Hawthorne, working up his English essays for publication, inserted a passage into "Outside Glimpses of English Poverty" for which there is no notebook source:

Nothing, as I remember, smote me with more grief and pity . . . than to hear a gaunt and ragged mother priding herself on the pretty ways of her ragged and skinny infant, just as a young matron might, when she invites her lady-friends to admire her plump, white-robed darling in the nursery. Indeed, no womanly characteristic seemed to have altogether perished out of these poor souls. It was the very same creature whose tender torments make the rapture of our young days, whom we love, cherish, and protect, and rely upon in life and death, and whom we delight to see beautify her beauty with rich robes and set it off with jewels. (*Centenary*, X, 283)

The image goes beyond the gaunt and ragged mother, beyond the young matron, and even beyond Elizabeth Hathorne to the archetype, the Magna Mater enthroned in a blaze of jewels in her son's imagination. Even at this late date the imagination remains centrally possessed of and by her image. Elizabeth had been dead for fourteen years. Hawthorne would be dead within a year himself. In this ardent image, he indicates that her presence will survive with him to the end.

From *American Literature* 54, no. 1 (March, 1982): 1-27. Copyright © 1982 by Duke University Press. Reprinted by permission of Duke University Press

Notes

1. See Hubert H. Hoeltje, "The Writing of *The Scarlet Letter*," *New England Quarterly*, 27 (1954), 326–46, and Stephen Nissenbaum, "The Firing of Nathaniel Hawthorne," *Essex Institute Historical Collections*, 114 (1978), 57–86.

2. Arlin Turner, *Nathaniel Hawthorne, A Biography* (New York: Oxford, 1980), p. 208; Julian Hawthorne, *Nathaniel Hawthorne and His Wife* (Boston: Houghton Mifflin, 1884), 1, 353–54 (henceforth cited parenthetically).

3. Jean Normand, *Nathaniel Hawthorne: An Approach to an Analysis of Artistic Creation*, tr. Derek Coltman (Cleveland: Case Western Reserve Univ. Press, 1970), and John Franzosa, "'The Custom-House,' *The Scarlet Letter*, and Hawthorne's Separation from Salem," *ESQ*, 24 (1978), 5–21, find the biographical significance of the romance to reside in the maternal figure of Hester, as I do. But both subsume this figure into larger, abstract schemes, Jungian and quasi-Freudian, respectively, and ignore biographical detail.

4. Mark Van Doren, *Nathaniel Hawthorne* (New York: Sloane, 1949), p. 9.

5. Norman Holmes Pearson, "Elizabeth Peabody on Hawthorne," *Essex Institute Historical Collections*, 94 (1958), 256–76; Randall Stewart, "Recollections of Hawthorne by His Sister Elizabeth," *American Literature*, 16 (1945), 316–31; Manning Hawthorne, "Hawthorne's Early Years," *Essex Institute Historical Collections*, 74 (1938), 1–21; "Parental and Family Influences on Hawthorne," *Essex Institute Historical Collections*, 76 (1940), 1–13; "Nathaniel Hawthorne Prepares for College," *New England Quarterly*, 11 (1938), 66–68; "Maria Louise Hawthorne," *Essex Institute Historical Collections*, 75 (1939), 103–34; "Nathaniel Hawthorne at Bowdoin," *New England Quarterly*, 13 (1940), 246–79; "A Glimpse of Hawthorne's Boyhood," *Essex Institute Historical Collections*, 83 (1947), 178–84; Gloria Ehrlich, "Hawthorne and the Mannings," *Studies in the American Renaissance 1980* (Boston: Twayne, 1980), pp. 97–117.

6. *Love Letters of Nathaniel Hawthorne* (Chicago: Society of the DOFOBS, 1907), II, 78 (henceforth cited parenthetically).

7. Pearson, "Elizabeth Peabody on Hawthorne," pp. 266–68.

8. James R. Mellow, *Nathaniel Hawthorne in His Times* (Boston: Houghton Mifflin, 1980), p. 13.

9. *At Odds: Women and the Family in America from the Revolution to the Present* (New York: Oxford, 1980), p. 20.

10. Pearson, "Elizabeth Peabody on Hawthorne," p. 268.

11. Manning Hawthorne, "Nathaniel Hawthorne at Bowdoin," p. 87.

12. Manning Hawthorne, "Nathaniel Hawthorne Prepares for College," p. 77.

13. "Nathaniel Hawthorne Prepares for College," pp. 69–70.

14. Nathaniel Hawthorne, *English Notebooks*, ed. Randall Stewart (New York: Modern Language Association of America, 1941), p. 23; *French and Italian Notebooks*, ed. Thomas Woodson (Columbus: Ohio State Univ. Press, 1980), p. 570. Subsequent references to Hawthorne's works citing the Centenary Edition published by the Ohio State Univ. Press will be parenthetically included in the text, noting volume and page number of the edition.

15. *Hawthorne and his Wife*, I, 123–25; Stewart, "Recollections of Hawthorne by His Sister Elizabeth," pp. 323, 327–28.

16. Mellow, pp. 185–86.

17. Turner, p. 141.

18. Turner, p. 142.

19. Louise Hall Tharp, *The Peabody Sisters of Salem* (Boston: Little, Brown, 1950), p. 185.

20. William C. Spengemann, in *The Forms of Autobiography: Episodes in the History of a Literary Genre* (New Haven: Yale Univ. Press, 1980), makes *The Scarlet Letter* a sort of ultimate "self-reflexive" autobiographical statement, but in his definition autobiography need not refer to any real-life happenings.

Agnostic Tensions in Hawthorne's Short Stories

Bill Christophersen

Literary history is marked by a number of moments of convergence, when two great authors come together. Bill Christophersen opens his essay with one of these moments, when Herman Melville reviewed *Mosses from an Old Manse* and *The Scarlet Letter* in 1850. Melville, argues Christophersen, was fascinated by Hawthorne's interest in religion—not the Puritanism that is so obvious in Hawthorne's major works, but rather the nature of spiritual belief itself.

Most readers have assumed Hawthorne was a more or less conventional Christian, but one not much interested in theology. Of course he was interested in Puritanism but, as Christophersen sums up the conventional wisdom, "Hawthorne's fiction concerns Puritanism but not God." For Christophersen, though, that conventional wisdom is wrong. Melville, he argues, "surely saw in Hawthorne a fellow skeptic, . . . a writer of agnostic fictions." Both of these canonical nineteenth-century American authors were deeply interested in questions of belief, and their works reveal their own struggles between faith and skepticism, against the background of the Second Great Awakening, as Protestant Christianity was increasingly being viewed as the American national religion.

Hawthorne realized, Christophersen argues, that "belief must sometimes be struggled for and that unbelief *is* an option." "Matters of faith are rarely brought to the fore, but when they are they are often scrutinized in an unorthodox light." Hawthorne's literary "mode based on indirection, irony, and veiled suggestion" was perfectly suited to this kind of exploration of conventional pieties, and we see it especially in the short tales, "The Gentle Boy," "Young Goodman Brown," "David Swan," "The Great Stone Face," "Sylph Etherege," "The Wives of the Dead," and "Rappaccini's Daughter."   — J.L.

Herman Melville, in his review of Nathaniel Hawthorne's *Mosses from an Old Manse*, remarks its "blackness, ten times black," as well as Hawthorne's tendency to tell the truth "covertly, and by snatches."[1] For modern readers, this early appreciation has resonated. Throughout his fiction Hawthorne, we know, was preoccupied with the unconfessed sin in the minister's breast, the selfishness underlying the philanthropist's schemes, the haunted house encompassing the sweet shop. His generally pessimistic take on the world—never much offset by the breezier passages and sketches with which he leavened his oeuvre—is doubtless part of what Melville had in mind. In a much cited passage he holds that Hawthorne's blackness "derives its force from its appeals to that Calvinistic sense of Innate Depravity and Original Sin, from whose visitations . . . no deeply thinking mind is always and wholly free" ("MM," 243). The insight points up Hawthorne's divergence from the more optative (Emerson) and sentimental (Longfellow) writers he lived among and neatly plumbs such tales as "Egotism; or, The Bosom-Serpent" and "Earth's Holocaust," the second of which explicitly suggests that the heart is the source of evil. But Melville's elaboration doesn't completely satisfy. For one thing, Hawthorne's Calvinistic strain isn't especially "covert." He often tempers it with a wry humor (as in "Earth's Holocaust"), but he doesn't disguise it. Moreover, although Calvinism was a gloomy religion, it was not downright black. A just God, it presumed, was in his Heaven and had taken the trouble to redeem his chosen, even if one's membership in that select company was moot. No, as the remainder of his review suggests, Melville was fascinated by something less conventional in the tales—and far less Calvinistic—than their chagrin over human fallibility.

Perhaps out of respect for Hawthorne's discretion, Melville seems reluctant to be more explicit about the blackness he identifies, but eventually he associates what he admires in the tales with sentiments uttered by Shakespeare's most nihilistic characters—Timon, Iago, Lear. He singles out "Young Goodman Brown" as the preeminent illustration of the blackness to which the stories he has already lauded contribute "the mere occasional shadow" ("MM," 244). He cites this passage: "'Faith!' shouted Goodman Brown, in a voice of agony and desperation; and the echoes of the forest mocked him, crying—'Faith! Faith!' as if bewildered wretches were seeking her all through the wilderness" (251). The writer of *Moby-Dick, Pierre, or the Ambiguities*, and *The Confidence-Man* surely saw in Hawthorne a fellow skeptic,[2] a "seeker, not a finder" (250), a writer of agnostic fictions that (as Melville wrote in a letter to Hawthorne) said "NO! in thunder" to more than the heady affirmations of Transcendentalist and Whig.[3] "This black conceit," says Melville, "pervades him, through and through. . . . [E]ven his bright gildings but fringe, and play upon the edges of thunderclouds" (243). The image echoes the story Melville praises alongside "Young Goodman Brown," "A Select Party," which for all its fanciful charm—its setting is a mansion in the clouds—burlesques the Heaven of the Elect.[4]

Yet Hawthorne's tales—with the major exception of "Young Goodman Brown," which Marius Bewley has termed "one of the most deeply agnostic works of art in existence"—have not typically been seen to display so pervasive a vein of religious skepticism as Melville seems to have discerned.[5] Yes, "Roger Malvin's Burial" is understood to be a story of one generation's sins visited remorselessly upon the next; yes, Father Hooper in "The Minister's Black Veil" goes to his grave wearing a symbol of guilt and alienation that no gospel has been able to mitigate. The brooding New England tenor of many of the stories, in short, is well appreciated, much as their historical ironies are appreciated, as the mark of a writer whose genius lay in scrutinizing rather than celebrating nativist themes and cultural shibboleths. But Hawthorne's fictions have rarely been seen as airing religious doubts or posing theological challenges.

Unlike Melville, whose anguished skepticism has been detailed by Lawrance Thompson,[6] Hawthorne has usually been judged a conventional, if somewhat indifferent, nineteenth-century Christian. Most literary biographers and critics depict him as pious, although unchurched

(F. O. Matthiessen, Hyatt H. Waggoner), or as disengaged from spiritual concerns (Henry James, Mark Van Doren).[7] Even so recent a commentator as Alfred Kazin observes matter-of-factly in *God and the American Writer* (1997) that Hawthorne "does not seem to have been much interested in 'God.'"[8] The involvement with his forefathers' Puritan heritage that fueled *The Scarlet Letter*, Kazin notes, was another matter—a preoccupation that often intersected with theological concerns over sin, atonement, and redemption. That heritage, Kazin grants, included a Calvinistic distrust of human nature that informs much of his fiction. But Hawthorne, he stipulates, cared little, either artistically or personally, about matters of faith; his relationship to the Puritan conscience was (as James said more than a century ago) intellectual, not theological.

The view that Hawthorne's fiction concerns Puritanism but not God seems to me to fit, by and large, *The House of the Seven Gables* and *The Scarlet Letter*—though the latter is a more complex case.[9] But it does not, I think, account for a number of the short stories, some of which were written almost a quarter century prior to the novels. Melville, I believe, read Hawthorne's blackness aright: many of the tales covertly exhibit doubts about God, the Bible, and Christian belief. This skepticism shows itself in the equivocating metaphors for the godhead that Hawthorne creates and in the often subversive use he makes of biblical subtexts and motifs. Matters of faith are rarely brought to the fore, but when they are they are often scrutinized in an unorthodox light.[10]

Hawthorne's personal writings afford only a modicum of support for this thesis. His letters exhibit little soul-searching and allude repeatedly and without irony to Providence, particularly in the years following his 1842 marriage to Sophia Peabody. Of a piece with these, on the whole, is the often cited passage from *The English Notebooks* (20 November 1856) in which Hawthorne, then a consul in Liverpool, recounts a visit from Melville:

Melville, as he always does, began to reason of Providence and futurity, . . .
and informed me that he had "pretty much made up his mind to be annihilated." But he still does not seem to rest in that anticipation; and, I think,
will never rest until he gets hold of a definite belief. . . . He can neither believe, nor be comfortable in his unbelief; and he is too honest and coura-
geous not to try to do one or the other.[11]

The tone is that of a man unvexed by metaphysical questions. Yet the
writer, for all his equanimity, clearly empathizes with the seeker caught
in spiritual limbo. Hawthorne recognizes that belief must sometimes
be struggled for and that unbelief *is* an option. The passage also pre-
supposes prior discussions between the two men about spiritual matters—discussions, that is, of a subject to which Hawthorne is widely
supposed to have been indifferent.

Earlier journal entries confirm such conversations: "After supper, I
put Julian to bed," Hawthorne noted on 1 August 1851, "and Melville
and I had a talk about time and eternity, things of this world and of the
next." *The American Notebooks* suggest, in fact, that Hawthorne rel-
ished such confabs long before he met Melville. On 24 July 1837, for
instance, he wrote of sitting up late with Horatio Bridge's friend and
French tutor, one Monsieur Schaeffer, talking "of Christianity and De-
ism, of ways of life, of marriage, of benevolence—in short all deep
matters of this world and the next." On a trip to Vermont the following
summer he recorded having passed the time of day discussing "predestination and free will, and other metaphysics" with a butternut vendor
(11 August 1838). More revealing is a notebook entry of 30 July 1849,
made as his mother's death approached and showing a man not merely
engaged by spiritual questions but stung by doubts about God and the
afterlife: "[Una] talks of her [grandmother] being soon to go to God,
and probably thinks that she will be taken away bodily. Would to God it
were to be so! Faith and trust would be far easier than they are now."[12]
The writer of this meditation sounds very like the skeptical writer Melville discerned behind the conventional personas of the "Mosses."

Something of this Hawthorne may be inferred as well from the plans he formed for publishing his early stories.

Michael J. Colacurcio, in exploring the historicity of Hawthorne's short fictions, focuses on his unsuccessful attempts to publish them in unified collections. During the late 1820s and early 1830s, Hawthorne assembled several collections of tales organized along thematic and narrative lines—"Seven Tales of My Native Land," "Provincial Tales," and "The Story-Teller." This third and most ambitious was to be a two-volume work whose contents, though not fully known, included many of the stories that were placed with the *New England Magazine* and elsewhere in the mid-1830s, when Hawthorne, at his publisher's behest, broke up the collection (1834). Apparently "The Story-Teller" was to have taken its narrative frame and controlling premise from "The Seven Vagabonds" and "Passages from a Relinquished Work," both of which, Colacurcio notes, set up an opposition between a storyteller and an evangelist:

> An odd couple, surely. Yet henceforth the two will itinerate together, the one preaching salvation to all those who have ears to hear, the other seeking variously to amuse or mildly edify whoever happens to have the price of admission to some village theater. The dichotomy is too cruelly and humorously perfect to be anything but Hawthorne's satiric yet not quite self-pitying version of the problem of secular or "historical" literature in a puritanic or "typological" culture.

With Hawthorne's proposed framework in mind, Colacurcio revisits "Mr. Higginbotham's Catastrophe," which is announced in "Passages from a Relinquished Work" as the Story-Teller's first public performance. He views this story about a peddler who retails an idle rumor of a farmer's death less as evidence of Hawthorne's incidental fascination with local color, the usual critical tack,[13] than as "an outrageous parody of the philosophical problem of 'testimony,' particularly as it relates to the Christian story of a miraculous resurrection."[14] The narrative context Colacurcio reclaims and applies, with its ironic contrasts between the spiritual and the secular, suggests a writer intent on treating religious concerns in a sustained, dialectical, open-ended, and unorthodox fashion.

Nor ought such an intention—or the disguises in which it often manifested itself—surprise us if we grant that Hawthorne in his early tales was, as Colacurcio argues, deliberately analyzing and critiquing his culture. America in the 1820s and 1830s was caught up in the Second Great Awakening, a multidenominational evangelical juggernaut that braided Protestant Christianity with a sense of ordained national purpose. The result, critics have observed, was the de facto establishment of a civil religion, or, as Reverend Heman Humphrey, president of Amherst College, put it, "the true American union, that sort of union which makes every patriot a Christian, and every Christian a patriot."[15] This revivalist impulse, instances of which Hawthorne apparently witnessed while a college student in Brunswick, Maine,[16] carried forward the New England Puritan view of an elect people building the New Jerusalem under God's auspices but broadened the Elect to incorporate, in effect, the electorate—preparing the way, as religious historian William G. McLoughlin notes, for the rise of Jacksonianism.[17] Any writer fixing a critical eye on America circa 1830, much less its New England origins, would have been hard-pressed to do so from an exclusively social or historical perspective, so intertwined had history and the Bible, secular culture and Christianity, become. By the same token, with Christianity becoming culturally enshrined, small wonder if a fiction writer bent on criticizing or questioning its assumptions were to choose a mode based on indirection, irony, and veiled suggestion.

Several critics have documented biblical echoes in Hawthorne's fiction. W. R. Thompson has done so for "Roger Malvin's Burial," "The Gentle Boy," and "The Great Carbuncle,"[18] and a number of critics have done so for "The Minister's Black Veil," "Rappaccini's Daughter," and a few other stories.[19] Sacvan Bercovitch, in a discussion of "Endicott and the Red Cross," has affirmed Hawthorne's familiarity with biblical exegesis.[20] Matthew Gartner, who recently argued that *The Scarlet Letter* reworks elements of the Book of Esther, writes: "It cannot be said too often that Hawthorne belonged to a culture for which the Bible was still the book of books. Admission requirements for [Hawthorne's alma mater] Bowdoin College included a translation from the Septuagint, the Greek translation of the Hebrew Bible, and the Bowdoin curriculum included regular Bible study."[21] "Regular" meant recitations every Sunday throughout the school year.[22] Hawthorne often cited the Scriptures in his letters home. The Bible, according to Hawthorne's publisher, James T. Fields, was the authority to which he routinely referred semantic questions.[23]

Hawthorne, in short, knew his Bible and drew upon it extensively, particularly in his short fiction. Not every story exhibiting biblical or religious elements treats God and faith. "Roger Malvin's Burial," its Old Testament echoes notwithstanding, is primarily about psychology and history, not theology. "Endicott and the Red Cross" is, to echo Kazin, about Puritanism, not God. But consider "Young Goodman Brown," Melville's exhibit A, a tale preoccupied with biblical *and* teleological concerns. A gloss on Puritan New England as well as on a mid-nineteenth-century America mesmerized by its own dubious errand into the wilderness, it is even more fundamentally a nightmare of spiritual doubt and disillusionment. When Goodman Brown adjures his wife Faith, who, he dreams, is about to be inducted into the witches' communion, to look up to Heaven, he awakens alone in the woods. His spiritual solitude is the more ominous for occurring in a story that ironically inverts several images from Exodus (the wilderness errand, the serpentine staff, the cloud, the pillar of fire).[24] The (presumably) good news for Goodman Brown, after he has envisioned the corruption of his community and the unfaithfulness of his wife, is that it has all been a dream. But the bad news—bad beyond the traumatizing glimpse he fancies he has received into the unholy communion of his race—is that it may *all* be a dream: Heaven as well as Hell, God as well as the Devil. Faith is lost, for all practical purposes: "Often, awaking suddenly at midnight, he shrank from the bosom of Faith," Hawthorne writes; "his dying hour was gloom."[25]

The question "Young Goodman Brown" asks—Is faith justified?—hovers above the action of a number of Hawthorne's stories. It is there in "The Gentle Boy," for instance, a story set in Massachusetts Bay in 1659 concerning a six-year-old boy named Ilbrahim, the son of Quaker parents. Puritan magistrates have hung his father, banished his mother to the wilderness, and left him to fend for himself. Tobias and Dorothy Pearson, a Puritan couple whose children have died, adopt the child, a kindness for which they are ostracized, reviled, and threatened. When they bring him to church, the minister denigrates them from the pulpit. Before long Ilbrahim is assaulted by a group of Puritan children. He recovers, but his health declines. At last his natural mother returns to his side, but only in time to receive his dying words.

One of Hawthorne's early "Provincial Tales," "The Gentle Boy" is very much about Puritanism at its most vindictive and intolerant. It is also, as critics have observed, about the masochistic, goading fanaticism of Quakerism. Ilbrahim's persecution-courting parents fail him as manifestly as the Puritans victimize him.[26] One critic has argued that Hawthorne revised the story expressly to balance the mutuality of guilt, the two sects exhibiting, at last, a kind of perverse symbiosis.[27]

But the tale is about Christianity as well as social history and sectarian psychology.[28] If Hawthorne's patriarchal Puritans overemphasize the Law, his evangelical Quakers overemphasize the Spirit; if the Puritans focus too exclusively on God the Father, the Quakers cleave too exclusively to the Holy Ghost—both, the story implies, at the expense of the Son and his gentler message. This contrast is reflected, W. R. Thompson has observed, in the way Hawthorne deploys biblical allusions throughout the story. The sequences characterizing the Puritans tend to allude to the Old Testament; those characterizing the Quakers evoke New Testament passages.[29] A triune God and integrated Christianity, a creed closer to the charitable faith of the Pearson family, is needed, Hawthorne seems to suggest.

There is also, however, an almost anti-Christian strain in this tale, whose most humane and Christlike characters are religious outsiders.[30] Tobias Pearson, we learn, took part in the Puritan revolution in England but became disaffected with its ambition. Emigrating to Massachusetts Bay for economic reasons, he and his wife have not been graciously accepted. By ministering to Ilbrahim, Tobias alienates himself further, taking on the role of Good Samaritan.[31] Ilbrahim is even more of an outsider. His Turkish name, given him because his parents were persecuted throughout Christendom but treated civilly in the Moslem realm, says it all. Such background details and paradoxes implicate not only the Massachusetts Bay theocracy but the Christian Church in general.

Beyond this strain is an even grimmer one springing from the "gratuitous cruelty" (to borrow the narrator's phrase) that infuses the tale.[32] The narrative pivots on the moment when Ilbrahim is attacked by the Puritan children whose fathers have executed his father. In that episode an injured child whom Ilbrahim has befriended, nursed, and all but come to worship turns on him treacherously. "Fear not, Ilbrahim, come hither and take my hand" (92), says the child; then, when Ilbrahim tries to do so, he strikes him in the mouth with his staff. It's the last straw for Ilbrahim; betrayed by his intercessor, he stops defending himself and is beaten almost to death. As cruel as the treachery itself is the irony with which the would-be protector's words recall God's assurance to Abraham, "Fear not, Abram: I am thy shield" (Genesis 15:1)—an assurance Christ later repeats to his followers ("Fear not, little flock"—Luke 12:32). Beyond all else, "The Gentle Boy" forces us to meditate the unavailability of the God of Ilbrahim.

Nor is the boy's spirit the only one broken as a result of the encounter. Tobias Pearson undergoes a spiritual crisis during Ilbrahim's final illness. An upright believer who is as humane as he is conscientious, he has been visited with Job-like afflictions, including the loss of friends, prosperity, property, and children.[33] At the prospect of losing his foster son, he spurns the Bible's comfort because his burden seems heavier than he can bear. Similarly, Ilbrahim's natural mother Catharine, who returns from banishment to find her son dying, asks: "[W]hat has God done to me? . . . Hath He crushed my very heart in his hand?" (102). As the two parents agonize, a furious wind rages outside Pearson's house.[34] But no divine voice issues from it; one blast "laugh[s] in the chimney" (96) and another extinguishes a lamp.

Several less baleful stories also revolve around matters of faith. "David Swan," for example, a little-remarked tale about a protagonist who, like Young Goodman Brown, pauses during a journey to rest among the trees,[35] purports to "argue a superintending Providence."[36] But the events it relates, though more mundane and blithely narrated than those of the stygian "Young Goodman Brown," call Providence into question.

David Swan, a young man on his way to Boston where a clerical apprenticeship awaits him, takes a midday nap beside a spring in a grove of maples that materializes "as if planted on purpose for him" (184). While he sleeps, a carriage breaks down on the road nearby. As the coachman and a servant repair the carriage, the passengers, an aging, well-to-do merchant and his wife, take shelter from the heat in the grove where David lies. The man is gouty; both he and his wife are troubled in mind. They have recently lost their only son. As they stare enviously and admiringly at the blissful sleeper, they notice that he resembles their deceased son. "Providence seems to have laid him here," the woman says to her husband, "and to have brought us hither to find him" (185). The couple almost decide to wake David and settle their fortune on him, but their servant interrupts to say that the coach is fixed, and they depart.

Next a young girl whose garter has come undone slips into the grove to fix it and notices David. She thinks him handsome. When she spots a large bee about to perch on his eyelid, she leans over him to shoo it away. The two young people, Hawthorne informs us, were made for each other. What's more, her father needs a clerk. David sleeps on, however, and the girl goes her way. She is soon succeeded by a pair of rogues who spy David and resolve to rob him and, if he should wake, to kill him. But as they are poised to carry out their plan, a dog wanders into the grove, and the men, deducing that his master can't be far behind, abandon their plan. Moments later David awakens, unaware of all that has passed, and hails a stagecoach to Boston.

"Does it not argue a superintending Providence," the narrator concludes, "that, while viewless and unexpected events thrust themselves continually athwart our path, there should still be regularity enough, in mortal life, to render foresight even partially available?" (190). Perhaps it does, though the reasoning seems labored. Perhaps there is a Providence acting an apparently laissez-faire part yet working behind the scenes to keep life's upsets to a minimum. But a reader may be forgiven for inferring the opposite. For one thing, a different and less reassuring deity, Fortune, is more palpably at work. Hawthorne has Fortune "bending over" the sleeper at one moment and "brush[ing] against him" with her garments at another (186, 187). Fortune aside, a superintending Providence had only to awaken a sleeper at an auspicious moment to confer great blessings. Instead, wealth and love pass David by; he barely escapes with his life.

These ironies don't directly challenge Providence. God, after all, may have sent the dog to foil the thieves, may have commissioned Fortune or stayed her hand, may have scripted the entire sequence for an inscrutable purpose. Hypothetical possibilities aside, however, the story leaves the impression that chance alone determines fate. The universe, it would seem, confers good (love, sympathy, shady dells) and evil (gout, large bees, murderous thieves) indiscriminately. We survive or perish, thrive or bear up. The scenario may be precociously naturalistic, but it is not remarkable, except insofar as Hawthorne thrusts Providence to the fore. By broaching the subject first in the old woman's observation to her husband and later in the conclusion, Hawthorne activates a tension that might otherwise have lain dormant. And although he does so with a flourish of affirmation, the effect is to amplify rather than mute the tale's unsettling implications.

These are further amplified by the protagonist's biblical name.[37] Behind Hawthorne's David is the shadow of another comely youth of the same name whom God raised up to be king of Israel, according to 1 Samuel. While yet a shepherd, the Old Testament David was anointed of the Lord. He entered the service of King Saul, whose troubled spirit he soothed with his lyre, whose enterprises he advanced, and whose daughter he wed (1 Samuel 16:12, 21–23; 1 Samuel 18:27). Wealth and prosperity followed, as David's life unfolded under divine aegis. David Swan—whose last name strengthens the biblical echo by denoting not only a person of unusual grace but also a poet—seems on the verge of receiving like blessings: patronage and wealth, a situation and wife. The onomastic echoes, however, like the apostrophes to Providence, create expectations the story disappoints.

"The Great Stone Face," a more frequently anthologized fable and one whose optimism few critics fail to remark,[38] treats the nature of goodness but, like "David Swan," attends as well to the nature of God. The tale concerns a New England village at the foot of a mountain whose outcropping rocks sometimes resemble a face. Legend has it that a great man with such a face will one day appear in the village. Over the years, the villagers hail various visitors—a successful merchant, a general, a politician, a poet—as the man foretold, only to discover at last that the man they've been waiting for has been living humbly in their midst.

The narrative builds rather mechanically (as Hawthorne, according to his son, recognized) to its "manifest moral."[39] But before the spring-winding gets under way, Hawthorne introduces his key image:

> The Great Stone Face, then, was a work of Nature in her mood of majestic playfulness, formed on the perpendicular side of a mountain by some immense rocks, which had been thrown together in such a position, as, when viewed at a proper distance, precisely to resemble the features of the human countenance. . . . True it is, that if the spectator approached too near, he lost the outline of the gigantic visage, and could discern only a heap of ponderous and gigantic rocks, piled in chaotic ruin one upon another. Re-

tracing his steps, however, the wondrous features would again be seen, and the farther he withdrew from them, the more like a human face, with all its original divinity intact, did they appear; until, as it grew dim in the distance, with the clouds and glorified vapor of the mountains clustering about it, the Great Stone Face seemed positively to be alive.[40]

The "divinity" with "wondrous features" suggests God. Hawthorne massages the image with divine attributes throughout the story, alluding to its "benign aspect" and "glorious features" and to its "look of grand beneficence [that] seemed to embrace the world" (27, 33, 48). And the prophecy of its incarnation, a prophecy whose fulfillment the human community awaits with "enduring faith" (28), evokes not just a generic, Emersonian deity but the Judeo-Christian God who covenanted with Abraham and Moses on a mountain.[41]

But this divinity, Hawthorne makes clear before adorning it with "glorious vapors," is patently "a work of Nature" (27), a "grand natural phenomenon" (26), a heap of rocks "piled in chaotic ruin one upon the other" (27). The face is a trick of light the villagers have invested with significance. Hawthorne doesn't emphasize the unorthodox implications; rather, he lets the stone image objectify a God who is alternately visible and invisible, manifest and elusive—a God who "seemed positively [deft paradox, that!] to be alive" (27). Beneath the shimmering appearance, however, there is never any question that the face is an illusion. And so a tale that seems to rehearse the Christian mystery undermines it at the outset.

"Sylph Etherege," another tale about illusion and belief, is darker.[42] It concerns an orphan, Sylvia Etherege, who has been brought up by her uncle, then sent, upon his death, to be cared for by a Mrs. Grosvenor. While an infant, Sylvia became the destined bride of a cousin, Edgar Vaughan, whom she has never seen but with whom she has corresponded. Shy, solitary, and romantic, she has "made a vision of Edgar Vaughan" (113); he, inferring her ethereal nature from her letters, has rechristened her "Sylph." Sylvia now learns that Vaughan, having completed his education abroad, is coming to marry her. One Edward Hamilton precedes him, bearing letters from him.

Sylvia abhors Hamilton on sight. He has, however, brought her a miniature of her cousin, with which she becomes enraptured. "[T]he pictured countenance," we are told, "was almost too perfect to represent a human creature" (114). What Sylvia does not know is that Hamilton and Vaughan are one. With Mrs. Grosvenor's consent, her betrothed has got up the enticing miniature along with the alias to cure the girl of her romantic ways.

Word soon arrives that Vaughan, just in from France, is on his way to Mrs. Grosvenor's house, where he expects to meet his bride-to-be that evening. The women await him in an apartment lit by a lamp in an anteroom. At last he enters the house and climbs the stairs. Taking up the lamp, he cries out "Dearest Sylph!" At the sound of his voice Sylvia begins to shake. Vaughan, an evil smile on his face, strides into the room where she sits. She drops the miniature in horror; he crushes it underfoot. "Awake, Sylph Etherege," he says, "awake to truth! I am the only Edgar Vaughan" (117).

One might expect the melodrama to end here, but it continues. Sylvia, who has fainted at the awful epiphany, recovers. Nuptials are announced. Although her appearance becomes gossamer-like as the wedding approaches, she apparently accommodates herself to the prospect. Then one evening Vaughan drops in and finds her sitting in a shadowy recess by the window. He jokes that she appears ready to fade away, to which she replies: "Farewell. . . . [Y]ou cannot keep me here!" (119). She has, we gather, allowed herself to waste away to the point of death. Vaughan answers her, however, in words that boost this Radcliffean tale into a blacker realm: "Can our sweet Sylph be going to Heaven," he says, "to seek the original of the miniature?" (119).

What's remarkable here is not (as Randall Stewart concludes) Vaughan's realization that his sadistic prank has backfired and that his devastated victim has escaped him.[43] It's that his words suggest not a romantic but a spiritual reversal whose drama wouldn't be fully realized until Katherine Anne Porter's "The Jilting of Granny Weatherall." Vaughan's remark conflates Sylvia's victimizing bridegroom with the New Testament figure of the Heavenly Bridegroom.

John the Baptist likens Christ to a bridegroom (John 3:29), and Christ elaborates the figure (Matthew 9:15; Mark 2:19–20; Luke 5:34–35), most memorably in the parable of the ten virgins (Matthew 25:1–13). There he speaks of the kingdom of heaven in terms of a bridegroom who has been delayed on his way to the wedding. Ten maids have been charged with lighting the bridegroom's way into the house. Five of them, anticipating delay, procure extra oil with which to trim their lamps through the night; the remainder neglect to do so. All ten are asleep when the bridegroom arrives. The unprepared maids, whose lamps have expired, must go in search of oil and are shut out of the wedding. The parable admonishes Christians to keep the lamp of faith trimmed and to be ready to encounter Christ.[44]

Hawthorne's story, in which a lamp and a summons to awake figure prominently, is about a young girl who has spent her life waiting for a "promised bridegroom" (112), the "distant and unseen" lover (115) whom she has invested with ideal, even religious attributes—"heavenly eyes," for instance, that "gazed for ever into her soul" (115). This spiritualized lover prompts a "blissful . . . ecstasy" and even "wile[s] Sylvia away from earth" (116). When she announces her imminent death and Vaughan suggests she has gone to look for her envisioned bridegroom in heaven, we can but imagine Sylph Etherege, her faith in an earthly bridegroom shattered, going with the same implicit and possibly naïve faith to meet Christ. Hawthorne out-Vaughans Vaughan, offering readers a sentimental romance that transmogrifies abruptly into a parable of disillusionment.

Absent groom and anxious woman recur in duplicate in "The Wives of the Dead," another story of faith flickering like lamplight as night descends.[45] Mary and Margaret, the newly wedded wives of two brothers, one a soldier and the other a seaman, both receive word within a two-day period that their husbands have perished—one in battle, the other in shipwreck. The neighbors and a minister stop by the house the sisters share to whisper "comfortable passages of Scripture" (192), but these are answered, Hawthorne tells us, by more tears. As evening approaches, the visitors depart, leaving the women to their grief. Mary, having gotten a grip on her emotions, submits herself to God, but Margaret cannot. When Mary says, "Come, dearest sister; you have eaten not a morsel today. Arise, I pray you, and let us ask a blessing on that which is provided for us," Margaret replies, "There is no blessing left for me, neither will I ask it!" (193).

In the course of the night each woman independently receives or imagines she receives word that her husband is alive and returning home.[46] But the sudden joy each experiences at this virtual resurrection is tempered by sorrow, for each believes the other's husband is still dead. These parallel episodes provide the framework for the delicately balanced contrasts the tale sets up. So ambiguous does Hawthorne render the events of his arabesque that we can't be sure whether it is a story of faith rewarded, faith frustrated, disbelief ratified, or disbelief reproved. (Both visitations are convincingly detailed; yet dreams and hallucinations can be convincing too, and the story's title is an anchor dragging against hope.) What's clear, however, is that bereavement, like night itself, becomes a spiritual metaphor: the question of whether or not the husbands live is bound up with that of whether or not the God Mary trusts and Margaret spurns is there.[47]

This is the context in which the central image—the lamp that illumines the mourners' house during the night, casting shadows on the wall—resonates. A recurring and sometimes explicit symbol of faith throughout Hawthorne's oeuvre (albeit one with secular echoes as well, the lamp of hope and Aladdin's lamp),[48] it sparks a range of biblical associations, from the parable of the bridegroom to the psalms of David ("Thy word is a lamp unto my feet and a light unto my path" [Psalms 119:105], and "Yea, thou art my lamp, O Lord, and my God lightens my darkness" [2 Samuel 22:29]). Perhaps the lamp brings to mind as well the calling of Samuel, another narrative of repeated nocturnal visitations conveying blessing (Samuel's election as a prophet and judge) but also doom (the destruction of Eli's house). This episode, in which God appears and speaks to Samuel, occurs, we are told, "when the lamp of God had not yet gone out" (1 Samuel 3:3).

The names of the women, meanwhile, recall Mary and Martha of the New Testament, whose brother Lazarus Jesus raised from the dead, according to John 11. (That story of miraculous reprieve, like Hawthorne's, opens with a scene of mourning in which two sisters are comforted by members of their religious community.) Mary and Margaret resemble their counterparts in more than name and circumstance. The biblical Mary personifies piety, faith, submission, and an unerring sense of spiritual priorities; Martha, by contrast, doubts that Christ can raise Lazarus from the dead (John 11:25–7; 38–40) and, on another occasion, allows earthly concerns to preempt Christian duty. While Mary listens to Christ's teaching, Martha fusses with the chores, contends with her sister for not assisting her—and with Jesus for not reproving Mary—and incurs Christ's rebuke that Mary has chosen the better part (Luke 10:41–42).

These overlapping allusions presuppose a story whose theme is the obligation to maintain faith, to keep one's lamp trimmed in the dark hours of doubt, and to cultivate Christian priorities. Yet "The Wives of the Dead" confounds so straightforward a reading—and not only because we don't know for sure whether the midnight visits are imagined or experienced. Its central drama concerns how the sisters-in-law cope with the "deluge of darkness" (195) that has overwhelmed them. Their differing spiritual reflexes aside, they cope by cleaving to each other in a figurative marriage born of grief. The two "joined their hearts," Hawthorne tells us (193). When Margaret receives word of her husband's preservation, she shrinks from awakening Mary, "as if her own better fortune, had rendered her involuntarily unfaithful" (196).[49] In the husbands' absence and in what may be God's absence, the wives bond.[50]

Edward R. Stephenson has remarked on the "human solidarity" achieved by the grieving women.[51] To the extent that this solidarity represents a strategy for coping in an unblessed world, the tragedy the wives suffer has a bronze, if not quite a silver, lining. Loss tries their trust in God but fosters their trust in each other. It also renews their faith in other people. Assuming that what seems to happen actually happens, an innkeeper, Master Parker, goes out on a stormy night to inform Margaret of her husband's imminent return. Mary's former lover Stephen makes a similarly selfless trip to bring her news of her husband's preservation. With these unexpected demonstrations of compassion the chain of human sympathies makes itself felt in ways it would not otherwise have had occasion to.

Unfortunately, the contrast Hawthorne sets up between Margaret's rebellious attitude toward her fate and Mary's stance of pious submission is never resolved. We don't know what happens, so we can't draw any conclusions concerning the power of faith or the presence of God. It seems all too possible that both visitations are fantasies, that there is no resurrection to celebrate. But assuming either of the husbands lives, Mary's ethic of pious submission may not necessarily represent the better part. If Margaret's good tidings are to be believed, her husband and a dozen companions saved themselves by fighting off the French and Indians who were presumed to have slaughtered them. And if Mary hasn't dreamt her good news, her husband and three other sailors "saved themselves on a spar, when the Blessing turned bottom upwards" (198). Saving oneself is a far cry from "Thy will be done."[52] New Testament precept, the story just barely suggests, may not suit the New World wilderness, where the survivors are likely to be those who struggle hardest against fate, stick together, and resign themselves to nothing.

"The Wives of the Dead," then, acknowledges the possibility that the human condition is one of darkness and spiritual bereavement, and it floats the possibility that a humanist alternative to the Christian gospel may be the better part. "The Great Carbuncle" is less tentative; its protagonists deliberately embrace such an alternative.[53] The title refers to a large gemstone that, according to Indian legend, occupies a pinnacle of the White Mountains. Eight characters intrigued by it—six individuals and a newly married couple—have come in quest of the stone. They meet halfway up the mountain and camp together for the night. After their meal, one of the adventurers, the Cynic, proposes they each explain their interest in the gem. The Seeker, we learn, pursues it because the desire to possess the stone has become an obsession. The chemist wants to analyze its makeup and crown his reputation by publishing the result. The merchant wants to sell it to the highest bidder. The poet craves the inspiration it will afford and the consequent literary fame. The aristocrat wants it to enhance the glory of his family seat. The newlyweds want it to brighten their cottage during long winter evenings and to impress their neighbors.

The story's meaning is at least as varied as its characters' motives (and we have yet to consider the Cynic's). But behind the allegory these suggest, a religious allegory glimmers. The Cynic characterizes the searchers as "fellow-pilgrims," and his address beginning "Here we are, seven wise men" (153) conjures up the Magi's pursuit of the star of Bethlehem. Light, indeed, is so pervasive a New Testament motif (Christ as the light of the world, the gospel as light) that when one adventurer announces plans to hide the jewel under his cloak—a phrase the Cynic reiterates: "Hide it under thy cloak, say'st thou?" (156)—we are reminded of Christ's injunction to believers not to hide their light under a bushel (Matthew 5:15).[54]

The religious allegory becomes more pronounced when the Cynic vows to show that "the Great Carbuncle is all a humbug." Hawthorne writes:

> Vain and foolish were the motives that had brought most of the adventurers to the Crystal Hills, but none so vain, so foolish, and so impious too, as that of the scoffer with the prodigious spectacles. He was one of those wretched and evil men, whose yearnings are downward to the darkness, instead of Heavenward, and who, could they but extinguish the lights which God hath kindled for us, would count the midnight gloom their chiefest glory. (157)

The fact that this "impious . . .scoffer" is singled out for the greatest reproach (and punishment) suggests that the tale—its more obvious moralizing about vanity, selfishness, and greed aside—is ultimately about belief. The "unbeliever" (162), as Hawthorne later terms the Cynic, sees no light, even when the carbuncle is right in front of his bespectacled eyes. When his glasses are removed, the light sears his eyes; he is later burned to death in the Great Fire of London, the hell into which his blindness leads him.

But the story's religious implications are not as unambivalently pietistic as the Cynic's fate might suggest. Its protagonists are the newlyweds. Their vain desire for the jewel, less obsessive and egoistic than the desires of the others, is venial. They alone are permitted to behold the gem without harm. Having beheld it, however, they decide that, all things considered, they would rather not possess it. Having climbed so high that "Nature herself seemed no longer to keep them company," they long for "blessed earth." In fact, the narrator continues, "the lovers yearned to behold that green earth . . . more intensely, alas!, than, beneath a clouded sky, they had ever desired a glimpse of Heaven" (160). And so, forgoing "visions of unearthly radiance" for "the more blessed light of one another's eyes," the two return to their cottage, there to enjoy the humble pleasures of sunlight, moonlight, hearth, and matrimony (158).

Hawthorne allows his affectionately drawn protagonists to walk away from the lustrous relic that, at least in part, suggests the Pearl of Great Price, and to prefer instead the household of earthly delights.[55] To be sure, he frames their decision innocuously enough: "[T]wo mortals had shown themselves so simply wise, as to reject a jewel which would have dimmed all earthly things" (165). More important, he avoids assigning a precise meaning to the carbuncle, making it impossible to specify just what it is the couple have rejected. In fact, as if to veil his unorthodox parable, he strews conflicting meanings like clouds about the carbuncle, characterizing it not only in material as well as spiritual terms but also in words that carry alternately infernal and divine associations: Its "awful blaze" (163) glows "dusky red" (161) and is linked by the merchant's congregation with "the evil one" (155), but "a ray of glory flashe[s] across its surface" when the pilgrims stumble across its "shrine" (161). Even the word *carbuncle*, as Patrick Morrow points out, has oppositional meanings—the geological one that the story is most obviously concerned with (a garnet) and the medical one (a pus-filled boil), which he reads as "an external manifestation of an inner sickness" and relates to the questers (the carbuncle, he says, is "each man's personal folly made manifest").[56] To acknowledge these swirling meanings is only to recognize the tale's complexity, for Hawthorne, here as in "The Minister's Black Veil," stretches allegory to the verge of symbol.

Nonetheless, the stone's unearthly aspect is paramount.[57] Its lofty, luminous grandeur, like that of the Great Stone Face, connotes divinity. Many of the spiritually connotative adjectives and nouns used to describe the Great Stone Face—"wondrous," "splendor," "radiance," "glorious"—are applied to the carbuncle. The Christian framework outlined earlier is reinforced by the biblical echoes of the protagonists' names.[58] The tale, in short, invites us to view the carbuncle as what the narrator terms one of the "lights which God hath kindled for us" (157). In turning away from the relic, the newlyweds ostensibly reject the material temptations of wealth and renown, but they also implicitly reject the Christian vision of life as a pilgrimage upward to a better world, a spiritual reward. They choose earth over heaven.

Their decision is made easier, of course, by the idyllic earthly paradise they are afforded: a lovers' hideaway at the foot of the White Mountains.[59] In "Rappaccini's Daughter" there is only the frying pan of Padua (with its Dantesque rivalries and insidious professional jealousies) and the fire (Rappaccini's sinister garden, a kind of inverted Paradise).[60] In this much interpreted story, a young man, Giovanni Guasconti, falls in love with the poisonous but ravishing Beatrice Rappaccini, whose scientist father has nurtured her on poisons so that she alone is inured to the deadly garden he has created as a laboratory.

An elderly professor named Baglioni, a friend of Giovanni's father and rival of Rappaccini, warns the youth to shun the beauty lest he become part of her father's experiment. When Giovanni refuses, Baglioni gives him what he claims is an antidote to her poison. Giovanni, upon discovering that he has been infected by Beatrice's poison, flies into a rage, spurns Beatrice, and produces the antidote, insisting that she drink it. She does, and it kills her.

Critics have identified two main problems with the tale.[61] Beatrice's character is the first. A composite of the Eve of Genesis and Dante's Beatrice (and perhaps Beatrice Cenci, victim of paternal incest),[62] she comprises both purity and pestilence, but to what end? Given the story's allegorical nature—and Hawthorne identifies it as an allegory in a preface—she ought to represent, as Richard Harter Fogle points out, "a contrast between outward beauty and inner ugliness and evil."[63] Instead, she is the soul of goodness, a gracious victim both of her father's scientific zeal and later of Giovanni's rejection. What, then, does her toxicity signify?[64]

The second problem concerns Hawthorne's orchestration of themes. "The real theme," says Fogle, "arises from Beatrice and Giovanni and concludes with a demonstration of Beatrice's spiritual superiority. . . . The theme of Rappaccini [the scientist who ignores all other values in his quest for knowledge] is secondary, but encroaches on the first."[65] And yet the tale's dramatic unity, it would seem, braids the two themes. The lovers' tragedy is a result of Rappaccini's science. The themes converge seamlessly in the conclusion, where Beatrice's death is followed immediately by Baglioni's cry, "Rappaccini! Rappaccini! And is *this* the upshot of your experiment?" (128).

Beyond a point, the complexities of Hawthorne's allegory refuse to parse. Beatrice says of herself, "though my body be nourished with poison, my spirit is God's creature" (125). Perhaps then her poison is her humanity? (So *in*humane are the nontoxic characters that one is tempted to see the tale as an antiworld of reversed symbols.) But an allegory that asks us to equate human nature with poison seems nothing less than medieval. Frederick Crews suggests that Beatrice's toxicity is her sexuality, a reading the tale's garden imagery and story line support.[66] But a Freudian gloss seems limiting as well as illuminating; it marginalizes moral and theological issues that ought, surely, to be central.

Alloyed though the story is with elements of Dante's *Commedia*, the Garden of Eden motif is so prominent—what with forbidden shrub, serpent, Giovanni/Adam and Beatrice/Eve, and the austere creator, Rappaccini, hovering in the wings—that any reading, it would seem, must begin here. But what is the application? Waggoner suggests that Beatrice is a symbol of mankind's "situation in a fallen world."[67] Why, then, should she be set apart so dramatically from the other characters? Fogle contends that the story "reasserts the fundamental justice of Providence."[68] But can Beatrice's death really be said to vindicate Providence? No doubt, as critics invariably point out, the tale incriminates the scientist for aspiring to the role of God. But does it not also indirectly incriminate God?

"Rappaccini's Garden" impeaches a creator who engineers an experimental world tainted by evil and whose noblest creature, deliberately exposed to the taint, partakes of it. The experiment is conducted at the creature's expense, whose fulfillment is made all but impossible by the poison that has been allowed to flourish. The only available "antidote" to this state of affairs is death. The tale amounts to a rather unflinching parody of the Creation and the Fall.[69] "My father," says Beatrice just prior to her death, "wherefore didst thou inflict this miserable doom upon thy child?" (127). To be sure, Hawthorne allows Rappaccini to answer her (he did it, he explains, for her own good, her own empowerment) and gestures toward assigning blame for the tragedy elsewhere, to Giovanni, for instance, whose spurning of Beatrice is certainly the tale's dramatic climax. But Giovanni has a right to his anger, however misdirected and incontinent. He has been poisoned. Baglioni too is a candidate for blame. His rivalry with Rappaccini, we infer, may have goaded him to murder. But Baglioni is an accessory after the fact. The fatal experiment is of Rappaccini's devising. Diffuse as the allegory is, it ultimately implicates the creator, the aloof bio-engineer Rappaccini.[70]

*   *   *

Hawthorne, we know, quarried in Cotton Mather's works. As a young man he savored the *Magnalia Christi Americana*, Mather's ecclesiastical history of seventeenth-century New England.[71] What he got from Mather, one suspects (F. O. Matthiessen to the contrary notwithstanding), was more than the stories.[72] In the profiles of exemplary New Englanders upon whose lives Mather superimposed those of biblical characters, suggesting a providential continuity between Israel and the self-styled New Jerusalem, Hawthorne found distilled the Puritan mindset with its conviction of election. But perhaps he also discovered in Mather's biographical reductions and redactions a strategy for enriching contemporary or historical fictions. Whereas Mather, however, used biblical allusions to demonstrate Providence at work, Hawthorne uses them to question Providence. Working both in and against the grain of the Massachusetts Puritan tradition, he hints that religious faith may be a lamp that distorts as well as illumines—that life may be less a pilgrimage than a sojourn, history less an alembic than a lottery, God less agent than image.

If some of Hawthorne's tales are "twice-told" in that they rehearse New England's history, others are twice-told in that they ironically revisit Scripture and doctrine. Writing such tales risked scandalizing readers wholesale, and Hawthorne went about it cautiously, blurring his intent, offering multiple interpretations, distracting our attention with one immaculately gloved hand while flashing disturbing pictures with the other. (In the unfinished fiction *Etherege*, he cautions himself: "Now, if this great blackness and horror is to be underneath the story, there must be a frolic and dance of bacchanals all over the surface; else the effect would be utterly miserable. There may be a steam of horror escaping through safety-valves, but generally the tone must be joyous.")[73] He used the same strategies, of course, in stories such as "The Gray Champion" and "Endicott and the Red Cross," in which he qualified or controverted patriotic constructions of New England's heritage while seeming to celebrate them. But even as those stories show a profound involvement with history, the stories I have discussed show a profound involvement with, rather than indifference toward, God and the Christian teleology, an involvement whose underlying doubts swirl, at moments, with a blackness akin to Melville's own.

Notes

1. Herman Melville, "Mosses from an Old Manse," in *The Piazza Tales and Other Prose Pieces*, ed. Harrison Hayford, Alma A. MacDougall, G. Thomas Tanselle et al., vol. 9 of *The Writings of Herman Melville*, 15 vols. (Evanston, Ill.: Northwestern Univ. Press and The Newberry Library, 1968–1993), 243–44. Subsequent quotations from this work will be cited parenthetically within the text as "MM."

2. Lawrance Thompson makes the same assumption in *Melville's Quarrel with God* (Princeton, N.J.: Princeton Univ. Press, 1952), 127, 137, noting that the phrase "blackness of darkness," which Melville uses elsewhere in his essay (243) to describe Hawthorne's tales, is "the term which Jude used in the Bible (verse 13) to condemn the devilishness of heresiarchs" (136).

3. Herman Melville, *Correspondence*, vol. 14 of *The Writings of Herman Melville*, 186.

4. Nathaniel Hawthorne, "A Select Party," in *Mosses from an Old Manse*, vol. 10 of *The Centenary Edition of the Works of Nathaniel Hawthorne*, ed. William Charvat et al., 23 vols. (Columbus: Ohio State Univ. Press, 1962–1994), 57–73. The one unwelcome guest at this exclusive rendezvous in the sky is the Wandering Jew.

One other story Melville praises in his review, "The Intelligence Office," shows a similar audacity. This mostly benign allegory of man's suppliant relationship to God depicts a cosmic Lost-and-Found office superintended by a mysterious, bespectacled official. He is visited daily by characters who have lost such items as their hearts, their place in life, or, in one case, the Pearl of Great Price. The avuncular "spirit" (as Hawthorne terms the Intelligencer) listens to their pleas and dispenses advice, aid, and an occasional reprimand. At last the godlike Intelligencer is visited by a Seeker of Truth, who, brushing aside all superficiality and bending a penetrating eye, asks the Intelligencer, "[W]hat is . . .your real agency in life, and your influence upon mankind?" The answer: "Know, then, the secret. My agency in worldly action—my connection with the . . . development of human affairs—is merely delusive" (*Mosses from an Old Manse*, 336). Melville's review likens Hawthorne to the Truth-Seeker ("MM," 250).

5. See Marius Bewley, *The Eccentric Design* (New York: Columbia Univ. Press, 1957), 124. Bewley is more attuned than most critics to a "sense of intolerable spiritual isolation" in Hawthorne's writing (122).

6. See Thompson, *Melville's Quarrel with God*.

7. F. O. Matthiessen, *American Renaissance* (New York: Oxford Univ. Press, 1941), 199; Hyatt H. Waggoner, *Hawthorne: A Critical Study* (Cambridge: Harvard Univ. Press, 1963), 6, 13; Henry James, *Hawthorne* (London: Oxford Univ. Press, 1879; reprint, Ithaca, N.Y.: Cornell Univ. Press, 1956), 46; Mark Van Doren, *Nathaniel Hawthorne: A Critical Biography* (New York: Viking, 1949), 214–16.

8. Alfred Kazin, *God and the American Writer* (New York: Knopf, 1997), 28.

9. *The Scarlet Letter*, it seems to me, stops just short of engaging questions of faith, though they are surely in the air. Pearl's "I have no Heavenly Father" rings eerily in the margins of the novel but never attains the status of a theme. Hester's "labyrinth of doubt" and its counterpart, the "moral wilderness" she is said to wander in, while recalling Young Goodman Brown's spiritual isolation, do not undermine her love for Pearl and Dimmesdale or the links, however tenuous, that she maintains to the Christian community (*The Scarlet Letter*, vol. 1 of the *Centenary Edition*, 98, 99, 183). And though her freethinking portends the eclipse of patriarchy and a patriarchal Christianity, it does not, I think, portend the eclipse of Christianity. The novel's subversive aspects (Hester's "Be it sin or no, I hate the man [Chillingworth]!" [176] is almost as defiant a sentiment, given the Puritan context, as Huck Finn's resolve to help Jim get free even if it means going to hell) are finally subsumed by the aura of redemption that attends Hester at the close. Matthew Gartner, whose "*The Scarlet Letter* and the Book of Esther: Scriptural Letter and Narrative Life" (*Studies in American Fiction* 23 [fall 1995]: 131–51) investigates an Old Testament motif in the novel, arrives at a similar conclusion concerning Hawthorne's attitude and intent. Hawthorne, Gartner decides, is not ironically recasting a biblical theme but rather reanimating a source text. By the time Hawthorne wrote his first two major novels, he was a married man, a father, and a fairly well-established author who seems to have struck a truce with the cosmos that had perhaps eluded him earlier. Hence the change of tone between "Young Goodman Brown" and *The Scarlet Letter*, and between the stories and novels in general (although *The Blithedale Romance*, which concerns a suicide in the sort of enlightened community Hester is said to anticipate and which ends in a mood approaching despair, qualifies this generalization).

10. In taking this tack, I acknowledge as antecedents not only Melville but literary biographer Edwin Haviland Miller to the extent that he departs from mainstream biographers in calling Hawthorne's relationship to God "uneasy" and in remarking that Hawthorne "was too skeptical to place much confidence in Christian . . . idealism" (*Salem Is My Dwelling Place: A Life of Nathaniel Hawthorne* [Iowa City: Univ. of Iowa Press, 1991], 11, 189).

11. Nathaniel Hawthorne, *The English Notebooks*, vol. 22 of *Centenary Edition*, 163.

12. Nathaniel Hawthorne, *The American Notebooks*, vol. 8 of *Centenary Edition*, 448, 58, 109, 430.

13. See, for example, B. R. Brubaker, "Hawthorne's Experiment in Popular Form: 'Mr. Higginbotham's Catastrophe,'" *Southern Humanities Review* 7 (spring 1973): 155–66.

14. Michael J. Colacurcio, introduction to Nathaniel Hawthorne, *Selected Tales and Sketches* (New York: Penguin, 1987), xxi–xxii. See also Colacurcio's *The Province of Piety: Moral History in Hawthorne's Early Tales* (Cambridge: Harvard Univ. Press, 1984), 502–4.

15. William G. McLoughlin, *Revivals, Awakenings, and Reform* (Chicago: Univ. of Chicago Press, 1978), 106.

16. In a letter of 26 November 1824 to his aunt Mary Manning, Hawthorne remarks, "There is a considerable revival of religion in this town" (*Letters*, vol. 15 of *Centenary Edition*, 189).

17. McLoughlin, *Revivals, Awakenings, and Reform*, 130, 139. See also Russel Blaine Nye, *The Cultural Life of the New Nation* (New York: Harper & Row, 1960), 220–21; and Sacvan Bercovitch, *The American Jeremiad* (Madison: Univ. of Wisconsin Press, 1978), 172.

18. W. R. Thompson, "The Biblical Sources of 'Roger Malvin's Burial,'" *PMLA* 77 (March 1962): 92–96; "Patterns of Biblical Allusions in Hawthorne's 'The Gentle Boy,'" *South Central Bulletin* 22 (winter 1962): 3–10; and "Theme and Method in Hawthorne's 'The Great Carbuncle,'" *South Central Bulletin* 21 (winter 1961): 3–10.

19. See Frederick Newberry, "The Biblical Veil: Sources and Typology in Hawthorne's 'The Minister's Black Veil,'" *TSLL* 31 (summer 1989): 169–93; Judy McCarthy, "'The Minister's Black Veil': Concealing Moses and the Holy of Holies," *Studies in Short Fiction* 24 (spring 1987): 131–38; Edgar A. Dryden, "Through a Glass Darkly: 'The Minister's Black Veil' as Parable," in *New Essays on Hawthorne's Major Tales*, ed. Millicent Bell (Cambridge, Eng.: Cambridge Univ. Press, 1993), 133–50; J. Hillis Miller, *Hawthorne and History* (Oxford, Eng.: Basil Blackwell, 1991), 62, 83–84. In addition, Hyatt H. Waggoner has traced biblical elements in "The Man of Adamant" (*A Critical Study*, 108–9), and interpreters of "Rappaccini's Daughter" regularly note Edenic parallels.

20. Sacvan Bercovitch, "Endicott's Breastplate: Symbolism and Typology in 'Endicott and the Red Cross,'" *Studies in Short Fiction* 4 (spring 1967): 289–99.

21. Gartner, *"The Scarlet Letter* and the Book of Esther," 133.

22. Miller, *Salem Is My Dwelling Place*, 65.

23. Gartner, *"The Scarlet Letter* and the Book of Esther," 133.

24. See Bill Christophersen, "'Young Goodman Brown' as Historical Allegory: A Lexical Link," *Studies in Short Fiction* 23 (spring 1986): 203–4.

25. Nathaniel Hawthorne, "Young Goodman Brown," in *Mosses from an Old Manse*, 90.

26. Arlin Turner (*Nathaniel Hawthorne: An Introduction and Interpretation* [New York: Barnes and Noble, 1961], 28) and Terence Martin (*Nathaniel Hawthorne* [New York: Twayne, 1965], 57–58), among others, stress the tale's rebuke to both the Puritan and Quaker camps.

27. See Seymour L. Gross, "Hawthorne's Revision of 'The Gentle Boy,'" *American Literature* 26 (May 1954): 208.

28. William Tremblay holds that "the real forces impinging on Ilbrahim are . . . 'rational piety' . . . and 'unbridled fanaticism'" ("A Reading of Nathaniel Hawthorne's 'The Gentle Boy,'" *Massachusetts Studies in English* 2 [spring 1970]: 87). Roy Male contends that the story is about "the agonizing difficulty of finding an integrated, fruitful religious experience in America" (*Hawthorne's Tragic Vision* [Austin: Univ. of Texas Press, 1957], 45).

29. W. R. Thompson, "Patterns of Biblical Allusions," 3–10. Thompson pays particular attention to the many New Testament allusions that characterize Catharine's speech.

30. Michael Colacurcio emphasizes Ilbrahim's role as Christ figure in *The Province of Piety*, 180–87.

31. See Frederick C. Crews, *The Sins of the Fathers: Hawthorne's Psychological Themes* (New York: Oxford Univ. Press, 1966), 67.

32. Nathaniel Hawthorne, "The Gentle Boy," in *Twice-Told Tales*, vol. 9 of *Centenary Edition*, 74. Subsequent quotations from this story will be cited parenthetically within the text.

33. See Louise Dauner, "The 'Case' of Tobias Pearson: Hawthorne and the Ambiguities," *American Literature* 21 (January 1950): 469.

34. Agnes M. Donohue remarks, "Around all the violence of the tale roars the wind of desolation" ("'The Fruit of That Forbidden Tree': A Reading of 'The Gentle Boy,'" in *A Casebook on the Hawthorne Question*, ed. Agnes M. Donohue [New Haven, Conn.: Crowell, 1963], 161).

35. James K. Folsom views the tale as a comment on the subjective nature of reality (*Man's Accidents and God's Purposes: Multiplicity in Hawthorne's Fiction* [New Haven, Conn.: College and Univ. Press, 1963], 22–24). Male calls it an example of Hawthorne at his most disengaged (*Tragic Vision*, 6). Mark Van Doren likewise dismisses it (*Hawthorne: A Critical Biography*, 95), and Lea Bertani Vozar Newman writes, "Perhaps the best use that 'David Swan' can serve is to identify, by its shortcomings, what makes the better stories as good as they are" (*A Reader's Guide to the Short Stories of Nathaniel Hawthorne* [Boston: G. K. Hall, 1979], 59).

36. Nathaniel Hawthorne, "David Swan," in *Twice-Told Tales*, 190. Quotations from this story will be cited parenthetically within the text.

37. Hawthorne's strategy of choosing biblical names for his characters has been remarked by W. R. Thompson ("Biblical Sources," 92–96) and Matthew Gartner ("*The Scarlet Letter* and the Book of Esther," 134), among others.

38. Randall Stewart characterizes its moral as Emersonian: "the power of an ideal to shape an individual life" (*Nathaniel Hawthorne: A Biography* [New Haven: Yale Univ. Press, 1948], 93). Richard Harter Fogle seconds its "Transcendentalist flavor" (*Hawthorne's Fiction: The Light and the Dark* [Norman: Oklahoma Univ. Press, 1952; rev. ed., 1964], 187). Morris Murphy notes its "Wordsworthian" tenor ("Wordsworthian Concepts in 'The Great Stone Face,'" *College English* 23 [February 1962]: 364–65). Nancy Bunge says that, other Hawthorne stories notwithstanding, this one "implies the world struggles toward benevolence" (*Nathaniel Hawthorne: A Study of the*

Short Fiction [New York: Twayne, 1993], 77). James J. Lynch sees it as an allegory of the progressive stages of life ("Structure and Allegory in 'The Great Stone Face,'" *Nineteenth Century Fiction* 15 [September 1960]: 140, 144).

39. Julian Hawthorne, *Nathaniel Hawthorne and His Wife: A Biography*, 2 vols. (Boston: James R. Osgood, 1884), 1:354.

40. Nathaniel Hawthorne, "The Great Stone Face," in *The Snow Image and Other Tales*, vol. 11 of *Centenary Edition*, 27. Subsequent quotations from this story will be cited parenthetically within the text.

41. Genesis 22:2–18; Exodus 19:20. Leo B. Levy suggests, for example, that Ernest, the prophecy incarnate, "is modeled upon the character and way of life of Christ" ("Hawthorne and the Sublime," *American Literature* 37 [January 1966]: 396).

42. Nathaniel Hawthorne, "Sylph Etherege," in *The Snow Image and Other Tales*, 111–19. Quotations from this story will be cited parenthetically within the text. Lea Newman summarizes the meager critical consensus on "Sylph Etherege" as follows: "It is innocuous enough to avoid controversy and too insipid to warrant commendation" (*Reader's Guide to the Stories*, 298).

43. See Randall Stewart, ed., *The American Notebooks by Nathaniel Hawthorne* (New Haven: Yale Univ. Press, 1932), l.

44. New England divines made much of this figure, particularly in the seventeenth century. They used it to describe Christ's relationship not just with the Church but with the individual believer. See Michael F. Winship, "Behold the Bridegroom Cometh! Marital Imagery in Massachusetts Preaching, 1630–1730," *Early American Literature* 27, No. 3 (1992): 170–84, especially 171.

45. Nathaniel Hawthorne, "The Wives of the Dead," in *The Snow Image and Other Tales*, 192–99. Quotations from this story will be cited parenthetically within the text.

46. Interpretations of what actually happens have ranged from Mark Van Doren's and Nina Baym's unqualified acceptance of the reality of the messengers (Van Doren, *Hawthorne: A Critical Biography*, 82–84; Baym, *The Shape of Hawthorne's Career* [Ithaca, N.Y.: Cornell Univ. Press, 1976], 32) to Hans-Joachim Lang's and Harry Levin's flat assertions that the widows dream the news of their husbands' return (Lang, "How Ambiguous Is Hawthorne?" in *Hawthorne: A Collection of Critical Essays*, ed. A. N. Kaul [Englewood Cliffs, N.J.: Prentice Hall, 1966], 86–98; Levin, *The Power of Blackness* [New York: Vintage, 1958], 58). Patricia Ann Carlson, tilling a more fertile middle ground, holds that the story mixes the actual and the illusive, but she contends—dubiously, I think—that "all the action taking place within [the lamp's] light is illusion" ("The Function of the Lamp in Hawthorne's 'The Wives of the Dead,'" *South Atlantic Bulletin* 40 [May 1975]: 62–64). During the past two decades, critics have tried hard to resolve the ambiguity. John Selzer's psychological reading is not a case in point, but his observation that Margaret, unlike Mary, has not been asleep when her summons arrives has suggested a practical resolution to the mystery of what is and isn't a dream ("Psychological Romance in Hawthorne's 'The Wives of the Dead,'" *Studies in Short Fiction* 16 [fall 1979]: 311). Gloria C. Erlich, pursuing the point, contends that Margaret's message is real, and that her husband, but not Mary's, lives (*Family Themes in Hawthorne's Fiction: The Tenacious Web* [New Brunswick, N.J.: Rutgers Univ. Press, 1984], 107). John McDermott agrees with Erlich ("Hawthorne's

'The Wives of the Dead,'" *The Explicator* 54 [spring 1996]: 145–46), and Mark Harris reaches the same conclusion, although by different reasoning. In his view, Mary too is awake to receive her news, but her messenger, unlike Margaret's, is untrustworthy ("The Wives of the Living? Absence of Dream in Hawthorne's 'The Wives of the Dead,'" *Studies in Short Fiction* 29 [summer 1992]: 323–29). But dreaming, it seems only fair to point out, isn't the only mental state that can warp reality. Just as surely as Mary is asleep when her summons arrives, Margaret is "disturbed and feverish" (194) when hers arrives. Her experience, therefore, like Mary's, remains suspect. I believe that, as Richard Poirier ventured a generation ago and as G. R. Thompson reiterates, Hawthorne deliberately suspends the events of the tale in a limbo of uncertainty (Poirier, *A World Elsewhere* [New York: Oxford Univ. Press, 1966], 113; Thompson, *The Art of Authorial Presence: Hawthorne's Provincial Tales* [Durham, N.C.: Duke Univ. Press, 1993], 76). That limbo extends to the vague pronouns of the final sentence.

47. I develop this thesis at greater length and with slightly different emphases in "Hawthorne's 'The Wives of the Dead': Bereavement and 'the Better Part,'" *Studies in Short Fiction* 20 (winter 1983): 1–6.

48. I have noted the lamp in "The Gentle Boy" and in "Sylph Etherege." Owen Warland, the spiritually inclined jeweler in "The Artist of the Beautiful," is associated from the first with a watchmaker's lamp. In "Main-street," Hawthorne says of the first-generation Massachusetts Puritans, "[T]he zeal of a recovered faith burned like a lamp within their hearts" (*The Snow Image and Other Tales*, 58). And "Night Sketches" concludes: "And thus we, night-wanderers through a stormy and dismal world, if we bear the lamp of Faith, enkindled at a celestial fire, it will surely lead us home to that Heaven whence its radiance was borrowed" (*Twice-Told Tales*, 432).

49. The word "unfaithful" may further suggest a twinge of spiritual remorse on Margaret's part. For she can hardly fail to reflect that if her husband lives, the God she (but not Mary) refused to pray to may have preserved him.

50. By speaking of the wives' figurative marriage, I don't mean to turn the story into a lesbian escapade (though there is some hint of yearning in Margaret's insomniac "impulse . . . to . . . gaze into Mary's chamber" [194]) but simply to attend to Hawthorne's language. The story is about plighted trust, faith, "faithfulness," and absent bridegrooms. Marriage is central to it, and the rhetoric of matrimony imbues the phrase "joined their hearts." To be sure, we might characterize the wives' bond differently; we might say, for example, that in their grief the sisters-in-law become sisters. (And in fact at the moment when Margaret's perceived good tidings separate her lot from Mary's, Hawthorne, who has been referring to the two as "sisters," writes, "Margaret shrunk from disturbing her sister-in-law" [196].) But if we ignore the marriage trope, key associations Hawthorne has bid for are lost.

51. Edward R. Stephenson, "Hawthorne's 'The Wives of the Dead,'" *The Explicator* 25 (April 1967): Item 63.

52. This contrast is sharpened by other New Testament subtexts the husbands' trials call to mind. Margaret's husband and his twelve scrappy comrades ironically recall Christ and the twelve apostles accosted by the Romans in Gethsemane. On that occasion Christ, whom the Romans had come to arrest, tells Peter *not* to fight but to "Put up

again thy sword" (Matthew 26:52). Mary's husband and his storm-ravaged shipmates likewise call to mind Christ and the apostles crossing the Sea of Galilee at night in a storm. The apostles become frightened as water fills their boat, but Christ rebukes them for not putting their trust *in God* (Luke 8:25).

53. Nathaniel Hawthorne, "The Great Carbuncle," in *Twice-Told Tales*, 149–65. Quotations from this story will be cited parenthetically within the text.

54. W. R. Thompson cites this last Scriptural reference in "Theme and Method" (6). He contends the story is about "the second great principle of the Christian religion, the concept of the brotherhood of man" (7).

55. See Colacurcio, *Province of Piety*, 510. See also Matthew 13:44–46: "The kingdom of heaven is like unto treasure hid in a field. . . . Again, the kingdom of heaven is like unto a merchant man, seeking goodly pearls: who, when he had found one pearl of great price, went and sold all that he had, and bought it." Christ's figures—the hidden treasure, the precious gem—seem likely cognates for Hawthorne's carbuncle.

56. Patrick Morrow, "A Writer's Workshop: Hawthorne's 'The Great Carbuncle,'" *Studies in Short Fiction* 6 (winter 1969): 161.

57. Leo B. Levy, for one, takes it for granted that the stone symbolizes the Deity, though he would extend its meaning to include "any spiritual principle that puts aside primary human considerations" ("Hawthorne and the Sublime," 394).

58. W. R. Thompson links Hannah's name to 1 Samuel (the Israelite Hannah followed her husband on an unselfish pilgrimage) and Matthew's to the book of Matthew ("Theme and Method," 5–7).

59. On the other hand, "The Ambitious Guest," a story linked to "The Great Carbuncle" by setting and meant to be its companion piece in "The Story-Teller," places ironic brackets around the idyll. In that tale the inhabitants of precisely such a house in the White Mountains, a young couple among them, are annihilated by a midnight landslide.

60. Nathaniel Hawthorne, "Rappaccini's Daughter," in *Mosses from an Old Manse*, 91–128. Quotations from this story will be cited parenthetically within the text.

61. I'm oversimplifying, of course. Criticism of "Rappaccini's Daughter" has become almost as much of an industry as that of *Moby-Dick*; current approaches range from intellectual history to gender studies to autobiographical criticism. It is beyond the scope of this paper to survey the terrain comprehensively. For a concise synopsis of recent interpretations, see Carol M. Bensick, "World Lit Hawthorne: Or, Re-Allegorizing 'Rappaccini's Daughter,'" *New Essays on Hawthorne's Major Tales*, 67–82.

62. Robert White, "'Rappaccini's Daughter,' *The Cenci*, and the Cenci Legend," *Studi Americani* 14 (1968): 63–86.

63. Fogle, *Hawthorne's Fiction*, 91.

64. One of the more intriguing answers is Carol M. Bensick's: syphilis (see *La Nouvelle Beatrice: Renaissance and Romance in 'Rappaccini's Daughter'* [New Brunswick, N.J.: Rutgers Univ. Press, 1985]). Bensick bases her interpretation on a scrutiny of the tale's historical setting. The question behind the question, of course, is, What does Giovanni's rejection of the toxic Beatrice signify? Male proposes that it demonstrates the skepticism he has imbibed from Baglioni and his consequent unworthiness of the redemption Beatrice offers (*Tragic Vision*, 54–70). But, as Crews points out, the

prospective marriage of two chemical freaks is a dubious redemption (*Sins of the Fathers*, 118). Waggoner suggests that Giovanni represents the classical as opposed to the Christian world view, since he lacks a "spiritual sense," an appreciation of evil (*Hawthorne: A Critical Study*, 113–17). That description, however, seems more appropriate for Donatello in *The Marble Faun*.

65. Fogle, *Hawthorne's Fiction*, 92. See also Waggoner, *Hawthorne: A Critical Study*, 118.

66. Crews, *Sins of the Fathers*, 119–121.

67. Waggoner, *Hawthorne: A Critical Study*, 124.

68. Fogle, *Hawthorne's Fiction*, 103.

69. Crews, who perceives the various characters as projections of Giovanni's conflicted psyche, takes a related tack: Rappaccini, he says, is "the God of Giovanni's latent atheism, the God of a godless world" (*Sins of the Fathers*, 134).

70. I ventured earlier that the agnostic tensions I have been tracing in the stories do not, by and large, characterize the novels. But surely one of the darker elements of *The Scarlet Letter* is the way in which it replays the disturbing allegory of "Rappaccini's Daughter." The novel, like the story, is set in an ironic Eden (not a toxic garden but a New World already polluted by sin) and features a trio consisting of a young man, a tainted if admirable woman, and an older man. In both works the older man is at least indirectly responsible for the fatal outcome the young man and woman court. And in both works the older man is portrayed as godlike, a possessor of inscrutable knowledge and power over life and death. So diabolical is Chillingworth rendered in the course of the novel that the reader is liable to overlook his identity as the One Who Is Sinned Against (not to mention the benevolence and solicitude that, Hester acknowledges, were once part of his character). But to the extent we overlook it we miss the Promethean aspect of Hester's rebellion against the merciless soul-searcher he becomes, whose intelligence and will seem to narrow, like those of the Calvinist god, on discovering, then visiting the iniquity of the sinner: "'Yes, I hate him,' repeated Hester. . . . 'He betrayed me! He has done me worse wrong than I did him!'" (176).

71. See James R. Mellow, *Nathaniel Hawthorne and His Times* (Boston: Houghton Mifflin, 1980), 40.

72. Matthiessen, *American Renaissance*, 116.

73. Nathaniel Hawthorne, *Etherege*, in *The American Claimant Manuscripts*, vol. 12 of the *Centenary Edition*, 292.

RESOURCES

Chronology of Nathaniel Hawthorne's Life_____

1804	Born on July 4 in Salem, Massachusetts, the second child of Nathaniel Hathorne (Nathaniel later changes spelling to *Hawthorne*) and Elizabeth Clarke Manning Hathorne.
1808	Father dies. Second sister is born. Nathaniel, his mother, and two sisters move in with relatives. Mother becomes more and more withdrawn, eventually becoming nearly totally secluded.
1821–1825	Attends Bowdoin College. Some classmates are Longfellow and Franklin Pierce. In 1825 his poem "The Ocean" is published in the *Salem Gazette*. Continues to have poetry, stories, reviews, and other material published in periodicals through 1863.
1825–1836	Lives in mother's house in Salem; spends much time reading and writing. In 1828, finances publication of his novel, *Fanshawe: A Tale*, which appears anonymously.
1836	Employed from January through August as editor of *The American Magazine of Useful and Entertaining Knowledge*.
1837	*Twice-Told Tales* is published. The work is a collection of stories that had appeared in periodicals.
1839–1841	Works at Boston Custom House until January, 1841. Spends some months in 1841 living communally at Brook Farm, West Roxbury, Massachusetts.
1842	*Biographical Stories for Children* is published. Marries Sophia Peabody. They move to the Old Manse in Concord. Associates with nearby inhabitants Ralph Waldo Emerson, Henry David Thoreau, Margaret Fuller, and Louisa May Alcott.
1844	First child, Una, is born.
1845–1853	Lives with family at various locations in Massachusetts.

1846	Works from 1846 as a surveyor at the Salem Custom House, until after the Whigs win the presidential election in 1848. *Mosses from an Old Manse*, which contains previously published pieces, published. Second child, Julian, is born.
1850	*The Scarlet Letter* is published.
1851	*The House of the Seven Gables* published. Third and last child, Rose, is born. *A Wonder-Book for Girls and Boys* and *The Snow-Image, and Other Twice-Told Tales* published.
1852	*The Blithedale Romance* and *Life of Franklin Pierce* published.
1853	Through August, 1857, works as American consul at Liverpool, England. Lives there with family nearly two years and then in various locations. *Tanglewood Tales* published.
1860	*The Marble Faun* published. Returns with family to live in Concord, Massachusetts.
1863	*Our Old Home* published.
1864	Dies in Plymouth, New Hampshire, during a trip with Franklin Pierce. Buried in Concord, Massachusetts.

Works by Nathaniel Hawthorne

Long Fiction
Fanshawe: A Tale, 1828
The Scarlet Letter, 1850
The House of the Seven Gables, 1851
The Blithedale Romance, 1852
The Marble Faun, 1860
Septimius Felton, 1872 (fragment)
The Dolliver Romance, 1876 (fragment)
The Ancestral Footstep, 1883 (fragment)
Doctor Grimshawe's Secret, 1883 (fragment)

Short Fiction
Twice-Told Tales, 1837 (expanded 1842)
Mosses from an Old Manse, 1846
The Snow-Image, and Other Twice-Told Tales, 1851

Nonfiction
Life of Franklin Pierce, 1852
Our Old Home, 1863
The American Notebooks, 1932
The English Notebooks, 1941
The French and Italian Notebooks, 1980
Letters of Nathaniel Hawthorne, 1984-1987 (4 volumes)
Selected Letters of Nathaniel Hawthorne, 2002 (Joel Myerson, editor)

Children's Literature
Grandfather's Chair, 1841
Biographical Stories for Children, 1842
True Stories from History and Biography, 1851
A Wonder-Book for Boys and Girls, 1852
Tanglewood Tales for Boys and Girls, 1853

Miscellaneous
Complete Works, 1850-1882 (13 volumes)
The Complete Writings of Nathaniel Hawthorne, 1900 (22 volumes)
The Centenary Edition of the Works of Nathaniel Hawthorne, 1962-1997 (23 volumes)

Edited Text(s)

Peter Parley's Universal History, 1837

Bibliography

Abel, Darrel. *The Moral Picturesque: Studies in Hawthorne's Fiction*. West Lafayette, IN: Purdue University Press, 1988.

Amireh, Amal. *The Factory Girl and the Seamstress: Imagining Gender and Class in Nineteenth Century American Fiction*. New York: Garland, 2000.

Auerbach, Jonathan. *The Romance of Failure: First-Person Fictions of Poe, Hawthorne, and James*. New York: Oxford University Press, 1989.

Barlowe, Jamie. *The Scarlet Mob of Scribblers: Rereading Hester Prynne*. Carbondale: Southern Illinois University Press, 2000.

Bell, Michael Davitt. *Hawthorne and the Historical Romance of New England*. Princeton, NJ: Princeton University Press, 1971.

Bellis, Peter J. *Writing Revolution: Aesthetics and Politics in Hawthorne, Whitman, and Thoreau*. Athens: University of Georgia Press, 2003.

Bensick, Carol Marie. *La Nouvelle Beatrice: Renaissance and Romance in "Rappaccini's Daughter."* New Brunswick, NJ: Rutgers University Press, 1985.

Bercovitch, Sacvan. *The Office of "The Scarlet Letter."* Baltimore: Johns Hopkins University Press, 1991.

Bloom, Harold. *Hester Prynne*. Philadelphia: Chelsea House, 2004.

Boswell, Jeanetta. *Nathaniel Hawthorne and the Critics: A Checklist of Criticism, 1900–1978*. Metuchen, NJ: Scarecrow Press, 1982.

Budick, E. Miller. *Engendering Romance: Women Writers and the Hawthorne Tradition, 1850–1990*. New Haven, CT: Yale University Press, 1994.

Carlson, Patricia Ann. *Hawthorne's Functional Settings: A Study of Artistic Method*. Amsterdam: Rodopi, 1977.

Carton, Evan. *The Rhetoric of American Romance: Dialectic and Identity in Emerson, and Dickinson, Poe, and Hawthorne*. Baltimore: Johns Hopkins University Press, 1985.

Coale, Samuel Chase. *In Hawthorne's Shadow: American Romance from Melville to Mailer*. Lexington: University Press of Kentucky, 1985.

Colacurcio, Michael J., ed. *New Essays on "The Scarlet Letter."* New York: Cambridge University Press, 1985.

Crowley, J. Donald, ed. *Hawthorne: The Critical Heritage*. London: Routledge & K. Paul, 1970, 1997.

Davidson, Edward H. *Hawthorne's Last Phase*. New Haven, CT: Yale University Press, 1949.

Dolis, John. *The Style of Hawthorne's Gaze: Regarding Subjectivity*. Tuscaloosa: University of Alabama Press, 1993.

Doubleday, Neal Frank. *Hawthorne's Early Tales: A Critical Study*. Durham, NC: Duke University Press, 1972.

Dryden, Edgar A. *The Form of American Romance*. Baltimore: Johns Hopkins University Press, 1988.

_____. *Nathaniel Hawthorne: The Poetics of Enchantment*. Ithaca, NY: Cornell University Press, 1977.

Easton, Alison. *The Making of the Hawthorne Subject*. Columbia: University of Missouri Press, 1996.

Elder, Marjorie J. *Nathaniel Hawthorne, Transcendental Symbolist*. Athens: Ohio University Press, 1969.

Erlich, Gloria C. *Family Themes and Hawthorne's Fiction: The Tenacious Web*. New Brunswick, NJ: Rutgers University Press, 1984.

Fogle, Richard Harter. *Hawthorne's Imagery, the Proper Light and Shadow in the Major Romances*. Norman: University of Oklahoma Press, 1969.

Greenwald, Elissa. *Realism and the Romance: Nathaniel Hawthorne, Henry James, and American Fiction*. Ann Arbor: UMI Research Press, 1989.

Haggerty, George E. *Gothic Fiction/Gothic Form*. University Park: Pennsylvania State University Press, 1989.

Harris, Kenneth Marc. *Hypocrisy and Self-Deception in Hawthorne's Fiction*. Charlottesville : University Press of Virginia, 1988.

Hutner, Gordon. *Secrets and Sympathy: Forms of Disclosure in Hawthorne's Novels*. Athens: University of Georgia Press, 1988.

Idol, John, and Melinda M. Ponder, eds. *Hawthorne and Women: Engendering and Expanding the Hawthorne Tradition*. Amherst: University of Massachusetts Press, 1999.

Kaul, A. N., ed. *Hawthorne: A Collection of Critical Essays*. Englewood Cliffs, NJ: Prentice-Hall, 1966.

Lee, Robert A., ed. *Nathaniel Hawthorne: New Critical Essays*. London: Vision Press; Totowa, New Jersey: Barnes & Noble, 1982.

Levin, Harry. *The Power of Blackness: Hawthorne, Poe, Melville*. New York: Alfred A. Knopf, 1958, 1976.

Mani, Lakshmi. *The Apocalyptic Vision in Nineteenth Century Fiction: A Study of Cooper, Hawthorne, and Melville*. Washington, D.C.: University Press of America, 1981.

Martin, Terry J. *Rhetorical Deception in the Short Fiction of Hawthorne, Poe, and Melville*. Lewiston, NY: Edwin Mellen Press, 1998.

Millington, Richard H. *Practicing Romance: Narrative Form and Cultural Engagement in Hawthorne's Fiction*. Princeton, NJ: Princeton University Press, 1992.

Person, Leland S. *The Cambridge Introduction to Nathaniel Hawthorne*. New York : Cambridge University Press, 2007.

Rohrberger, Mary. *Hawthorne and the Modern Short Story: A Study in Genre*. The Hague: Mouton, 1966.

Stern, Milton R. *Contexts for Hawthorne: "The Marble Faun" and the Politics of*

Openness and Closure in American Literature. Urbana: University of Illinois Press, 1991.

Stubbs, John Caldwell. *The Pursuit of Form, a Study of Hawthorne and the Romance.* Urbana: University of Illinois Press, 1970.

Swisher, Clarice, ed. *Readings on Nathaniel Hawthorne.* San Diego: Greenhaven Press, 1996.

Thickstun, Margaret Olofson. *Fictions of the Feminine: Puritan Doctrine and the Representation of Women.* Ithaca: Cornell University Press, 1988.

Thompson, Gary Richard. *The Art of Authorial Presence: Hawthorne's Provincial Tales.* Durham: Duke University Press, 1993.

CRITICAL INSIGHTS

About the Editor

Jack Lynch is Associate Professor of English at Rutgers University in Newark, New Jersey. He has published both scholarly and popular books and essays, mostly on British and American culture in the long eighteenth century. He is the author of *The Age of Elizabeth in the Age of Johnson* (Cambridge University Press, 2003), *Becoming Shakespeare: The Unlikely Afterlife That Turned a Provincial Playwright into the Bard* (Walker & Co., 2007), and *Deception and Detection in Eighteenth-Century Britain* (Ashgate Publishing, 2008). He is also the editor of *The Age of Johnson: A Scholarly Annual* and co-editor of *Anniversary Essays on Johnson's Dictionary* (Cambridge University Press, 2005). His essays and reviews have appeared in scholarly forums such as *Eighteenth-Century Life*, *The Review of English Studies*, and *Studies in Philology*, as well as in *The American Scholar*, *The New York Times*, and The *Los Angeles Times*.

About *The Paris Review*

The Paris Review is America's preeminent literary quarterly, dedicated to discovering and publishing the best new voices in fiction, nonfiction, and poetry. The magazine was founded in Paris in 1953 by the young American writers Peter Matthiessen and Doc Humes, and edited there and in New York for its first fifty years by George Plimpton. Over the decades, the *Review* has introduced readers to the earliest writings of Jack Kerouac, Philip Roth, T. C. Boyle, V. S. Naipaul, Ha Jin, Jay McInerney, and Mona Simpson, and published numerous now classic works, including Roth's *Goodbye, Columbus*, Donald Barthelme's *Alice*, Jim Carroll's *Basketball Diaries*, and selections from Samuel Beckett's *Molloy* (his first publication in English). The first chapter of Jeffrey Eugenides's *The Virgin Suicides* appeared in the *Review*'s pages, as well as stories by Edward P. Jones, Rick Moody, David Foster Wallace, Denis Johnson, Jim Shepard, Jim Crace, Lorrie Moore, Jeanette Winterson, and Ann Patchett.

The Paris Review's renowned Writers at Work series of interviews, whose early installments include legendary conversations with E. M. Forster, William Faulkner, and Ernest Hemingway, is one of the landmarks of world literature. The interviews received a George Polk award and were nominated for a Pulitzer Prize. Among the more than three hundred interviewees are Robert Frost, Marianne Moore, W. H. Auden, Elizabeth Bishop, Susan Sontag, and Toni Morrison. Recent issues feature conversations with Salman Rushdie, Joan Didion, Stephen King, Norman Mailer, Kazuo Ishiguro and Umberto Eco. (A complete list of the interviews is available at www.theparisreview.org) In November 2008, Picador will publish the third of a four-volume series of anthologies of *Paris Review* interviews. The first two volumes have received acclaim. *The New York Times* called the Writers at Work series "the most remarkable and extensive interviewing project we possess."

The Paris Review is edited by Philip Gourevitch, who was named to the post in 2005, following the death of George Plimpton two years earlier. Under Gourevitch's leadership, the magazine's international distribution has expanded, paid subscriptions have risen 150 percent, and newsstand distribution has doubled. A new editorial team has published fiction by Andre Aciman, Damon Galgut, Mohsin Hamid, Gish Jen, Richard Price, Said Sayrafiezadeh and Alistair Morgan. Poetry editors Charles Simic, Meghan O'Rourke and Dan Chiasson have selected works by Billy Collins, Jesse Ball, Mary Jo Bang, Sharon Olds, and Mary Karr. Writing published in the magazine has been anthologized in *Best American Short Stories* 2006, 2007 and 2008, *Best American Poetry*, *Best Creative Non-Fiction*, the Pushcart Prize anthology, and *O. Henry Prize Stories*.

The magazine presents two annual awards. The Hadada Award for lifelong contribution to literature has recently been given to William Styron, Joan Didion, Norman Mailer and Peter Matthiessen in 2008. The Plimpton Prize for Fiction given to a new voice in fiction brought to national attention in the pages of *The Paris Review* was presented in 2007 to Benjamin Percy and to Jesse Ball in 2008.

The Paris Review won the 2007 National Magazine Award in photojournalism and the *Los Angeles Times* recently called *The Paris Review* "an American treasure with true international reach."

Since 1999 *The Paris Review* has been published by The Paris Review Foundation, Inc., a not-for-profit 501(c)(3) organization.

The Paris Review is available in digital form to libraries worldwide in selected academic databases exclusively from EBSCO Publishing. Libraries can contact EBSCO at 1-800-653-2726 for details.

For more information on *The Paris Review* or to subscribe, please visit: www.theparisreview.org.

_____

Jack Lynch is Associate Professor of English at Rutgers University in Newark, New Jersey. He is the author of *The Age of Elizabeth in the Age of Johnson* (2003), *Becoming Shakespeare: The Unlikely Afterlife That Turned a Provincial Playwright into the Bard* (2007), and *Deception and Detection in Eighteenth-Century Britain* (2008). He is also the editor of *The Age of Johnson: A Scholarly Annual*.

Frank Day is Professor Emeritus of English at Clemson University and was Fulbright Lecturer in American Literature at Cuza University in Iasi, Romania, in 1980-1981, and at Dhaka University in Bangladesh, in 1986-1987. He was a long-time editor of *The South Carolina Review* and has published books on William Empson and Arthur Koestler.

Elaine Blair is the author of *Literary St. Petersburg* (2007). She writes about books for *The New York Review of Books*, *The Nation*, and other publications.

Bridget M. Marshall is an Assistant Professor in the English Department at the University of Massachusetts, Lowell, where she teaches courses in American literature, the horror story, the gothic novel, and disability in literature. She earned her Ph.D. at the University of Massachusetts, Amherst, with a dissertation on legal themes in the gothic novel. She has recently published articles on a seventeenth-century witch in Hadley, Massachusetts, and on witch-themed tourism in Salem.

Matthew J. Bolton is a professor of English at Loyola School in New York City, where he also serves as the Dean of Students. Bolton received his Doctor of Philosophy in English from The Graduate Center of the City University of New York (CUNY) in 2005. His dissertation at the university was entitled: "Transcending the Self in Robert Browning and T. S. Eliot." Prior to attaining his Ph.D. at CUNY, Bolton also earned a Master of Philosophy in English (2004) and a Master of Science in English Education (2001). His undergraduate work was done at the State University of New York at Binghamton where he studied English Literature.

Margarita Georgieva is a post-graduate research student at the Université de Nice Sophia Antipolis (France). She is working on her Ph.D. on the image and representation of the child figure in the gothic genre from 1764 to 1824. She has contributed to the Facts on File, Inc. encyclopedia of literary themes to appear in 2009. Interested in translation and creative writing, she is also the author of various non-academic articles and short stories published by AUBG, Bulgaria and Janet-45 Press, Bulgaria.

Jennifer Banach Palladino is a writer and independent scholar from Connecticut. She has served as the Contributing Editor of *Bloom's Guides: Heart of Darkness* and *Bloom's Guides: The Glass Menagerie* for Facts on File, Inc. and is the author of the forthcoming volumes *Bloom's How to Write about Tennessee Williams* from Facts on File, Inc. and *Understanding Norman Mailer* from The University of South Carolina Press. Palladino has also composed teaching guides to international literature for Random House's Academic Resources division and has contributed to numerous literary reference books for academic publishers such as Facts on File, Inc. and Oxford University Press on topics ranging from Romanticism to contemporary literature. Her work has appeared in academic and popular venues alike; her fiction and nonfiction have appeared under the *Esquire* banner. She is a member of The Association of Literary Scholars and Critics.

Hugo McPherson taught at McGill University where he served as Director for the Graduate Program in Communications. McPherson also served as Film Commissioner for the National Film Board of Canada. In addition to writing extensively on Canadian art and literature, McPherson's publications include *Hawthorne as Myth-Maker* (1969).

Clark Davis is Professor of English at the University of Denver where he has also served as Associate Chair of the department and Director of English Graduate Studies. He is the author of *Hawthorne's Shyness: Ethics, Politics, and the Question of Engagement* (2005) and *After the Whale: Melville in the Wake of* Moby-Dick (1995) and his essays and articles have appeared in numerous journals including *the Southern Review, ESQ: A Journal of the American Renaissance, Studies in American Fiction, Literary Imagination*, and *South Atlantic Review* among others.

Evans Lansing Smith is Professor of English at Midwestern State University. He is author of several books including *Rape and Revelation: An Archetypal Poetics of the Underworld in Modernism* (1990), *Ricorso and Revelation: An Archetypal Poetics of Modernism* (1995), *The Hero Journey in Literature: Parables of Poesis* (1997), *Figuring Poesis: A Mythical Geometry of Postmodernism* (1997), and most recently *The Myth of the Descent to the Underworld in Postmodern Literature* (2003).

Thomas R. Moore taught rhetoric at Boston University. He is the author of *A Thick and Darksome Veil: The Rhetoric of Hawthorne's Sketches, Prefaces, and Essays.*

Kathryn B. McKee is Associate Professor of English at the University of Mississippi. Her essays have appeared in *Southern Literary Journal, Studies in American Humor, Southern Quarterly*, and *Mississippi Quarterly.*

Claudia D. Johnson was Professor of English at the University of Alabama-Tuscaloosa where she also served as Chair of the Department for 11 years. Her books include *To Kill a Mockingbird: Threatening Boundaries* (1994), *The Social Impact of the Novel: A Reference Guide* (2002), *An Annotated Bibliography of Shakespearean Burlesques, Parodies and Travesties* (1976), *Nineteenth-Century Theatrical Memoirs* (1982), *American Actress: Perspective on the Nineteenth Century* (1984), and *The Productive Tension of Hawthorne's Art* (1981).

John Gatta, Jr. is Dean of the College and Professor of English at Sewanee: The University of the South. He has taught at the University of Connecticut and the University of Missouri and he has been a Woodrow Wilson Fellow and a Fulbright professor. His books include *The Meditative Wit of Edward Taylor* (1989); *American Madonna: Images of the Divine Woman in Literary Culture* (1997), and *Making Nature Sacred:*

Literature, Religion, and Environment in America from the Puritans to the Present (2004).

John G. Bayer has taught at St. Louis University and St. Louis Community College, Meramac. His publications include *The Shifting Function of Rhetoric in Early Nineteenth-Century American Education and Belles Lettres* (1982).

Leo B. Levy taught at Arizona State University. His essays appeared in *American Literature, Nineteenth-Century Fiction, The Journal of English and Germanic Philology,* and other scholarly journals. With Waldo F. McNeir he edited *Studies in American Literature,* and his books include *Versions of Melodrama: A Study of the Fiction and Drama of Henry James, 1865-1897* (1957).

Melvin W. Askew taught literature at Kansas State University. He wrote on a wide variety of literary subjects for publications such as *Psychoanalytic Review, American Literature, The Tulane Drama Review,* and *The University of Kansas City Review.*

Nina Baym is Center for Advanced Study Professor Emerita at the University of Illinois at Urbana. She is the author of numerous books including *American Women of Letters and the Nineteenth-Century Sciences* (2002), *American Woman Writers and the Work of History, 1790-1860* (1995), *Fiction: A Guide to Novels by and about Women in America, 1820-1870* (1978, 1993), *The Scarlet Letter: A Reading* (1986), *Novels, Readers, and Reviewers: Responses to Fiction in Antebellum America* (1984), and *The Shape of Hawthorne's Career* (1976). She has held fellowships from the John Simon Guggenheim Foundation, the National Endowment for the Humanities, and has served as the general editor of the *Norton Anthology of American Literature.*

Bill Christophersen is a freelance writer and copy editor living in New York City. His essays and reviews have appeared in *Studies in Short Fiction, Poetry, American Literature, Modern Language Studies, The Yale Review, Newsweek,* and *The New York Times Book Review.* Christophersen is also the author of *The Apparition in the Glass: Charles Brockden Brown's American Gothic* (1994).

Acknowledgments _____

"Nathaniel Hawthorne" by Frank Day. From *Dictionary of World Biography: The 19th Century* (1999): 1064-1067. Copyright © by Salem Press, Inc. All rights reserved.

"Introduction to Nathaniel Hawthorne's Work" by Elaine Blair. Copyright © 2008 by Elaine Blair. Special appreciation goes to Nathaniel Rich and Christopher Cox, editors for *The Paris Review*.

"The Scarlet Letter" by Hugo McPherson. From *Hawthorne as Myth-Maker: A Study in Imagination* (1969) by Hugo McPherson. Copyright © 1969 by University of Toronto Press. Reprinted by permission of Toronto University Press.

"Chiefly about Coverdale: *The Blithedale Romance*" by Clark Davis. From *Hawthorne's Shyness: Ethics, Politics, and the Question of Engagement* (2005): 105–117. Copyright © 2005 by The Johns Hopkins University Press. Reprinted with permission of The Johns Hopkins University Press.

"Re-figuring Revelations: Nathaniel Hawthorne's *The Scarlet Letter*" by Evans Lansing Smith. From *ATQ* 4, no. 2 (June 1990). Copyright © 1990 by University of Rhode Island Press. Reprinted by permission of University of Rhode Island Press.

"Hawthorne as Essayist: *Our Old Home* and 'Chiefly about War Matters'" by Thomas R. Moore. From *ATQ* 6, no. 4 (December 1992). Copyright © 1992 by University of Rhode Island Press. Reprinted by permission of University of Rhode Island Press.

"'A Small Heap of Glittering Fragments': Hawthorne's Discontent with the Short Story Form" by Kathryn B. McKee. From *ATQ* 8, no. 2 (June 1994). Copyright © 1994 by University of Rhode Island Press. Reprinted by permission of University of Rhode Island Press.

"Hawthorne and Nineteenth-Century Perfectionism" by Claudia D. Johnson. From *American Literature* 44, no. 4 (January 1973): 585-595. Copyright © 1973 by Duke University Press. All rights reserved. Used by permission of the publisher.

"Progress and Providence in *The House of the Seven Gables*" by John Gatta, Jr. From *American Literature* 50, no. 1 (March 1978): 37-48. Copyright © 1978 by Duke University Press. All rights reserved. Used by permission of the publisher.

"Narrative Techniques and the Oral Tradition in *The Scarlet Letter*" by John G. Bayer. From *American Literature* 52, no. 2 (May 1980): 250-263. Copyright © 1980 by Duke University Press. All rights reserved. Used by permission of the publisher.

"Hawthorne and the Sublime" by Leo B. Levy. From *American Literature* 37, no. 4 (January 1966): 391-402. Copyright © 1965 by Duke University Press. All rights reserved. Used by permission of the publisher.

"Hawthorne, the Fall, and the Psychology of Maturity" by Melvin W. Askew. From *American Literature* 34, no. 3 (November 1962): 335 -343. Copyright ©1962 by Duke

Beecher, Lyman, 211
Beethoven, Ludwig van, 72
Bell, Michael Davitt, 72-73
Bell, Millicent, 38, 45, 164, 166
Bellingham (*The Scarlet Letter*), 84;
    armour, 84, 92; mansion, 84
Benis, Monte. *See* Monte Benis (*The
    Marble Faun*)
Bense, James, 153
Bercovitch, Sacvan, 278
Berlin, Isaiah, 109
Best American Essays 1990, The, 135
Bewley, Marius, 274, 298
Biblical allusions, 232, 279-280, 289,
    296, 300; definition of sin, 53; in *The
    Scarlet Letter*, 53, 55, 115, 118-119
Bier, Jesse, 201
"Birth-Mark, The" (Hawthorne), 3;
    Aylmer in, 67, 69, 232, 238; fall of
    man theme, 231; Georgiana in, 54,
    66, 106; myth of maturity in, 237;
    science themes in, 69; sin in, 54
Bjelajac, David, 115
Blair, Hugh, 202, 211-212
Blithedale Romance, The (Hawthorne),
    26, 40, 42, 95, 137-138, 181, 269;
    class tensions in, 111; friendship in,
    101, 105; narrative, 99-102; political
    implications in, 11, 96, 100, 106-107;
    preface in, 97-98; self-limitation in,
    97-98, 107
Bloom, Harold, 66
Booth, Wayne, 203
"Bosom Serpent" (Hawthorne), 179,
    273; Roderick Elliston in, 178-179
Boswell, Jeanetta, 38
Bowdoin College, 6, 9, 12, 22-23, 27,
    30, 39, 173, 184, 211
Bridge, Horatio, 27, 174, 276
Brodhead, Richard, 99-101
Brontë, Charlotte, 4, 64

Brontë, Emily, 64
Browne, Nina E., 38
Brownson, Orestes, 28
Budd, Louis, 38
Budick, Emily, 46
Bunyan, John, 4, 189, 232
"By a Peaceable Man" (Hawthorne),
    149
Byron, Lord, 64, 72, 227

Cady, Edwin H., 38
Calhoun, John C., 211
Calvinist, 65, 86, 174, 212, 273, 275,
    304
Calvinist teleology, 104
*Cambridge Companion to Nathaniel
    Hawthorne, The* (Millington), 39
Canby, Henry Seidel, 71
"Canterbury Pilgrims, The"
    (Hawthorne); fall of man theme in,
    231; Josiah in, 232, 237; Miriam in,
    237; myth of maturity in, 237
Cantwell, Robert, 245
Captain Hunnewell ("Drowne's Wooden
    Image"), 166
"Celestial Railroad, The" (Hawthorne);
    social reform in, 195
Chandler, Elizabeth Lathrop, 44
Channing, William Ellery, 11, 140, 143,
    211
Cheever, Susan, 47
"Chiefly about War Matters"
    (Hawthorne), 98, 102, 136, 149-153,
    156
Chillingworth, Roger. *See* Roger
    Chillingworth (*The Scarlet Letter*)
Chopin, Frederic, 72
Christian themes; in *The House of the
    Seven Gables*, 188, 198; of
    perfection, 174-179, 181-185; in *The
    Scarlet Letter*, 41, 80, 95, 279, 298; in

Lamb, Charles, 135
"Leamington Spa" (Hawthorne), 134, 140-141, 144, 147, 153
Leavis, Q. D., 84
Lectures on Art, and Poems (Allston), 222
Lectures on the Works and Genius of Washington Allston (Ware), 223
Letter A symbolism in *The Scarlet Letter*, 11, 15, 92, 128, 180, 208
Lewis, R. W. B., 45, 232
"Lichfield and Uttoxeter" (Hawthorne), 137
Liebman, Sheldon W., 67
Lincoln, Abraham, 149, 152, 156
Lindsey, Mr. *See* Mr. Lindsey ("The Snow-Image")
"Literary Reputation and the Essays of *Our Old Home*" (Anhorn), 137
"London Suburb, A" (Hawthorne), 147
Longfellow, Henry Wadsworth, 6, 9, 22-24, 26, 32, 39, 150, 273
Lowell, James Russell, 150
Lueck, Beth L., 136
Lyrical Ballads (Coleridge and Wordsworth), 63

MacDonald, John J., 160
McFarland, Philip James, 47
McLoughlin, William G., 278
McPhee, John, 135, 150
Magnalia Christi Americana (Mather), 296
Mahan, Asa, 176
"Main-Street" (Hawthorne), 203, 206, 267
"Man of Adamant, The" (Hawthorne); Mary Goffe in, 179, 239; Richard Digby in, 178-179, 239; transgressions in, 221
Manning, Mary, 136, 249-250, 253, 255

Manning, Richard, 249, 253, 255
Manning, Robert, 249, 253, 255
Marble Faun, The (Hawthorne), 12, 42, 95, 137, 269; Donatello in, 182-183, 232, 237; fall of man theme in, 231; gothic themes in, 68; Hilda in, 182, 269; Kenyon in, 182-183, 269; Miriam in, 182-183, 241; Monte Benis in, 182, 237; myth of maturity in, 237; perfectionistic values in, 182
Martha ("The Shaker Bridal"), 179
Martin, Robert K., 46
Martin, Terence, 70
Marxist criticism, 37
Mary Goffe ("The Man of Adamant"), 179, 239
Mather, Cotton, 296
Matthew ("The Great Carbuncle"), 220
Matthiessen, F. O., 45, 170, 275, 296
Maule (*House of the Seven Gables, The*), 187, 189
Maule's Curse: Seven Studies in the History of American Obscurantism (Winters), 44
"Maypole of Merry Mount, The" (Hawthorne), 71; Edgar in, 232-234, 237, 240; Edith in, 233-234, 237, 240; Endicott in, 233; fall of man theme in, 231, 233; myth of maturity in, 237
Mellow, James R., 38, 245
Melville, Herman, 6-7, 22, 29, 31, 36, 40, 42, 47, 62, 65, 101, 103, 110, 114, 120, 224, 273-276, 279, 297-298
Miles Coverdale (*The Blithedale Romance*), 95, 181; autobiographical figure, 99; motivations, 99; murderer, 99; principle of responsibility, 103-105; speech, 104; unreliable narrator, 99, 101; voyeurism, 101, 106; weaknesses, 101

scene in, 54, 115-119, 125, 180, 215; setting, 69; sin in, 10-11, 52, 54-55, 71; structure of, 45, 115-116, 265; symbolism in, 169; writing of, 243

Scharnhorst, Gary, 38, 43

Schubert, Franz, 72

Science themes, 67, 294-295

"Select Party, A" (Hawthorne), 274, 297

Selected Letters (Hawthorne), 38

"Seven Tales of My Native Land" (Hawthorne), 277

"Shaker Bridal, The" (Hawthorne); Adam Coburn in, 178-179; Martha in, 179; transgressions in, 221; village in, 178

Shakespeare, William, 7, 41, 88, 108, 144, 197, 273

Shelley, Mary, 64

Shelley, Percy Bysshe, 64, 72

Short story, 3-4, 231; agnostic tensions in, 274, 304; dissatisfaction with, 31, 158-159, 163-165

"Sights from a Steeple" (Hawthorne), 22, 102, 140

Simpson, Claude M., 141, 155, 213

Sin themes in Hawthorne's work, 54, 71, 187, 273; definition of, 53-55; knowledge of, 52, 55, 57-58, 60; secret, 52, 58-60; unpardonable, 10-11

Sketch Book of Geoffrey Crayon, Gent., The (Irving), 134

"Snow-Image, The" (Hawthorne); Mr. Lindsey in, 168; Peony in, 162, 168; snow child in, 168-169; view of the artist in, 159; Violet in, 162, 168

Socialism, critique of, 97, 107

"Some of the Haunts of Burns" (Hawthorne), 154

Stephen, Leslie, 43

Stephenson, Edward R., 289

Stevenson, Robert Louis, 135

Stewart, Randall, 44, 244-245

"Story-Teller, The" (Hawthorne), 277, 303

Sublime traditions; false, 222-226; imagery, 221, 225; intolerable, 226; moral, 222-223, 226, 230

"Sunday at Home" (Hawthorne), 140

Surveyor Pue's manuscript, 205-206

Swann, Charles, 100

Swift, Jonathan, 135

"Sylph Etherege" (Hawthorne), 285, 287, 301-302

Sympathy theme in *The Scarlet Letter*, 202, 205-206, 208, 211, 213

Tales of a Traveller (Irving), 136

Taylor, Zachary, 27

Tempest, The (Shakespeare), 197

Tharpe, Jac, 56

Theodore ("The Minister's Black Veil"), 105

Theroux, Paul, 135

Thompson, Lawrance, 274, 297

Thompson, W. R., 278, 280, 300, 302-303

Thoreau, Henry David, 7, 11, 22, 40, 150, 218

Thurber, James, 135

Ticknor, William, 27, 30

"To a Friend" (Hawthorne), 137, 144

Tobias Pearson ("The Gentle Boy"), 280-281

Token, The (Hawthorne), 22-23, 39, 150

Tourism industry, 33

Transcendentalism, 11, 40, 52, 86-87, 115-116, 150, 274, 300

Trollope, Anthony, 43

Tuckerman, Henry A., 142, 150